MARKETING
PLANNING
BY DESIGN

MARKETING PLANNING BY DESIGN

Systematic Planning for Successful Marketing Strategy

Ralf E. Strauss

A John Wiley & Sons, Ltd., Publication

Copyright ©2008   John Wiley & Sons Ltd, The Atrium, Southern Gate, Chichester,
West Sussex PO19 8SQ, England
Telephone (+44) 1243 779777

Email (for orders and customer service enquiries): cs-books@wiley.co.uk
Visit our Home Page on www.wiley.com

Other Wiley Editorial Offices

John Wiley & Sons Inc., 111 River Street, Hoboken, NJ 07030, USA

Jossey-Bass, 989 Market Street, San Francisco, CA 94103-1741, USA

Wiley-VCH Verlag GmbH, Boschstr. 12, D-69469 Weinheim, Germany

John Wiley & Sons Australia Ltd, 42 McDougall Street, Milton, Queensland 4064, Australia

John Wiley & Sons (Asia) Pte Ltd, 2 Clementi Loop #02-01, Jin Xing Distripark, Singapore 129809

John Wiley & Sons Canada Ltd, 6045 Freemont Blvd. Mississauga, Ontario, L5R 4J3 Canada

Wiley also publishes its books in a variety of electronic formats. Some content that appears in print may
not be available in electronic books.

Library of Congress Cataloging-in-Publication Data
Strauss, Ralf E.
    Marketing planning by design : systematic planning for successful marketing strategy / by Ralf E.
Strauss.
       p. cm.
    Includes bibliographical references and index.
    ISBN 978-0-470-72167-4
    1. Marketing—Management. 2. Strategic planning. I. Title.

    HF5415.13.S8789   2008
    658.8′02—dc22

                                                                2008046995

British Library Cataloguing in Publication Data
A catalogue record for this book is available from the British Library

ISBN 978-0-470-72167-4

Typeset in 10/12 pt Bembo by SNP Best-set Typesetter Ltd., Hong Kong
Printed and bound in Great Britain by TJ International Ltd, Padstow, Cornwall

For my little son Victor –
With the promise that a more efficient planning
will give us more time to play

CONTENTS

ABOUT THE AUTHOR

Dr. Ralf E. Strauss is the global head of product management for CRM Marketing at SAP. For the previous five years he was the CMO for SAP in Central Europe and Germany. Before becoming the head of marketing, Dr. Strauss had already had many years of experience in marketing and sales projects in management consulting before he came to SAP Germany in 2002 as head of business development. As a result of his work as management consultant, and in line management at SAP, he can look back on a diverse range of project experience in the areas of strategic planning, marketing transformation, reorganization, company and new-product launches, and IT implementation. He has several years of professional experience with projects and project leadership in the areas of telecommunications and media, one-to-one marketing, e-business, customer relationship management, networked enterprise structures, and the transformation of traditional companies. He is also the author of more than 60 publications in these subject areas.

He graduated with a higher degree in business economics and administration from the University of Passau, and received a PhD from the Institute of Computer Science and Social Studies/Telematics from the University of Freiburg in Breisgau for his work on the subject of "Determinants and Processes of Organizational Learning". In 1995, he was nominated deputy member of the "Multimedia Enquête" commission of the State Parliament of Baden-Württemberg, and in 1997 he was appointed as a member of the Multimedia Innovation Forum. He is the author of a total of three of the largest and most representative studies in Germany and Europe on the subject of e-business. The book that he co-wrote with Professor Schoder (University of Cologne/Germany), *e-Reality – Das e-Business Bausteinkonzept. Strategien und Erfolgsfaktoren für das e-Business-Management* [e-Reality – Building Blocks for e-Business. Strategies and Success Factors for the e-Business Management], was published in October 2001.

Contact address:
Dr. Ralf E. Strauss
SAP AG
Dietmar-Hopp-Allee 16
D-69190 Walldorf, Germany

Cell phone: +49 (0160) 88 96 910
E-mail: Ralf.Strauss@Hamburg.de
E-mail: Ralf.Strauss@sap.com

PREFACE

Numerous books have been written about marketing and marketing planning. Most of them have contributed a great deal of important information to the discourse on and further development of marketing as a professional discipline that contributes to the success of sales and companies as a whole. However, no marketing book has yet examined marketing from within the company as closely as this book does – as a function that is under immense pressure to perform. It is required to submit reports to management; is judged by the sales department based on whether it helps sales; it is scrutinized by financial control regarding how efficiently it uses budgets; and last, but not least, it is under constant review by customers, markets, and the public.

Marketing faces more dilemmas and conflicts of interest than any other part of a company. This, however, is not entirely undeserved. Even those involved in marketing often underestimate the usefulness and opportunities inherent in systematic planning as a foundation for successful marketing. The reason for this lies in the *lack of a plan for marketing planning*. This book not only identifies numerous examples of this problem as experienced by businesses, but it also offers ways of solving the problem.

The goal of this book is as follows: marketing as a corporate function must finally be put in a position to prove what it can do, what it can achieve, and what it is worth. However, for this to happen, it must also be prepared to be measured – and no longer hide behind a semi-commercial "arty" image. In the end, marketing, too, must formulate its goals as precisely as, say, production does, and it must allow those goals to be evaluated with equal precision.

Another point in which this book differs significantly from many others is that it systematically integrates the increasingly broad field of online marketing. This area does not just increase the responsibility of marketing within the enterprise, but it also extends the opportunities to link marketing with company success – and vice versa. With that in mind, this book and the examples it contains address both the business-to-business (B2B) as well as the business-to-consumer (B2C) area.

A book cannot replace the professionalism, motivation, and commitment of its reader – but it can help to cultivate all these qualities. Consequently, while this book can be viewed as academic literature, it is primarily intended as an aid (and a survival tool) for marketing theorists and marketing professionals – as well as for those not involved in marketing directly, such as financial controllers, buyers, managers, and executives who must evaluate the work and the effects of the marketing strategies deployed. In other words, the same principle applies in marketing as in all other areas of (professional) life: only by gaining a better understanding can we work together to achieve more. And this is precisely the objective to which this book intends to contribute.

Ralf Strauss
Walldorf/Hamburg, Germany, March 2008

FOREWORD

The role of the marketing professional has changed dramatically over time. Once an intuitive art form that prided itself on creative design, marketing has become an applied science with a new focus on measurement and analysis. This emphasis on quantitative results enables marketers to better answer the fundamental business question: "What practical, measurable value does marketing add to a company?"

The evolution of marketing science has generated demand for new skillsets in corporate marketing: strong analytical skills are necessary to effectively execute new marketing strategies. Today's marketing professionals must be able to target specific audience segments with content that is tailored to clear objectives and delivered through effective communication channels.

Marketing communication remains one of the last arenas to benefit from the evolution of analytical marketing methods. It is the responsibility of the marketing department to drive the innovations necessary to maintain a consistent level of quality communication with prospects and customers. Efficient internal processes supported by integrated technology are fundamental to ensuring that customers enjoy a consistently reliable experience in all their interactions with a company.

The integration of technology and marketing processes has been a major factor in the evolution of marketing's role within the corporate enterprise. The marketing department must take the lead in defining internal business processes and ensuring that IT can support these processes. Today's marketing managers must be able to show how measurable marketing activities are directly linked to bottom-line results – regardless of whether these results were attained through traditional sales channels or by means of technology-enabled customer interactions.

Innovative technologies offer new possibilities for future interaction with prospects and customers who have become increasingly difficult to reach by traditional channels. To effectively leverage these new technologies, however, marketing management must establish a systematic methodology for marketing planning.

This book demonstrates in practical terms the importance of marketing planning for efficient utilization of resources and consistent measurement of marketing results.

I am convinced that the insights it offers are essential to meeting the challenge of measuring marketing's contribution to the success of the corporate enterprise.

Marty Homlish   *New York, March 2008*
Global CMO, SAP AG

INTRODUCTION:
THE "LACK-OF-EVIDENCE TRAP"

*I*t is difficult to know whether Henry Ford's renowned comment on marketing was a result of cynicism, skepticism, or simply a realistic outlook: "Fifty percent of my marketing dollars are wasted – I just don't know which half." Whatever the case, such dark humor is of little use to anyone with marketing responsibilities today. What is needed instead are convincing answers to questions such as:

- How can I prove that increases in sales as a result of addressing new customer segments and winning new market potential can be directly attributed to marketing activities?
- How do increased customer focus and addressing a target group more specifically actually affect customer loyalty?
- What do targeted marketing activities to differentiate between competitors really achieve?

Marketing as a classic business function is increasingly being forced to prove that its budgets and expenditure can be associated with objectively verifiable, measurable results.

CMOs, their employees, and the next generation cannot complain about a lack of specialized books, articles, studies, and, increasingly, online publications. The operational reality, on the other hand, looks quite different. Instead of lofty business theories, sober cost/benefit analyses are required. This leads not only to critical questions from the executive board, controlling and purchasing, but also prompts uncertainty in other company areas beyond marketing and sales. This is because there is a danger that even the simplest questions cannot be answered conclusively:

- Are the marketing measures and tactics used suitable for effectively addressing the target groups identified and for actually reaching the goals that have been set?
- Do the chosen marketing activities constitute the cheapest, fastest, and most secure way of reaching the intended goal?
- Does the selected content actually reach the intended audience by means of the selected tactics and communication measures?

- Is the content to be communicated described in sufficient detail, and is it easily understandable?
- Or even: Does marketing – that is, its content, how it addresses target groups, selected tactics, key figures (known as key performance indicators or KPIs), and so on – comply with company strategy at all?

At the same time, marketing is being confronted with new challenges. Increasing individualization in the delivery and communication of services, as well as new Internet-based applications (such as consumer-generated content within Web 2.0), mean that uncertainty around these issues is increasing rather than decreasing. If you ask heads of marketing – who are known as **Chief Marketing Officers** (CMOs) in both the business-to-business (B2B) and the business-to-consumer (B2C) areas – about deficits in marketing today, the conclusion drawn is usually this: the main reason for the prevailing uncertainty about the effectiveness and efficiency of marketing strategies and tactics is often shown to be inadequate marketing planning or a lack of marketing planning altogether. This means that marketing planning is often:

- inadequately synchronized with business planning as a whole;
- too limited to the planning of strategies and measures, while neglecting content-based planning at a topic level and program level;
- nothing more than an adaptation of planning from the previous year, with minor modifications in terms of content and scheduling (known as the "binder-off-the-shelf syndrome");
- lacking in accurate KPIs agreed between marketing and other affected company areas (such as sales and distribution, international branches, etc.).

Insufficient and non-systematic planning lands marketing in the *lack-of-evidence trap*. One consequence of this is that the added value generated from marketing expenditure and effort is nearly impossible to account for within the company in the sense of a return on marketing investment (ROMI). As a result, the efficiency of future company-external marketing activities is very difficult to prove. Qualitative and quantitative studies show that around three-quarters of all marketing activities barely meet the expectations set for them. The reasons for this are numerous and complex, but again can be ultimately attributed to insufficient marketing planning. However, critique of the functionality of marketing and the arguments mentioned here are not new. Such criticism was made as early as 1980 – but a sustainable solution has not been found until now (Müller 2008). And as early as 2000, Doyle similarly referred to the "marginalization of marketing professionals" (Doyle 2000).

This deficit extends to insufficient briefings for *agencies* of all types: Content is not sufficiently defined, communication channels for addressing target groups are not precise enough, and campaign-specific success factors are not, or are only roughly, identified. This unsatisfactory situation is then perpetuated by the agencies. Often, agencies ask too few questions and compensate for a lack of content in the briefing with their own interpretations of content and target groups. This means that the negative effects of poor marketing planning are intensified, with, consequently, several rebriefings that require additional time and resources for the client and the agency, an overall inefficient planning and implementation process, and marketing campaigns and activities that produce results that fall short of expectations.

What appears to be an inevitable evil of business marketing is in fact avoidable and can be turned around to become a sustainable process for success. This confident and positive claim derives from contextual and practical knowledge, which we have systematically acquired and prepared for this book. It is based on numerous projects from the last 10 years – a qualitative analysis of success factors using detailed interviews to develop a procedural model for marketing planning. In addition to conducting a qualitative survey of 43 CMOs in Europe, the analysis was supplemented further with personal interviews to follow up on selected issues until the end of summer 2007. The findings were checked and developed using more than eight projects on marketing strategy, planning, and implementation at companies in many different industries. The identification of demonstrably successful concepts, their critical success drivers, and, above all, the definition of objectively verifiable key indicators for the success of marketing form the basis of a tried-and-tested procedural model. Comprehensive literature research at the level of current marketing knowledge forms a comprehensive network of expertise as a back up. The following are some of the methodological activities carried out in the development of the procedural model:

- Numerous approaches and implementation concepts from theory and practice were filtered out in accordance with exacting qualitative and theoretical factors.
- Many empirical studies were evaluated and the results that are relevant for practical application were summarized.
- The most important experience gathered from additional examples of implementation projects from business practice was analyzed.

The findings from this multifaceted and complex subject were translated into a procedural model for successful marketing planning. The procedural model is designed as both a basis for management and as an instrument for quality assurance – for executive management and for marketing teams responsible today and tomorrow. Proof that the model works in practical application can be found in the fact that it has been tested in practice and updated using results and experiences drawn from a series of strategy and implementation projects that we have assisted.

The goal of the marketing procedural model proposed in this book is to pinpoint the decision-making problems that companies encounter when developing and implementing effective, efficient marketing planning, to present practical options for structuring marketing planning, and to contribute to the achievement of greater potential in marketing. The results-based and activity-oriented presentation of empirical values and best practice examples helps to illustrate the options for designing marketing planning and to enable readers to develop their own ideas. The value proposition of this book and its procedural model for systematic marketing planning lies in tapping the structural options and potential for success for company marketing activities. The use of empirical values is intended to do more than help readers to adopt best practice examples. With the new challenges facing marketing today as a premise, it should also act as a stimulus for developing ideas and structural options for planning and implementing marketing activities. And the ultimate objective is to ensure that no one from the exciting and fascinating world of marketing ever gets caught in the lack-of-evidence trap again.

PART I

CHALLENGES TO THE MARKETING FUNCTION: IMPERATIVE FOR CHANGE

CHAPTER 1

NEW CHALLENGES IN MARKETING

1.1 THE CHALLENGE: ONE SIZE DOESN'T FIT ALL – QUALITY NOT QUANTITY

Intermezzo: A brief evaluation of the term *marketing*

Literature on the subject offers countless definitions of the term *marketing*, while marketing in practice also offers many interpretations of the term. Yet, to expect, let alone formulate, a single, ubiquitously valid definition is simply too much to ask. A historical analysis of the term makes clear that it has come to mean more in both its significance as a commercial function and in its related areas of activity.

While at the beginning of the twentieth century the terms marketing and sales were still considered synonyms, the part of that definition that involved sales gradually incorporated the tool of advertising in its broadest sense. The backdrop for this development was the change from comparatively static supply-driven markets to increasing competition as early as in the 1930s. The most significant contributions to marketing theory at that time were made in the United States.

It was not until the economy had revived after the Second World War that the marketing function, which had taken a back seat to production for so many years, was able to reaffirm itself as an independent business discipline. During the economic prosperity that developed in numerous countries on both sides of the Atlantic, and the emergence of the *marketing mix* (4 Ps: **P**roduct, **P**rice, **P**romotion, **P**lace), the term *marketing* gained further in complexity and breadth.

As part of the discourse on *market-oriented management* in the 1980s, the primacy of an economic theory that was predominantly production-oriented and focused on individual transactions was replaced by a new perspective that emphasized the customer relationship. This approach to marketing focuses less on completing individual sales, but more on a systematic and lasting relationship with the customer (relationship marketing, Stevens *et al.* 2006).

In its most recent definition of marketing, the American Marketing Association (AMA) broadened and vitalized the term accordingly:

> *Marketing is an organizational function and a set of processes for creating, communicating, and delivering value to customers and for managing customer relationships in ways that benefit the organization and its stakeholders.*

In recent years, relationship marketing has been summed up by the term *Customer Relationship Management* (CRM) – due in no small part to the inclusion of modern IT systems. It should be mentioned, however, that in everyday business language, CRM often only refers to software applications that can support systematic, lasting relationship management. This is too limited and offers further options for developing our understanding of marketing in the future.

Ideally, a definition of marketing that is suitable for the present day would include an *activity-oriented* component (the activity itself), a *relationship-oriented* component (the result of all customer interactions and activities), and a *management-oriented* component (the focus of all company activities) – and each component would change its meaning and form depending on context. After all, for marketing activities to be successful *outside* a company, conditions have to be suitable *inside* the company (e.g. organizational structure and coordination mechanisms along all required processes). They must be designed by everyone involved to form an integral whole if customer relationships are to be developed in an optimal way – this is equally true both for "customer retention" as well as for customer acquisition.

If we use the marketing definitions we have outlined so far as a foundation for analyzing the marketing principles that underlie them, we see that they too have changed a great deal over time. While business marketing activities followed a Mass Marketing principle until the 1960s, it was replaced by a *target group-based approach* in the form of Direct Marketing no later than the 1970s. Beginning in the early 1990s, concepts of *Database Marketing*, which features a strong focus on databases and analysis systems, alongside modern information techniques (together increasingly summarized under the term *Customer Relationship Management* – CRM), have been discussed and implemented to facilitate a comprehensive, highly standardized, yet simultaneously individualized approach to customer management ("Mass Customizing" – Diller 1999, 2001; Seybold 2001 – see Figure 1.1).

Consequently, CRM means improving customer loyalty and profitability in terms of both acquiring new customers and optimizing existing customer relationships. While

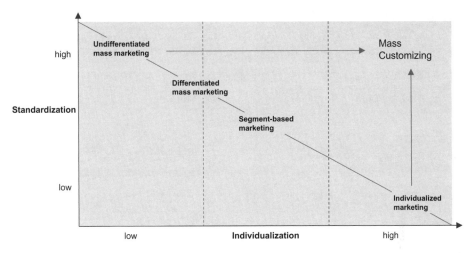

Figure 1.1 Stages of development of marketing concepts (Jung & Wiedmann 1998; reproduced by permission of Wilde & Hippner).

traditionally structured marketing tends to concentrate on generating sales in the short-term market shares and unidirectional customer information, the relationship-based approach focuses on establishing long-term business relationships, knowledge of individual customers and interacting with customers. The focus on individual transactions discernible in part is replaced by an emphasis on business relationships. The expression *share-of-wallet* is used to indicate that selling the largest possible quantity of product to a buyer (in some cases by means of aggressive advertising) is far less important than finding out as much as possible about a buyer's problems and needs in order to offer appropriate solutions and ultimately to gain a large "share" of the customer's "wallet" by becoming the customer's problem-solver of choice (Seybold 2001).

The reason for the increase in focus on the customer comes from the realization that *dissatisfied customers* are usually gone for good and, more importantly, they can have considerable negative repercussions on their respective market. Retaining satisfied customers, on the other hand, requires far less expenditure and resources than customer acquisition and opens up the potential for additional sales (known as *cross-selling*, see Figure 1.2).

Numerous studies show that customer satisfaction is less a result of one specific interaction with a company, and more the outcome of the entire business relationship (Homburg *et al.* 1999). At the heart of the matter is the comparison between what the customer actually experiences when a service is rendered and the customer's particular standard for the service (what the customer expects). If the customer perceives that the ACTUAL service is (approximately) equal to the expected level of the (expected) TARGET service, his existing expectations will have been met (known as *confirmation*). The opposite case leads to a satisfaction level that is below expectations. A high degree of customer satisfaction has a positive effect on customer loyalty – besides purchasing again, those customers may also purchase other items (cross-selling and up-selling) or promote the company or product by making a recommendation to people they know.

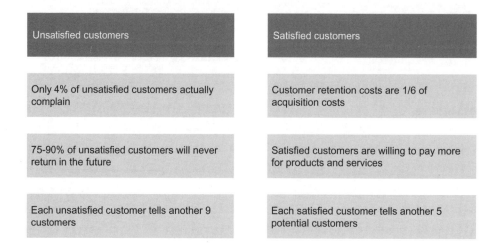

Unsatisfied customers	Satisfied customers
Only 4% of unsatisfied customers actually complain	Customer retention costs are 1/6 of acquisition costs
75-90% of unsatisfied customers will never return in the future	Satisfied customers are willing to pay more for products and services
Each unsatisfied customer tells another 9 customers	Each satisfied customer tells another 5 potential customers

Figure 1.2   Comparing the impact of satisfied and unsatisfied customers (Strauss & Schoder 2001; Homburg *et al.* 1999; Tiwana 2001).

The strength of the relationship between customer satisfaction and customer loyalty depends largely on the following critical factors (Coyles & Gokey 2002; Schnaars 1998):

- Features of the business relationship (such as how long the relationship has existed);
- Customer-specific features (such as the level of risk with which they are comfortable);
- Product features (like product complexity and product introduction expenditure);
- The intensity of competition.

The effect of the Internet on customer satisfaction and customer loyalty has been discussed in a wide variety of ways in recent years. The fact that more and more people are using the Internet and the specific characteristics of the Internet itself allow for an efficient, more affordable implementation of the CRM-based approach – by collecting basic customer data and addressing customers individually and interactively with personalized websites and e-mail, for instance. Customers can use advertising on the Internet to communicate with companies directly, without switching media. In terms of customer loyalty, however, the Internet can be a double-edged sword. On the one hand, individualized, interactive customer relationships can improve customer retention. On the other hand, the transparency of information and the direct availability of alternative offers as well as (manufacturer-independent) comparisons of products and prices can reduce customer loyalty. Consequently, the intensification of Internet-based competition generally results in a broader range of alternative offers, which in turn leads customers to refine their expectations of the products offered by providers in an industry sector (Strauss & Schoder 2001).

With this in mind, many companies have tended to view the Internet as a means of accelerating a downward trend in customer loyalty (Strauss & Schoder 2000;

Seybold 2001). Increased company activity online heightens the customer experiences related to online business, which is often considered to entail a further loss in customer loyalty. The only effective way for a company to retain customers in the intensely competitive environment of the Internet is by addressing customers on an individual level and using innovative services and comprehensive information to raise the *retention effect* of the Internet above the *loss effect* brought about by attractive offers from other providers. Studies show that a high degree of interchangeability of the services offered by different providers can, at least in part, be compensated with stable distribution structures (and consequently stable customer relationships, as in the case of insurance providers) and the (technical) uniqueness of products (in areas such as chemicals and pharmaceuticals – Strauss & Schoder 2001). There is also the option of working closely and networking with the customer, and involving them, for instance, in product development and the overall value chains of the company, particularly in the B2B area (Fleisch 2001; Strauss & Schoder 2000).

Amazon.com has managed to generate long-term customer loyalty. At the heart of its success is quick, free delivery (even for comparatively low order values) and a very large selection, combined with the technical sophistication of personalized lists of recommended products and "1-click ordering", which saves customers a great deal of time. After the first purchase, the system "recognizes" a returning customer, welcomes him or her by name and allows easy ordering of every single product with a single mouse click, without requiring any other activity or data entry.

Other companies have integrated forums into their Internet presence for this purpose, such as the agricultural group **BayWa** wich its *Farmers Forum*, where in-house experts answer questions on products and applications and chat about new developments in biology, chemistry, and technology.

The pharmaceuticals corporation, **Fresenius**, offers customers visiting its website a "guided tour" with experienced employees in the role of "tour guide". These company representatives not only introduce online guests to the most important pages of the site, but also provide their contact information to answer any questions the visitors may have. This has resulted in an unequivocal increase in Internet customer loyalty.

1.2 THE CHALLENGE: CRM – FROM THE BUZZWORD TO SYSTEMATIC CUSTOMER MANAGEMENT

Ideally, CRM allows companies to optimize customer relationships with the retrieval of real-time customer information and a continual innovation cycle induced by markets and customers for products and processes (Muther 2000; Seybold 2001; Peppers & Rogers 1997; Sterne 1996). In a standard CRM process, customer feedback and

Figure 1.3 CRM cycle (Strauss & Schoder 2001).

additional customer information (e.g. from after-sales support) form the foundation for better customer understanding, which in turn can be used as the basis for better marketing and sales activities.

It is common to reduce CRM concepts to the immediate customer interface (e-mail marketing, call center integration, training for sales personnel, creating innovative websites), but a wider understanding of the term shows that such an approach is insufficient. Traditional approaches from marketing and sales form the foundation for CRM, further supplemented by technologies such as data mining and sales support applications with web access (known as "Sales Force Automation").

The development of sustainable customer relationships can be described in the form of a **CRM cycle** as a long-term, revolving process. The initial emphasis lies in knowing (*analyzing and identifying*) existing customers (Figure 1.3) and their needs. A technical platform based on a *data warehouse* as well as various applications, such as *error-tolerant synchronization tools* and *data mining* are available for that purpose (Wieken 1999; Mena 1999). Such tools use existing customer data to enable users to draw conclusions about customer profitability, preference models and the likelihood of customers to switch to another provider (called "churn", Seybold 1998).

As the example of **BMW USA** (www.bmwusa.com) illustrates, data from existing customer relationships can be combined with information about potential new customers as part of a comprehensive approach. BMW aggregates customer data from every customer interaction (such as use of the online product configurator, participation in vehicle presentations and product consultations) and analyzes it in terms of purchase probability. Customers classified as potential buyers receive personalized information in the form of e-mail, direct mail, invitations to special events at dealerships, etc. After a sale is completed, the cus-

tomer evaluates the dealership, vehicle delivery and all related purchase experiences. This evaluation is then added to a database with
existing customer data. As a result, it is reported that the purchase
probability for that customer group tripled (Strauss & Schoder 2001).

Marketing professionals can use their knowledge of the existing market and customers to develop and position specific customer offers (*strategy and offer*). The emphasis
here should be on developing a market strategy and integrating the various distribution
and communication channels. Different ideas need to be worked out for conveying
the advantages of the service being offered, structuring customer preferences with
regard to products and services, and addressing different customer interests. The systematic, permanent, flexible development of specific customer offers nearly always
requires an immediate adjustment of existing organizational structures and processes in
the context of reorganization and training; this is usually referred to as *customer-focused
organization*.

These concepts are implemented in sales and service to include all customer
interfaces. Sales information systems include functions such as customer analyses, deadline monitoring, scheduling shipments, sales forecasts, support for offer creation, and
sales profitability checks. Insurance providers, for example, use what are known as sales
support systems to calculate complex insurance products as well as to train internal
sales associates. The sales process is complete when order data and customer data have
been integrated into existing systems for billing and order management. Services that
take place after the sales process has been completed include loyalty programs, measures
to improve the effectiveness of the service organization, or services that use a communication center. A *communication center* or *interaction center* is a call center that has
been enhanced to accommodate Internet applications.

A call center agent, like the agents active in the added value telephone
services of **Deutsche Telekom** (www.dtag.de), can assist customers by
opening the same web page that the customer is viewing and help them
to enter any missing information or answer their questions (known as
browser sharing).

Design options for a CRM cycle with telecom support range from simple contact
person qualification to systematic, permanent customer support in *Telecoverage to Telesales* and simple *Tele-Partner Support* concepts (Figure 1.4).

Whereas the term *Telemarketing* includes activities in the areas of data qualification,
contact person qualification and qualification of specific potential buyers (known as
lead qualification), the term *Telecoverage* involves the systematic, permanent support of
customers via telephone and support for company–internal partner management in the
sense of an internal telephone sales team (Naudi 2003). *Tele-Partner Support* comprises
all activities for active sales support and partner tracking as well as support services in
the form of an internal sales team (as a sort of outsourced function) for partners. This

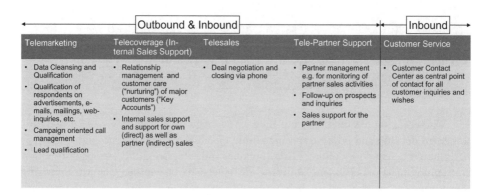

Figure 1.4 Different forms of Telemanagement.

includes contact qualification for partners through the respective company. All Tele-management functions can be deployed *inbound* (reactive, initiated by customers or partners) and *outbound* (active, initiated by your own company) (Krumm & Geissler 2005). A Customer Service Center is usually understood to be the central channel for incoming calls for (reactive) processing of customer inquiries, such as those in response to marketing campaigns. The Telemanagement tool outlined here, however, is not meant to be exclusive. Depending on how internal processes, customer categories and market segments are structured, Telecoverage functions can also be used to cover Telemarketing tasks, such as in the business-to-business segment (B2B), when generating qualified leads for larger key accounts. The following criteria should be used when selecting and designing Telemanagement functions:

- **Customer relationships:** Maintaining existing customer relationships, as performed by Telecoverage agents, for example. Case studies in the B2B area clearly demonstrate that changing telephone contact persons causes an above-average drop in customer retention and willingness to make subsequent purchases.
- **Qualifications:** Qualifications of agents to process individual tasks. This includes a wide range of activities, from simple data qualification in Telemarketing which requires a relatively low level of qualification, to more complex inquiries regarding products and sales in Telesales which require the relevant level of product knowledge and skills.
- **Resource situation:** The quantity of resources present in a specific task area, derived from detailed planning of required telecom capacities during campaign planning, for example.

The term *customer retention*, one of the essential concepts in CRM, subsumes classic customer retention programs such as loyalty points as well as web-specific retention measures such as actively designing online communities (Seybold 2001). The CRM cycle allows us to integrate customers to a point where they are even involved in product development, as in web-based *electronic product clinics*, where customers can test and evaluate products before they come on the market (Chesbrough 2003, 2006; Ulrich *et al.* 2003).

Fiat (www.fiat.de) got customers virtually involved in the product development process when it was developing the *Punto*. Using a variety of designs and fitting options, customers could put together and see their ideal car. Within three months, Fiat received more than 3,000 responses, which it used in the development process (Bliemel & Fassott 2000).

With IdeaStorm (www.dellideastorm.com), **Dell** maintains and manages a community that has contributed almost 9,000 ideas to date, which serves as a discussion platform where innovative customers can engage in a dialogue with Dell experts. Through collaboration with their customers, companies like Dell are able to cultivate an external information and human capital resource that participates in the company's value creation with the same enthusiasm as the company does itself (Schoder *et al.* 2008).

A prominent example for co-innovation jointly with customer has been established by **BMW**, which receives more than 1,000 innovative ideas from its customers per year without any further promotions or advertisements. The "Customer Innovation Lab" offers each customer, employee as well as further interested persons the possibility to insert ideas in an easy way and post them for further discussions. All proposals following the theme on "How to further enhance my BMW car?" will be valuated through an internal expert team.

Webasto AG, one of the world's leading suppliers of sunroofs and heaters for the automobile industry, involves end customers directly as partners in product development. Their collaboration ranges from simple customer input and classic market research to lead user workshops and the integration of Internet communities (Lang & Reich 2008).

Most recent approaches in Japan even go so far as to give registered members the opportunity to test all sorts of products (cosmetics, ketchup, etc.) in a **Sample Lab** (www.samplelab.jp) and take home the ones they like. The opportunity to test products before purchase appeals to customers, while the opportunity to receive diverse customer feedback, usually before the products are available to the general market, appeals to manufacturers. Similar approaches are used in England, where *Brand New You Tube* sends cosmetics to consumers for them to test at home (www.brandnewyoumagazine.com/bnytube). Consumers are then asked to provide detailed feedback on the products.

The range of activities outlined here for the CRM cycle extends to *complaint management* (Stauss & Seidel 1998; Pepels 2001b). Sales and service include applications that support customer-focused business processes (such as those for automating marketing, sales and service), as well as the entire control, support and synchronization of all channels for communicating with the customer (e-mail, web, telephone – Hippner & Wilde 2001).

After sales and service has been implemented, the measures it introduced are checked (response tracking and controlling) – for example, by calculating the value of the customer throughout the customer relationship (known as *customer lifetime value*) or by means of a more comprehensive evaluation as part of a *balanced scorecard* procedure. This check allows us to collate all the experiences in the cycle and plan additional measures (Peppers & Rogers 1999). The results of this phase should be entered as additional customer information and retained for other measures in the CRM cycle. This analysis of all marketing activities along defined key performance indicators (KPIs) allows conclusions to be drawn about which of the marketing activities performed – some of which may already be established company practice – are actually bringing about the desired results, and which of them need to be stopped immediately.

After **Continental Airlines** narrowly escaped bankruptcy, it moved in a new direction that focused on collecting better information about the profitability of individual customers. Part of this involved generating data about how passengers were treated when their flight experienced a long delay, when they were bumped off a flight, or when they were negatively affected in some other way during their journey (Oldroyd & Gulati 2005).

The first insight gained from this CRM project was anything but positive. It revealed that customer support was disorganized, wasting millions of dollars each year. For instance, check-in personnel acted arbitrarily when providing compensation for delays and other deficiencies. One alarming revelation was the fact that, on average, customers who brought the company the *least* profit received the *most* compensation. In some cases, "stranded" passengers had even succeeded in receiving compensation more than once for the same incident. Customers who had been bumped from their flight received one voucher for a free flight from the check-in staff at the airport, and a second voucher when they called customer service to complain. Agents at the call center had no way of knowing that those customers had already received compensation at the time of the incident (Oldroyd & Gulati 2005).

Continental began viewing its customer information holistically; they gathered all data relevant to customer contact in a central database, then consolidated and analyzed it. This enabled them to provide the same kind and amount of compensation for delays and similar inconveniences. When a passenger receives a voucher for a free flight from the check-in staff at the airport, the occurrence immediately appears in the database along with all other information about that customer. Even if the customer calls the airline's customer service center immediately after making a complaint at the airport, the person will not receive a second voucher.

Compiling customer interactions in a centralized database also provided a much more sophisticated platform for subsequent measures.

In the mid-1990s, Continental Airlines had 35 to 40 US and another 50 international databases. A good half of these were intended for managing customer data, though almost all of them contained other important data about customers and transactions. The CRM project led to all the databases being consolidated into two. One was for usable information about customer relationships (customer analytics) and data modeling, and the other was for company data relating to order processing.

In the past, having various databases often meant having various answers to a single question. Even the simple question of "which customers were most profitable for Continental?" could not be answered conclusively. The answer varied, depending on whether the calculation basis was the number of miles flown or the ticket price. As a result of consolidating the customer databases, the calculation now includes both the number of miles flown and the ticket price and consolidates them in a unified customer value model.

The group of analysts at Continental also use feedback from 49,000 customer service representatives for continuously forming new hypotheses and pre-defining new measures. Their purpose is to maintain and expand the company's customer base. Dialog takes place during think tank meetings and training events led by project coordinators from marketing. The job of these marketing experts is to determine measures for improving customer focus at Continental. During these meetings, air traffic controllers, managers and flight attendants from domestic and international operations share their experiences. The marketing team responsible for customer focus then passes the information on to model developers. They, in turn, modify and improve their forecast models, hypotheses and interventions based on the customer database (Oldroyd & Gulati 2005).

This type of workshop has proved to be very successful for Continental and has already produced more than 600 suggestions for how customer data can be used to improve service quality. One suggestion, for example, was to expand the database of information that *President's Club* personnel have for frequent flyers to include such information as customers' favorite drinks.

One of the tests Continental performed involved different options for responding to customers who had been inconvenienced while traveling – by a delayed flight, for example. Customers in the control group received no response whatsoever from the airline. Some customers received an apology letter from the CEO, others received a letter and a voucher for a free flight, while others received a letter with a pass to the company's *Club Lounge*. Subsequent buying behavior was then evaluated for each group. The result was as astounding as it was simple. Although all (active) interaction with these customers was beneficial, the Club Lounge response was just as effective as the other, far more costly options (Oldroyd & Gulati 2005, reproduced by permission of Harvard Business Manager; Seybold, 1998).

1.3 THE CHALLENGE: FROM THE MASS MARKET TO ONE-TO-ONE

1.3.1 The Goals and Problems of Individualization

In the eyes of many CMOs, after direct marketing and telephone marketing had prepared the way, it was the Internet that ultimately broke down the barriers for businesses to individualize how they address target groups. Numerous studies predict a steady trend toward individualization in all areas of life and also for the near future. This is due to a growing awareness of quality and function, which demands products that meet specific consumer expectations, as well as a growing desire on the part of consumers for product variety (known as *variety seeking behavior*). As a consequence, many providers have been forced to employ marketing that addresses consumers on a more individual level or offer a more diverse range of products even to the point of made-to-order. Commensurate with this trend, sales markets are constantly becoming more segmented. Ultimately, many companies will be faced with the challenge of addressing and processing customers individually (Piller 2006; Schnäbele 1997).

Individualized services have traditionally been associated with an increase in revenue resulting from the added value generated by a solution that is tailored to a customer's specific needs (Kleinaltenkamp 1995). However, a number of competition factors prevent a company from being able to respond to fragmenting sales markets and the trend toward individualization simply by using the classic strategy of differentiating itself by means of variety or offering individualized services and communication – combined with a *premium price*. Challenges such as pricing pressure due to overcapacity, smaller and smaller differences between competitors in terms of technology and quality, and ever-increasing competition from abroad as a result of recent developments in IT all lead to growing market pressure that has changed many industries from sellers' markets to buyers' markets where consumers are in a much stronger negotiating position. The relationship between price and performance is also shifting. Even at low sales prices, consumers have relatively high demands with regard to quality, service, variety and functionality, or, conversely, in the case of products with a high degree of differentiation, they have very specific additional requirements that must be met within a certain budget (Kaluza 1996). The solution to this area of tension has been to replace small-scale individualization at premium prices with *mass individualization* at costs and prices that are approximately equal to those of standard products already available, while at the same time offering a higher degree of interaction with individual customers (McKenna 1997; Pine *et al.* 1995; Mayer 1993). See Figure 1.5.

Since the beginning of the 1990s, more and more companies have been turning away from classic mass production and segment-based marketing and opting instead for an **individualized approach**. This approach is based on perceiving all customers as independent market segments and serving their needs accordingly, both in marketing and in service delivery. Consequently, individualization has a bearing on the fields of marketing (one-to-one marketing, Peppers & Rogers 1993) and service delivery (**Mass Customization** – Pine 1993; Schnäbele 1997). In both cases, the starting point of individualization is determining what customers want and transferring those needs into specific marketing activities or product and service specifications, which makes it

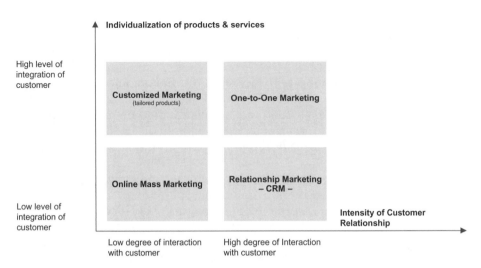

Figure 1.5 Intensity of customer relationship and individualization of range of services (Strauss 2008; Link & Hildebrand 1993).

absolutely necessary to increase the intensity of the information exchange between providers and customers.

The basis for individualization is a customer database for saving, analyzing and supplying all available customer data. The permanent collection of customer information builds on this type of customer database, leading to a continuous process of learning and adjustment in marketing and service delivery (known as a *learning relationship* – Peppers & Rogers 1997). On the one hand, CRM, as an approach to systematic relationship management, prepares the foundation for subsequent individualization, while, on the other, individualization is a natural, consistent form of CRM implementation.

Cortal Consors, as a "customer-driven investment bank", is an organization built around its customers. Each week, they check the assignment of customers to different customer group segments using an analytical process. Customers whose behavior and profile have changed are moved to a customer segment that better suits their profile. The only thing customers in this learning relationship see is that they are receiving service that best supports their activities – keeping with the company's own motto for customer focus in terms of *"knowing what the customer wants without asking them"*. Using sophisticated mathematical and statistical procedures based on high-quality, comprehensive customer data, the company can put together an extensive customer profile. In this comprehensive CRM model that includes analytics, marketing, sales, finance, call centers and IT, information technology helps to address and support customers at an individual level. The sales channels Cortal Consors uses are investment advisers (in the field), call centers and an online portal. This makes each of its customer support units a multichannel unit. Maintaining customer data is a task shared by everyone who has contact with customers. A structured authorization concept controls who is responsible for maintaining specific data records and who can use specific customer information. With "customer intelligence", a new customer's registration data can be used to assign them to an appropriate customer segment group. In this way the customer receives the best possible support from the very beginning (Alvarez *et al.* 2006).

The decisive factor for aggregating customer knowledge is the interaction between a data warehouse and the operational customer database in the CRM system. Call center agents proactively receive customer value reports that contain asset classes as well as soft factors such as estimates of how willing the customer might be to buy other products. The likelihood of individual customers switching to another bank is also forecasted. Customer data queries are supported in real time so that call center agents can immediately retrieve all the information about a customer in the event of a call (Martin 2006; Strauss 2008).

Last year the lingerie brand **Women's Secret** had limited insight into the particular shopping behaviors and preferences of individual customers. As with many companies, much of the brand's marketing and planning was based on overall historical sales and intuition. Competition being what it is, Women's Secret realized that it needed to offer its wide range of customers a more personalized experience. By learning more about each customer, the company could tempt her with specific offers that matched her spending profile, increasing loyalty, sales and the entire customer base at the same time. As the use of its data warehouse progressed, the group integrated all data in its centralized data warehouse from across different marketing channels, while also introducing analytics, to better understand and manage customer transaction behavior. Customers who join the club receive "wow-money" – vouchers equaling 5% of their purchases – which they can use toward future purchases at Women's Secret for the subsequent year. Additionally, loyalty club members receive a "birthday surprise" on their birthdays, along with other discounts and special offers. *Club WOW* also treats its members to free exclusive concerts, festivals and trips. The data warehouse also allows the lingerie brand to launch timely, individualized promotions based on sophisticated CRM customer event triggers.

Advantages of individualization for the customer result from: saving time when searching for relevant information, the option of storing user experiences, and receiving products that match individual requirements exactly.

From a company's perspective, individualization in multifaceted concepts promises (Piller & Schoder 1999):

- Sustainable strengthening of the *competitive position* with increased customer focus and differentiation of the product range *vis-à-vis* competitors, combined with increased revenue;
- *Greater market know-how* by systematically collecting all available customer data and using it for product development and marketing, with the option of in-depth, one-to-one marketing and cross-selling other products that fit the customer's user profile;
- More *targeted placement* of advertising and with it a reduction of losses due to stray ads;
- *Customer-specific solutions*, for which customers may be willing to pay higher prices, compared to standard products at standard prices;
- *Greater customer satisfaction*, which tends to entail greater customer loyalty, results from selectively offering products and services that have been tuned to individual preferences. For example, a screen could include all of the user's previous orders, similar new products, and products that the user has not yet seen but which buyers with a very similar interest profile have found (*collaborative filtering*).

1.3.2 One-to-One Marketing

One-to-One Marketing involves making all marketing activities customer-centric, with the goal of addressing those customers at an individual level (Peppers & Rogers 1993; Strauss & Schoder 1999b). An example of One-to-One Marketing is the manner in which *Amazon.com* recommends products by showing items that customers with similar product preferences have already bought. Individualized electronic newsletters are also common now, such as the ones sent by online CD stores (*CDNow!*, www.cdnow.com) that provide recipients with custom content (Figure 1.6).

The emphasis of the offer is added value that "fits". For example, an offer will present a user with performers and groups that have a similar musical style, or, based

Dear Ralf,

Because you're a fan of Aretha Franklin we thought you'd want to know that for a limited time only, her entire catalogue is available here at CDNow for up to 30% off our regular prices.

To see Aretha Franklin's entire discography go to:

http://cdnow.com/aretha/from=rex:x:cdn:af.

Your friends at CDNow

Figure 1.6 Example of a simple e-mail based on One-to-One Marketing.

on what is known about a music lover's entire collection, an offer will contain the CDs that that person does not yet own, but which would fit right in with the CDs the person already has.

Other ways for implementing mass communication at the level of individual customers include:

- Greeting and addressing customers by name;
- Managing customer-related data, such as credit card numbers and delivery addresses, to spare customers the inconvenience of providing that information each time they place an order.

A new CRM system at **Porsche Cars North America** displays all customer-related information and vehicle histories, which helps to simplify campaigns, mailings and how customer concerns are processed. In the highly competitive automobile industry, the success of a make no longer depends solely on performance, design and safety. Instead, customer loyalty and brand trust are becoming the most important factors. So it is only logical for Porsche to take a 360-degree view of data concerning potential buyers, customers and vehicles the center of its customer relationship management. Transferring the approach to the company's largest market, the United States, was the next logical step. The data pool at Porsche Cars North America (PCNA) in Atlanta contains around 2.7 million completed business transactions, 1.2 million customers and potential buyers, and more than 650,000 vehicles. In the past, all information about customers and vehicle histories was stored in 10 different databases that were not connected with one another. This made it practically impossible to implement total customer and vehicle support. Porsche decided to introduce an integrated CRM system within 10 months in order to have a panoramic view of all its data ("360-degree view of the customer").

In addition to key functions, the project team also introduced new processes, including predictive complaint management. This provides Porsche's customer commitment specialists with early warnings in cases such as when a vehicle is in service for an extended period of time due to delayed delivery of replacement parts, or when a vehicle needs a safety-relevant repair. The system also allows Porsche to follow, without interruption, the relationship between a vehicle and its owners over the course of time: Where was the vehicle purchased? Which dealers delivered services? Is a new purchase planned? When does the leasing agreement expire? etc. Changes to address data or specific customer requests are transferred from the integrated database to the relevant locations automatically and processed. This allows Porsche to implement central campaigns, follow-up processes in sales management and service activities in a customer-specific manner using up-to-the-minute information. Previously, for example, mailing campaigns had always been selected and performed manually. This meant that a great deal of time was spent for each selection. Introducing the CRM system reduced selection time to 15 to 30 minutes. At the same time, the number of letters returned due to incorrect contact information went down considerably (SAP 2007).

- Product presentation tuned to customer preferences and skills, achieved by involving users in purposefully designed dialogs on the web (giving experts more detailed information, for example);
- Information services that tell customers about areas that might be of interest to them, either because they have explicitly expressed an interest in those areas already or because previous dialog with the customer suggested they might be interested in those areas, for instance;
- Recommendation services with the optional inclusion of profiles and evaluations from third parties with similar preferences, such as in the banking sector (Strauss & Schoder 2001). See Figure 1.7.

Using or not using one-to-one marketing has serious consequences for the future of traditional purchase advice. Empirical findings can be summarized as follows (Strauss & Schoder 2001; Strauss 2008): more and more companies that have already implemented a way of addressing customers individually increasingly expect that one-to-one marketing will replace traditional purchase advice (at least in part), supplemented by quality data from neutral third parties such as Consumer Reports in the US

Source of Information \ Source of Rules	Bank	Customer	Automatically Generated
Legacy Data — Bank	• Development of different security alternatives → Alerts and new recommendations • Segment → Direct Marketing • Anniversary → Greetings / -Mail • Product Usage → Individual conditions	• Location → offer for local events • accounts, deposits → mailing of quotations • Transactions → order acknowledgments	• Automatical segmentation of customer base according to product evaluations and product assessments → offers / cross-selling • "Comprehensive" advising / offer through expert systems
Profile Data — Customer (explicit)	• Stockwatch list→ information about IPOs of "similar" companies • Preferences → Recommendations for new products	• Stockwatch lists, preferences → short infos / analysis, industries, markets companies • Stock limits → e-mail notification • Preferences for realty → real estate offerings, mailing lists	• Collaborative filtering according to preferences and web usage → offers for articles / news in finance • Analysis of web usage (preferences) → Change of navigation path (short-cuts)
Web Activities — Customer (implicit)	• Visited categories → recommendations • Used tools, downloads → Offer / hint for further tools / downloads • Reduced logins, period of time without logins → e-mail with information on innovations / news / enhancements		

Figure 1.7 Personalization at a bank (project example).

(www.consumerreports.org) or the consumer association, *Stiftung Warentest*, in Germany. Individual marketing with its higher degree of IT-driven automation brings with it the chance to record and maintain a greater number of business relationships. Though real life examples show that a personalized marketing approach can help to significantly improve customer loyalty, as was the case at *Xerox* (www.xerox.com), many companies are still not fully aware of the link between loyalty and individualized marketing (Seybold 2001; Peppers & Rogers 1999; Strauss & Schoder 2001).

Companies that have not yet been able to solve the problem of base customer data records that are distributed over several systems will not be able to implement individualized marketing in the near future – they must first solve the more basic problem of information management. Once data consolidation has taken place, one-to-one marketers can (Strauss & Schoder 2001):

- Make more individual evaluations in the data records;
- Define customer segments more clearly to identify key accounts;
- Start determining at an earlier date the total value of customers over the course of their life cycle (known as *customer lifetime value*).

Germany's **Postbank** has shown how to implement individualization successfully. "e-Design", a personalized, individualized campaign for customer communication, offers impressive evidence that one-to-one dialog is technically feasible and can be extremely efficient even with a very large number of customers. When a person requests product information from the Postbank call center or Internet site, he or she receives material that is more specifically tailored to his or her interests than ever before. For a demander who needs a credit card for travel, there are product flyers and literature with images and text aimed at travelers. Both the flyer and the image of the credit card on the flyer show the customer's name. The application for the card is already filled with the data provided to the call center, making it almost completely personalized. If the inquiry concerns products for savings and invest- ments, additional building blocks are added, such as the amount the person wants to invest, the duration of the investment and the motive. The customer receives his/her own special offer including the current interest rate and the total payout immediately in "black on white". With a standardized procedure, Postbank individually compiles each piece of printed matter according to the customer's needs. The foundation for this consists of building blocks from the company's own parameter pool, which allows for every possible combination. This starts with appropriately addressing the target group, progresses with socio- demographically tailored images and text blocks for the product, and concludes with personalized calculation examples for each investor. The aim is to make every customer feel as if he/she is being addressed directly in every channel of communication. This strategy has brought Postbank tangible, measurable success. Depending on the product, sales improved by 20% to 30%, and process costs were cut in half (Dreihues-Uter 2005).

In a similar way, the American banking entity **First Union** recently launched a complex strategy to segment its customer portfolio, assigning them importance according to their current value and potential lifespan in the heart of the bank. The bank's sales reps have a scorecard in which customers are rigorously classified by these two factors, and the scorecard also invites the reps to offer maximally personalized treatment to those customers of greatest interest. At First Union's customer service center, operators have weather information for each state in the United States at their disposal at all times, so that the first thing they do is ask the most potentially "interesting" customers about the weather in the place they're calling from. It is perceived as being a curious and intelligent way of making customers feel that their financial entity is following their steps very closely (Daemon Quest 2005).

1.3.3 The Challenge of Mass Customization – From Individualized Marketing to Individualized Products

Customer-specific mass production or *Mass Customization* attempts to combine the advantages of mass production (cost advantages from large lot sizes) and customer-specific production (competitive advantages from product diversity) at a cost level approximately equal to that of mass-produced standardized goods (Downes & Mui 1998; Piller & Schoder 1999; Pine 1993).

The following are examples of Mass Customization:

* The *Original Spin* program by **Levi's Jeans**, which manufactures jeans according to customers' individual measurements. It offers a total of 49,500 different sizes and 30 different styles for a grand total of 1.5 million possible combinations of jeans at a cost of USD 55 each. Orders are filled and shipped within two weeks;
* **3billionbooks**, which implemented "print-on-demand" including bookbinding (www.3billionbooks.com/; McCloskey 2001);
* **Creo-Shoes.com**, which provides personalized shoes (www.creo-shoes.com/);
* The printing and publishing sector, which provides personalized printed matter such as personalized daily newspapers (Conniff 1993; Consoli 1993);
* **Dolzer**, which offers custom-tailored clothing at an affordable price using a multichannel system (online, telephone, stores);
* **xaaaz.de**, Germany's first online department store for individualized products (Piller 2006).

The point is not necessarily to manufacture a lot size of 1 for customers. Rather, the concept of Mass Customization, as it applies to industrial goods for instance, is more about manufacturing a large number of identical products – which have already been adjusted to suit individual customers – for a single consumer.

Literature on the subject sometimes characterizes Mass Customization using terms that clearly suggest conventional made-to-order production (preliminary costing, generation of customer-specific work plans and bills of material, a low degree of preproduction). However, the two need to remain distinct. Mass Customization is neither a case of configure-to-order nor do the products it offers have different basic structures. This type of individualization is about a few small differences in the details, which from the point of view of the customer, however, are of crucial functional importance. All the products normally have the same price or follow a clearly defined pricing structure. Bills of material are dynamic and should be generated automatically; the same is true for production and assembly instructions. Unlike made-to-order, Mass Customization aims at a large sales market whose customers differ with respect to the specific features they want in a product (Piller & Schoder 1999).

Perhaps no other newcomer to Web 2.0 mass customization has harvested so much favor in Europe recently as **Mymuesli.com**. Yet only a few weeks after business started, public enthusiasm became a problem, as response to the site exceeded all expectations. The consequence: delivery problems. Still, fans of the German company based in Passau did not walk away. This is a lesson for how to communicate successfully on the web (Kolbrück 2007).

The business idea is simple. Customers can put together their very own breakfast cereal by choosing from around 70 different organic ingredients. "Custom made cereals" is their slogan. The entire site makes a highly personalized, friendly impression. Customers are addressed with the German informal form ("du"). The three founders introduce themselves as "the guys". Customers who create their own mixture can give it a name. The principle of Mass Customization has electrified the blogosphere more than any other space, and it's no wonder – self-determined content and brands are part of that space's core values. Bloggers also helped to make the site popular on the Internet. The search engine *Technorati* now counts almost 300 links to the site. Radio and printed media reported the story, providing additional PR – at no cost (Kolbrück 2007).

Yet the founders attribute their quick success to more than just web logs; it was also the use of conventional media to reach traditional target groups. The print media reacted to the blogs. Bloggers then responded to those articles, starting a ping pong effect. There are no plans for a marketing campaign, however. Instead, the hope is that no-compromise transparency will win people over and generate new customers. The most important tool is the company blog, which was also where the company clearly explained the reasons for the delivery problems as they arose. This made Mymuesli even more curious and popular to people (Kolbrück 2007).

Customers even provided suggestions about how to fix the packaging bottleneck or proposed new products and additional supply sources for ingredients. The muesli makers promptly respond to e-mails and similar offers made by bloggers. According to company information, not even being sold out of muesli had hurt the company image. The blog continues to remain an essential part of their PR work. It is intended to create transparency and announce new products and features.

Once the logistics problem is solved, we can expect to see many new developments. The company is to extend its business to further European countries soon, and a relaunch of the website is in progress. The plan is to make it more interactive so that it can develop into something like a community. Then customers might be able to present and evaluate their own mixes. Until now, the mix gallery focuses primarily on the favorite mixes of the founders themselves (Kolbrück 2007; reproduced by permission of Horizont).

Alternative forms of mass customization range from customization that does not interfere in manufacturing (known as *soft customization*), as in the following examples (Piller 2001; Pine 1993):

- *Service individualization:* Individual services are added to standard products, as at *Hertz Gold Service*, which enhances its standard service, car rentals, with additional services like bus transfers or road maps for the trip that the customer has planned;
- *Self-individualization:* Customers modify products, like making their own birthday cards at *Hallmark*;
- *Point of delivery customization:* Products are adjusted according to customer needs, like *Dynafit*, which makes the molds for the insoles of its ski boots in the store, or *Build-A-Bear* (www.buildabear.de), which offers limited customization of teddy bears;

Soft Customization: No intervention in manufacturing process	Hard Customization: Manufacturing oriented variety
Service individualisation Enhancement of standard products with individualised secondary services	Modularisation according to a construction set Development customer specific products out of standardised components
Self-Individualisation Construction and manufacturing of standardised products with built-in flexibility, which might be adapted by the customer himself	Mass manufacturing of single products Cost efficient individualised manufacturing of a product across the whole value chain via standardised processes
Customer specific final or pre-production	
Individualised final assembly in retail store / sales channel Delivery of a uniform raw product, which will be finalised according to customer preferences at the point-of-sale	Individualised pre/final production with standardised finishing Either the first or the last parts of the value chain are customer specific, all others are highly standardised.

Figure 1.8 Different forms of Mass Customization (Piller & Schoder 1999; reproduced by permission of the authors).

At the other end of the spectrum is *hard customization* (Figure 1.8). Hard customization means:

- *Modularization*, as at *Ohaus*, which uses a modular system to manufacture precision scales; or custom, paper-based daily newspapers, like at *First!* and the *Wall Street Journal*;
- *Mass-produced one-offs* that use standardized processes, as at *Sandvik Coromant*, which manufactures custom tools;
- *Standardized manufacturing that employs customized pre/postproduction*, where either the first process steps (such as metalworking) or the last process steps (such as assembly) are customer-specific. One example is the clothing retailer *Dolzer*, whose custom-tailoring involves cutting cloth to custom sizes at the beginning of the manufacturing process and standardized mass production for the rest of the process.

Intelligent customer interfaces in the form of design tools help to customize products and services for individual customers by enabling them to quickly and intuitively find a combination that offers them the most value. The Internet has *online product configurators* that lead buyers to the optimal product, harmonizing their needs with the capabilities of the company. Without tools of this sort, customers (or their representatives in retail and sales) often face so many basic designs and combinations of options that the resulting over complexity may well prevent them from finding a suitable solution (Piller & Schoder 1999; Pine 1993; Reichwald & Piller 2001).

Find the right kit to install your **Lintech** hands-free system in any car model with just a few clicks – that is what the German company Lintech promises with its new online configurator. Installers, for instance, can use the company's database to access information about nearly any established make and model (www.lintech.de/fse-konfigurator/). The user chooses a vehicle and the tool recommends the installation kit that fits. The same page offers users the option of downloading an installation guide. The configurator is currently available for two of the company's hands-free Bluetooth systems, *Basic* and *Comfort*. In the future, however, the tool will support more products, says LinTech (*Telecom Handel* 2007).

Verpackung24 GmbH (www.verpackung24.com) has a new online store for corporate customers. The portal can be used to purchase boxes, plastic foil, bags and pallets, plus items for worker safety. An online packaging configurator completes the offer. The tool plans and calculates packaging solutions based on specific customer data. This makes it possible to configure special packaging that goes beyond standard solutions.

Inframa (www.inframa.de) offers an online configurator that helps users to select a look for their banquet chairs, from different frame models, colors and even fabrics and patters. The assortment includes stackable banquet chairs made of aluminum and steel, folding banquet tables, accessories like carts for moving chairs and tables, personalized consultation and custom-fabrication. The company has developed chairs and tables for events such as the World Expo 2005 in Japan (*Allgemeine Hotel- und Gastronomie-Zeitung* 2006).

The foundation of manufacturing-based Mass Customization is the use of flexible manufacturing systems such as universal CNC machines, flexible transfer lines, flexible production cells and flexible manufacturing systems using different degrees of flexibility (Doringer 1991; Wildemann 1994; Mayer 1993). However, Mass Customization does not necessitate state of the art production technology. For instance, one part of the manufacturing process could employ the advantages of mass production, while custom manufacturing would only be used for specific value-adding activities.

1.4   THE CHALLENGE: THE CHANGED CONDITIONS OF MARKETING STRATEGY

Companies face a variety of changes that affect their business strategy and marketing strategy – the rise of Web-based applications is just one example for such changes (Hartman & Sifonis 2000; Porter 2001). See Figure 1.9.

On one hand, the rise of virtual company networks and customized products promote a virtualization of organizational structures and products. Examples can be found in the manufacture and marketing of customized CDs via the Internet (Piller 2001; McCloskey 2001). *Virtual organizations* come into being when independent companies collaborate for a limited period of time, involving parties such as suppliers, distributors, customers and even competitors (Fleisch 2001).

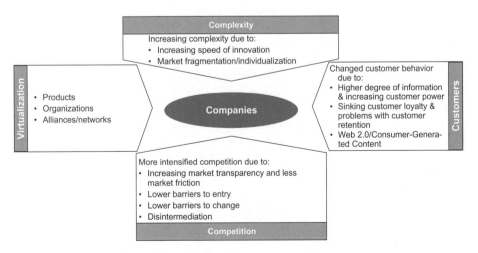

Figure 1.9   Changes affecting company strategy (Porter 2001; Fitz-Enz 2001; Wirtz 2000; Hartman & Sifonis 2000).

One frequently cited example is **Dell** (www.dell.com), which custom assembles and delivers all of its computer systems within 12 days. Production takes place in tightly woven value chains and in sync with supplier procurement and customer procurement. Supplier warehouses were positioned near production areas for this very purpose.

The increasing *complexity* in developing and implementing company strategies can be traced back to two different phenomena. Firstly, an increase in *innovation* speed leads to an immediate and significant *decrease in product life cycles* (Brown & Engelhardt 1998).

Leica offers one example of shorter product life cycles and the "digital threat". Leica revolutionized photography when it invented the small-format camera in 1913 and then mass produced it in the 1920s. The cameras were lightweight with excellent technical execution. Yet this traditional company has been having serious problems. Its losses have been piling up since 2003. The reason for the crisis is that the company, once a technological leader, appears to have failed to accurately assess the importance of digital photography. Management assumed for a long time that demanding customers would not be interested in megapixels, but in the photographic experience – meaning top quality, from optics to mechanics to final images (Koch 2005).

Leica did not decide on a *hybrid strategy* until much later. It developed a digital back for what were originally analog single-lens reflex cameras. In doing so, the company intended to enable customers to continue using the lenses and cameras they had been collecting for decades. Despite increasing economic pressure, management refused to allow any compromises that would affect the quality of the new product. The consequence: The module, which had been announced at Photokina 2004, did not appear on the market until mid-June 2005 – significantly later than expected (Koch 2005).

Despite these economic troubles, Leica remains a cult brand that continues to attract customers. Principal shareholders, however, are losing patience and demanding that the company change its strategy. The concern is that the company's downward spiral will only get worse and become a vicious circle. Yet the phenomenon of *self-fortification* was also what played a central role in establishing and maintaining Leica's unique expertise (cf. Schoder 1995). An item that succeeds on the market becomes an easy sell. A product that sells well draws more and more customers, who trust the decisions other consumers have made or because the commercial channels really only support one particular standard. When a brand has a good reputation, the effect is even stronger. Yet expertise in a particular area – in the case of Leica, first-class analog photography – can also lead to a situation where management is no longer capable of doing anything but what it has always done. Then management is locked in its own success. Straying from the path that made it successful would seem foolish for the short term and would be difficult to communicate to the market and its own shareholders (Koch 2005).

Even when the company is very successful, management judges developments in the market against the backdrop and in the context of its own, highly developed capabilities. Leica executives were almost forced not to take digital technology seriously, because objective criteria showed that when the technology was in its infancy, it was far from matching the quality of analog photography. The problem with assessing developments in a technology or market is the fixed frame of reference – here it was the company's high degree of expertise in its field. In situations like this, companies end up using what they know to block their own path, which makes it necessary for them to "unlearn" insights and knowledge that took years to acquire (Koch 2005; Strauss 1996; reproduced by permission of Harvard Business Manager).

As demand increases for customized products and services, so does *complexity in market reach and production* (Zerdick *et al.* 2001). Implementing one-to-one marketing requires more than a detailed analysis of customer data; it requires using that analysis to target even very small customer segments, and then changing the manufacturing process to accommodate very small lot sizes. Customization increases market fragmentation, in turn increasing the complexity required in marketing management.

Customer behavior is changing more with time and is acting as both a cause and a catalyst for the type of changes in company strategy just mentioned. An increase in the amount of customized information together with better options for collaboration and coordination like those provided by groups of people with common interests (*virtual communities* and *blogs*) lead to more finely-tuned approaches for demanders. The exchange of positive and negative experiences with products and companies (e.g. the customer service department) concentrates demander power in virtual communities and blogs and increases the amount of information on specific topics within the virtual group. The increase in information that is available to consumers along with the removal of barriers that prevented new providers from entering the market leads to a gradual drop in customer loyalty, which causes companies to introduce customer retention measures (Eggert 2001). In the 1970s, in the context of the use of independent test reports (like Stiftung Warentest or Consumer Reports), experts foresaw an archetypical customer who would have access to a comprehensive, independent source of information and who would be very willing to switch brands or dealers (an *information seeker*); today it is the information transparency of the Internet that offers an easily accessible information platform for making that type of consumer a reality (Thorelli *et al.* 1975; Tölle *et al.* 1981; Silberer *et al.* 1984).

Results from the current online shopping surveys show that the number of consumers who consult the Internet before making a purchase has risen in various countries by more than 8% in the last year. In the case of travel services, the Internet influences up to 70% of the buying decisions online users make. The biggest increase in pre-purchase research versus the previous year was in comparisons of retailers, say the results of various online shopping surveys. The group of online users who use the Internet as a source of information before buying products has risen by almost 10% compared to the year before. This means that the Internet has gained more strength as an influential purchasing factor than as a sales channel, since the number of actual online buyers has only risen by 6% during the same time period. The purchase of travel services such as airline tickets and accommodation was most strongly affected (GfK, June 2007).

Toyota's approach is a good example of the systematic use of information transparency on the Internet. For most people, buying a car is associated with taking a great deal of time to reach a decision. Toyota responded to this behavior by offering a link on its website to *Edmunds*, a reliable source for car reviews. Customers trust the objectivity of the *Edmunds* site, which is independent – and Toyota trusts in the fact that its cars do well in those reviews, compared to the competition. In this way, Toyota gives a third party the job of supporting customers during the decision-making process. When customers have the information they want and they know the precise differences between the makes and models they are considering, the *Edmunds* site guides them back to the Toyota site, where they begin the purchasing process (hopefully with greater peace of mind that Toyota is the right choice). Some dealerships, such as **Boch Toyota** in Boston (USA), went even further by showing the vehicles they have in stock with their suggested retail prices and information about dealer costs, asking customers to make them an offer online. Dealers believe that today's (unbound) customers have access to a great deal of information about dealers' acquisition costs. In light of this fact, the best thing a provider can do is maintain the connection to the customer throughout the process. Traditional sales channel logic would suggest that the company should define certain customer segments (like in-store buyers and online buyers) and then use that supplier-side definition as a foundation for building up a direct, indirect or hybrid sales channel for each segment. Instead, Toyota, like other companies, concentrated on and recognized the buying behavior of customers as a whole. This (plus the special features of products and logistics in the markets of partner companies) enabled them to build up distribution channels that best met customer needs (Nunes & Cespedes 2004). **Progressive Insurance** takes a similar road, when honestly sharing both their prices and their competitors' – even when they are not as good. The result: customers respond and acknowledge by placing trust in the new collaborative web (Tapscott & Ticoll 2003).

The availability of comprehensive information and the improved capacity to compare products and services increases the level of knowledge of substitution options from other providers, and in turn, the intensity of competition. One consequence is a drop in the importance of market friction – in the form of fewer barriers that prevent a switch to a new provider, for instance. In traditional (offline) markets, information asymmetry between vendors and demanders with regard to the actual quality of products and services can be significantly reduced by improving general information transparency, as well as with specific services such as *expert forums* and *opinion portals*. Automatic price comparisons from autonomous agents, for instance, further improve market transparency for specific product selection criteria and further limit the room that companies have for pricing and price differentiation. In theory, the only factors stopping markets that are completely transparent (with regard to price) from becoming a reality are:

- Alternative company strategies;
- An individual's limited ability to process information ("information overload");
- The inefficiency of available search methods.

The result is that companies focus more and more on differentiation strategies to avoid being compared to rivals purely on the basis of price, which is often perceived as being unfair (Collins *et al.* 2005).

A search for a **Fujitsu-Siemens Amilo Xi2428** laptop returned 39 matches with prices ranging from EUR 980.50 to EUR 1,133.43 (idealo.de). That is a saving of over EUR 150.00. A search for a **Panasonic NV-GS320** camcorder on Geizkragen.de returned prices between EUR 388.99 and EUR 599.00. This means a potential saving of over EUR 210.00.

Other barriers preventing customers from switching from one provider to another (switching barriers) are technological (systems are not completely compatible, for instance), knowledge-related (as when existing knowledge or additional knowledge is required) and psychological, as in the case of brand loyalty (Schoder 1995; Skiera & Garczorz 2000). All these barriers result in and even increase *switching* costs, which can lead a customer who is rationally considering the pros and cons to not choose an objectively better alternative that is only marginally below the switching costs because that person already has their mind set on the alternative that they already chose.

One example of such a *lock-in* arose when **VHS** was becoming the standard for video recorders in the early 1990s. Even though experts deemed VHS to be technologically inferior to other formats of the time (e.g. Betamax and Video 2000), VHS prevailed as the standard. The reason: VHS managed to establish itself as the standard for video rentals; consequently, the demand for players gradually shifted to VHS-compatible devices, even though they really did not work as well (Schoder 1995).

The situation is similar for the various providers of coffee pad and coffee capsule systems on the market. These are general terms for coffee machines that work with single and double portions, known as coffee pads and coffee capsules. The essential feature of these coffee systems is that they make coffee quickly and easily. The most established coffee pad systems are *E.S.E.* (Illycafe, in Switzerland: Amici), *Cafissimo* (Tchibo), *Caffita* (Gaggia and Ècaffè), *Dolce Gusto* (Krups and Nestlé), *MyCup* (Melitta), *Nespresso* (Nestlé), *Senseo* (Philips and Douwe Egberts) and *Tassimo* (Braun and Kraft Foods). These systems are not compatible with one another, so each system requires specific coffee pads and coffee capsules. At the beginning they were only available from the manufacturer, which greatly limited the choices available. Now, even the coffee packs are available from other providers. When a person buys a particular manufacturer's coffee system, to avoid switching costs he/she must also buy the pads that that system requires for operation. Critics claim these coffee systems exploit price capturing. This means that while the cost of acquiring these coffee machines is relatively low, the subsequent cost for the coffee pads is higher than the cost of traditional coffee – sometimes several times higher.

It can be assumed that such obstacles will gradually erode as a result of new technical standards (that offer the option of easily integrating various technologies), a broader diffusion of knowledge, decreasing loyalty to brands and dealers and increasingly product homogeneity (Seybold 2001).

At the same time, changes in institutional framework conditions as part of the liberalization and deregulation of markets further lower existing barriers to market entry. The intensity of competition will increase in proportion to the time that customers use the Internet and experience what is available there (Strauss & Schoder 2001). As web-based direct distribution (known as *disintermediation*) replaces traditional retail structures, the focus will shift to differentiating the competition.

1.5 THE CHALLENGE: MARKETING STRATEGY FOLLOWS CORPORATE STRATEGY... OR VICE VERSA?

A company's basic goals are the starting point for determining its marketing strategy. At the highest level of a company's goal hierarchy, the **mission** describes its long-term goals and provides a basic framework for all its activities.

The mission of **Merck**: "To provide society with superior products and services by developing innovations and solutions that improve the quality of life and satisfy customer needs, and to provide employees with meaningful work and advancement opportunities, and investors with a superior rate of return." (Reproduced by permission of Merck.)

The mission of **Microsoft**: "A computer on every desktop and in every home, running Microsoft software." (Reproduced by permission of Microsoft.)

The mission of **Novartis** : "We want to discover, develop and successfully market innovative products to prevent and cure diseases, to ease suffering and to enhance the quality of life. We also want to provide a shareholder return that reflects outstanding performance and to adequately reward those who invest ideas and work in our company." (Reproduced by permission of Novartis.)

The vision of **Credit Suisse**: "It is our vision at Credit Suisse to become the world's premier and most admired bank, renowned for our expertise in private banking, investment banking and asset management, and valued for our advice, innovation and execution." (Reproduced by permission of Credit Suisse.)

The mission of **Credit Suisse**: "Our mission is to set new standards in partnering with our clients and providing them with innovative, integrated financial solutions. As a global bank serving clients in every region of the world, cultural diversity is essential to our success. We strive to create an open, respectful workplace that encourages people to work together and with our clients to deliver superior products, services and results and support the success and prosperity of all our stakeholders." (Reproduced by permission of Credit Suisse.)

A company's goal pyramid is a visual expression of how to further operationalize its goals, right down to the level of instrumental goals (Figure 1.10). At the same time, the functional goals at the lower levels – including marketing goals – represent a means of achieving the superordinate goals of the company. While goals tend to remain relatively abstract at the corporate level, it is better to make them more concrete and measurable all the way down to the instrumental goals.

This is used to define the actual *corporate goals* on the next level (Level 2). These goals can be formulated more precisely as financial or non-financial targets. While financial targets are usually defined in terms of return on investment (ROI) or dividends, non-financial targets tend to include dimensions such as improving customer satisfaction or improving the company's ability to innovate (Jenner 2003).

BP, for example, included employee satisfaction as one of its corporate goals, reporting on how it developed in the company's annual review for 2006 (www.bp.com/liveassets/bp_internet/annual_review/annual_review_2006/).

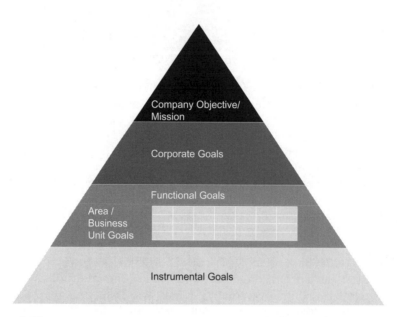

Figure 1.10   Corporate goal system (Jenner 2003; Backhaus & Schneider 2007; Kreikebaum 1989; Homburg & Krohmer 2006).

Tesco reported in a similar fashion about non-monetary KPIs such as employee turnover rate in its annual review for 2007: (www. tescocorporate.com/images/TESCO_FULL%20low.pdf).

UBS strives to increase shareholder value. It proclaims goals such as a sustained return on equity of 15–20% after taxes and average growth of (undiluted) earnings per share in the double-digits – regardless of how the market is performing at any given time.

In most planning scenarios, the strategy follows superordinate corporate goals. In their groundbreaking book, *The Discipline of Market Leaders*, Treacy and Wiersema describe the overarching goals of a company as *value disciplines* (Treacy & Wiersema 1995a, 1995b). It says that successful companies do not serve all heterogeneous customer needs, but rather focus specifically on a unique service promise. That promise is aimed at one of three known customer types: (a) customers that prefer tried-and-true services; (b) customers that prefer innovations; and (c) customers whose individual needs must be met as satisfactorily as possible. A total of three strategies, called *disciplines*, can be derived from those customer types (Schnaars 1998):

* *"Operational excellence" companies:* Distinguish themselves with optimized and rationalized processes. This enables them to guarantee services at a low price and fixed quality. Doing so puts them in a position that competitors in their market cannot reach. Their focus is on having the best prices – setting price standards – as

well as on a relatively limited range of services, average quality, limited service and short value process chains.

One example for this approach comes from **Wal-Mart**, which focuses on very low prices and high efficiency in all its internal and external processes (e.g. its relationship with suppliers). Companies such as Aldi, McDonald's and Toyota have adopted a similar approach.

The Neumarkt plant of Delphi Deutschland GmbH (a subsidiary of the Delphi Corporation) received a gold medal for operational excellence. Plant director Johann Lang bowed to his employees, who received the medal with him. His plant produces high-quality contact parts and plug connections for the car industry. To guarantee the highest quality, the company has been emphasizing insourcing and process excellence for the past seven years. The result: No complaints and zero defects since 2001, as well as no occupational accidents and a below-average number of staff on sick leave (less than 3%) for the past five years. Auditors were impressed with how seriously everyone at the plant takes the guiding principle of "exceptional quality". In recent years, the company has won many awards, such as Factory of the Year in 2005 and the 2007 Prize for Quality, as well as numerous internal distinctions. The chance to be audited by outside experts was what motivated the company to apply for external distinctions. The target: To find areas of the company that could still be improved in spite of all previous efforts (www.cetpm.de/).

- *"Product leadership" companies:* These companies encourage the development of innovative products, which enables them to regularly bring out products that redefine technological standards. They focus on the core processes of innovation, product development and research into market availability, and are always on the look-out for the "first mover" advantage. They emphasize performance, not price. Their essential characteristics can be summarized as (1) having the best products, (2) setting product standards in (3) waves of innovation, and (4) achieving premium prices.

Intel can be cited in this section as an example of a company with a large number of innovative products. **BASF** received the 2005 Product Leadership of the Year Award. The award was presented for the development of a new method of delivering triphenylphosphine (TPP); BASF was the first company in the world to offer it in the form of pellets. The pellets generate less dust than the conventional flakes, which makes them easier to handle and process while also significantly improving safety. Besides pellets, BASF also markets TPP in the form of a meltable mass. In this form, the product can be pumped, allowing it to be processed in a closed system – eliminating the need for costly manual labor. BASF produces TPP using the largest system of its kind in the world, located at its headquarters in Ludwigshafen, Germany. It is the only company in the world to manufacture TPP using a single-strand process, which prevents cross-contamination with other products. The consequence: Consistent, high product quality (www.bankkaufmann. com).

- *"Customer intimacy" companies:* These companies focus on the greatest customer proximity possible. They focus on (1) developing solutions, (2) implementing those solutions and (3) maintaining relationships. They emphasize long-term relationships, not individual transactions.

A good example for a customer intimacy strategy with a superior customer service strategy is **HyperFit** (www.hyperfitusa.com), addressing customer needs on a personalized basis. When new members join HyperFit, they fill out forms that highlight their fitness goals and any health issues. The information is stored in a database so all experts on staff have access to their records. The gym also helps clients to stick to their regimes. If a customer doesn't show up for three weeks, he automatically gets an e-mail alert. Sometimes trainers phone with a pep talk. It is reported from the company that recently a man joined the gym planning to run a marathon, but stopped coming during a messy divorce. After three weeks an alert went out. The gym followed up by e-mailing an article about marathon training to the client. The man soon returned to the gym.

Quite the same way is taken by **SimplySoles** (www.simplysoles. com), dedicated on customer service and intimacy. Shoppers who call the toll-free customer-service number can even reach the founder, Kassie Rempel, directly. For certain customers SimplySoles will send out a selection of shoes – no charge, no commitment. These shoppers can try on shoes in their homes to see which pair looks best with a particular outfit – still being in the top price range where the average pair of shoes goes for $275. They are billed only when they make a purchase and can send the remaining shoes back to SimplySoles in prepaid mailers at a cost of about $12 a returned pair roundtrip. SimplySoles also sends out handwritten thank-you notes to every customer who orders shoes. The notes address the customer and shoe by name – a little touch that builds loyalty.

As part its customer care activities, the English real estate agent **Foxtons** (www.foxtons.co.uk/) offers customers everything they need when searching for real estate. The agency focuses on the strong demand for temporary property for people who spend time in London on business. Some of these people do not have the option of viewing real estate in person. The website solves that problem by using every option available to provide a virtual impression of the property, such as numerous detailed photos and a 360-degree video, a map that identifies the location of the property as well as directions to a particular destination (e.g. the city center), a detailed description of the area's infrastructure (schools, public transportation, etc.) and a planning tool that calculates the way to the customer's workplace. The provider also uses technology to stay in contact with its target group. SMS Property Alert, for example, sends customers text messages with new offers that match their search criteria and e-mails with brochures.

To have a position that effectively differentiates it from competitors, a company must focus on one of the three disciplines – Product Leadership, Customer Intimacy or Operational Excellence (Figure 1.11). While the three disciplines present positioning options at their highest levels, each discipline also contains an off-limits zone area that should be avoided (i.e. a performance minimum is required in each discipline). According to Treacy & Wiersema, a successful company must be excellent in at least one discipline and at least on the same level as their most important competitors in the other two. The following empirical analyses show that companies are most successful when they follow one of the three value disciplines mentioned and systematically and consistently use that same value discipline to determine the content for their strategic marketing planning (Tomczak *et al.* 2008; Stevens *et al.* 2006).

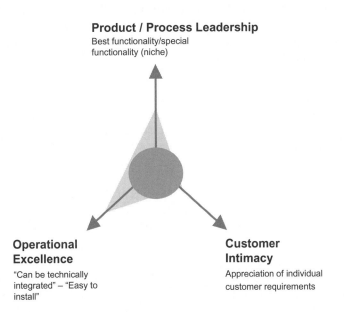

Product / Process Leadership
Best functionality/special functionality (niche)

Operational Excellence
"Can be technically integrated" – "Easy to install"

Customer Intimacy
Appreciation of individual customer requirements

Figure 1.11 Competitive positioning according to Treacy & Wiersema (1995a, b).

According to Treacy & Wiersema, one company that breaks down its corporate goal according to the "value disciplines" is the US pharmaceuticals corporation **Eli Lilly**. It emphasizes "product leadership" (Stevens *et al.* 2006).

- *Corporate goal:* To maintain product leadership in all new markets.
- *Functional goal at the level of the strategic business unit:* To protect a market share of 80% in a certain segment of the pharmaceuticals market (non-narcotic analgesics) for the next five years. *Strategy:* Introducing new products to replace profitable products (known as "blockbusters") after their patents expire.
- *Instrumental goal at the product market level:* Using telemarketing to explain to doctors and pharmacists the advantages of these new medicines and offer them introductory discounts. *Strategy:* Extend the product line and employ aggressive pricing to protect market share when replacing products.

Automobile maker, **Saturn** (a General Motors company) has an entirely different approach: This company focuses on *customer proximity*. The Saturn Family came into being after Saturn recognized that people often feel uncomfortable going to car dealerships and believe that dealers have an excessive number of preconceptions about customers (Dirkes *et al.* 1999). New *Saturn* owners are automatically enrolled in a club whose benefits include access to a variety of information. Being a member of this special club improves brand loyalty while at the same time making visits to the dealership much more pleasant. Combined with other activities, the customer club has helped Saturn to sell nearly twice as many vehicles as other General Motors brands (Court *et al.* 1999).

The further operationalization of corporate goals takes place at a third level, in *functional areas* (such as marketing, production, etc.) or strategic business units. However, functional goals, such as those of marketing, are not necessarily the same as the goals of specific organizational units. This is why some marketing tasks and goals can be carried out by other functional areas outside of marketing. Examples include holding events or creating sales brochures.

At the lowest level of the goal hierarchy are *instrumental goals*, which can refer to components in the marketing mix, such as improving product quality, improving price differentiation versus competitors or improving the company image in the relevant target segment.

In the example from **Eli Lilly**, the instrumental level included goals, like numbers of doctors and pharmacists to contact in a certain time period.

At this level we can distinguish three different goal categories for marketing (Schnaars 1998; Homburg & Krohmer 2006):

- *Economic marketing goals:* Relate to common economic references as found on a profit and loss statement, e.g. revenue directly attributable to marketing campaigns or number of qualified leads with (at least an indirect) reference to revenue and, by extension, to the profit and loss statement.
- *Marketing goals relating to market success:* Relate to target values that represent the actual success of a company or strategic business unit, using customer behavior as the foundation. An example is increasing relative market share.
- *Marketing goals relating to potential:* Relate to variables that precede actual customer behavior, such as using a measurement of customer satisfaction to determine revenue for a later time.

These goal dimensions can be interdependent – improved customer satisfaction (a potential-oriented goal) can lead to greater market share (a goal relating to market success) when satisfied customers make repeat purchases.

Whereas a *corporate strategy* defines the basic long-term direction of a company (for instance, by stating goals for KPIs, the further development of strategic resources or the distribution of resources within the corporation as a whole), a *business area strategy* describes the direction of a strategic business entity and a *functional strategy* describes the strategic orientation of individual business functions (Jenner 2003).

There are at least three different ways of viewing the *marketing strategy* within this categorization (Homburg & Krohmer 2006):

- *As a functional strategy:* The marketing strategy is determined to be one of several, equal, functional strategies. In so doing, the corporate strategy defines the strategic framework for activities in the marketing strategy over a long period of time. The marketing strategy then focuses on optimal implementation of marketing instruments (such as communication policy).
- *As being equal to the corporate strategy:* Strategic marketing is equal to the core strategic tasks of the company.
- *Dominant marketing strategy:* The marketing strategy dominates other functional strategies by virtue of its role as an interface to the company environment and a supplier of information for other functional areas in the company.

Empirical studies and real-life examples show that the dominant marketing strategy has some advantages over other functional strategies. It ensures that the corporate strategy is systematically geared toward the requirements of customers and the market ("Customers.com") and that the marketing strategy becomes a key element in the corporate strategy (Seybold 1998; Rayport & Jaworski 2005). This perspective tends to allow marketing to move beyond its immediate functional area so that it plays a central role in the corporate strategy. In practice, what role the marketing strategy takes depends heavily on the product portfolio, the market segment (B2B or B2C) and the industry. Consequently, the marketing strategy has tended to also dominate the corporate strategy in B2C environments with strong brand management.

Regardless of what role of the marketing strategy plays in a company's goal hierarchy, the results from empirical studies of the marketing situation in various companies shows that the decisive factor when developing a marketing strategy is the process-related perspective. This means systematically aligning the marketing strategy with other functional areas (*horizontal*) as well as with corporate goals (*vertical*) in all its important dimensions, KPIs and content (*marketing programs*).

CHAPTER 2

FOCUS ON THE CHIEF MARKETING OFFICER (CMO): A JOB DESCRIPTION

T he marketing planning process, including the systematic preparation and execution of a marketing plan, must have a secure place in a company to be able to make a professional contribution toward achieving the higher-ranking revenue targets, profit targets, and corporate goals. The natural responsibility for marketing planning lies with the Chief Marketing Officer (CMO). Representative, quantitative, and qualitative studies carried out by the CMO Council, Palo Alto (USA) among 1,500 marketing managers, CEOs, managers, and recruitment consultants show that there is plenty of room for improvements in the working conditions and organizational involvement of the CMO in many companies (CMO Council 2007). Simultaneously, these studies clearly indicate that increasingly higher demands are being placed on the CMO's professionalism, versatility, and personality.

2.1 A YOUNG PROFESSION: A DEMANDING SPECIALIZED AREA WITH C-LEVEL CALIBER

The title of Chief Marketing Officer (CMO) first appeared in the 1970s as brand owners promoted their marketing managers to the management team of their company. In the early 1990s, another advance in establishing the position of CMO was made in Silicon Valley.

At first, the role of the CMO was closely associated with expertise in brand engineering and spectacular advertising campaigns, so that some CMOs were considered to be celebrities. This fact must have seemed dubious to many managing directors, CEOs, and even to CFOs, leaving an effect whose traces can still be seen today. At the same time, the last 15 years or so have witnessed a fundamental expansion of the job portfolio of a top CMO far beyond brand and advertising. The requirements

Specific skills, expertise, and qualities companies are requiring from CMO candidates

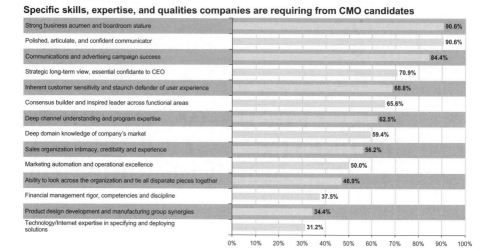

Strong business acumen and boardroom stature	90.6%
Polished, articulate, and confident communicator	90.6%
Communications and advertising campaign success	84.4%
Strategic long-term view, essential confidante to CEO	70.9%
Inherent customer sensitivity and staunch defender of user experience	68.8%
Consensus builder and inspired leader across functional areas	65.6%
Deep channel understanding and program expertise	62.5%
Deep domain knowledge of company's market	59.4%
Sales organization intimacy, credibility and experience	56.2%
Marketing automation and operational excellence	50.0%
Ability to look across the organization and tie all disparate pieces together	46.9%
Financial management rigor, competencies and discipline	37.5%
Product design development and manufacturing group synergies	34.4%
Technology/Internet expertise in specifying and deploying solutions	31.2%

0%   10%   20%   30%   40%   50%   60%   70%   80%   90%   100%

Figure 2.1   Statements from recruitment experts on the characteristics a company particularly looks for in a potential Chief Marketing Officer (CMO) (CMO Council 2007; reproduced by permission of the CMO Council).

catalogs of leading recruitment experts for candidates are more strongly influenced by management qualities, strategic strengths, and leadership skills than by the ability to develop advertising campaigns (Figure 2.1). This trend is developing against the background of a change in how marketing is understood – no longer an "art", but as an ever increasingly detailed science.

2.2   THE SITUATION: THE DISCREPANCY BETWEEN EXPECTATIONS AND CORPORATE REALITY

Marketing managers are often still hired according to conventional expectations. They should be responsible primarily for all marketing plans, programs and measures. In addition, it is their job to act as the ombudsman for brands, their values, consistency and culture, and they should have a certain degree of competitive intelligence for developing preventive strategies. Then again, managing directors, CEOs, and board members see the CMO as a valuable, strategically-oriented member of the management team (73.1%) – but ultimately do not really trust him or her with full acknowledgment of this role. This discrepancy is made even more acute by the fact that marketing is often only insufficiently incorporated into the company organization as a function. This means that products are often developed without integrating marketing, which is then to manage successful promotion of the product (Kotler 2005). It is easy to see that there is only a limited chance of success in these cases.

However, if, in the rare case, the CMO is intensively incorporated into company management and leadership, the more the CMO is valued by executives and colleagues from other functional areas (Figure 2.2).

Along with intensified use of the web and the related *richness* of the communication channel, an important driver for the change in the role of marketing managers

Estimation of the CMO's performance as a valued member of the senior management team

Grading by members of the executive board or upper management whose marketing managers are involved in most or all strategic decisions:

Grading by members of the executive board or upper management whose marketing managers are not at all involved in strategic decisions or are involved only to a limited extent:

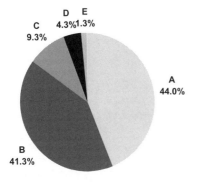

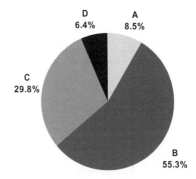

Figure 2.2   Relationship between the integration of the marketing function into the strategic and organizational work of the company and its rating (CMO Council 2007, A = very good, B = good, etc.; reproduced by permission of the CMO Council).

also lies in the increasing number of communication channels and interaction points for customer contact (Court 2007). *User-generated* content (such as blogs and *YouTube*) or also comparatively new advertising possibilities (such as search engine optimization) require not only "integration" with the widest possible and most cross-functional knowledge for shaping an efficient 360-degree communication, but also specialists who have a detailed understanding of the individual disciplines. The CMO is faced with the challenge of building the understanding and knowledge required in the field of marketing. This requires a shift in focus. Topics such as brand management or the implementation of revenue-generating activities must be supplemented with concepts and activities for the further development of the company–internal marketing organization and the knowledge presented here. Concepts for transferring functions and tasks within the framework of outsourcing were discussed and implemented in IT years ago, and many companies now are increasingly following a marketing outsourcing strategy with respect to cost efficiency and the need for specialized knowledge (Court 2007).

2.3   THE GREATEST CHALLENGE FOR HEADS OF MARKETING: LEGITIMACY AND CREDIBILITY AMONG COLLEAGUES AT THE MANAGEMENT LEVEL

As the majority of CMOs are appointed to corporate management with the support of the CEO, having a good relationship to the boss is a deciding factor for success. However, it is still worth while for marketing managers to build and maintain a good relationship with other board members and management executives. Since preconceptions about marketing are more pronounced in these executive circles, which may have little to do with marketing, establishing the legitimacy of the function of the

Credibility with the officers and directors of other functional areas

Self-Estimation on a Scale from 1 (very low) to 5 (very high)

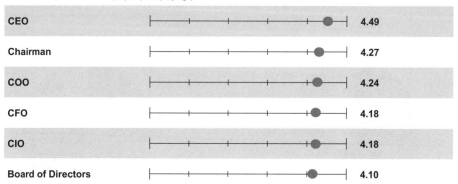

CEO	4.49
Chairman	4.27
COO	4.24
CFO	4.18
CIO	4.18
Board of Directors	4.10

Figure 2.3 Assessment of the credibility of the marketing function (CMO Council 2007; reproduced by permission of the CMO Council).

Performance Criteria for a Top Marketing Executive's Scorecard

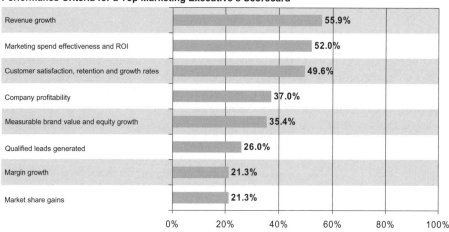

Revenue growth	55.9%
Marketing spend effectiveness and ROI	52.0%
Customer satisfaction, retention and growth rates	49.6%
Company profitability	37.0%
Measurable brand value and equity growth	35.4%
Qualified leads generated	26.0%
Margin growth	21.3%
Market share gains	21.3%

Figure 2.4 Desired measures of success for marketing (CMO Council 2007; reproduced by permission of the CMO Council).

CMO and the CMO's own credibility here is particularly difficult (Figure 2.3). The next biggest challenge is educating colleagues at the executive management level about the special functions and potentials of marketing. After all, it is not always easy to convince the CFO that the marketing budget is justified (CMO Council 2007).

2.4 THE CMO'S NEW IMAGE: GUARANTOR FOR "RETURN ON MARKETING"

When asked about their particular causes for complaint, those most critical of marketing at the executive level will cite a lack of objective data on the success of marketing activities as one of their main criticisms. When asked whether the CMO provides sufficient information about the return on investment, more than 62% answer "no" (CMO Council 2007; Court *et al.* 2005).

When considering the professional skills and characteristics that a CMO should have now and in the future, executives place requirements such as a "strong sense of business" and "long-term strategic vision" at the top of the wish list. Classic competencies such as "communication" and "success with advertising campaigns" are markedly less important than they were before.

The new image of a marketing executive or a CMO is that of a management generalist with special knowledge concerning proximity to target groups ("customer advocate") and marketing, particularly using innovative IT and online solutions. The CMO's strengths lie in strategic planning, business development and general management, including the readiness and ability to deliver "hard data" on the "return on marketing" (Figure 2.4). What puts the CMO in a position to do so is, among others, a systematically planned and implemented marketing planning strategy, which serves as a basis not only for executing and achieving the announced targets in the future, but also for in-house, content-driven communication with other functional areas and executive colleagues (CMO Council 2007; Court *et al.* 2005).

CHAPTER 3

PLANNING COMES FIRST ...

3.1 RESULTS OF THE CMO MARKETING PLANNING SURVEY

In the summer and fall of 2006, another survey was carried out among marketing executives in some European countries. The goal of this survey (Strauss 2007) was to research questions including:

*   Which approach to marketing planning was selected?
*   What are the differences between marketing best practices and current marketing planning in the companies that participated in the study?
*   What are the key influencing factors and upheavals for the marketing function?
*   Which solution approaches have already been identified in the various companies and how have these solutions been implemented?
*   What subjects do marketing managers fundamentally regard as important for further developing marketing at their companies?

The main focus of this empirical investigation was not to perform a statistically representative study, but to gather benchmarks and best practices from different companies in a wide variety of industries. In such a way, the conclusions of the US analysis of the CMO Summit were to be validated and analyzed for European countries – that is, the aim was to discover in particular whether insufficient marketing planning is also the main reason for many follow-on problems in marketing. To this aim, 43 marketing executives participating in a CMO Summit were questioned (Strauss, 2007, 2008). The answers of a web-based survey are listed below in eight different subject areas:

*   Positioning of marketing;
*   Key marketing objectives;
*   Planning process;
*   Budgeting;

- Organizational structure;
- Fact-based planning and controlling;
- Standardization and automation;
- Innovations in marketing.

These points were explored in greater detail with 12 in-person interviews. The most important topic in the interviews was always the basic question of "What has the greatest influence on the success of the respective marketing organization?"

If we compare the information in the marketing executives' self-assessment in relation to (1) existing capacities in the company with (2) the significance of each of these dimensions for the function of marketing, we can summarize the main issues among the marketing executives as (Strauss 2007):

- Fact-based planning and controlling;
- The entire marketing planning process;
- Standardization and automation.

In the survey, the greatest difference exists in these dimensions between the assessment of the significance on the one hand and the self-assessment of existing capacities and capabilities within the company on the other (Figure 3.1). The participants see these areas as those with the greatest need for action.

Comparison of the rating of actual abilities vs. their significance

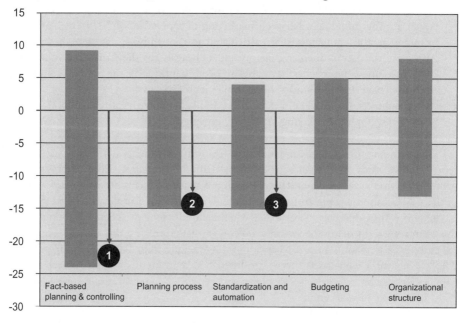

Figure 3.1 Comparison of the most important questions (each with assessment of *current capabilities* vs. *importance* – Strauss 2007).

The detailed analysis and the subsequent personal interviews convincingly proved that the other subject areas in the analysis can be subsumed far below these three factors.

Similar to the CMO Council analyses in the United States, it reveals that the situation of marketing in many companies is contradictory. Although marketing topics are definitely on the CEO's agenda, the marketing function itself is often not represented at board level (also known as "C level"). For example, two-thirds of the CMOs who participated in the interviews stated that their topics were worthy of discussion by the board, but only in one-third of cases was the CMO represented at board level. Although company management perceives marketing as an important topic, marketing executives rarely have direct access and seldom report to the CEO directly. Company executives are usually involved within the framework of large (media) campaigns, but rarely have anything to do with the wide range of other marketing activities, let alone in terms of the various contributions marketing makes to business success. As a result, marketing in Europe is facing a similar dilemma to that in the United States. Despite the fact that marketing is expected to contribute decisively to business success, the positioning of marketing in the company hierarchy seldom corresponds to the great (but possibly only superficial) interest in marketing issues at board level (McDonald 2005; Strauss 2007).

Marketing is mainly positioned purely as a *service function* for supporting sales, or even as an *"industrialized factory"* for cost-effective communication services. This usually puts marketing in the role of the tactical implementer. In only 25% of the companies questioned do the executives responsible see marketing as a "driver for securing sales today and tomorrow". In the future, marketing is increasingly expected to be positioned as a "business value creator" and therefore "critical success factors" are also expected (Strauss 2007). Linked with this is a departure from the traditional role in the area of marketing communications (and thus from the role as a pure service provider for executing tactical communication measures) toward a role as a driver, integrated with business strategy. In view of the tendency toward sinking marketing budgets, it is becoming increasingly necessary to address the market efficiently and to target specific groups.

In the majority of marketing organizations, a top-down budget process dominates, which is geared toward reaching quantifiable monetary goals (Figure 3.2).

More than half of the marketing executives interviewed state that the *performance metrics* used in their companies focus purely on quantifiable monetary performance indicators (such as generated sales or the number of leads). Barely a quarter is focused on indicators that have only an indirect impact on sales (such as customer satisfaction). In the majority of cases, budget planning is an annual process, which means that companies have only limited flexibility to react to short-term changes in business needs (Strauss 2007; Harter et al. 2007).

At the same time, the underlying target systems within the company as a whole are highly heterogeneous: many marketing executives stated that the *marketing* target system is contrary to the target systems in other areas, such as sales or top management, or the higher-ranking financial goals. Therefore, the empirical study underlines the necessity of aligning target systems and the underlying indicators across different functional areas within a company as part of the marketing planning process.

The reason that the head of marketing is inadequately positioned within the company, and that the efficiency of implemented marketing activities is often critically

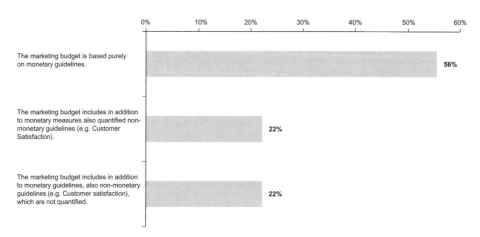

Figure 3.2 Comparison of marketing budget with marketing specifications (Strauss 2007).

questioned, can usually be attributed to an inadequately planned and executed marketing planning process. More than two-thirds of the marketing executives judge the planning process as "*important*" or "*very important*" – but at the same time refer to existing shortcomings in this initial marketing task (Figure 3.3). As a result, efforts focus on planning specific (tactical) campaigns and individual activities, followed by the marketing mix and plan and rough customer segmentation. Only a handful of marketing executives state that they focus on an explicit customer strategy – even though this is destined to become much more important in the future. Customer focus, which has until now been insufficient, is also regarded as one of the greatest tasks and challenges for the future (Strauss 2007). In this respect, the greatest challenges within the marketing mix can be found in the area of communication strategy. While other elements of the marketing mix (such as price or product) tend to be planned carefully and in great detail, the planning and design of marketing campaigns and activities is neglected in comparison.

Because an explicit customer strategy is not usually the focus of marketing planning, detailed analyses of customer segments, customer needs and subsegments are performed only to a lesser extent (Figure 3.4). The general inadequacy in the alignment of the marketing planning process with other company areas, and the minimal strategic foundation, resonates consequentially to the level of individual tactical measures. The rather neglectfully defined and implemented customer strategy brings about only a minimal level of alignment between marketing expenditure, target systems, market segments and cross-area market reach strategy.

As well as strategic alignment, the *implementation* of the selected strategy within the framework of marketing planning proves to be critical. The CMOs surveyed see an immense need for aligning global, regional and local marketing planning and follow-on activities. This makes it virtually impossible to align all contents, strategies and tactics within the planning process across different levels and company areas. In some of the interviews, it was made clear that the (*company-internal*) alignment of global, regional and local organizations in some places ties up more resources and attention than the (*company-external*) addressing of customers, for example, as part of campaigns.

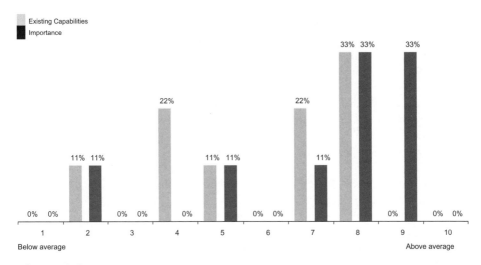

Figure 3.3 Quality of marketing planning process execution vs. importance of this topic and capability compared to competition (Strauss 2007).

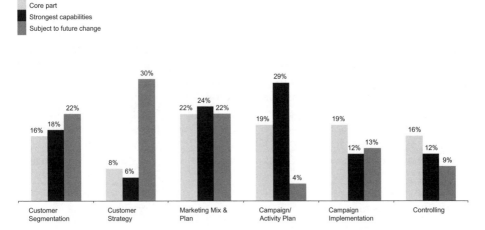

Figure 3.4 Focus in the marketing planning process – focus area, capabilities, and expected changes (Strauss 2007).

Consequently, company-internal alignment usually focuses on individual activities, such as placing advertisements or carrying out an individual direct mail campaign. A content-based discourse and alignment are not priorities here. The approval and coordination of all measures is highly centralized – and the logical results are: bottle-necks while the processes are being performed; reduced motivation of the employees involved; and bottlenecks due to the central instances in the upper echelons of the hierarchy being overloaded, all of which result in delays in the approval of content and measures. It seems virtually impossible for marketing employees to extensively organize and coordinate the planning and execution of measures personally owing to the number of people who have a say in these matters. The consequence: protracted alignment processes and loss of employee motivation.

The greatest potential for efficiency has been identified as being in a greater "standardization within the framework of the marketing planning process". This is precisely where many companies have the greatest discrepancy between what they aspire to do and what takes place in reality: activities between different business units are barely coordinated or aligned. A high level of decentralization in the marketing organization ensures that the central (country) units usually make their own decisions, driven by individual (local) interests. The result is that marketing activities are developed several times over. The lack of coordination and standardization within the planning process makes it almost impossible to eliminate the often lamented shortcomings. Due to differing concepts, processes and supporting instruments, best practices cannot be systematically set up and exchanged. Cross-area marketing planning and the leveraging of synergies across different countries therefore do not happen. A lack of standardization – in the planning process, supporting tools and underlying concepts – is regarded by the majority of marketing executives as one of the most important obstacles to efficient marketing planning.

Many of the marketing managers questioned point to the *planning process as being only professionalized to a limited extent and having only rudimentary IT support*. Marketing plans are usually drawn up in the form of spreadsheets, presentations (Microsoft PowerPoint), or continuous text. Marketing plans are created at all levels (global, regional, local), but the lack of a standardized and automated process often makes it difficult to compare different plans, let alone aggregate local and regional plans to form a global marketing plan. Accordingly, the marketing executives who were surveyed place the main focus on cross-country harmonization at the level of marketing program planning and in terms of the performance indicators used. An integrated and stringently calculated marketing planning process – from the market reach strategy to the level of individual measures and the associated KPIs – is often nothing more than wishful thinking (Strauss 2007; Reinecke & Herzog 2006). In many cases, the focus of planning efforts involves the discussion of individual activities and tactics, rather than a strategic planning approach (derived from company strategy). This insufficient standardization means that although people talk about the same metrics (such as sales potential or leads) on a superficial level, they are defined very differently in terms of content (semantically) and are thus used in different ways.

The analysis based on the survey and further interviews clearly underlines the fact that marketing executives have started numerous projects for improving the planning process. Some of the initiatives include the development and implementation of improved marketing controls and audits, as well as increased process automation and standardization with the aid of integrated IT applications. However, in some cases, an attempt is being made to substitute the lack of a coordinated and standardized business planning process with the use of integrated software applications. "Process follows IT" evidently applies here – even though all those surveyed are equally aware that aligning business processes to the requirements of the available IT applications is objectively insufficient and tends to lead to suboptimal results. It seems that the less successful efforts in standardizing the process are to be revitalized with the help of IT.

The survey of the marketing managers shows that (in addition to inaccurate forecasts about the effectiveness of individual measures and marketing campaigns) considerable conceptual and strategic weaknesses can be found, even in companies with high marketing expenditure. In many cases, marketing engagement is based on fairly imprecise statements and platitudes, such as "tapping new markets", rather than such specific objectives as "increasing customer satisfaction by $x\%$" or "increasing sales by EUR x million". Even if the corresponding strategies and concepts exist, they are characterized in many companies by a combination of time-consuming analysis and little practical relevance, or they focus only on individual functional and task areas (such as media expenditure). As a result, these (partial) designs often remain unimplemented and the procedure orients itself more toward the (tactical) necessity of operative, day-to-day business or the intuition of the people involved.

Conceptual bases that are non-existent, poorly founded, or lacking in practical relevance have the effect that marketing strategies are frequently only implemented in very limited and specific forms (*lack of integration*). One consequence is, for example, the emergence of numerous different applications (e.g. customer databases) and of competition with other functional areas (e.g. service and sales). An integrated consideration of potential along the entire value chain from marketing (contact generation), sales and distribution, through service in the sense of the CRM approach outlined above, remains in most cases a noble yet unattainable goal (Strauss 2007).

Often, success cannot be adequately proven in the business. Such problems of proof may be caused by difficulties in measuring success or by delays between the cause and the effect. The accountability and the measurability of a marketing activity's successes are often made more difficult by the lack of adequate procedures. The great complexity and the *independencies* between the different influencing factors mean that successes in the market (such as increases in sales) can rarely be clearly linked to one specific marketing measure. Further problems arise in the B2B area, in particular with regard to the extent to which sales successes should be attributed to (personal) direct sales or marketing activities. Finally, delays between cause and effect (also known as "time lags") can occur if activities do not have a positive impact until a later phase – such as an increased awareness in the customer's "relevant set" for upcoming buying decisions.

3.2 "THE PARADOX OF THE MARKETING FUNCTION" AND "THE 10 HURDLES OF MARKETING PLANNING"

If we combine the results of the survey of German-speaking countries and comparable studies by the CMO Council, *the paradox of the marketing function* manifests itself (Harter *et al.* 2007; Kreutzer & Merkle 2008a; Müller 2008).

- *Formal vs. perceived significance:* While the marketing function is deemed by the majority as "important and strategic", it is rarely valued as such within enterprises.
- *Hierarchical level vs. assessment of performance:* The position of the CMO in the company hierarchy and the related involvement in strategic corporate decisions correlate positively with the assessment of performance of this area. As the marketing function is not usually ranked at top level, both of these indicators currently still tend to be rather low.

- *Budgets vs. the transparency of planning and activities:* High budget expenditure in marketing contrast with relatively little transparency with regard to alignment with strategic goals at the planning stage and the stringency of the activities derived from these goals. There is a total lack of an internal connection mechanism – in the thinking of the key players as well as in the IT tools used.

The surveys and additional interviews clearly indicate the underlying cause of the paradox of the marketing function: *inadequate marketing planning*. The 10 problem areas of marketing planning comprise the following (McDonald 2005; Homburg & Schenkel 2005; Strauss 2007):

- *Content:* An inadequate grounding in terms of the content of the advertising messages and activities to be communicated.
- *Relevance:* Marketing planning that is not sufficiently up-to-date or detailed. As a result, marketing planning is strictly aligned with the annual planning cycles, while tactical measures – with no significant basis in the marketing strategy – are constantly adapted to meet business needs.
- *Alignment:* Inadequate alignment with other functional areas such as sales and distribution or partner management, which inevitably leads to the duplication of planning and activities – often coupled with highly centralized coordination (approval) for all measures, which leads to bottlenecks in internal processes.
- *Customer perspective:* Too little integration of the customer perspective. Planning and the marketing activities derived from it are motivated by a definite inside-out approach.
- *KPIs:* Inadequate operationalization of marketing planning and subsequent activities in the form of key performance indicators (KPIs).
- *Planning transparency:* Little transparency in terms of the status and progression of marketing planning.
- *Project management:* Either too few planning activities (with a tendency to be carried out incidentally) or uncontained planning activities without milestones or precise start/end dates.
- *Tools:* Different bases for planning, templates and tools used (for example, CRM system, Microsoft Excel, PowerPoint, or similar).
- *Acceptance:* Minimal acceptance from the employees affected, because revision of existing plans by top management tends to be seen as arbitrary and barely serious.
- *Use:* Insufficient use of planning as the specification for subsequently drawing up programs and campaigns, as well as updating and adapting existing plans during the year.

As a result, inadequately systematic and strategically aligned marketing planning causes a poor understanding within the company of marketing's value contribution to corporate goals, an internal image of this area that can be described as negative and – as a direct consequence – the positioning of marketing well below the top management level. Studies in the United States and case studies in European countries show that, in view of this, a comprehensive transformation process can be expected in many companies. With high-quality marketing planning as a starting point, many operational processes and functional areas will need realignment (Court 2007; Strauss 2006).

PART II

THE PATH TO THE PLAN

SEVEN PHASES FOR DEVELOPING MARKETING STRATEGY AND SYSTEMATIC MARKETING PLANNING (SEVEN-PHASE MODEL)

C ase studies show that a marketing planning process that is systematic, strategic and well-grounded in terms of content should be based on a seven-phase procedure (Figure 4.1; Strauss, 2007). In the first step – that of the ***planning and budgeting cycle (Phase 1)*** – for each level in the marketing planning process, all the interfaces, milestones, and activities in the planning project are defined in the form of a project plan and project organization. It has become apparent that a decisive factor for success is to combine all existing planning initiatives within the company right from the start. At the same time, the interfaces to other areas and contact persons, each of the target groups addressed, and the content should be consolidated as early as possible.

After the overall project planning, ***budget planning (Phase 2)*** takes place. Here, once the total marketing budget available (material and personnel costs) has been determined, this budget is roughly divided according to different segments and areas. Although, in theory, the discussion of corporate goals, strategies pursued (value disciplines), and positioning should take place before the marketing budget is discussed, in reality, most companies at the beginning of the planning process take a top-down approach to discussing and calculating the total available budget – derived from revenue quotas etc. The initially calculated budget and its distribution to different areas or product segments must then be further revised or refined during the course of the marketing planning process, based on the scheduled activities and measures.

As the results of the CMO survey show, a customer-centric strategy is increasingly becoming the focus, even though its realization so far is still lagging behind the claimed aspirations. In keeping with this, we can expect that, in the future, the marketing planning process will definitely be discussed in the light of increased customer

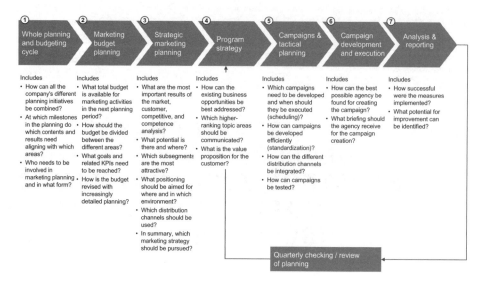

Figure 4.1 Seven-phase model for systematic marketing planning (Strauss 2007).

orientation. Following analysis of the initial strategic situation (environment, market, and company situation), all the available customer and market knowledge about this is consolidated for *strategic marketing planning (Phase 3)*. The strategic prioritization of different product/market scenarios performed as part of this phase in the dimensions *market attractiveness* and *intensity of competition* then enables all the resources deployed (budgets, employees) to be focused precisely on objectives.

A systematic and sound *analysis of the initial situation* provides the basis necessary for the development of marketing strategies. The procedures for the market, enterprise, and competitive analysis must meet fundamental requirements, such as the information used being reliable and realistic. The information basis for drawing up the marketing strategy must be sufficiently detailed and precise to prevent purely intuitive decisions from being made. However, the information and analyses used must focus on the essentials and not generate an information overload as part of the strategy discussion.

Formulation of the *marketing strategy* is then related to specific goals, target groups, or the design of the marketing mix for reaching the objectives set. In this phase, alternative marketing strategies are formulated as options, which are then further evaluated and consolidated as part of the continuing process, with one of the options finally being selected and adopted as the marketing strategy to be pursued. Through the systematic and well-grounded design of the marketing planning process – with customer needs and market potential as the starting point – the alignment with different company areas (such as sales and distribution or service) and with global, regional, and local units becomes easier. Case studies reveal that, by using the approach outlined here, within a few weeks, marketing planning in its entirety – across all the areas involved – can be aligned in detail in terms of the most important dimensions:

- Cross-area strategy;
- Marketing programs and content;
- Campaigns and tactics.

The marketing programs are defined for each customer segment or product in the next process phase (*program strategy, Phase 4*). This stage in the formulation of the strategy contains statements about:

- The precise objectives of a program according to priorities;
- The key performance indicators (KPIs) used as a basis;
- The target groups to be addressed;
- The target customer benefits including an all-encompassing selling idea;
- The content to be communicated in this respect;
- The first indications of the fundamental design of the marketing and communication mix for the (more tactical) level of marketing planning that follows later.

In this respect, and for the further planning process, it is crucial to differentiate between the different levels of marketing planning.

Marketing program:
- Defines the goals for addressing a target market;
- Gives an overview of the marketing strategies for addressing this target market;
- Is defined as the spectrum of integrated marketing and sales activities under the umbrella of a content-based, relevant, and goal-oriented concept.

Campaign:
- Contact flow for meeting the goals of a program using all communication instruments and a wide variety tactics;
- Campaigns usually take place over a period of several months.

Marketing tactics:
- Marketing tactics for communicating with the target group within a campaign;
- In turn, different marketing tactics in a given time period form a campaign wave;
- Examples of marketing tactics include telemarketing, sending e-mails, or staging an event.

In this structure, a *program* usually comprises several campaigns and brings content to the market. The communication channels used may vary here, as may the goals or the content itself. However, a program does not necessarily have to comprise several campaigns – for example, in the case of a sales program. While a program can have several goals, a campaign focuses on one specific goal.

The differentiation of the different stages of marketing planning outlined above has a relatively trivial goal. Only once the content of one phase has been adequately clarified can the design of the next phase begin. For example, all target groups, content, and goals pursued must be sufficiently specified at a program level (Phases 3 and 4) before the discussion can start about the individual *tactics* for reaching goals (Phase 5).

The programs that are established are developed further in the next step in the form of campaigns. If required, the campaigns can be executed in different waves (of time) as part of integrated marketing communication planning (*integrated marketing communication planning, Phase 5*). On the basis of empirical values and panel tests, *best-practice campaign architectures* can be used as a basis for addressing different target groups and goals in campaign planning. Ideally, all marketing and communication activities are aligned not only with the different geographical units (global, regional, and country) but also with other affected functional areas (such as sales and distribution or service) from the level of programs through campaigns and individual tactics and measures.

After the ***development and execution of the campaigns (Phase 6)***, the implementation of the selected strategy at the level of tactical measures requires systematic feedback loops in the upstream phases of the strategy process within the framework of the ***analyses and reports*** in the final stage (***Phase 7***). Here, the issue at hand is not so much to question the adopted strategy as it is to systematically track the results achieved and to operationalize and fine-tune the detailed content for subsequent periods. A *marketing audit* – which can be defined as a sporadic analysis of all marketing activities and processes, and of the marketing organization – enables the re-evaluation of all process phases and of all the tasks performed.

Even though a sequential approach to marketing planning seems to make sense in terms of clarity and ensuring a strictly adhered to method, case studies show that a parallel or rolling procedure should rather be the norm in the phase model presented here. While traditional annual planning takes place in one single planning session for one planning horizon (for example, a fiscal year), the plans are continually adjusted and updated at quarterly intervals based on new information or market developments as part of *rolling marketing planning* (Figure 4.2). Across the quarters, the plan is fine-tuned in stages for the subsequent periods. The advantage of rolling planning – apart

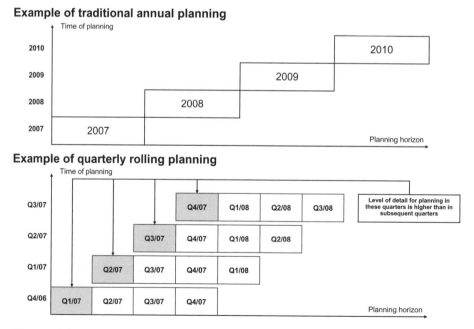

Figure 4.2 Traditional annual planning versus rolling planning (Homburg & Schenkel 2005; reproduced by permission of the authors).

from permanently improving marketing planning – is that the quantitative results of marketing reporting and the related KPIs are (necessarily) included systematically. Once established, the ongoing effort required for revising and fine-tuning planning remains manageable.

Project experience shows that, once implemented the standardization of marketing planning and of the entire process enables:

- Higher quality content at the program and campaign level;
- As a result, a systematic and well-grounded alignment with all the areas and contact persons involved;
- The possibility to make binding agreements in the form of KPIs (such as the number of leads generated or contributions to revenue) as an integral part of the planning process;
- As energies are not misdirected in the planning process, all marketing planning activities are completed in a timely manner.

To illustrate this more clearly, the most important key points of marketing planning will be examined later in the book using the example of a hypothetical case study in which the company *NatureLabs* launches its product *alpha*.

CHAPTER 5

PHASE 1: PLANNING THE PLANNING

At its core, a market planning project follows the same principles and rules as other projects. The majority of the time-limited project is dedicated to planning and executing the identified tasks, mostly in cross-area project teams. Therefore, target-oriented planning and effective implementation are fundamentally important for the duration and the costs of the project. Experience shows that the following elements are essential for optimizing the costs and duration of the marketing planning project:

- A *systematic method* from strategy development to the implementation of individual measures, such as the seven-phase model for marketing planning;
- A *structured approach* for developing content, programs, and campaigns;
- A carefully defined *team and project structure* with coordinated project planning including precise milestones, well-defined work packages, end-to-end project monitoring, and a project organization that incorporates all important task managers.

Project objectives for implementing the seven-phase model of marketing planning must also be determined. These objectives should satisfy the SMART requirements:

- **S**pecific, as in "we want to define concrete KPIs for all marketing activities in the program planning content and tactical campaign planning";
- **M**easurable, as in "the rating of the quality of our agency briefing will increase by 10% in the external agency assessment";
- **A**ttractive, as in "through clearly structured tasks and responsibilities within the seven-phase model and end-to-end planning focused on content, unnecessary activities and duplication of work can be avoided during the subsequent execution process, and the entire planning will be carried out and approved within three months";
- **R**ealistic, as in "if we follow the planning method and carefully prioritize content and market segments, we can increase next year's sales by 20%, while keeping the same marketing budget";

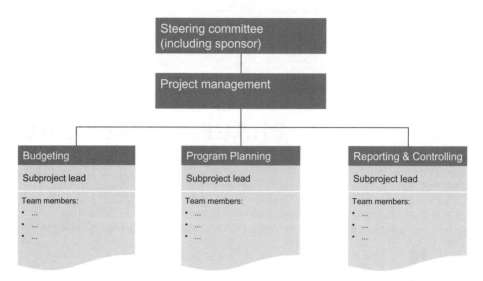

Figure 5.1 Example of a project organization for marketing planning.

- **T**argeted, as in "we want to have the marketing planning for the next year completed by October 30 of the current year and next year's campaigns fully developed by and presented on November 30".

Subprojects (also called work streams) can be derived from the project objectives (or task areas). The subprojects can, for example, be grouped according to "budgeting" or the content of "program planning", or subdivided for the development of performance indicators and assessment procedures tracked later in *Reporting & Controlling* (Figure 5.1).

From the beginning, various roles must be defined for the implementation of the project as part of *Project organization*. The *Project sponsor* is the chair of the steering committee. The sponsor actively supports the success of the project, assists the project management team in overcoming resistance, and is the spokesperson of the project idea at the senior management level. Due to the importance of marketing planning for the success of this function, this role must be performed by the CMO (Dibb *et al.* 1996; Cohen 2006).

The *Steering committee* is responsible for the success of the project, gives the project coordinator the project charter, and acts as the initiator of the project idea and the selected procedural model for marketing planning. Within the scope of implementing the project, the steering committee is also the highest authority in de-escalation and makes fundamental decisions, such as on final prioritization in strategic planning or in the approval of the stated marketing performance indicators for the subsequent periods (e.g. revenue targets, customer satisfaction, or awareness level). The steering committee will meet regularly during the course of project to monitor project progress, risks, and benefits. If necessary, this authority will approve changes in the project procedure, project charter, project costs (budget), or project duration. Along with the sponsor, the steering committee should include other marketing managers. Furthermore, participants from other company areas such as sales or business development should be involved in the marketing planning process where needed.

Linked to the role of *project coordinator* are expectations including coordinating and controlling all subprojects and informing the sponsor and steering committee. The project coordinator's tasks include removing implementation obstacles (de-escalation and decision making) and securing communication within the project and with other projects. Experience has shown that the quality of marketing planning is highly correlated with the project coordinator's availability during the planning period. Shortest possible project cycles, an effective planning approach, the necessity of understanding marketing/strategy, and the subsequent implementation of all strategies and activities call for the skills of experienced *project managers*. Knowledge of (1) the basic marketing concepts and (2) the content to be communicated as well as (3) proficiency in project management are needed for this. Therefore, a manager who, from a professional, methodical, and management-oriented point of view, will remain with the planning project until its implementation in the scope of campaign execution should be appointed as the project coordinator (see Eggers & Hoppen 2001).

The support of *external consultants* is helpful for implementing the marketing planning project (Nippa 1993). Their support is especially beneficial as they can:

• Bring in objectifying statements in relation to customer requirements and competitors;
• Contribute cross-company and cross-industry know-how to the planning process and to target group-specific know-how;
• Use interdisciplinary competencies and the resulting possibilities for creating cross-functional solution approaches beyond the areas of marketing, sales, and production;
• Integrate project management and methodological skills for the transition to the future implementation in the scope of campaign execution;
• Provide the necessary resources and alleviate capacity bottlenecks;
• Ensure the greatest independency from company-internal structures and power-political constellations.

Company-internal project coordinators, on the other hand, have a better familiarity with one's own organization, facilitate easier recognition among lower levels of the stated strategies and decisions that were made, and can transfer the broader identity of the value expectations to those involved. In both cases, the focus is on better empathy in the social structure and political power fields, and the key figures acting in these areas.

The *subproject manager* (e.g. marketing intelligence manager) takes subject-specific responsibility and makes decisions within the transferred task area, identifies the necessary resources for this, and defines resource planning. The subproject manager reports to the project coordinator on project progress, status, problems, and changes, and initiates decision and escalation processes as needed. Experience with various planning projects has shown that this is a very important role – for example, to ensure that the experience and knowledge of different employees are incorporated into marketing planning and that the developed marketing planning is subsequently and accepted both for its content and on a personal basis. This would also include knowledge of online specialists or knowledge of market potential from the field of market analysis.

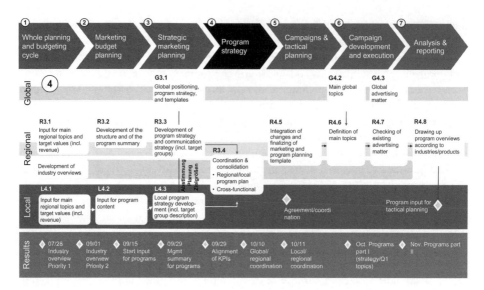

Figure 5.2 Excerpt of a simple project planning process including all alignment points in the seven phases (example of program strategy).

Team members bring know-how of various target groups, product/industry areas, methods, procedures, or processes to the planning project. Team members actively take responsibility for defined work packages within the subproject, as well as specify and evaluate solution alternatives and their ability to be implemented. Various roles within and outside of marketing, such as product managers, telemarketing managers, and industry managers, are incorporated in the team.

Project control and the identification of all milestones are found to be the most important success factor for securing a strategic and content-oriented planning and its subsequent execution. One of the first steps according to the seven–phase model is to determine all important interaction points between different functional areas (such as sales, business planning, etc.) and between different national and international marketing organizations and their respective marketing plannings (Etzel *et al.* 2000; Figure 5.2).

It is often beneficial to specify precisely the activities, decisions, roles, and tasks of the involved persons or areas within the planning process. The acronym RACI can be used to identify which person:

- Performs the activity (**R**esponsibility);
- Is authorized to make routine decisions without the further involvement of the steering committee and takes the overall responsibility for all results generated (**A**ccountability);
- Should be consulted before a decision is made or an activity is performed (**C**onsulted);
- Must be informed about a decision/activity (**I**nformed).

At the beginning of the planning process, the project team must agree on the assignment of all activities and important work packages and communicate with all

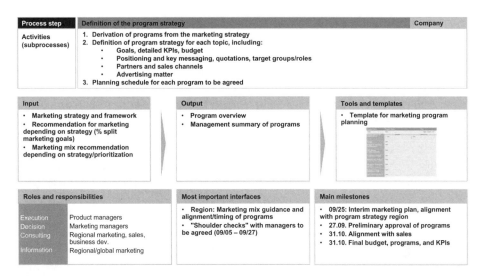

Figure 5.3 Description of the process steps in marketing planning (example of program strategy).

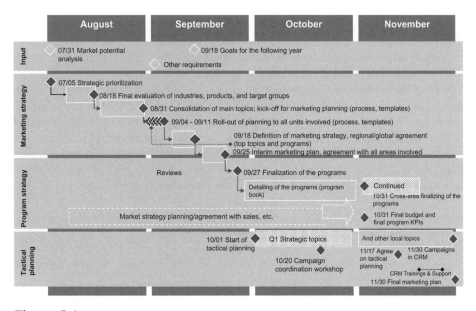

Figure 5.4 Project plan for marketing planning in the seven-phase model (example).

areas involved and with contact persons at an early stage. Determining the most important activities and subprocesses prevents:

• Multiple responsibilities;
• Unnecessary duplication of activities in the planning process;
• Too stringent a division of tasks between different project areas;

- Lack of responsibilities;
- Too much or too little information within the project team.

As a result, delays and the loss of motivation of the persons involved can be prevented. A tried and tested method is to adhere to each of the process steps with all input/output relationships including the tools and templates intended for this purpose (such as in form of a PowerPoint template; Figure 5.3).

Translating the simple procedural model into a ***project plan*** within the seven-phase model of marketing planning should also comprise interim communication with the areas that are affected in the wider environment in every project step (Figure 5.4). Along with sending simple e-mail newsletters, etc., this is a place to consider how advisable it is to hold an *information fair*. In practice, holding an information fair has shown to be a highly effective means of communication. All persons directly or indirectly affected by the planning process are taken through a display (for example, using DIN A2-sized paper on partitioning walls) containing the most important content of the planning process. As an information fair, the presentation has the advantage that it eliminates the (perceived) distance of a presentation and that it usually sparks a lively discussion among the participants.

Experience shows that, in many cases, the project plan for marketing planning

- Is either non-existent or too vague;
- Is too detailed, making it hardly accessible; or
- Has not been communicated at all or well enough to the project participants or areas and contact persons to be involved.

In all cases, planning and the milestones to be followed, with the exclusion of the project plan, are set up at the project coordinator's request. The result is generally that the originally stated planning time period exceeds the predetermined time period and that marketing planning is seen as excessive and even superfluous from within the company. This is especially the case when planning in other functional areas is faster than planning in the marketing area. Taking this into account, it is advisable to devise at least a project plan with the most important milestones (Figure 5.4).

CHAPTER 6

PHASE 2: APPROACHES TO MARKETING BUDGET PLANNING

*B*udgeting determines the total expenses that will be needed to carry out all marketing activities (particularly the marketing communication and advertisement budget) for each subsequent planning period. Most companies plan their budget in an annual cycle. There are two broad approaches to budgeting: *heuristic* methods and *analytical* methods for budget planning (Reinecke & Fuchs 2006). While heuristic approaches tend to be based on plausibility considerations and experiences from previous years (for example, based on revenue or profit), analytical budgeting approaches are founded more on shaping a relationship between the committed budget and the KPIs to be achieved (for example, revenue or brand awareness).

6.1 HEURISTIC BUDGETING APPROACH: PRAGMATIC BUDGET CALCULATION

Heuristic budgeting methods can be based on the budget of the previous period, revenue/profit, the available means, the estimated budget for various competitive activities, or communication policy objectives. The main advantage of a heuristic approach is the simplicity of its calculation and the understanding of clear budget drivers. There are, however, a few basic conceptual limitations that should be kept in mind for heuristic approaches, which facilitates a more in-depth view of the different approaches.

- *Based on the budget of the previous period:* The simple update of an existing budget amount for the following period is attractive on account of its simplicity and practicability. However, underlying is the (at least implicit) assumption that the budget of the previous period was a (halfway) reasonable amount. At the same time, a budget based on the previous period does not take into consideration the changes in the competitive, marketing, and customer environment that would make it appear advisable to adjust the marketing budget.

- *Based on revenue or profit:* A marketing budget based on revenue or profit is determined as a percentage of revenue and profits from either the previous period or for the following period (plan value). Determining the percentage value is, in turn, based on historical, empirical values or values benchmarked against the competition or comparable companies.

> For example, in the **car industry**, the estimated sales price for each vehicle serves as a reference point for determining the marketing budget; in the **petroleum industry** a set portion of the budget is allowed for marketing expenses for each liter of gasoline sold (under the company's own brand).

- Even in this case, the advantage of easy implementation and reference to marketing expenses in relation to purchase price and profit is also countered by the restriction that actual values of the previous period cannot be included as a basis for the plan values of the following period without further consideration. When the budget is based on the previous period, there is the risk that the company will behave pro-cyclically. For example, if the sales in the previous period are below the originally stated value, this would mean a decrease in the marketing expenses for the following period, leading to a repeated decrease in sales, around which a negative, self-reinforcing development trend manifests itself. For this reason, the best use of this approach is for determining a reference value for benchmarking.
- *Based on available financial means:* In this approach, the budget for marketing communication is calculated as the residual amount of the (planned) profit after all other costs have been deducted. Similar to the approach based on revenue, this method also bears the risk of a pro-cyclical budgeting process and structure of communication activities. If, in the case of a crisis situation with decreasing profit, a more convincing and broad-based market communication had been recommended, this budgeting approach would result in a far-reaching reduction of communication activities. Consequently, the company would lose the chance to improve awareness through communicative measures and indirectly with it, to improve the revenue and profit situation. The various short-term, medium-term, and long-term effects of measures to promote sales would be ignored, making continuous marketing reach impossible.
- *Based on competitive activities:* In this case, the marketing budget is benchmarked against the competitor's budget. The budget for marketing measures is based on the strength of a company's "share of voice" among the competition (Diller 1998). In this approach, budgets are determined as either absolute amounts or as a share of the marketing budget in revenue or profit. Also in this approach, the focus on the competition and on efforts to organize at least the same scope and amount of communication effort and expenditure starts to take the focus of the budget away from the communication objectives of the company. An inefficient use of the competition's marketing budget would inevitably lead to "over-budgeting".
- *Based on communication objectives (objectives and tasks method):* Marketing budgets in this approach are calculated on the basis of predetermined communication

objectives (such as increasing the level of awareness, number of qualified leads to be generated, or the desired market share and market penetration). In this approach, at least rough estimates of the required communication measures and tactics are defined and multiplied by the expected implementation costs. An early estimation of the required communication activities makes way for a bottom-up estimation from the perspective of actual cost drivers from empirical values. If the rough forecast predicts that the communication objectives can barely be achieved, either the set goals need to be revised or the budget needs to be adjusted accordingly. This type of budgeting requires profound knowledge of the relationship between the main cost drivers, such as advertising expenditure, the type and number of qualified contacts with the target groups, the initial purchase rate, and repeat sales. These parameters can usually be determined as part of marketing analysis from the dates of the previous period.

In terms of the seven-phase model for marketing planning, this approach anticipates the activities and measures to be specified in later phases. Accordingly, it may be that the early forecast based on past experience about the measures that need to be taken to reach the communication objectives is still flawed. Incremental budgeting with the option to revise the initially set values using the planned activities according to the progress of marketing planning can offset the disadvantage that this approach has when applied in practice. Due to its orientation toward communication objectives and its foundation in market strategy, this approach can also be classified as uniquely conceptually reasonable and practicable. The other approaches described for budget planning should assume a more supporting role (Rahders 1989).

Since 1998, the term *beyond budgeting* has been used to discuss a management method in controlling to overcome the disadvantages of rigid, annual budgeting processes. This approach is briefly taken up here due to its prominence in business literature. The Swedish bank, Svenska Handelsbanken, can be referred to as one of the first organizations to apply the "beyond budgeting" concept; it started to use the fundamentals of beyond budgeting in the late 1980s. A beyond budgeting approach is supposed to reduce the commonly lamented high levels of expenditure and resource involved in classic budget preparation and/or the questionable relationship between budget compliance and company objectives, and so on (Hope & Fraser 1999, 2001; Gleich & Kopp 2001). In reality, the postulated basic failure to carry out budgeting planning rarely occurs in most cases – rather, a variety of instruments for controlling and flexibility (with principles of self-coordination) often accompany a rigid, annually set budget (Rieg 2007).

6.2   ANALYTICAL BUDGETING APPROACH: MODELING USING THE ADVERTISING IMPACT FUNCTION

In contrast to a heuristic approach, an analytical budgeting approach attempts to estimate the correlation between a communication budget and a target value by using several influencing factors either statistically or dynamically (over several time periods). This target value can have either a *potential-related* effect (in terms of the awareness level of a certain product, brand awareness, etc.) or a direct *market success-related* effect (such as the communication activity of attributable sales, the number of qualified leads, etc.). These types of advertising impact functions assume that there is a positive correlation between the communication budget, the activities based on this budget, and sales.

Further *dynamic budgeting approaches* allow the incorporation of any number of (previous) time periods and response correlations, such as the following (Schmalen 1985; Diller 1998):

- *Goodwill* established over several time periods (as a positive brand image);
- *Wear-out effects* (diminishing effect of advertisements over the course of time as a result of the advertising affect aging);
- *Carry-over effect* (advertisement does not make an impact until later periods);
- Forget rate of communication measures;
- *Reactance* due to "over-advertising".

The basis of an analytical budgeting approach is estimating the influence of advertising measures based on mostly historical (mathematically formal) advertising response functions. The estimation of the advertising response is, therefore, based on previous data. In practice, this means that all incoming parameters must be identified and estimated as accurately as possible, which hardly seems possible in reality – and, if so, only with considerable time and expenditure. As communication measures mostly have a delayed effect, it is usually hard to make a precise, functional correlation between, for example, revenue and advertising effort.

For reasons of practicability, the preferred approach to budget planning is mostly heuristic, based on communication objectives. Interviews with marketing executives support this conceptual assessment. In practice, budgeting is characterized mostly by a heuristic approach and an incremental method. The company continues to follow the budget allocation model from the previous years, usually with consideration of company–internal political concerns, with a short-term budget buffer for reactions to interim market developments. A systematic review of the budget resources used, and of the objectives achieved ex post in terms of a systematic marketing intelligence approach, is often not carried out, which means that knowledge as to how resources could be used more efficiently remains undisclosed. Consequently, not enough experience with the efficacy or efficiency of planning and measures used is acquired for planning periods in the future.

CHAPTER 7

PHASE 3: STRATEGIC MARKETING PLANNING

7.1 SYSTEMATIC PROCEDURE FOR STRATEGY DEVELOPMENT

The foundation of the marketing strategy should be an analysis of current and future market conditions and an assessment of your own core competencies and resources. A three-phase procedure is an ideal method for devising the strategy (Figure 7.1 – Aaker 2001; Goodstein *et al.* 1993).

Besides analyzing the company environment and general market conditions, the most important factors and changes in the customer environment and competitive environment are important when formulating a marketing strategy. In addition to general market analyses (like market growth), changes in customer behavior must also be determined. With the help of an in-house analysis of existing competencies, processes, and the company's market situation (such as current market share, customer loyalty, etc.), future positioning options and their feasibility can be examined and discussed. Based on the positioning of choice and the business potential associated with it, you can work out points in the marketing strategy, such as specific customer benefits, positioning with respect to the competition, specifying a distribution channel strategy, and designing the marketing mix.

The procedure outlined and discussed below uses key questions to help to further systematize the procedure, correctly operationalize deployment of the different concepts, and thereby improve the quality of the results (Homburg & Krohmer 2006).

7.2 ANALYSIS OF THE INITIAL STRATEGIC SITUATION

7.2.1 Market and environmental analysis

7.2.1.1 *Market analysis: differentiating and evaluating markets*

In market and environmental analysis, you must identify all those developments in the social, legal, political, and technological area that are significant for the strategic aspect

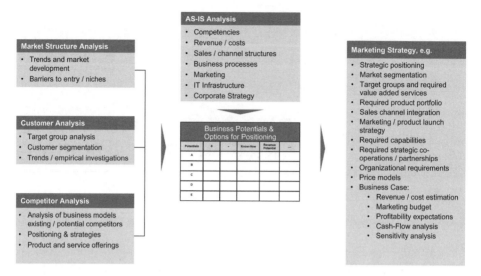

Figure 7.1   Ideal procedural model for developing marketing strategy.

of marketing. Apart from general market characteristics, such as estimated market growth, particular attention needs to be paid to the causes of these changes, such as changes in customer needs or behavior. This general action framework for market strategy is predetermined by the global company environment and can barely be influenced. Overall commercial, technological, and social developments and legal changes are key (Götz 1998).

The area of **general social developments** refers to changes in the general values, attitudes, standards, values, and principles of a society (Strauss 1996). At least four major trends can be identified for this area:

- **"Evolumania":** The scientific explanation of the world is experiencing a popular renaissance. The theory of evolution in particular is being used as a comprehensive metaphor that can also interpret individual, social, and even political, economic or technical developments (Zaltman & Zaltman 2008). What is new is that the theory of evolution is not being viewed as a principle of extinction, but as a positive principle of development. Each status quo that has been reached is seen as a preliminary peak of selection and simultaneously as an intermediate step toward even higher quality. Evolutionary thought strongly resembles the way in which, for example, small and mid-sized enterprises view themselves. Small and mid-sized enterprises are structures that emerge and continue to evolve by means of a "natural" selection process (Figure 7.2), combined with tradition and experience. Abstract, theoretically-oriented, purely logic-based thought and action tend to be alien to this market segment (Ries & Ries 2005; Simon 2007).

The media reacted to this trend about 10 years ago. The world of science, technology, and research has always been appealing to

Figure 7.2 Example for natural evolution as used in a "Mini" advertising campaign (reproduced by permission of Mini/BMW Group).

television, and subject-based television shows are a standard format of this medium. However, they received little formal acknowledgment. Since the mid-1990s, however, there has been a noticeable increase in scientific reporting in all media. This is true for both printed media and television. By now, it is feasible to talk of a veritable "science boom" on major TV channels, which has also reached private commercial channels, such as *Abenteuer Forschung* [Research Adventure] (ZDF), *Welt der Wunder* [World of Wonders] (Pro7), or ScienceTV (www.science-tv.com). Cable networks have capitalized on the entertainment value of science and technology to become prolific purveyors of scientific television shows, such as *Beyond 2000* (Discovery Channel) and *Science and Technology Week* (CNN). Science programs have become a staple ingredient on education-oriented cable channels such as The Discovery Channel. Recently, cable has also directed its attention back toward the scientific community with the development of professional programing such as Lifetime's Medical Television (science.discovery.com/). Science is "in"; channels are offering a broad range of shows and viewers are watching.

- *Machine–machine analogies:* Neurosciences, as well as nano and genetic technologies are offering a new utopia of constantly developing ways to rationalize and control life. Biochemical processes are being used to *explain* "soft" factors like will, faith, and emotions. "Neurotheology" is simply a continuation of this world view in the area of ethics and religion. The vision of finding a means to control the intangible side of human existence centrally is fascinating, but simultaneously awakens our deepest fears. This "Aesthetic of Pure Reason" (highly efficient, seamless processes free of human error) is also fascinating for business professionals. At the same time, this vision contradicts our own life experience (see "Evolumania"). We fear that this type of accuracy can only be achieved at the cost of a personal and corporate "abandonment of identity" (Gehirn & Geist 2006).

In 2006, the US security firm, **RSA Security**, unveiled a new product that uses speech recognition for authentication for telephone banking. Their "Adaptive Authentication Package" was supplemented with speech biometrics. The new product is intended to reduce telephone banking fraud. The solution assesses risk with a point system that analyzes voice expression and other parameters, such as telephone number and user behavior. Low-risk transactions can be carried out directly, whereas high-risk transactions are carried out with extra verification using an additional security function. This can be a secret question, for example. According to RSA, current technology for telephone authentication is only moderately secure as it still requires some manual execution.

- *"Optionism – Simplicity":* In today's world we have countless options in almost every area of life. Individuals are constantly finding themselves in different roles and decision-making patterns. This results in an (excessive) strain on mental resources. In our quest for the "essential" facts, we increasingly and consciously tend to choose the option that reduces our options. Clarity and simplicity play an ever greater role in design, how we shape our life, and commerce and industry (Küstenmacher *et al.* 2004). Simplifying processes, increasing efficiency, streamlining, overviews, clarity and transparency are all business challenges. At the same time, a market filled with options demands the ability to react quickly and flexibly. A firm command of business processes enables us to concentrate on more essential things (Brandes 2005).

At the assortment level, for example, consumers are experiencing an overload; few can easily find their way around the wide range of offers available. For instance, a major electronics store in Europe – such as a **Media-Markt** store – may carry between 94 to 134 cameras from more than 20 brands. However, more offers do not necessarily lead to more purchases: 60% of customers stop in front of a shelf with 24 types of jelly, but the percentage of purchasing customers is only 2%; 40% of customers stop when there are six types, and 12% of them make a purchase. Moreover, customers often feel overwhelmed and frustrated in front of a larger shelf because they worry they might make the wrong choice. This form of disorientation and the rising unease that this triggers also manifests itself in the results of polls, which revealed that about one-third of people who wanted to buy could not find what they were looking for – despite a huge selection (Esch 2007; Riemenschneider 2006).

But the optionism might also backfire from a company's perspective if the brand has to suffer too many extensions in one category in order to satisfy different optionistic customer demands, such as is the case for **Gatorade**. The brand that created the sports-drink category continued to reinvent it with new products and strategies that kept it sprinting past rivals. But lately, the $3 billion-plus Gatorade brand has been getting winded. While it controlled 82% of the category last year, that's down more than 10 share points from two decades ago, when it owned 93% of the market (Zmuda 2008; AdAge.com). It's getting more volume out of existing consumers but losing a nearly equal amount to rivals at the same time. And while sports-drink volume gained 2.5% last year, volume for the Gatorade family was reported to be up just 1%. One of the reasons: much of the blame is pinned on aggressive rivals who try to satisfy customer optionism. The result: the so-called "hydration category" has seen more than 200 new brand introductions in the past two years. At the same time, Gatorade is said to have moved too far off its core athletic positioning with an "everything-but-the-kitchen-sink" plethora of products under the brand banner. Today it markets a "performance series" (consisting of energy drinks, energy bars and nutrition shakes); a "thirst quencher" series (Rain, Frost, Fierce, X-Factor, Xtremo, A.M. and Tiger, in addition to the standard formula); Propel Fitness Water; and G2 (for off-the-field hydration). With this, Gatorade might be losing its historically strong messaging around its authenticity as a sports drink as a key point of differentiation at a time when the beverage aisle is becoming increasingly crowded.

The trend toward flat rates is another vivid example of the desire for simplicity (and a counter-movement against optionism) in an option-filled environment. Globalization and the permanent flood of news on the Internet shower consumers with more information and variety than ever before. This new flood of information has made it more arduous and laborious for consumers to find the right information and make the best possible (subjective) decision for their particular situation than ever before. If the post-modern individuals in industrial nations flung themselves eagerly into the delights of a complex, unbridled consumer world during the New Economy boom, that world is increasingly falling under the control of centrifugal forces. Searching through a literally endless variety of information has made the lengthy process of comparison an increasingly dull but central part of everyday life. The daily struggle through the confusing maze of rates, general terms, and conditions (fine print) is increasingly becoming a source of consumer irritation, as potential buyers get lost in the information jungle and hold off making a purchases (Berke *et al.* 2007). Cognitive relief is sought in simplified product and price models. Fixed prices offer complete cost transparency and control. In addition to the flat rate models established since 2001 in the telecommunications area, the fixed price wave is increasingly spilling over into other industries. Since the beginning of 2007, **Ford** has been selling a service package known as the *"Ford Flatrate"* that consists of a four-year product warranty, roadside assistance, maintenance and inspections as well as a financing model with a low interest rate. Customers can return their car after four years or continue financing. According to the manufacturer's statements, just under 40% of private customers are already taking advantage of this flat rate offer. Other providers like **VW** are including full and partial comprehensive insurance policies with their "all-around satisfaction" packages. The Deutsche Telekom subsidiary, **Musicload**, offers customers unlimited listening access to a portion of its music library for a monthly fee of EUR 8.95. Similar models are also being pushed by software providers. **SAP**, for example, offers a fixed price software rental called *Business ByDesign* that customers can order on the Internet.

- *"Deep support":* The swift change of external parameters forces businesses to adjust their own identity constantly. This necessitates highly individualized support. "Deep support" is personalized coaching and support for specific capabilities and the development of existing capabilities. "Deep support" identifies, promotes, and responds to individuality. This development is based on trust, reciprocity, authenticity, and reliability. Using "Deep support" means preserving one's own identity while continuing to develop. The pressure to change and innovate also forces small and mid-sized enterprises to adapt to developments. At the same time, they must preserve their own identity, which is often seen as a critical competitive advantage (Simon 2007). Consequently, companies seek bilateral exchange with other businesses (e.g. at trade fairs and forums), individual coaching, and *"sensitive consulting"*, which respects the fact that a company perceives its own situation as something very special (Maxmin and Zuboff 2004; Whitmore 1993).

Nivea implemented deep support in the form of a campaign. With the slogan "Beauty is what you make of yourself", Nivea created a workshop for teenagers, NIVEA Camp 2007. It focused on the question of what really makes a person beautiful. The aim was to teach participants that beauty is in the eye of the beholder, and what really counts in life is personality, not just external beauty. Thirty participants met to learn about themselves in three different workshops. The workshops focused on topics like personality, performance, and look & style. Professional coaches and prominent mentors such as TV presenters and boy groups gave the participants valuable tips.

Like social developments, *general economic development* affects marketing strategy, in terms of general economic growth, distribution of private household income, and the general willingness of companies to invest, for example. *Political and legal developments*, such as liberalization of the telecommunications market or amendment of telecommunications data protection laws, lead to having to rethink entire marketing strategies or just elements of planned communication channels (e.g. the use of telemarketing and telesales).

Technological developments open up new opportunities or threats that must in turn be taken into consideration during strategy development. From the perspective of modern IT as an important strategic enabler, this means in particular the enhancement of business design options for in-house operations and cooperating with suppliers or new distribution channels (Strauss 1996). The most obvious example is in-house use of the Internet as well as externally tapping new business fields and sales markets within the scope of IT-based virtual networks.

A striking example for how technological developments and raised environmental awareness affect marketing can currently be found in the automobile industry. From the standpoint of the industry, the discussion about CO_2 emissions that began in mid-2007 was a surprise. Nevertheless, with its *Prius* model, **Toyota** managed to present a hybrid vehicle with new technology, although the current generation had already been modified more than once. The Toyota *Prius* was the world's first large-scale production vehicle to be powered by a hybrid gasoline-electric drive. The first generation of *Prius* arrived on the market in Japan at the end of 1997. The third generation model has been on sale around the world since 2000.

Various methods are available for analyzing the global business environment, such as:

- *Early warning systems:* Based on the premise that *weak signals* announce essential changes in the company environment in advance. These signals are mostly unstructured qualitative information from the business environment that point to a substantial change (Simon 1985; Krystek & Müller-Stewens 2002). Quantitative leading indicators can be economic figures or mood indicators (such as the Purchasing Managers index), which can be supplemented by qualitative and quantitative studies from research institutes. Problems can arise when using an early warning system if leading indicators that have proven effective in the past are also used to forecast future changes.
- *Forecasting techniques:* Estimates of future developments are made based on the experience of *experts*. This procedure lends itself particularly to developments for which there is not sufficient data for a quantitative description. In the best-known approach, the *Delphi method*, experts answer several rounds of questions in writing about their estimates of future environmental development. The group then discusses their answers. Ideally, the iterative process will produce a unified opinion from the group of experts. The main disadvantage of the relatively small number of formal requirements for this forecasting technique is that strong discontinuities in the environmental development may in some cases receive insufficient attention.
- *Scenario technique:* In contrast to forecasting techniques or foresight systems, the scenario technique focuses not only on one possible future development but on several. In addition to describing various future developments ("scenarios"), these

are weighted by conclusions drawn regarding their respective likelihood of occur-rence. Rating these scenarios from a company standpoint ("best case", "worst case", and "base case") enables businesses to represent factors in non-contradictory combinations (von Reibnitz 1996; Jenner 2003). In practice, discussing different scenarios and the assumptions at the root of them can yield important insights. The approach that is usually chosen for devising a marketing strategy involves planning with the most probable scenario (*leading scenario*) in mind. A strategy based on the leading scenario must be created with enough flexibility so that other scenarios can also be carried out if there is a change in strategy. It follows that this approach can also be used to select alternative marketing strategies (Götz 1998; Hansmann 1995).

These relatively general environmental analyses can form the foundation for a more detailed description of the relevant market. *Relevant market* refers to the market in which the company wants to be active. A relevant market can be defined on the basis of groups such as (Freter & Obermeier 2000):

- *Providers* (e.g. the IT market as a market served by companies in the IT sector);
- *Products* (e.g. a market for enterprise software solutions);
- *Demanders* (e.g. the SME/mid-market with less than EUR 80 million in annual revenue);
- *Needs* or needs categories (e.g. a market for flexible financial software).

You will normally need to combine several categories together to differentiate the relevant market. Seen from a customer-oriented marketing perspective, the focus should be on demanders, and customer segmentation and a detailed needs analysis should be used as aids.

Seen from the perspective of a differentiated marketing strategy, a purely provider-oriented approach, which defines the area of small and mid-sized enterprises based on a specific revenue (e.g. less than EUR 80 million annually) is not very beneficial and seems overly simple. Customers of upper mid-size enterprises tend to have preferences (in terms of product design and types of communication in marketing campaigns) associated with large enterprises, while customers of smaller SMEs (less than about EUR 10 million in annual revenue) tend to have very different preferences. Following a simple, provider-oriented categorization of the relevant market in this way is hardly a suitable manner of sufficiently modeling the heterogeneity of the needs structure of demanders.

Using a value chain with its respective process phases and the main activities that take place there is a common method of analyzing and determining the relevant market (Figure 7.3). This allows you to:

| | Concept | Adress based services | | Production | Execution of activities | Response Handling |
		Provisioning of target group segments	IT services			
Companies	• Database marketing agencies • Direct marketing agencies • Media consulting	• Address brokers • Listbrokers	• Software provider • System integrators • Database marketing agencies	• Print • Lettershops • Telemarketing agencies • Web design agencies	• Lettershops • Call center • Internet provider	• IT service provider • Listbroker • Lettershops
Work areas	• Target group determination • Marketing concepts • Text / copy development • Creative services • Media consulting	• Renting of qualified business addresses • Renting of qualified private addresses • Listbroking	• Address management & error analysis • Address qualification • Development of databases & address management • Customer structure and potential analysis	• Design of marketing communication material • Production • Print services (personalisation and mailing) • Coordination of all activities	• Address based mailings • Mailings with no specified addresses • Active / passive telephone marketing • Interactive services	• Response reception • Response processing • Response fulfillment • Response controlling • Analysis of captured data (response qualification)

Figure 7.3 Example of a value chain analysis in the market segment for address-based dialog marketing services.

- Categorize companies whose core competencies are in that area;
- Conduct a differentiated analysis of overall market volume and (future) market growth in the different value-adding stages;
- Subsequently conduct a differentiated analysis of competitors' activities in various fields of activity.

Above all, the analysis of general market characteristics includes information about the size of the market and expected (past or future) market growth (see Figure 7.4). An estimate of profit margins and profit development in various value creation levels provides information about their relative attractiveness, as well as about possible risk due to the emergence of a new competitor. The emergence of a new competitor is, of course, more the rule in market segments that have a high profit margin. The required foundation of data can be obtained from studies by external analysts or by interviewing a small number of experts.

The following *key questions for market analysis* need to be answered adequately (Paley 2000; McDonald 2005; Homburg & Krohmer 2006; Hiebing & Cooper 2000):

- What characterizes the relevant market and how can it be differentiated?
- Which services and value-adding stages exist in this market segment, based on a value chain analysis?
- How large is the market volume and the current/expected future market growth?
- What is the current profit situation of providers in the market and what future developments can be expected?

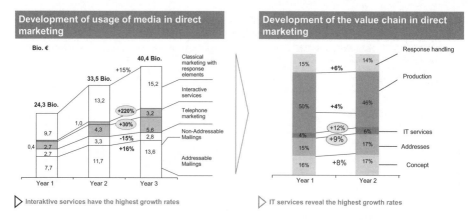

Figure 7.4 Estimating market volume and market growth at different value-adding stages in the area of direct marketing (example).

- What profit margins come from different services and value-adding stages, and what can be expected in the future?
- What changes are expected among current market participants? Can it be expected that new providers will enter the market or that the established distribution channels will change in this market segment? Can it, for example, be expected that competitors from another market will enter this market segment because they offer similar competencies (as in the telecommunications market)?

7.2.1.2   Customer analysis: what does the customer want?

The most important questions in customer analysis are: Who is a demander in the market segment in question? Which customer segments can be distinguished? What types of behavior do those customer segments manifest? and Which underlying preferences can be identified? A marketing strategy that is differentiated according to customer segments will only be useful if sufficiently differentiated customer segments exist and can be identified. The basic needs and behavior of customers are the foundation for devising the marketing strategy. Both their current behavior and the changes and developments expected in their future behavior are of interest.

For this purpose, customer segmentation can fall back on various tools of *classical market research*. In terms of content, there are two key aspects:

- *Identifying market segments* to distinguish between buyers and potential buyers based on certain criteria;
- Creating the *information base* needed to continue to devise and implement marketing strategies that best describe the segments identified in advance and allow for subsequent implementation in the marketing mix.

Segments should ideally be as similar as possible (homogeneous) internally, but as different as possible (heterogeneous) when compared with other segments. In order to ensure that a segmentation can also be used later to devise differentiated marketing strategies, some basic requirements must be placed on segments (Dibb *et al.* 1996; Paley 2000), including:

*   **Behavioral relevance:** The criteria for differentiating segments should reflect actual customer behavior and reveal clear differences between segments (with regard to buying behavior);
*   **Responsiveness:** It should be possible to specifically address customers in the segments, by using communication measures for instance (reachability);
*   **Distinctiveness:** Segments can be clearly distinguished from one another and described according to their characteristics. Segments should respond differently to different marketing programs and elements of the marketing mix;
*   **Measurability:** You should be able to accurately measure the criteria underlying segmentation to be able to determine size, buying power, and other characteristics that are important for subsequently devising marketing programs;
*   **Time-based stability:** The devised segments should have time-based stability – with regard to the segment structure as a whole and the affiliation of individual demanders to those segments;
*   **Cost effectiveness:** The creation and processing of these segments should be presentable in economic terms. A segment must be sufficiently large (substantial) in terms of size and potential for revenue and profit. In terms of marketing planning, a segment is to be defined as the largest homogeneous target group for which a specific marketing program is worth while. It must be ensured that addressing and service provision remains economically viable even for individualized addressing within one-to-one marketing.

A number of procedures exist for customer segmentation (in the B2C area) in the context of marketing strategy, each with its own advantages and disadvantages (see Figure 7.5).

Benefit-oriented segmentation (or *needs based segmentation*) was common practice in many companies until the beginning of the 1990s, but was later used much less frequently. The main reason for this was that while this segmentation procedure was very helpful for identifying differentiated demander segments, from an economic perspective, it offered little help when addressing those segments. The implementation of a benefit-based segmentation has only proven successful in the past when all company units were involved and an effective strategy was also established for serving articulated customer needs.

Ice.com, the leading online retailer of high-end diamond and gemstone jewelry, has about a million subscribers in its e-mail-marketing program. With numbers like those, and given the intensely personal and individual relationship its customers have with their jewelry, a single e-mail message sent to the entire database was not going to deliver the results

Segmentation Procedure	Starting Point	Advantages	Disadvantages
Socio-demographic	Using demographic criteria (e.g. age, sex, industry) or socioeconomic criteria (e.g. income)	• Segments accessible for address • Simple data collection	• Low relevance to buying behavior
Geographic	Categorization of demanders by country and city (*macrogeographic*) or residential area in a city (*microgeographic*)	• Identifies similar lifestyles and buying habits, result is tendency toward higher behavioral relevance	• High cost of data acquisition • Segments are stable for a limited time
Psychographic	Categorization based on attitudes, personality traits, or lifestyles	• High behavioral relevance • High time-based stability	• Product-dependent • Requires time/resources to develop • In some cases, segments may be difficult to address
Behavior-oriented	Using actual behavior patterns	• High behavioral relevance	• Approach is more symptom-oriented than cause-oriented. • May find causes of behavior in psychographic or sociodemographic characteristics • Tends to be a more retrospective analysis • Segments difficult to address
Benefit-oriented	Categorization according to benefit structure with regard to products or services	• High relevance to buying behavior	• Segments difficult to address • Benefit criteria require high degree of reference to product • Requires time/resources to create

Figure 7.5 Overview of different procedures for customer segmentation in B2C area (Dibb *et al.* 1996; Green & Tull 1982; Homburg & Krohmer 2006).

the company needed. Previously, Ice.com only utilized two segments: those who had purchased and those who had not. Using a more differentiated segmentation function, however, the company can create personalized e-mails based on what each customer tells the company he or she most wants to receive. By being able to add any kind of variable – product, lifecycle position, etc. – to any customer record, Ice.com can create a relevant segment based on that variable and build a targeted campaign around it. Using segmentation and other functions, Ice.com was able to report a 10% increase in average sale and triple the number and variety of email campaigns – proving once and for all that diamonds really are a girl's best friend. (Obermire, rrwdatabasemarketing.blogspot.com).

While psychographic, behavior-oriented and benefit-oriented segmentations exhibit a high relevance for describing actual buying behavior, segmentation based on sociodemographic and geographic criteria facilitates greater ease for marketing measures to address segments. For this reason, it is normally advisable to use psychographic, behavior-oriented, and benefit-oriented criteria to differentiate segments and then use more specific characteristics to describe them in greater detail. In this way, different marketing activities can be used to customize addressing (Backhaus & Schneider 2007).

At this point, a special feature in the area of business-to-business marketing should be mentioned. Market development is determined less by direct customers than by the behavior of the *customers of customers*. Consequently, an analysis should focus not only on the behavior of direct customers, it should also include the behavior of your customers' customers.

Key questions for *customer analyses* include (McDonald 2005; Hiebing & Cooper 2000; Paley 2000):

- Who are the customers on the market?
- Which customer segments can be distinguished on the market?
- What are the basic needs of the customers?
- How will those needs change in the future?
- How are the needs of customers actually reflected in customer behavior and buying behavior?
- What changes in customer behavior are expected in the future as a result?

Three procedures will be presented below that use market potential analysis and a customer typology/target group matrix for high-quality, high-value market and customer analyses. While the focus of market potential analysis is the quantitative description of the market (market volume, development) in the dimensions "top-down/bottom-up" and "individual market share vs. competitors", typologies and target group matrices focus on qualitative description. Here the focus is on analyzing the special features, styles, and motivators of different customer segments.

7.2.1.3 Market potential analysis: which market and customer segments are the most attractive?

7.2.1.3.1 Market potential analysis: is it worth performing a differentiated analysis?

Market potential analysis (MaPo) is a comprehensive method for the joint analysis of markets (such as market volume, market growth) and the behavior of individual consumers (such as spending patterns of individual customers; Cornelsen 1998; Kuss *et al.* 2007). Market potential analysis provides precise information about market potential in different product and industry areas. Although it is admittedly a laborious procedure for analyzing markets and customers, market potential analysis is of special interest for devising marketing strategy. The combination of different procedures, such as qualitative expert interviews, general market studies, behavior-oriented customer segmentation, and quantitative buying power factors, permits an extremely differentiated market description and a subsequent address utilizing different tools in the marketing mix. Market potential analysis consists of a total of three different analyses:

- *Top-down analyses:* Summarily encompass market potential from the view of external analyses – the same as the market analysis.
- *Share-of-wallet analysis:* Describes market potential while taking into consideration past product purchases and reinvestment cycles on the basis of individual customers. Share-of-wallet, therefore, provides information about the percentage of demand that the company has met to satisfy the needs of a customer in a certain product segment.
- *Top 20 analysis:* Describes potential in 20 customers or customer groupings that have been identified as important based on expert interviews regarding product satisfaction or customer loyalty.

Customer surveys may be carried out to supplement analytical, database-supported buying power analyses. They can validate existing assumptions and allow insights into how market potential is currently being addressed to influence the subsequent description of the market and the actions that should follow. Additional market potential estimates – by persons in the company who are responsible for target groups (such as product managers or sales managers) – help to further validate the potentials determined and assumptions made in the analysis. They also help to ensure that the results of the analytic approach will be accepted when they are presented later (Figure 7.6). Contrasting in-house and external analyses and discussing their underlying assumptions in this way promotes the alignment of different market perspectives (such as in product management, marketing, sales, and beyond).

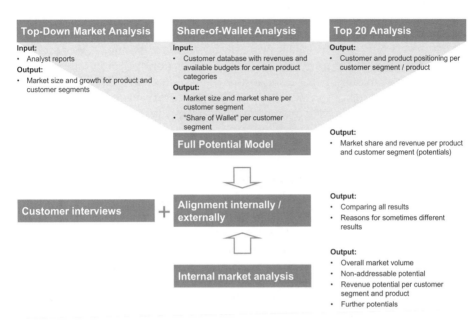

Figure 7.6 Possible levels for examining a market potential analysis.

Car repair shops can retail parts and accessories to supplement the revenue generated by normal operations. In most countries, however, there is a surplus of parts retailers. There is hardly a spot on the map without a retailer for parts and accessories. Car manufacturers have also discovered the lucrative accessories business, urging many of their retailers to integrate attractive stores into their dealerships. Not only can customers find sport mufflers and antifreeze, but many of these shops actually resemble fashion boutiques. In addition to a range of classic accessories, many retailers offer a complete range of travel accessories, jewelry, watches, and even high-priced jackets – all with the car manufacturer's logo. The arts and accessories section of independent, non-dealership workshops, in contrast, often appear dreary in comparison. Replacement parts are issued over a neglected counter or a small window with a bell, while the goods sit around in a gloomy warehouse. In Germany, for example, four spare parts collaborations, **Carat, Coparts, ATR**, and **Temot**, are now acting as system vendors for a workshop concept as well as a specialist store concept. To determine if founding a specialist store for replacement parts will pay off, they each carry out a simple market potential analysis. First, the trading area of the business is determined jointly with the respective interested parties for expanding the service range. Existing billing systems can be useful for this purpose because they usually allow users to request information about customer origin, assuming that customer data has been maintained accordingly. Then the chosen vehicles from the chosen area and the average vehicle age enter into the calculation. The competition in the trading area is also taken into account during a potential analysis (Väthröder 2005). Similar analyses are also employed by European wood trade companies such as **Hagebau Holzhandel** to determine the market volume in the trading area of a business location.

7.2.1.3.2 Top-down analysis: the market "from above"

At the focus of top-down market analysis is the market size in different customer segments and product segments, as based on analyst reports. A top-down market analysis presents a view of markets "from above". Unlike a "bottom-up" analysis in the context of a "share-of-wallet" analysis, which aggregates data of individual (potential) consumers and consolidates it in an overall view, a top-down analysis uses external sources that already specify values for entire markets (Figure 7.7). This also includes industry reports by respective industry associations. The boundaries between different market segments, customer segments, and industry groupings in the studies must be examined in detail, as the criteria used by the different analysts for differentiation and ranking rarely comply with those used in one's own company.

The example in Figure 7.7 provides information not only on market volume or market size, but also on the respective distribution of market shares. As can be seen, a provider in market segment A has a market share of ~75%, while the market volume in market segment D in this graph (bar width) is actually almost twice as large as for A, where it represents a market share of only ~35%.

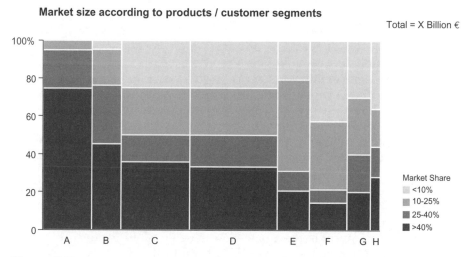

Figure 7.7 "Top-down" market potential analysis using market sizes and market shares for different providers in a market segment and a company's own market share (example).

7.2.1.3.3 Share-of wallet-analysis: the market "from below"

The basis for a share-of-wallet analysis is a database with all the potential consumers in a market segment, their average annual expenditure for a certain product category, and the share of your own company in the consumers' expenditure (i.e. revenue from each individual consumer). This means that the following are prerequisite for a "share-of-wallet" analysis:

• A comprehensive database with all the potential consumers in a market segment;
• Information on their spending patterns in relation to a certain product category – this information is provided in part by external analyst reports;
• Accurate assignment of your own revenue in a market segment to individual consumers. This requires differentiated company-internal information on all revenue per customer so far.

Analyses and calculations, such as the following, can be carried out if the above prerequisites are met:

• *Coverage per customer segment:* This answers the question: How large is the share of customers with whom the company generated revenue in year X in the respective segment (market penetration)? Possible conclusion: "50% of consumers in a segment are already our customers."
• *Market share per customer segment:* Shows the company share in total revenue in the respective product category in the respective segment. Possible conclusion: "We have 20% of the market share in the market segment in question."
• *Share-of-wallet per customer segment:* Shows the revenue share of your own company in the spending volume for a specific product segment – both in terms of individual customers and aggregated for a certain market segment. Possible conclusion: "We have a clearly lower share in the annual costs in customer segment A than in customer segment B."

Key points for determining consumer buying power and the spending behavior for a certain product category are found mostly in analyst reports or can be gained as information provided by interviews (for example, expert interviews or sampling in the relevant target group). Multiplying the determined buying power per customer segment by the number of customers from a "share-of-wallet" (SOW) database based on this data provides the respective buying power per market segment (this actually is the "market volume").

The market share of your own company is then defined for each segment as the share of your own revenue in the total customer buying power (market volume) in this customer segment for a particular period. The result allows conclusions, such as, "approximately 40% of the market in segment A has not been tapped by the company, while the company has a market share of less than 10% for the remaining almost 40% of the market that can be addressed" (Figure 7.8).

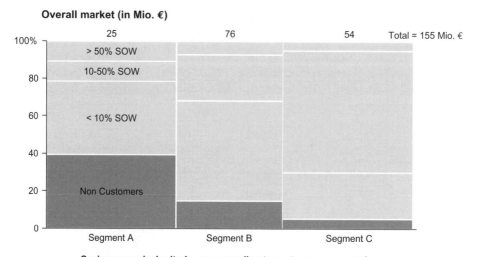

Figure 7.8   Result of a "share-of-wallet analysis" (example).

7.2.1.3.4   Top 20 analysis: learning from the most important customers

The goal of the top 20 analysis is to determine the degree of coverage of a company's product range to locate its position in relation to the competition in a particular customer segment. The criteria for determining customer position are current market shares, customer coverage, and existing customer relations within the relevant target group. Assuming that valid data is available, an analysis of customer value coverage by the company's existing range of services is carried out at this level. Relative positioning can be examined using a rating system. For example, "1 = greatest gap to best competitor" to "5 = far superior to best competitor". The product position can be determined on the basis of evaluations provided, for example, by questioning experts or areas dealing closely with customers or retailers (Figure 7.9). It is also worth while to record customer feedback (e.g. customer satisfaction, win/loss analyses) and analyst statements. At this point, simple ratings of "1 = unsuitable" to "5 = perfectly suitable" are usually sufficient.

As a result of the Top 20 analysis, the most attractive customer segment/product combinations, within which your company's offer is perceived to be superior to that of competitors, clearly emerge.

7.2.1.3.5   Market share development: the "full potential model"

In the "full potential model", the results of the "top-down" market analysis, share-of-wallet analysis, and the top 20 analysis is aggregated, and the revenue potentials are calculated per customer segment, target group, and product. The white spots are calculated first. This means the installed customer base minus the market share for the installed base; in other words, the difference between the total "wallet" of the installed base (market volume of the installed base) and the company's own share in this

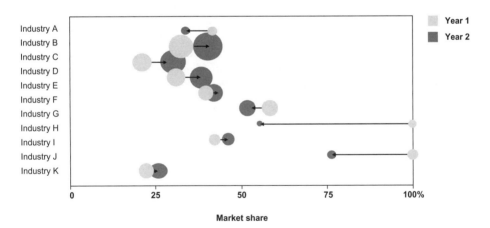

Figure 7.9 Result of a Top 20 analysis by customer segment and different product positionings for product positioning analysis (example).

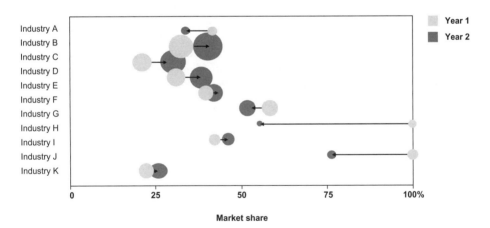

Figure 7.10 B2B example for determining projected market share development by customer segment (industry) in the "full potential model".

"wallet", which means the revenue for each customer. These "white spots" represent market shares still to be secured for base customers in a certain period of time.

Applying this logic to all customer segment/target group/product combinations, provides the market shares and the projected share development. In the example, the market volume (size of circle) will largely remain stable for a customer segment (in this case, industry A). However, the market share of the company will decrease significantly in the following year (circle is displaced; Figure 7.10).

7.2.1.4 Customer typologies and target group matrix: what is the best channel and content to reach a particular customer?

Project examples show that, often at the point when future marketing strategies and related communication strategies are being discussed, the information available is inadequate for optimum, target group-specific marketing communication and strategy (Krafft & Albers 2000). Some questions that need to be clarified concern the following points:

- *Customer typology or the role of customer in the buying decision process:* How can a customer best be typified and what is the customer's role in the (company) buying decision process (in the B2B area)? What is the customer's relationship to the respective product? What are the customer's topic preferences? and What is the language level that should be used to address the customer? Working out commonalities and differences between the respective customer typologies and roles in the company are important here.
- *Communication content:* This is often shaped by a more company-internal perspective, which is why it may only be of limited interest to the relevant target group and/or is not prepared with adequate differentiation within the overall marketing communication.
- The selection of *communication channels* used: An exact description of the information behavior and information likes and dislikes of different buyer types and roles is required. Many companies fail to carry out, even sporadically, a detailed check of the basic communication preferences of the target group (dependent on the product category in question). Preferences here range from active communication (initiated by the consumer), passive/reactive communication (as a response to company marketing activities) and the question of how often the consumer wants to be addressed or it is worthwhile to address the consumer (daily, weekly, monthly or similar).
- *Status of the customer in the buying decision process:* Which content must be communicated to which customer type or function in the company with which communication channels, depending on the respective customer status (e.g. new customer vs. base customer/repeat buyer, existing product knowledge vs. no product knowledge, and so on)?

Rather than trying to establish a presence in all market segments and target groups ("shotgun approach"), an efficient marketing approach requires identifying the most attractive market segments that can be supplied successfully (market segmentation). In a target group-oriented marketing approach, the market is divided into the most important segments. Segments are then selected from these, and specified products and marketing programs developed for them subsequently. There are many procedures for differentiating and characterizing market segments and target groups, such as those based on demographic segmentation already discussed or approaches based on consumer behavior (Schnaars 1998).

The *target group matrix* and the target group description used for addressing private customers based on *typologies* can be used as established methods for market and customer segmentation in both B2B and B2C environments. Typology means the classification of customers on the sole basis of empirical data. While typologies that figure in the business-to-business (B2B) environment are strongly characterized by classic business functions and their affiliated roles (e.g. purchasing manager, HR manager), the characterization of private users in the business-to-consumer (B2C) environment is infinitely more complex. Influence values, such as professional status, disposable family income, number of household members, private lifestyle, general spending behavior, political voting behavior, or social outlook shape the spending behavior (Kotler & Bliemel 2001).

At the end of the 1990s, the **Stollwerck Group** found itself in the situation of having high name recognition for chocolate (e.g. 95% for *Sprengel* chocolate), but only minimal loyalty value, which was also declining. Only 29% of chocolate connoisseurs considered the brand appealing. It was no wonder that the competition from television advertising, like *Milka* and *Ritter Sport* jointly shared over half the chocolate market, leaving *Sprengel* with a mere 1.4% of the market share. *Sprengel* was repositioned based on the target group typology of the sociologist Gerhard Schulze, who divides consumers on the basis of their leisure behavior into "experiences milieus". According to a consumer analysis (CA) incorporating the Schulze milieus, *Sprengel* consumers are represented over-proportionately in the "integration milieu". These consumers tend to be older, family-oriented conformists with a mid-level education, who spend most of their leisure time at home and in the garden. After detailed analysis, however, the brand was to be anchored in the *self-actualization* milieu. The reason: This slightly younger "milieu" of individuals between 20 and 45 harbors the most chocolate eaters beside the slightly less educated *entertainment* milieu (somewhere between soccer stadiums and action films).

As Stollwerck's single aim was a higher positioning of its product, the decision was made to target the active, more educated and diversely interested *self-actualizers*. Although this group has a hedonistic tendency, it strives for success and perfection at the workplace and on the sports field, which, in contrast to the pleasure principle, also demands discipline. The search for that "kick" in professional life and sports was associated with *Sprengel Top Choc*. The experiential world of this success-oriented group was to be reflected in display advertising and billboard images. A young, sporty snowboarder reflects the activities and dynamic of the self-actualizing individual just as the successful business guy. With the slogan "Reward for winners", the brand was positioned in the premium price segment, unknown terrain for the chocolate for winners. The media plan was also developed from the Schulze typology. It did not include any television activities – but not because of the limited advertising budget, rather because the active, mobile self-actualizers can be reached more easily with billboards and city lights in busy urban areas, movie theater advertisements, floor

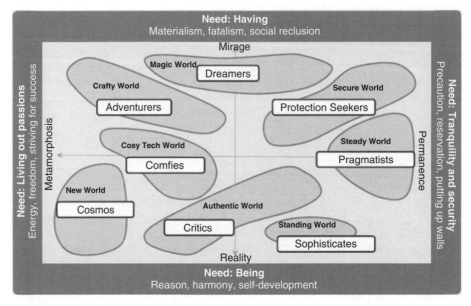

Figure 7.11   "Euro-Socio-Styles" of the German Society for Consumer Research as an example of a lifestyle typology (GfK 2005, reproduced by permission of GfK).

advertisements at points of sale, or selected publications in the sportive area (e.g. *Fit for Fun*), as well as the more serious journals and city magazines (Pfannenmüller 1999). In the meantime, *Sprengel* has come to stand for fine chocolate compositions (www.stollwerk.de).

In all cases, pyschographical typology for addressing private customers is of value due to its basis in empirical values and reasoning, which allows for accountability, even if the requirements on the psychographical and behavior-oriented data to be collected are extensive. Companies can develop their own typologies to obtain typologies that are tailored exactly to the needs of the respective company or the type of product in question. Alternatively, companies can use *standardized typologies* as provided by market research companies to save the substantial time involved and cost incurred by developing their company typologies. However, the advantage of lower costs is accompanied by the disadvantage of a potential inadequacy in satisfying specific requirements and questions. An established example for a standardized typology is the *lifestyle topology* (Lohmüller 2008). This typology uses basic questions on attitudes, values, buying habits, and further socioeconomic characteristics to represent groups with different lifestyles (Figure 7.11).

The respective lifestyles can be further characterized using the criteria on which they are based.

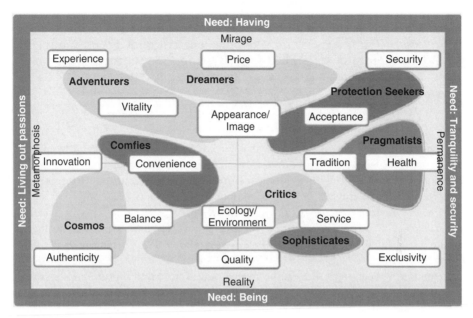

Figure 7.12 Market affinity and product expectations of GfK "Euro-Socio-Styles" (GfK 2005; reproduced by permission of GfK).

Secure world type consumers (the *protection seekers*) are mostly characterized by hedonistic families, tend to be traditional, seek security and financial independence, and are usually bargain hunters. They are driven by values, such as "a happy family life", "comfort and safety", "security" or "home owner". The *authentic world* type (the *critics*) comprises rational, moral and committed "cocoon families", seeking a harmonious and balanced life, with a rather pragmatic consumer behavior. Their core values are "prevent environmental dangers", "find yourself", "increase knowledge", "fight for a cause", "build your own home", or "put nature first".

Studies show that members of different typological groups not only use different communication channels and media, but can also be addressed with different communication content and topics (Figure 7.12).

A similar tool for analyzing customer needs and the subsequent devising of marketing strategy and communication measures is available in the form of the **target group matrix**. As for the lifestyle typology, collecting the required data for different target groups or roles in the company (e.g. purchasing manager or HR manager) is based on classic market research procedures: preferences are collected by conducting empirical investigations (questionnaires). To clarify, the target group matrix is presented in the context of a B2B environment, which most resembles its use in practical application, below.

Some tourist boards in Europe, such as the Regional Tourist Board of Western Pommerania, for example, use a target group matrix in the B2C area for differentiating between "day trippers and city tourists", "rivers and country vacationers", and "beach and seaside vacationers".

Due to cost reasons, it is usually advisable to collect and discuss basic hypotheses about preferences in terms of communication channels and content, for example, in an initial step with a (qualitative) survey of a small sample group of about 20 (potential) customers, before verifying these in a comprehensive (quantitative) empirical survey with several hundred people. In order to ensure that the resulting statements can be generalized, the empirical collection of data should fulfill fundamental qualitative requirements, such as statistical representativeness (Bortz 1993; Backhaus *et al.* 1994; Esser 1974; Kreutz & Titscher 1974; Green & Tull 1982). Project examples show that the empirical collection of data can be carried out using statistical procedures and with comparatively moderate effort and resources, as individual market research companies carry out studies at regular periods.

The target group matrix can be divided into at least three different dimensions:

* Role analysis;
* Analysis of the target group in the "buying center" and;
* With regard to the group's preferences for a certain communication channel.

A *role analysis* is used to obtain cross-industry role descriptions, and to be able to make conclusions about the following points, for example:

* Activities/core tasks of the role;
* Self-image, in other words, the function or status which the role assigns itself;
* Underlying personal goals (which the role pursues in working life), motivators and professional challenges (e.g. grievances/circumstances that impede the role in performing work);
* Relationship of the role in handling/use of certain product categories (drivers or barriers);
* Topics relevant for dealing with this role;
* Arguments that should be used when dealing with this role in terms of particular products; terminology/language style to be used for communicating with the role in question and terminology that should be avoided;
* The feeling that should always be conveyed when dealing with this role;
* Commonalities/differences between different roles.

While consumers generally make their decisions individually (they may be influenced by other members of the same household), the buying decision process (buying center) in a company involves several persons and functions (formal). A *buying center* refers to all individuals involved in the buying decision process. The different members of a buying center each have different functions in the buying process that range from

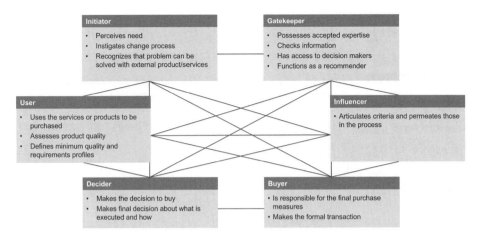

Figure 7.13 Different functions in the "buying center" process (Webster & Wind 1972; Bonoma 1985).

initiating the buying process, to influencing the decision, to the actual decision (Johnston & Bonoma 1981; Webster & Wind 1972). See Figure 7.13.

Besides offering more procedural descriptions of the functions and players involved along the "buying center" process, subdivision into the groups below provides further explanation for behaviors and procedures within the buying decision process:

- **Promoters:** Actively support purchasing a certain product;
- **Opponents:** Impede and slow down the buying process for a certain product.

From a provider's viewpoint, it is advisable to try to meet as many different needs of the players along the "buying center" process as possible. To do so, it is very important to clarify the following points:

- What do a typical decision process and its phases for certain product categories look like?
- Which different players are involved in the process ("buying center types"), what criteria can be used to differentiate between these types, and how great is the actual influence of each player on the buying decision?
- Which other influencing factors (such as, type of buying center, company size, organizational structure) exist?
- Which functions do the participating roles adopt in different phases of the "buying center" process?
- Which typical drivers, accelerators, barriers, and "hygiene factors" are important in the "buying center" process?
- What is the potential influence of communication within the scope of the buying process – what is the information and decision behavior of the various organization members and what are the consequences of this behavior for the decision process?

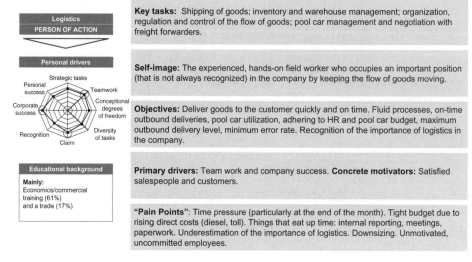

Figure 7.14   Excerpt from a role profile for a logistics manager (example).

The results allow not only for the development of differentiated *role profiles* that comprise a general role description (as seen in the example here for a logistics manager, Figure 7.14), the relationship of the role to each product category under consideration, its communicative requirements, and its function in the "buying center" process. Project examples show that the role profiles in the B2B environment (similar to the typologies in the B2C area) are not only highly stable in terms of time, but also have few significant deviations across different industries. In other words: certain types and characters in certain roles and genres (irrespective of industry sector) are shaped by the respective functional area (such as logistics) in which they are active and their underlying preferences, which are articulated by their choice of profession. Different roles may sometimes require an industry-specific address, and a role-specific address at other times.

An analysis of preferred communication channels helps answer the following points quite accurately:

- What is the criteria used in the selection of the communication channels (preferences/dislikes)?
- What should be the level of intensity of communication (significance and usage frequency of communication channels in terms of the role in the "buying center" process and depending on the individual product)?
- What are the dialog preferences (more active communication by the consumer or more reactive, and with which frequency in the address)?
- Which communication channels are the most suitable for the respective product for which type of communication ("channel profile")?
- How are different communication channels assessed from the perspective of the role in the "buying center" process (general use, professional/private and in relation to certain products)?

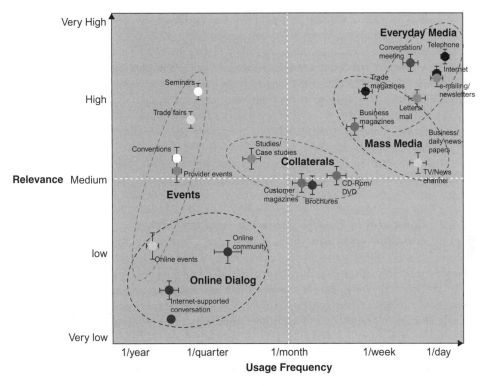

Figure 7.15 Example for analyzing communication channels (usage frequency vs. relevance for a certain product selection) in a certain target group (for role, see Schmitt 2004).

Studies show that everyday media are the most frequently used and most relevant tools for communication (Figure 7.15). These comprise the following access channels: mail, telephone, e-mail, personal meetings and the Internet. Mass media are frequently used but, in comparison, are less relevant for communicating product-relevant features. Product brochures ("collaterals") are significantly less relevant, as, from the perspective of the consumer, they are already more "promotional" by nature. However, they are deemed relevant for special informational events. The question of providing sources of information actively (*push*) or passively (*pull*) permits, among other things, differentiated conclusions to be drawn about the ideal frequency with which communication channels are to be used or when it is to be expected that the recipient will respond with reactance. This shows, for example, that even in the B2B environment, the telephone is a more suitable active communication channel than others for addressing some business functions.

By examining all roles, common criteria for selecting or rejecting channels can be determined, such as speed (requires little time expenditure, fast information), plausibility (honest, factual, competent), or the depth of information (selected information in detail).

A comprehensive *target group profile* is suitable for summarizing all collected data from the role analysis, preferred communication channels and "buying center" processes. This profile summarizes the following:

- **Role descriptions:** Consumer core tasks and needs, consumer self-image, educational background, private and professional goals and drivers for certain activities;
- **Relationship to certain product categories:** Relationship, use, drivers, and barriers;
- **Recommendations for communication:** Superordinate topics, arguments, and language to be selected;
- **Function in the "buying center" process:** Tends to trigger a need, negotiator or decision maker;
- **Preferred communication channels:** Criteria for channel selection, affinities, and rating of channels in terms of suitability;
- **Intensity matrix:** For usage of communication channels and dialog preferences (passive/active and with which frequency).

7.2.2 Competitive analysis: between cost leadership and differentiation

Besides analyzing existing market structures and customer requirements, the competitive analysis ultimately focuses on the business models, positioning, and offers of competing market participants (Aaker 2001; Wheelen & Hunger 2001). The attractiveness and average profitability of a market segment can be described by factors such as (Homburg & Krohmer 2006):

- **Competitive intensity arising from rivalry between current providers:** For example, between the providers on the PC market or the currently discernible high competitive intensity among automobile manufacturers, predominantly concerning price;
- **Market entry of new competitors:** For example, the new providers of telecommunication services;
- **Barriers to market entry:** For example, the monopoly of some former telecommunications and postal companies until recently;
- **Existence of substitute products:** For example, MP3 players as a substitute for CDs, even if, in this case, both the product and distribution channel (online) are substituted;
- **Power of suppliers and customers:** For example, of automobile manufacturers *vis-à-vis* their suppliers and their (independent) dealers.

At best, the different analyses in these areas already show potential market niches and positioning options in the respective industry segment (Kim & Mauborgne 1997). The level of competition determines the success (such as profitability) in this industry segment: If the level of competition increases, the profitability for providers in the respective market segment tends to decrease.

Rising competitive pressure forces companies to orient new goods according to customer needs even more closely, thereby meeting increased quality requirements **and** lower price expectations when compared to established or predecessor products, in order to satisfy the dictates of demand (Pine 1993). The choice of a suitable competitive strategy is largely responsible for later competitive positioning, which can in turn lead to increased company success. According to Porter (1980), there are two applicable, generic strategy types:

- Cost leadership strategy;
- Differentiation strategy.

The first strategy of *cost leadership* is aimed at gaining a competitive advantage over the competition by having lower costs (Burr 2003). A better cost position in comparison to the competition opens up more leeway for the provider for pricing (e.g. lowest price strategy). This cost position is mostly associated with a desire to gain high market shares and production in larger batches for greater economies of scale. With *differentiation*, the focus is on the uniqueness of the company service portfolio. In this case, a company's products are presented so that customers recognize them as unique when compared to the competition. The perceived uniqueness does not have to be limited to objective performance or service features, but can also include subjectively perceived advantages of the service offer (e.g. the brand image) or the special nature of the customer relationship.

Sunglasses manufacturer, **Oakley**, provides an example of using a differentiation strategy with product designs. Oakley achieved great popularity in the 1990s. The company focuses on modern sunglasses at premium prices with super-hardened polycarbonate lenses and unusual designs. Initially created as motorcycle glasses, the glasses were used by such well-known athletes as Greg Lemmond, winner of the Tour de France in 1985 and 1986, or by other VIPs, for example Michael Jordan (basketball). Aside from the product concept of unusual design and the option of replacing the lenses, the company's image for quality was reinforced by a carefully planned distribution strategy. This allows the glasses to be sold only by high-end retail businesses and not by large-scale discounters like Wal-Mart.

Mid-market companies – the so-called SMEs – offer a notable example for a differentiation strategy using niche marketing. Simon (2007) defines companies that have more than 50% of a world market share, are active in a niche segment, but are not well known as "hidden champions." Examples are *Tetra Food* with a 80% share on the market for tropical fish food or *Hohner* with a 85% market share for harmonicas. They are in spots such as Altavilla Vicentina (Italy), where the Zamperla family makes the rides found at Disneyland and other big amusement parks. Or in Stockholm, where Assa Abloy is the world's biggest lockmaker. The group of "hidden champions" range from near-giants like British packaging company **Rexam PLC** ($5.6 billion in sales) and French optical specialist **Essilor** ($2.9 billion in sales) to relative minnows like Norwegian recycling specialist **Tomra Systems** ($363 million in sales) or **La Sportiva**, an Italian maker of climbing shoes ($77 million). These "hidden champions" are mostly family-operated businesses active in stable markets and base their success on (Simon 2007):

- High customer orientation and knowledge, excellent services, fast service, punctual delivery, but not necessarily low prices;

> • Management in direct and regular contact with the most important customers;
> • High focus on continued innovation for the customer's benefit;
>
> The high degree of connection and orientation to the customer manifests itself among "hidden champions" in a high customer contact rate. In comparison to large companies, five times as many employees of "hidden champions" have regular customer contact. They pursue a clearer strategy, manage their finances more professionally, provide superior customer service, and invest more in research and development than their poorer-performing peers.

However, the competitive analysis faces challenges (Porter 2001; Aaker 2001; Timmers 1999; Slywotzky & Morrison 2000; Lammerskötter & Klein 2001) such as:

• Competitive analysis in an unclear competitive environment due to reduced barriers to entry and blurred industry boundaries (*convergence*). If the classic competitive analysis focuses still more on individual competitors, the complexity of strategy development increases, for example, by taking into account different company networks or competition "clusters" (Porter 1999);
• Identifying new market participants from segments that were previously different industry segments, such as infomediaries on the Internet or Internet pharmacies like DocMorris (Strauss & Schoder 2001);
• Necessity of identifying partners with complementary competencies, but who may appear in other product and market segments as competitors.

7.2.3 Enterprise analysis: what's the status quo concerning customers, competitors, and the market as a whole?

In addition to carrying out customer, market, and competition analyses, it is also necessary for a company to establish its location in this environment in order to devise a marketing strategy at a later stage. This requires at least three levels of consideration as part of the analysis:

• Company situation with its (base) customers;
• Company situation with the consumers in the broader market environment (the "not yet customers");
• Company situation in comparison to competitors.

The analysis of the company situation with its own existing customers primarily refers back to customer satisfaction and customer loyalty for the company. By comparing the actual customer experience (ACTUAL) when a service or product is used in comparison to a particular, predefined comparative standard of the consumer (TARGET), customer satisfaction emerges as a highly cognitively structured phenomenon (Beutin 2006): Satisfaction arises mainly from the customer's perceptory processes. Customer satisfaction indirectly influences customer loyalty, which manifests itself in (Schnaars 1998; Homburg & Schäfer 2006):

- Repurchase behavior;
- The willingness to purchase additional items (*cross-sell/up-sell*); or
- The willingness to recommend products to other consumers (*recommendation*).

Empirical studies show that customer satisfaction positively influences not only customer loyalty but also the willingness to pay higher prices (Kotler & Bliemel 2001). More detailed analyses within the scope of a sales segment calculation offer additional insight into the current profitability of existing customer segments. A customer value analysis ("customer lifetime value") not only shows the current value, but also aggregates the costs and revenue along the entire customer life cycle (from customer acquisition to customer loss) as an instrument for analyzing the situation with base customers (see section 11.2.3).

At least the following should be answered for the analysis of the company situation with base customers:

- What is the degree of customer satisfaction with the company's current services?
- How loyal are customers to the company and to the company's services?
- To what extent are base customers willing to recommend the company and its products to other consumers?
- What is the company's "share-of-wallet" (see market potential analysis, page 88) of total consumer expenditure in a certain service and product portfolio?
- How high is customer-specific profitability of the customers? What is the percentage of non-profitable customers?

Besides the analysis of the company situation in the customer environment, analysis of the company situation in the *total market* among consumers is a further prerequisite for subsequent formulation of a marketing strategy. Such an analysis orients itself strongly toward the image and name recognition of the company and its products. The analysis can be structured according to the steps of the **brand funnel** (see Section 7.2.3). Deficits in the perception or willingness to buy can indicate a need for more intensive communication activities with a more specific target.

The following should be answered for the *analysis of the company situation* with consumers in the market:

- What image does the company or its products have on the market?
- What level of name recognition does the company have with all consumers in the market?

- What are the company's values, for example, in the dimensions "awareness of the company and/or its products" or "willingness to buy" (see the "brand funnel" analysis)?

To determine the situation in relation to the most important competitors, differential characteristics that are not only important for customers, but can also be perceived and have a certain durability should be applied. Many of the required key points and information here are already used in market potential analyses or customer typology.

The following at least should be answered for the *analysis of the company situation in comparison to competitors*:

- What is the company's market share in the market as a whole?
- What are the company's strengths/weaknesses in comparison to competitors?
- What are the relevant, and, from the customer's point of view, important and sustainably differentiable competitive advantages? Which customer value is addressed in the sense of a "value proposition"?

Today's enhanceable *core competencies* must be identified to summarize and supplement the market and competitive analyses as part of a resource-oriented and competency-oriented approach. Core competencies require that imitation is only possible (if at all) with great difficulty by competitors and that the market lacks possible substitute products (from an input-oriented point of view). The results show core competencies with added value that can be clearly perceived by the customer, and the possibility of having the customer differentiate between one company and its competitors with products and services (Hamel & Prahalad 1994; Goodstein *et al.* 1993). Therefore, core competencies are the necessary prerequisite for creating the highly sought after customer value. Evaluation of the possibilities for differentiation between one company and competitors can only be carried out with adequately accurate knowledge of market development and (current/future) customer needs, which then results in a close interrelatedness between market and competency analysis. Simultaneously, it is also necessary to assess the extent to which technological innovations and market changes lead to core competencies becoming outdated and losing value. From a company viewpoint, this prompts the need either to further develop required core competencies systematically, restructure core competencies, or acquire core competencies by way of cooperations and mergers (Lensker 2008).

Virgin Atlantic Airways provides a successful example for how detailed customer analyses can be implemented in a dedicated, customer-driven differentiation strategy, and core competencies can be systematically created and structured. After emerging from the Virgin Group music conglomerate in 1984, the initially small British carrier has become a driver of innovation in the global aviation industry, particularly for the standard of service on long-distance flights. It is no news that airlines move in a market environment that is increasingly competition based and under increasing cost pressure, but in which real technological breakthroughs are a thing of the past. It's also no surprise that potential improvements generally target better service, lower prices, and increased punctuality and reliability. So what makes Virgin better than the competition?

The reason lies with consumer desires and needs, which would not necessarily be articulated explicitly in a survey or questionnaire, and which are only rarely discovered by market researchers. The challenge that Virgin handles so brilliantly is to understand the customer's situation – to get in the customer's shoes, so to speak. The company combines leading product innovations with excellent service and so creates a unique flight experience for its customers. Using an optimal mixture of investment in research and development, ground-breaking design, and the ability to anticipate customer expectations, Virgin Atlantic has become the market leader for upper-class air travel. In 2004 alone, one of the most difficult financial years for many airlines, Virgin's passenger figures increased by 26% in comparison to the previous year (*Absatzwirtschaft* 10/10/2006).

Virgin placed a clear emphasis on finding out the typical "pain points" that plague almost every passenger before, during, or after a flight in order to create relevant customer value by providing appropriate solutions. Consequently, a new lounge at Heathrow (London) offering stressed frequent flyers massages or beauty therapy was created. Flyers can also improve their golf stroke on their own driving range and then enjoy the latest sashimi creation in the recently open sushi bar. And the service innovations don't stop on the ground: even at an altitude of a few thousand meters, passengers can have their hair cut or get a manicure (*Absatzwirtschaft* 10/10/2006).

In order to get the most comprehensive picture of their customers, Virgin Atlantic places strong emphasis on the commitment of its employees and ethnographic processes in qualitative market research. Company employees, known internally as the "Virgin Tribe", are given a high degree of personal responsibility and independence to generate ideas that the company can implement in new and innovative services. With its customer-driven strategy, Virgin Atlantic Airways achieved outstanding success. In 2004, profits rose to USD 120 million, which meant almost triple that of the previous year. While many airlines had to record substantial losses in the past few years, Virgin Atlantic was able to increase sales by another 28% in 2005. Virgin is already crafting concrete plans for further future growth. The company is planning a new service and innovation offensive for the coming years to welcome customers with improved service and the latest technology, which is to surpass that of competitors by far. Achieving success comparable to that of Virgin Atlantic and sustained growth requires more than just the right, creative business idea. Rather, the main challenge is to orient the entire company and the core competencies toward customer needs across all areas. Marketing, sales, and research/development must subject themselves equally to this "demand first" orientation (*Absatzwirtschaft* 10/10/2006; reproduced by permission of *Absatzwirtschaft*).

Virgin is not alone in consistently focusing on customer needs and structuring the core competencies required accordingly. Case studies from other companies, such as the **Ritz Carlton Hotel Group**, exhibit similar characteristics (Kreutzer 2008).

The challenge of the competency analysis in dynamically changing markets (Aaker 2001; Handy 2000; Raub & Probst 2001; Fitz-Enz 2001; Lammerskötter & Klein 2001; Fellenstein & Wood 2000; Strauss 1996) lies in:

- Checking the actual *usability or value* of existing competencies;
- Permanently *comparing* (and adjusting) existing competencies with their usability or value in highly dynamic markets;
- Systematic control of company *knowledge management* (organizational learning) which extends to customers, suppliers, and competitors in terms of "co-opetition" (Picot & Neuburger 2000);
- The ability to *integrate* new employees and organizations as quickly as possible, and the ability to manage interfaces to external organizational units efficiently (Schein 1994).

For a pragmatic approach, analysis along the entire value chain, benchmarking, context analysis, and the SWOT analysis can be selected from the wide range of available instruments for conducting an enterprise analysis (Aaker 2001; Porter 2001). These procedures are mostly used in combination.

The advantage of a *value chain analysis* is a clear representation of a (potential) customer value, which consequently indicates potential competitive advantages along the process chain for diverse company activities (Aaker 2001; Kreikebaum 1989). Individual activities within the value chain are investigated as to the extent that they actually offer customers added value and which competitors offer similar services and activities. The "brown paper method" offers a simple approach for devising and visualizing the internal business value chain. As part of this method, all primary and supporting process steps are compiled on brown paper during a workshop. This form of visualization facilitates "plastic" discussion of possible sources for generating additional customer value and, consequently, potential competitive advantages (Figure 7.16).

Supplementing a process analysis with financial key figures (such as process costs) facilitates structured discussions and conclusions about the actual value contribution.

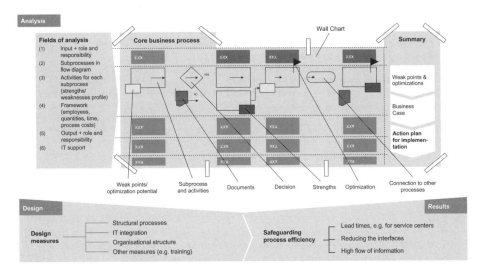

Figure 7.16   Manual method for analyzing the value chain ("brown paper method").

Practical examples show that the approach using a led workshop has substantial advantages in comparison to a purely IT-supported process modelling. The "high touch, low tech" approach forces a high degree of interaction and discussion between participants, and fosters the formation of a consistent group opinion both on the participants' own company and the location of competitors. Subsequently, the results on the company can be mapped for implementing process improvements and adjusting the associated IT in IT-supported modeling procedures (such as ARIS) as required. Process modeling that goes beyond the company to include recipients and suppliers as part of a cross–company value chain offers further potential for optimization, such as optimization of the interfaces between manufacturers and retailers (*efficient consumer response*).

A cross-company value chain was implemented by **Wal-Mart** and **Procter & Gamble**. The e-procurement solution of Wal-Mart uses the aggregated data of the cash registers, websites and sales planning of affiliated brand item manufacturers, such as Procter & Gamble (efficient consumer response, "ECR"). The integrated solution connects IT applications with customers and suppliers, existing ERP and planning systems, and comprehensive data warehousing/data mining (Wildemann 2000; Brehm & Ferencak 2001). Continual and flexible replenishment control by Wal-Mart lead to significant savings when compared to inventory and stock-keeping used previously. In order to avoid simply transferring additional transport resources and expenditure arising from increased delivery frequencies, and the supply risk to the manufacturer, the manufacturer receives comprehensive and independent control of the supply process (vendor-managed inventory). Based on current (ACTUAL) inventory data from Wal-Mart, the distribution centers, and sales forecasts beyond individual distribution steps, quantity structures and time frames are determined including all further process parameters. Inventories are reduced with realistic planning and control of all goods flows on a uniform IT platform with reduced safety stock and shortened replenishment lead times. For smaller retail companies, cross-docking points outside cities or transport centers allow efficient transport commissioning for products from different manufacturers (Werner 2000).

The emphasis of a cross-company value chain analysis, besides determining the location on the market, is more on efficiency-oriented targets, (Walther 2001; Thaler 2001; Wildemann 2000), such as uncovering potentials, for example:

- For improving *customer service* (as regards deadline and delivery reliability);
- For a possible decrease of *product development* and *lead times*;
- For reducing *stock* along the entire value chain;
- For increasing the *flexibility* of integrated delivery chains across several companies;
- Using *synergy effects* and additional business opportunities.

In an ideal case, a high degree of integration along the entire value chain reduces all costs associated with a transaction (as a result of reduced stock-keeping or fewer express deliveries, for example), times (e.g. wait times and lead times), secures high deadline reliability (as a result of integrating real-time planning models, for example), and serves as an early warning system, allowing all participating partners to react promptly to malfunctions and errors. Case studies show, for example, that the *synergy potentials* of a comprehensive value chain optimization are significantly higher than when individual segments of the value chain are improved, and manifest themselves in considerable *cost reduction potential*, such as the following (Holland 2001; Walther 2001):

- A reduction of **stock** (between −25% and −60%);
- **Forecast accuracy** (between +25% and +80%);
- **Logistics costs** (between −25% and −50%).

Therefore, the value chain analysis not only allows accurate conclusions to be made on the location of your own company in the competitive environment, but thereby also prepares the basis for a potential analysis of internal and cross-company process optimization. Given this context, the analysis of cross-company value chains would also be advisable for establishing the location of your own company in the competition.

The stationary manufacturer, **Herlitz**, communicates, for example, with suppliers and retailers (thereby, customers) in real-time about stock levels, delivery times and capacity bottlenecks (Strauss & Schoder 2001).

The disadvantage of the value chain analysis is that a comparison of the value chain with the most important competitors requires considerable knowledge of the internal structures of the competitors, and consequently demands considerable time and resources. In contrast, *benchmarking* is structured significantly more simply (Karlöf & Östblom 1993; Jentner 1998; Kricsfalussy & Meurer 2006). The focus of benchmarking is the systematic and structured comparison between companies using standardized benchmarks and values. Central attention is to be paid to companies that are considered exemplary in the area being examined (*best practices*).

In the 1990s, **ABB** concentrated heavily on external "best practice analyses, in other words, on comparisons with the competition or the process leader outside the industry sector. First, the benchmark object; that is, a subprocess from the value chain, is determined. In the next step, this subtask is analyzed using process mapping, and the required benchmarks are identified. Better understanding of your own company's processes and optimization frequently make best practices comparisons unnecessary. However, if analysis of your own company processes is insufficient, selecting and analyzing a suitable benchmarking pattern is a legitimate option. The results are then implemented in your own company. According to ABB, it is at this stage at the latest that having included those that have the greatest interest in process optimization, provided that they have been included from the beginning, proves to be extremely advantageous (*Absatzwirtschaft* 1996).

The direct comparison offers key points for improving services in individual business areas, activities, or product features. Criteria for benchmarking can be either costs (costs of sales activities and distribution channels), times (such as delivery times for purchase orders), or reachability and quality of responding to service questions (Schober 1998). Other areas within your own company, companies in the same industry, competitors, or companies with similar process can be used as benchmarks. The ability to carry out an objective comparison with the activities and structures of a competitor, for example, with the greatest accuracy possible speaks in favor of the benchmarking method. However, the emphasis of benchmarking lays more in improving operative efficiency and less at the level of strategic orientation and structure. Consequently, a common criticism of over-using benchmarking is that the focus falls purely on copying the solution approaches of other companies, while creating one's own creative solutions and strategies recedes far into the background (Jentner 1998).

The *context analysis* refines the benchmarking concept for establishing the positioning in the competitive environment, particularly in the area of marketing communication. This method compares the positioning profiles of the most important competitors with the company positioning. The goal of the context analysis is a systematic assessment of the promises communicated by competitors. All available and relevant marketing measures (such as placing advertisements, brochures, mailings) carried out by the most important competitors are used to determine this positioning

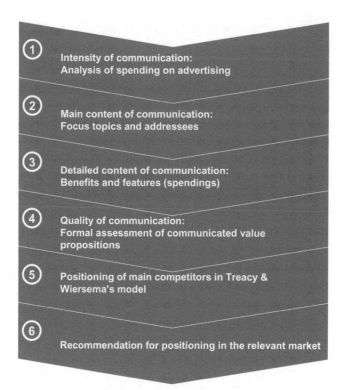

Figure 7.17 Procedure for context analysis (Strauss 2008; SKA Agentur für Relationship Marketing).

profile, and are analyzed in terms of the content (qualitative) statement and the generated (quantitative) advertising impact. Strictly speaking, all marketing activities and tactics should be taken into account equally for this procedure. However, it can hardly be assumed that, in reality, (a) all marketing measures of all competitors are broadly available and/or visible and (b) can be included in detail in the analysis, which would be far too costly. It is equally unrealistic to expect to be able to draw conclusions about the impact of these measures in the total marketing mix or the budget used by the competition in each case. For practical reasons, it is therefore generally advisable to focus the analysis heavily on marketing communication with a specific emphasis on advertising. Other measures, such as brochures, mailings, and websites can be integrated additionally and selectively in the analysis. This has the effect that advertisements are implicitly interpreted as representative tactics of the communication strategy of competitors – in other words, with this analytical focus, it is assumed that the advertisements reflect the content of the communication strategy of the respective competitor in the same way as in other communication measures. Ideally, the context analysis should have six steps, as shown in Figure 7.17.

Competition differentiation: In the first step, the advertising spending of the most important competitor is evaluated. For this, the advertising volume and the advertising expenditures of competitors in the area of display advertising, among other things, are calculated:

- Assignment of the identified market participants in the emerging competitor categories;
- Creation of a representative selection of market participants in the respective competitor categories;
- Definition of relevant competition and the market participants to be observed.

Collecting all promotional communication and evaluating the main content: During the second stage, main topics and addressees, including the respective detailed content, are statistically evaluated:

- Inspection and preparation (sorting, scanning, saving, organizing, etc.) of the entire marketing communication of the relevant competition;
- Creation of communication overview ("wall paper");
- Creation of a communication database that is updated with all the information on promotional communication (product/service, advertiser, advertising form, advertising medium, advertising launch date, volume, images, etc.);
- Collection of all advertising messages communicated in the competitive environment.
- Analysis of the communicated messages (benefits) according to the attributes used; which means assigning terms like "uncomplicated", "easy to manage", and "easy to use" to positive higher-level definitions, such as "easy manageability". Here, you can draw conclusions about how often a certain argument is used, for example:
  - Satisfied reference customers: For example, "works every day for thousands of customers";
  - Market leaders/experts: For example, "solution for product XY from market leader", "comprehensive industry know-how and execution expertise";
  - Address type: Pure "I/we" perspective, market perspective (" it's known that …") direct address ("you"), respective provider reports on customers;
- Target group language: For example, small companies, mid-sized companies, large companies/groups, housewives, or "best ager".

Evaluation and detailed content of communication: Customer benefits and product features are used to create a document and evidence function within the communicated benefits for the customer. The following, for example, are examined:

- How often a certain argument (customer benefit) is used;
- Percentage share of all advertising volume that contains benefit X;
- Weighting of advertisement placing with the list price (represents range, page positioning, size of advertisement, and so on) and the position of benefit X within the advertisement (such as headline, subline, or text/copy);
- Standardization using the most strongly communicated benefit (with index 100).
- The outlined example from the B2B environment (Figure 7.18) includes a broad spectrum of customer benefits; from technically-based, operational benefits to

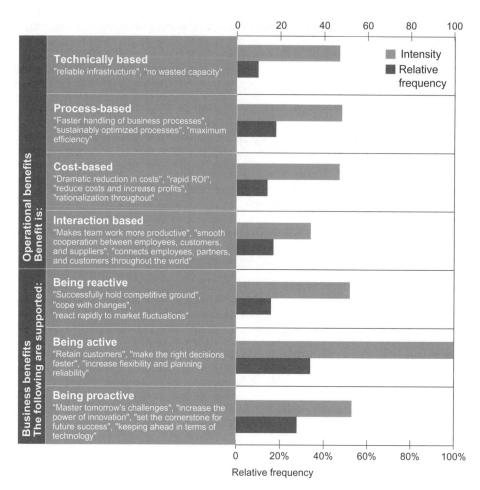

Figure 7.18   Relative frequency and intensity of the communicated benefits as part of the context analysis (B2B example).

future-proof business benefits. Supporting "active entrepreneurship" is the most intensively communicated customer benefit.

- On this basis, conclusions can be drawn regarding the most communicated customer benefits and the prioritization of different benefit categories, for instance. It is also possible to evaluate to what extent the needs that were determined as part of the customer analysis are already systematically addressed by competitors in terms of marketing communication.

- The aim of the context analysis is to determine and evaluate the content and quality of communicated promises systematically. To objectify (generalize) the evaluation and substantiate its claim, a point of reference with various reference categories is required. The *value proposition* provides this point of reference (Figure 7.19).

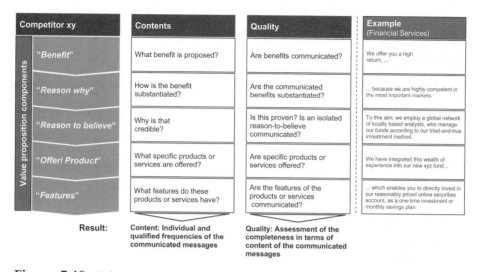

Figure 7.19 Value proposition as a point of reference for the evaluation of content and quality of communicated promises as part of the context analysis.

The "value proposition" describes the value that the relationship between a (product) brand and its customers generates, as well as the realization of this value in a chain of communicative arguments (Hühnerberg 1984) in the following dimensions:

- **Value:** The relevant and unique added value beyond the cost/benefit calculation for the target group;
- **Benefit:** The emotional or rational benefit that the customer gains directly or indirectly from the offering and on which the value is based;
- **Reason why:** The reason for the benefit based on the main features of the offering;
- **Reason to believe:** Credible confirmation of the benefit, such as external, independent sources, verifiable successes in the form of figures, objective/scientific proof.

Quality of the communication: Using the communicated value proposition, the quality of the communication can be evaluated in an informed manner. This raises the question – what is the percentage share of advertising that contains a "benefit", "reason why", "reason to believe", product reference or even certain product features?

- In Figure 7.20, only 77% of all advertisements communicate benefits at all. Quality deteriorates in the "reason to believe": 65% of advertisements provide no evidence. Approximately 80% of advertisements contain features. Therefore, features dominate the benefits.

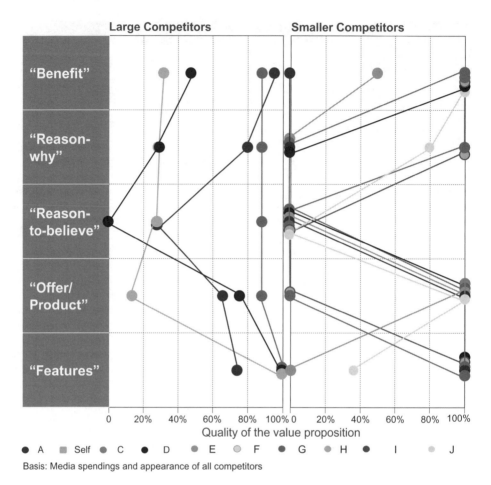

Basis: Media spendings and appearance of all competitors

Figure 7.20 Evaluation of competitive communication along the value proposition (example).

- The dominance of features indicates the product-heavy view the entire market has of itself. The profile as a whole documents the attempt to compensate for lack of evidence by making promises about the product.
- For your company ("Self"), it is advisable to provide clear evidence in order to be set apart positively from the market as a whole.
- High consistency and high effectiveness of the value proposition ("ideal communication") could be displayed in a vertical line graph on the right. The individual profiles show the average communication quality for each competitor. In Figure 7.21, competitor "C" has the highest communication quality.
- All other competitors are very different, especially in their weak or lack of evidence. There is a complete lack of evidence, particularly with small/mid-size competitors. The company's own quality profile shows an overload of communication through features. Substantiated value propositions are hardly

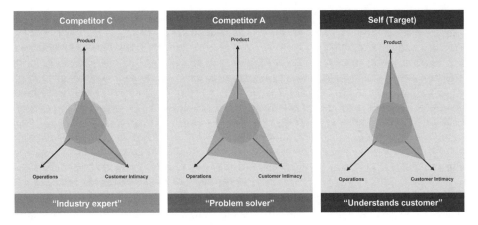

Figure 7.21 Positioning of competitors and own company's intended positioning in the model from Treacy & Wiersema (example).

communicated. Competitor "A" communicates benefit with substantiation, but gives no evidence for the claimed benefit.

Positioning of main competitors and your company's intended positioning: The results of the context analysis can be directly included in the development of your company's own positioning profile according to Treacy & Wiersema (see section 1.5 and Figure 7.21).

- Comparison of the vacant positions in the competition with your company's own offering potential;
- Consider whether your company's own offering is suitable for an attractive niche and whether it can force a competitor out of an occupied position.
- In Figure 7.21:
  - Competitor "C" focuses on customer intimacy and uses the messages in its campaigns to clearly position itself to that effect. An approach that emphasizes testimonials and the notion that "Finally, someone who speaks our language" signal that the company has a profound understanding of customer requirements. Products are named but there is no emphasis on specific features.
  - Competitor "A" also positions itself with customer intimacy, but lacks clear focus. Aspects of operational excellence are communicated well above the market average.

The next point to be discussed as part of the strategy discussion is the company's own TARGET positioning (for communication) in the target market. In this example, it seems advisable to focus on product leadership while also safeguarding customer intimacy (Figure 7.21).

A very common way of obtaining a general overview and evaluation of qualitative and quantitative factors is to perform a **SWOT analysis**, which analyzes strengths, weaknesses, opportunities, and threats (Thompson & Strickland 1990; Götz 1998)

(1) Internal **STRENGTHS** (... To be built upon)	(2) Internal **WEAKNESSES** (... Which need to be compensated)
• Good customer relationships • Knowledgeable product management • High quality of manufacturing •	• Low influence on customer retention • Lack of important competencies in new areas and product lines • ....
(3) External **CHANCES** (... Which might be utilized)	(4) External **RISKS** (... Which have to be managed)
• High awareness for brand • High quality sales channel network and high geographical coverage •	• Entrance of new competitors from other industries • Aggressive growth of existing competitors • ....

Figure 7.22 Example of a SWOT analysis.

(Figure 7.22). In so doing, a SWOT analysis combines content from other analytic tools and contrasts external opportunities and risks with in-house strengths and weaknesses in a systematic form. This can then be used as a foundation for structured discussion and decisions concerning different marketing strategies.

The great advantage of a SWOT analysis is its simplicity and its ability to integrate a variety of different perspectives directly (Beamish & Ashford 2006). However, it is important for subsequent discussion of marketing strategy that companies understand that even when they are particularly strong in one factor (a particular competency), that does not necessarily give them a competitive advantage. This may be the case when that strength appears irrelevant to customers, or when competitors provide an equal or higher level of service. It is, therefore, of crucial importance for the analysis and the later formulation of the marketing strategy that the company is comparatively stronger than its competitors in each (customer-relevant) factor (Nykiel 2003; McDonald 2005).

The following hypothetical example describes the step-by-step process of marketing planning for the fictitious company, **NatureLabs AG**. NatureLabs has been a successful organic cosmetics group since 1975 and is the 15th largest cosmetics manufacturer. The company's sales growth has dropped dramatically during the past two years, the most recent results being only 0.5%. To counteract this trend, the company is planning to enter a new market segment – men's cosmetics. The company is targeting a 5% sales growth in this market segment, and intends to improve its market position from 15th place to 12th place (*corporate goal*).

The market analysis shows that although the overall market for cosmetics has become stagnant, the market for men's cosmetics still has a double-digit growth rate, making it very attractive. The "care products" segment in particular still has great potential.

- *Market volume, market dynamics:* The market for men's cosmetics, e.g. in Germany, shows that in 2007 sales were EUR 806 million. The expected market growth is at an annual 19% until 2008

(Hamburger Trendbüro). In comparison, the general cosmetics markets is growing only at around 3–4% annually; 50% of men use cosmetic products daily; 55% of men between the ages of 18 and 59 spend EUR 5 to EUR 20 per month on cosmetic care products (Federal Statistical Office of Germany/Statistisches Bundesamt).

- *Market segments:* Shaving cream, shaving gel, and aftershave are declining most rapidly. Skin care creams stand out with double-digit growth for the third year in a row. Lotions currently account for only 6% of sales. Yet the "care products" market segment, with a current market volume of only EUR 49 million, is still capable of major expansion.
- *Special features, barriers to entry:* A significant barrier to entering the market is that competitors are already spending a large amount on advertising. At the same time, strict EU guidelines apply when launching any new product, which means that about 12–15 months must be calculated for development and approval. Discounter stores and brand names intensify the price war.
- The customer analysis shows that 45% of men who spend more than EUR 10 on cosmetic care products are between 30 and 49 years old. This target group equals a 37% share of the market potential (31 million). Users of men's cosmetics have a net monthly income of up to EUR 2,200. Men in technical professions, men in mid-level to upper-level salaried positions, and men employed by the government all have a particular affinity for care products. (TDW Intermedia 2002/03; 2004/05 Trend).

There is no "typical user" in terms of typology. However, there is a difference between men who view body care as something that is purely functional ("low involvers") and men who are intensive users ("high involvers") (Gesellschaft für innovative Marktforschung 2003). Three different segments can be identified, according to some studies (cf. Burda Study on Maennerkosmetik – Bericht ueber Kommunikation in Internetforen, Figure 7.23):

- Segment 1: *Trendsetters who like to experiment* – Low price elasticity, 3.45 million potential customers;
- Segment 2: *The undecided* – High price elasticity, 3.92 million potential customers;
- Segment 3: *The experienced mainstream* – Mid-level price elasticity, 3.17 million potential customers.

Image is important to the needs of all user segments. They want to appear a certain way. This is reflected in their use of cologne. The reasons for using these products include curiosity, openness, a desire to experiment, vanity, the "feel-good factor", as well a poorly developed ego and insecurity. In terms of buying behavior, when compared

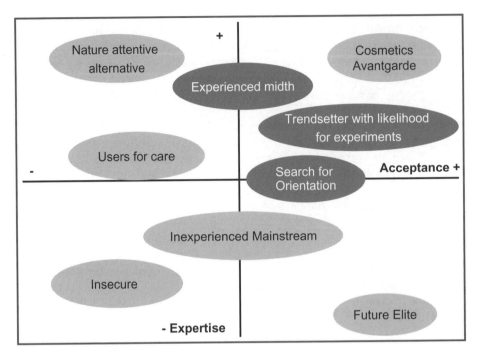

Figure 7.23 Customer typologies according to Burda Study on "Maennerkosmetik – Bericht ueber Kommunikation in Internetforen" 2007. (Reproduced with permission of Burda Community Network GmbH.)

with the "trendsetters who like to experiment", the "undecided" and the "experienced mainstream" tend to choose brands they know, and are open to advertising. Make-up and tanning products are an exception; all of the groups rejected them. NatureLabs is interested in introducing its new cosmetics line, *alpha*, to segments 1–3 because those segments have a high affinity for care products and because with about 12 million potential users, the target group is sufficiently large.

The analysis shows that men are paying more and more attention to their appearance because they know that looking good has a direct effect on professional success and is socially relevant (Customer insights, Trendbüro). Men think functionally – "I take my car to the car wash, so I'll use anti-aging cream on my face". Men are getting their information from consumer and lifestyle magazines (e.g. *Men's Health*), TV, radio (private stations, placement: masculine context and family shows) and, increasingly, from online shops (i.e. online pharmacies, Focus Medialine 2004). Only about 50% of the time do these men make their decision to buy on their own. The older the target group, the greater the influence of other people (usually the wife) when buying men's cosmetics. Men are not comfortable trying cologne in perfume stores; they prefer to make their purchases online or at stores in airports. Men's cosmetics trigger controversial discussions about social taboos (like gender roles), which can be seen as preconceptions and inhibitions. On the whole, men are more concerned about their looks and are ready to spend money on their appearance. However, they do not want too much of a good thing. Men want care products that emphasize masculinity, not care products that attack or belittle role models.

The **competitive situation** is characterized above all by a few companies that dominate the cosmetic market. The massive efforts that these cosmetic giants put into advertising and research make for tough competition. The groups with the greatest growth are **L'Oréal** (e.g. *Garnier, Lancôme*, sales growth of 8.9%), **Procter & Gamble** (e.g. *Wash & Go, Old Spice*), **Unilever** (e.g. *Axe, CD*), **Wella** (e.g. *WellaFlex, Crisan*, +11%), **Beiersdorf** (e.g. *Nivea, Gammon*, +7.2%), and **Henkel** (e.g. *Schauma, Seberin, Fa, Bac*, +1.5%). Those that provide leading brands have a competitive advantage. This allows multinationals to dominate the market. According to Sevenonemedia, the cosmetics market is one of the five most advertising-intensive industries (Sevenonemedia), with the advertising expenses of the top five enterprises in Germany totaling nearly EUR 650 million. This strongly polarizes the market. The most successful products are either premium brands or low-priced brands. Providers in the mid-priced market segment, on the other hand, have trouble winning market share (Focus Medialine). Attacking those market participants effectively would require a sum of tens of millions. Yet, there are success models in certain niches.

The market for cosmetic products is determined by five important trends:

- Trend 1: *Redefined roles* – Women are becoming more masculine and men are becoming more feminine. "Today's men are trying to live a patchwork identity. They want to bring together opposites, being hard on the job and soft in their relationships" (Wippermann, Hamburger Trendbüro).
- Trend 2: *"Metrosexual"* – Fashion-conscious, body-conscious men have been setting new trends since the mid-1990s. David Beckham is representative of this trend. According to estimates, approximately 30–35% of men aged 25 to 45 in the United States have metrosexual tendencies (*Economist*).
- Trend 3: *"Cosmopolitan, athletic man"* – Men who play sports are concerned about their bodies and are more open to personal care products (Communication Networks 6.0). The cosmopolitan, athletic man is fit, international, self-confident in his masculinity, and well-groomed. Examples of this type of man are swimmer Thomas Rupprath and actor Jude Law. This new masculine image will replace that of the metrosexual (manager-magazin).

- Trend 4: *"Lifestyle of Health and Sustainability"* – New values, new awareness, people focusing on their inner needs and changing their lifestyle to understand themselves, escape stress, decelerate, get healthy, and find sustainability and consistency. This generates a demand for efficient, healthy, economical products and services. This trend, known as LOHAS, includes around 30% of German consumers (Universität Hohenheim).
- Trend 5: *Body aesthetic of strength and fitness* – Today's aesthetic demands that men have a body that exudes an aura of strength and fitness (trend247). Looks are also playing a more important role in how men are judged in their professional lives (Trendbüro).

Biotherm Homme offers one example of how the "cosmopolitan, athletic" trend can be implemented interactively. Biotherm is the market's number two cosmetics provider with approximately 20% of the market share (AC Nielsen). It is positioned in the higher-priced segment of the market. As competitors have been winning market share, the company intends to improve customer retention and address new target groups. To help to achieve those goals, it has introduced a new product, *High Recharge*, and launched a new website (www.biotherm-active.de). The company's focus on the Internet lies in a seasonal sporting event and the search for people who want to participate – "... Active Experience 08 has begun. We're looking for a handful of guys to take part in the ultimate ice experience. Winners will receive everything they need for a four-day trip across water and ice – and have the time of their lives ...". The main feature here is not the product but the experience surrounding the brand – taking advantage of the extreme sports trend and associating it with the brand. Tips for physical fitness and personal care as well as information about Biotherm Homme products flesh out the website and help visitors to experience the brand.

The company motto and the mission of **NatureLabs** are specifically aligned with market trends: "At NatureLabs, our task is to promote beauty and well-being in harmony with nature. We combine the power of nature with the human experience. We use scientific knowledge and create products that are effective and become an invigorating experience." The SWOT analysis for NatureLabs points out:

- *Strengths:* Over 30 years of success in manufacturing cosmetics based on natural raw materials; three biotechnological research and development centers in Europe, and several multi-award-winning, innovative products, and ingredients.
- *Opportunities:* These arise in the market from the trend toward ecological products with a large selection of natural, powerful ingredients that can be used for men's cosmetics. The market for men's cosmetics also promises further growth.

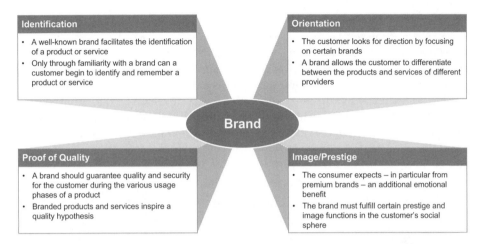

Figure 7.24 Brand functions.

- **Weaknesses:** Up to now, NatureLabs has no offering for or experience with the "men" target group.
- **Risks:** As the market for men's cosmetics matures, it has reached a rather sophisticated level. Diversification problems may arise for NatureLabs on account of the late entry on the market.

7.3   BRAND MANAGEMENT: A BRAND IS A BRAND

7.3.1   The advantages of systematic brand management

Brands represent a vendor's range of services and allow emotional differentiation, in the form of orientation and subjective creation of trust (Aaker 1996; Upshaw 1995; Esch & Wicke 2000). Essentially, a brand represents a perception anchored in the consciousness of the customer, which distinguishes the company's offering from others (Burmann *et al.* 2005a).

For the consumer, the brand serves as an orientation tool to help to identify products and services within a complex range of services more easily (Figure 7.24). Simultaneously, the signal effect of a provider's services represents a promise of quality, which in turn reduces the perceived risk in purchasing. Thereby, brands offer a form of cognitive relief in the purchasing process (Esch 2007). When there are several goods with same-level function, a brand can communicate additional emotional experiences (additional emotional *benefit*) or can be used for personal self-expression. Distinct branding helps the provider to achieve a profile in relation to the competition, and signalizing a certain quality creates particular preferences among the customers.

Empirical analyses have shown in the past that customers who remain loyal to their brand are less sensitive to prices (Krishnamurthi & Raj 1991). When distribution partners use manufacturer's brands, they can reduce their own sales risks: the brand loyalty of consumers and the assumption of quality with respect to the manufacturer's brand also extend to their own services and products. The result is that this usually helps to reduce the amount of explanation needed within the sales negotiation, among other things.

With its two toothpaste brands, *Aronal* and *Elmex*, **Gaba** has shown how systematic brand management can secure long-term market success. The products, which were introduced more than 60 years ago, have a share of 25% of the German toothpaste market. Unchanged in their appearance and positioning on the store shelves, they became the stars of the toothpaste market. *Aronal* and *Elmex* versus *Blend-a-med* is not just a competition for customers between two seemingly interchangeable products, it is also a competition between two models: radical concentration on the brand versus expansion of an established brand in the same segment (*line extensions*; Pletter 2007).

In contrast, **Procter & Gamble**, *Blend-a-med* manufacturer, focused on expanding its existing brand: "Exotic Energy, Extreme Green and Citrus Breeze – names like fruity cocktails, but for ... toothpaste!" position the "Blend-a-med complete impressions" as a teeth-brushing taste sensation. The brand had first established itself with the slogan, "Blend-a-med – that's what dentists give their families". Customers were informed that they could "still bite hard tomorrow" after using it, without bleeding on fruit. During the past years, *Blend-a-med* suffered a decline in market shares. Once an expensive product with a medicinal image, the standard toothpaste sold in stores today costs barely half as much as the tubes of *Gaba*, which competes with the simple message, "Aronal in the morning, Elmex in the evening". However, *Blend-a-med* is now available for mornings and evenings, and there are herbal, fruit cocktail, and naturally fresh series, as well as the classic version (Pletter 2007).

Whereas previously *Blend-a-med* still had a clear brand profile, it became increasingly diluted. Research in this market segment has shown that the customer acquires an impression that products can be interchanged arbitrarily – as a result, the orientation function of the brand declines. However, especially for medicinal trust products, such as toothpaste, it is precisely this orientation function and creditability that are important. *Blend-a-med* thus did basically the opposite of what *Gaba* did. At Gaba no product innovation was ever allowed to compete with an existing Gaba product (Pletter 2007; reproduced by permission of Brand Eins).

From the company's point of view, the areas of activity of brand management can be broken down into the areas of

- Brand strategy;
- Branding;
- Brand control.

In addition to these areas of activity, discourse on *internal branding* has emerged more recently. This discourse is motivated by the insight that effective marketing strategy and consistent branding can only be successful if the underlying brand values are reflected in every interaction with the customer. For example, if the brand image directed at the customer is not consistent, if the entire marketing communication is oriented toward the brand values and consistent branding but the activities of other points of interaction between the customer and the company (as in sales or service areas, for example) are perceived as diametrically opposed to this communication. Consequently, it is important that awareness and understanding of the brand value is broadly anchored in your own company (Kreutzer & Merkle 2008a; Schauer 2008; Burmann & Zeplin 2005).

7.3.2 Brand strategy: how should the brand be positioned on the market?

The brand strategy can be broken down into the dimensions of brand coverage, brand positioning, and brand architecture. In the context of *geographic brand coverage*, the extent to which a brand should appear and function as a point of orientation in a regional, national, or international market environment is determined. As concerns vertical brand coverage, the different value creation levels that a brand is to affect should be specified. When brand products are used in the production of other products and are not otherwise identified, it is a *pure manufacture brand* (for example, Kugelfischer ball bearings for automobiles). On the other hand, if a brand entering various value levels of production is identified, this is a case *of ingredient branding*.

Ingredient branding describes the branding policy for a product component that is usually an essential part of the end product, where it "is lost" and remains invisible for customers at subsequent levels (pure manufacture brand). To avoid this anonymity and, the related substitutability, component manufacturers try to practice a cross-level branding policy. Intel, one of the pioneers in this area, defines ingredient branding as the "promotion of a brand within a brand to the end user" (Sebastian & Simon 1995).

Examples in which the manufacturer managed to escape anonymity with intermediaries, consumers and users include *Nutrasweet* (beverage sweetener), *Shimano* (gearshifts and brake systems for sports bikes), *Gore-Tex* (textile lamination in sport and leisure clothing), *Teflon/DuPont* (non-stick coating for pots and pans) or *Tetra Pak* (milk and juice cartons). The most famous case of a metamorphosis from "unknown" supplier to "strong" brand owner is provided by **Intel**, the largest manufacturer of electronic semiconductor chips in the world. With the *Intel Inside* campaign that was launched in July 1991, the company addresses PC users directly and tries to encourage them to buy a PC, irrespective of make. The main thing is that it has an Intel microprocessor (Sebastian & Simon 1995; Clark 1994).

In the case of *co-branding*, several brands are presented in combination on the market, in the hope that both brands boost each other and open up new sales potential in their joint market appearance (Burmann *et al.* 2005a).

Porsche and **Adidas** are following a joint path. The sporting goods manufacturer and the Porsche Design Group want to establish a premium sports brand in a long-term partnership. Under the name "Porsche Design", the companies are developing sport shoes, as well as textiles and accessories for golf, tennis, and running with a co-brand of the two brands *Adidas* and *Taylor-Made*. The first products from the "Porsche Design" line have already been introduced on the market. Customers around the world can buy them in up-market sporting goods stores and exclusive Porsche stores. A competitor of Adidas, **Puma**, is taking a different path: Puma has been working together with **Ferrari** since the beginning of this year. Since then, the company has been responsible for equipping the F1 Scuderia racing team. In addition to fireproof racing products, Puma is also responsible for the team's apparel, shoes, and accessories. Puma also acquired the worldwide license for the official Ferrari goods collection (*Absatzwirtschaft*).

A vivid example of brand cooperation as co-branding is provided in the form of a toilet freshener jointly offered by **Alessi** and **Henkel**. While Henkel is mainly active in the areas of short-life consumer goods and covers the product categories of detergent, cleaning supplies, cosmetics, personal hygiene articles, and adhesives, Alessi offers exclusive design articles for kitchen and bath (Jenewein *et al.* 2007). By its own account, consumer goods manufacturer, Henkel, wants to use the cooperation mainly to reach consumers who, for aesthetic reasons, have never used a toilet bowl cleaner before. Market research conducted by Henkel revealed that a great number of consumers would like a toilet cleaner that does not spoil the look of luxury bathrooms, and is appealing to the eye. For its part, Alessi hopes that the cooperation will increase its awareness above all, and that it will help to boost sales. The result of this cooperation is the *FreshSurfer*, a toilet cleaner in the shape of a small man on a surfboard, which is to combine the proven performance of *WC Frisch* from Henkel with the visual appeal and exclusivity of an Alessi designer object. An examination of the target effect derived from this brand cooperation in an empirical study shows that the brand cooperation resulted in varying degrees of success for Henkel and Alessi (Jenewein *et al.* 2007). While Henkel's image was significantly improved in the dimensions of "attractiveness", "exclusivity", "aesthetics" and "design", and only incurred a loss in the criterion of "quality", Alessi's image was damaged by the *FreshSurfer* in all of the cited dimensions when comparing the before (i.e. before introduction of the *FreshSurfer*) with the after (i.e. after introduction of the *FreshSurfer*). Henkel enjoyed great benefits for its *WC Frisch* product range as a result of the co-branding with Alessi. The only down side was that Henkel lost ground in, of all things, the dimension that is so central for its brand, "quality". The cooperation also paid off for Henkel in the fiscal sense: *FreshSurfer* costs 1 euro more in stores than normal toilet fresheners, and Henkel was also able to increase its market share in the toilet cleaner product category by 5% to reach a current level of almost 40%. By contrast, the image of Alessi has suffered as a result of the brand cooperation, which has an especially critical impact on the "exclusivity" dimension, which is so important for a design company like Alessi (Jenewein *et al.* 2007).

The keys to success for brand cooperation are therefore:

- *Brand strengths* (e.g. appeal, purchase intention, willingness to recommend) of the partner. For a successful cooperation, both cooperation partners should possess enough strength and be renowned enough to be able to support each other.
- *Compatibility of the partner's image with your own brand:* The associations transferred or summoned by the cooperation must match each other in content and strengthen your own brand or add a new (desirable) dimension. Alessi's image stands for exclusivity and aesthetic design, whereas Henkel's image stands more for hygiene and quality. The "image fit" required for successful brand cooperation is lacking in this case.
- *Complementarity of brand cores:* The cores of the brands involved must remain clearly recognizable, despite the required image and product fit. The associations anchored in the memory of the consumers with the brands involved should complement each other so that both desirable and relevant associations are produced for the co-brand. Examples of brand cooperation that complement each other in their properties and capacities are consistently rated more positively than brands with properties that overlap.

Brand positioning is mainly a question of the definition and active management of the **brand core** (Figure 7.25). This represents the brand's identity most directly.

The **brand value** describes the value proposition that is to be suggested in the consumer's mind. The main goal is to anchor a brand with specific value propositions

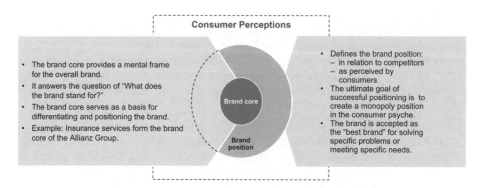

Figure 7.25 Definition of brand core and positioning.

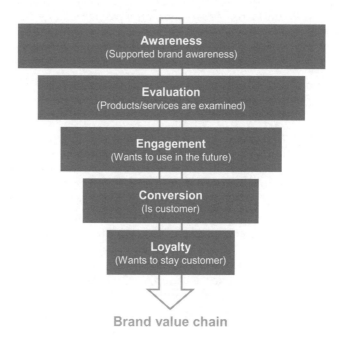

Figure 7.26 "Brand funnel" or brand value creation chain.

in the subjective perception of the consumer. There are at least three proven methods in business practice used to formulate the brand core, brand value, and brand positioning.

First, analysis of the **brand funnel** allows conclusions to be drawn about the actual strengths and weaknesses of a brand (Figure 7.26, Riesenbeck & Perry 2005). In the process, all brand dimensions – from awareness, to image, shortlist, and on to purchase and loyalty – are recorded quantitatively for each target group using performance indicators and compared with those of the competitors.

Considerable reductions in value during transition from one level of the "funnel" to the next are a sign that the brand has concrete problems. These can be overcome

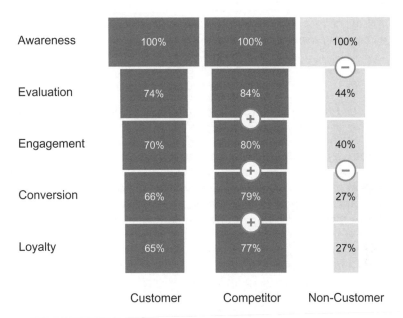

Figure 7.27   Brand funnel, differentiated by customer, non-customer, and competitor (example).

using specific marketing tools, such as activities to increase awareness or loyalty. The conversion rates (in %) for each level in relation to the surveyed random sample indicate the status quo of the brand in comparison to competitors – differentiated by customer and non-customer – for various target subgroups (Figure 7.27; Riesenbeck & Perry 2005). The example at hand shows that a strong brand funnel exists for the competitors: overall, there are very strong conversion rates from the level of evaluation to loyalty. On the other hand, for non-customers, there is a striking rupture between awareness and evaluation, as well as an additional inhibition threshold in the willingness to buy (conversion). Consequently, evaluation barriers and the attitudes that underlie them need to be deconstructed.

In addition to analysis of current brand positioning, this procedure affords direct conclusions about the effectiveness of the currently implemented communication measures. If, as in Figure 7.27, there is high brand awareness (level 1, "Awareness", 100%), but only a below-average willingness to buy ("Products/services are examined"; "Evaluation", level 2), activities for acquiring new customers (level 3) are hardly useful, since the basic willingness to buy does not (yet) exist. Deficits in awareness (level 1) can be compensated using broad-based mass communication, such as TV, posters, or even perimeter advertising. A substantial drop in the purchase intention as compared to the brand image can be countered by selective price promotions or a stronger presentation of the value proposition of the brand and suitability of the products along the value proposition. Problems with the purchasing rate can be countered, for example, by a more intense communication of the sales partners ("Where can I get the product?") and by direct mailing with specific purchase stimuli. Finally, at the lowest level of the brand funnel, loyalty programs facilitate an increase of the repurchasing rate and the number of regular customers.

The **Siemens Mobile** example (Figure 7.27) shows how sales and market share can be increased using a systematic brand funnel analysis. After mobile telephone vendors enjoyed high growth rates in the late 1990s, the market was saturated. Marketing was also examined as part of the search for potential ways to increase efficiency. The goal was to achieve the greatest possible effect using the annual advertising budget of several hundred million euros. **Siemens** examined its brand using the brand funnel, and in the first step it concentrated on the five core countries of Europe (Germany, France, Italy, Spain, and Great Britain). The result: although awareness of the Siemens brand was already fairly high in all of these countries, weak points were discovered in awareness of the individual products and in the brand's image. However, the greatest potential for improvement emerged in the areas of "shortlist" and "purchase". The driving factors for the decision to purchase emerged as product availability, product visibility, and a specific purchase recommendation. Further examinations of the point of sale (PoS) showed, for example, that some Siemens products were not available everywhere (despite central listing) or were not displayed where the customers could see them. At the same time, sales personnel did not make enough recommendations for the purchase of Siemens cell phones.

With this in mind, the marketing budget for 2001/2002 was radically restructured, and exploited the high awareness of the brand (funnel level 1). Siemens Mobile significantly reduced expenditures for classic advertising and launched a broad-based, European-wide PoS campaign. As part of this, care was taken to develop individual solutions for each problem – be it availability, visibility, or purchase recommendation. Refocusing enabled Siemens to increase its market share in sales by several percentage points in only six months, and even became the market leader in some countries during this period (*Absatzwirtschaft* 11/10/2002).

At the same time, the brand funnel analysis made it possible to develop alternative strategies. Whereas previously the budget was oriented one-dimensionally toward increasing store sales, now the focus was more on exploiting the available potential for product awareness and brand image. To do so, the company placed more emphasis on classic advertising. One reason for using this approach is that, from the customer's point of view, the technical features of the products from the various cell phone providers today are almost all the same. The product's emotional value, as communicated by "above-the-line" mass communication, is therefore becoming increasingly important (*Absatzwirtschaft* 11/10/2002).

By utilizing the brand funnel and examining the status quo in the respective funnel levels with empirical analysis, you can use a bottom–up approach (i.e. for each individual level of the funnel) to assess the costs and resources required to reach the specified brand goals and systematically plan communication measures. In practical terms, this means that the focal points of an advertising budget may have to be redefined. This increases the effect of the individual activities, and the budget can be implemented with a higher degree of efficiency (by an average of 15 to 25%).

Additional qualitative conclusions for brand positioning and the perceived value propositions are provided by the SWOT analysis discussed above, implemented here in relation to brand perception. They describe the respective strengths and weaknesses, and simultaneously indicate the opportunities and risks of the brand. The case examples show that even a small number of 10–15 customer interviews is enough to derive sufficient information for the measures required. Qualitative customer interviews (face to face), workshops with other areas (such as sales or service), or simple online surveys, usually offer amazing insight for brand positioning and required areas of action.

The brand funnel analysis and the strength/weakness analysis are both methods that are suitable for brand control. The central points here are brand strength (measured by brand awareness, for example, among demanders), the brand's market success (measured, for example, by the customers' loyalty toward the brand), and/or brand value (the brand's value in monetary units). There are many assessment techniques for measuring brand value as a purely monetary value, such as *Interbrand*.

To date, the brand assessment procedure developed by the **Interbrand** in 1988 has been used to appraise more than 2,000 brands world wide. This method, which is widely used in business practice, is based on a point system or scoring approach. The brand to be assessed is given a point score based on seven factors, which are subdivided into 80 to 100 criteria. The exact weighting of the criteria is considered to be a trade secret by Interbrand and is therefore not publicized. The determined brand strength is then transferred to an S-shaped multiplier. According to Interbrand, this multiplier reflects the fact that, as the brand increases in strength, the increase in brand value is at first exponential, then linear, and finally just marginal. This multiplier value can be between 1 and 20, depending on the brand strength, and is used to multiply the average value of the profit for the last three periods. This results in a monetary brand value according to Interbrand.

The Interbrand model thus tries to grasp the complex essence of the brand more in quantitative terms than other models. However, the high number of criteria risks correlation between the individual criteria; furthermore, the weighting and selection of criteria could solicit criticism. The "marketing support" criterion, for instance, is an input factor and implies that a high brand value can be realized alone with high investment in the area of marketing. Some specialists, therefore, deny that the Interbrand brand value is an exact value statement and instead refer to it as an estimate or tendency. Nevertheless, this method has established itself in the media: The Interbrand value for the most valuable brands in the world, for example, is published each year in the *Financial Times* (Wikipedia 2007).

Whereas the focus of the strength/weakness analysis is the more rational or articulated brand perception, a ***semiometric analysis*** allows assessment of emotional perception. Discussions can be held on both the ACTUAL and TARGET positioning of the brand awareness of a company's own brand as well as those of competitors (Sevenonemedia 2004). The adjectives used to describe a brand during qualitative interviews are transferred to a *semiometric space*. The focus here is not so much on mathematically correct positioning (in terms of multidimensional scaling), but more on the description of the perception areas along fixed attributes (Strauss 2006; Figure 7.28). The spatial distances between your own brand and those of competitors only serve to draw conclusions about the uniqueness of the positioning. Consequently, positioning models, such as a semiometric placing, are extremely useful for representing the current positioning in comparison to competitors, and for a discussion about which TARGET positioning should be strived for (derived from the corporate strategy). Practical experience shows, however, that changes in the positioning of a brand represent a considerable challenge, since in this case a brand image fixed in the minds of the consumers needs to be changed.

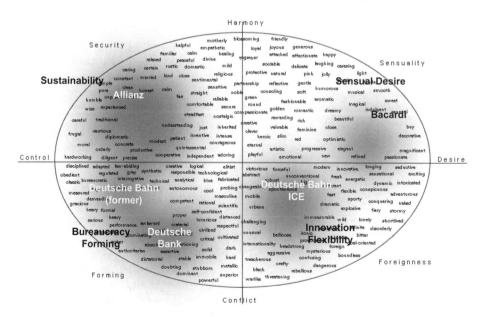

Figure 7.28 Mapping brand awareness with semiometry (example, Strauss 2006).

7.3.3 Brand presence: consistency on the market

After defining the brand strategy, the brand presence determines the actual appearance on the market. This involves both the design of the brand name (the actual brand name and logo) and the form of all marketing instruments (such as creative layouts).

It is important for the brand presence that the name and logo:

- Evoke *associations* in consumers which are compatible with the desired TARGET positioning according to the brand strategy (in the way that *Bionade* summons associations of an organic, healthy, refreshment beverage);
- Have a *concise design* that can be easily distinguished (high in contrast) from the competition, with simplicity and consistency along all customer interaction points. A negative example would be the previously mentioned *Brand New You Tube*, which practically forces confusion with *YouTube* (www.youtube.com);
- Clearly *stand out* from other brands (Paley 2000).

Communication tools can be deployed to ensure that the market presence is always unique, consistent, and characterized by high continuity.

Until the beginning of 2000, **Samsung** was characterized by a very heterogeneous market appearance. As a result of many different responsibilities, using many different agencies and too many ideas for the brand's presence, there was no consistent market appearance. For example, three Samsung advertisements were placed in a single newspaper, but all three had a different tone and appearance. Only the product, and not Samsung, was communicated. No consistent image reached the consumer – even most trade journalists knew only one product group each. Within the Samsung corporation, which in the meantime has reached the Top 20 in the *Interbrand* ranking for most valuable brands in the world, Samsung Germany scored last for a long time. Today, Samsung is well on the way to becoming a model brand itself. The reason for the lack of focus in their branding was ultimately due to internal structures: the autarchy of the marketing directors of individual product divisions led to a highly heterogeneous market appearance. Today, corporate marketing is responsible for the corporate identity, and therefore also for the texts used in campaigns (wording, one voice), and for the coordination of all promotions. The marketing heads of the divisions practice classic marketing and product management and keep corporate marketing up to date with simple briefings. The focus for Samsung is on "product value information" – away from pure product innovation, towards emotion. Communication should convey the value of the products and simultaneously pay into the account of the Samsung brand (Berdi 2006).

A similar situation prevailed at **Philips** in the early 1980s: a vague image, a weak position in the consumer paradise of the USA, and a comparably low ranking in the top 100 most important brands – far behind **General Electric, Intel, Sony**, and even **Samsung**. The first action of the newly appointed Chief Marketing Officer (CMO) was to revise and adopt the central marketing plan (Stippel 2005). As a result, he presented an action plan to the board of directors, which was defined in part by the following:

- Continued development of marketing and sales process tools: the best tools that are useful for introducing new products, and, at the same time, setup of a "marketing academy" to train approximately 3,000 in-house marketing professionals;
- Strengthening the CMO board with various company areas, which was expanded to become one of the most important panels in the decision-making process;
- Improvement of strategic alliances, global customer management and worldwide sponsoring (not a question of more banners, but technological cooperation instead). Philips was to take more initiative in partnerships and also select the companies on which it should focus;
- Creation of a corporate marketing strategy (agency, claim, policy, governance);
- Constant monitoring of marketing expenses and resources using a reporting system;
- Reorientation of marketing organization, development of target marketing functions and job descriptions, and benchmarking the organization.

To liven up the brand promise of "sense and simplicity", Philips developed the new marketing message in a corporate image appearance until September 2004. In December 2004, Philips founded the "Simplicity Advisory Board" (SAB). The SAB serves as a "think tank" and promoter within and outside the company. The founding members include English fashion designer Sara Berman, Chinese architect Gary Chang, MIT professor John Maeda, automobile designer Ken Okuyama, and Dr. Peggy Fritzsche, President of the North American Radiological Society (Stippel 2005).

Similar to Samsung and Philips, **SAP** also developed and implemented global branding guidelines to establish a consistent brand presence. In addition to detailed guidelines for advertisements and media appearances, these also include a comprehensive marketing infrastructure for detailed guidelines for using the logo, color schema, images, and "one voice" rules (tone).

Lufthansa provides another prime example for consistent branding along all customer interaction points. Their brand appearance is highly consistent, for example, from check-in, to lounges, to call-center employees (Eisenächer 2005).

At a one-day event at a "brand academy", **BMW** makes sure that employees and managers learn about the orientation of the **BMW Group** and its brand worlds. These training measures are supported by in-house coaching in the car dealerships (Schauer 2008).

A widely used systematization tool for describing brands is provided by the *brand personality model* (Figure 7.29; Hieronimus & Burmann 2005):

- The *brand strength* distinguishes from the competition and points out its relevance;
- The *brand stature* describes reputation and familiarity. The stature and strength reveal the development potential of the brand;
- Brand values include image and properties;
- *Brand appearance* is the implementation in signs, images and language.

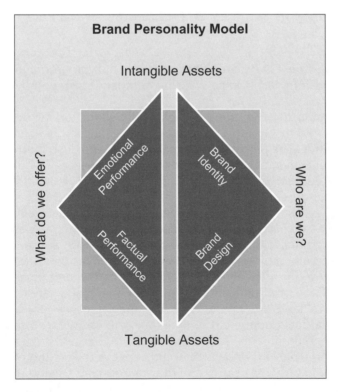

Figure 7.29 Brand personality model: modeled after *icon brand navigation* (brand steering wheel).

As far as brand personality is concerned, brands also possess "human characteristics" in the sense of an individual personality. With human attributes, artefacts are to be "brought to life", making it easier to describe and interact with these objects.

> The **Mini** brand as a lifestyle brand, for example, has a young, modern character, an unconventional appearance, and tries to communicate with target groups with wit and humor (for example, the evolutionary path of the Mini, Figure 7.2) (Burmann & Meffert 2005b).

The factors mentioned above – brand strength, brand stature, brand values, and brand appearance – provide the definition of brand personality. The brand personality is expressed in the four dimensions:

- *Brand identity:* Describes the characteristic properties;
- *Brand design:* Describes the visual/acoustic characteristics, such as name, colors, logo, claims, figures, music, symbols, such as the typical shape of Coca-Cola bottles;
- *Factual performance:* Rational differentiators that distinguish the brand clearly from the competition;
- *Emotional performance:* Makes the brand attractive beyond rational arguments.

> For the hypothetical case of **NatureLabs**, the brand personality model presents itself in accordance with the company's mission:
>
> - *Brand identity:* The brand combines the characteristic properties of nature and technology, well-being and science, it is ecological and innovative. The personality of the brand can be described as natural, curious, active, cheerful, innovative, and moral.
> - *Brand design:* Besides codes, such as name, color, logo, claim, people, figures, music, or symbols, the brand has the product name *alpha*, symbolizing "being first", "leadership", as well as having technical connotations, such as in space travel. Green as the main color symbolically reflects a closeness to nature and environmentally-friendly packaging. The claim is "Discover your nature".
> - *Factual performance:* The effectiveness of the products is emphasized as the rational differentiator for the brand, and in turn the products have been tested using special procedures. Only the essential facts apply, e.g. a small assortment with a maximum of 15 active ingredients in one product.
> - *Emotional performance:* The brand conveys the feeling of being the best thing for your beauty and the environment. Taking responsibility for your appearance and the environment stands out as the emotional factor that makes the product unique.

7.3.4 Brand management on the internet: does the customer manage the brand …?

There are two opposing effects to be expected for the orientation and trust functions of brands on the Internet: on the one hand, the variety of information that is available helps to create customers who are well informed (independent), and so less loyal to any particular brand. On the other hand, the overwhelming flood of offers and the loss of direct and binding personal contact to the dealer or manufacturer increase the perceived risk of an online purchase for the customer, thereby supporting the need for orientation and trust through known brands. In this case, consumers use the brand even more as an information filter and instrument of trust, and they use known (offline) brands to orient themselves, both to process information and to make the actual product selection. Newer business models and the associated brands in e-business, such as **Amazon** (www.amazon.com), **Google** (www.google.com) or **Auto-byTel** in the car industry (www.autobytel.com) have already demonstrated that the Internet spawns independent business brands (of intermediaries) with a high degree of awareness and familiarity. It is particularly debatable in Web 2.0 as to what degree known product brands or prominent Internet brands will assume the task of providing orientation and trust within the online purchase decision process in the future, and how important they will become in e-business as a consequence (see also Knapp 2001).

Insecurity about the future role of the brand in e-business results largely from the changed conditions of *Internet-based brand management*, such as those below (Aaker & Joachimsthaler 2000; Bongartz *et al.* 2005):

- *Interactivity and Colaboration:* Whereas brand companies in traditional marketing control not only the presented (product) content, but also the surrounding context, this influence is lost in e-business. The brand consumer, previously passive, becomes part of an interactive communication process and can directly communicate experiences and personal impressions of the product to other consumers, for example, in the context of virtual communities, expert forums or blogs (so-called "consumer-generated content" in Web 2.0) (Hagel & Armstrong 1997; Seybold 2001).

> The latest development using micro-bloging can be seen at **Amazon:** Amazon uses the micro-bloging service *Twitter.* Periodically Amazon refers to current offers or sends out coupons and codes to its followers in order to allow them to purchase specific products at special rates (www.twitter.com).

- *Wealth of information:* The informational content of the website becomes an immediate part of the consumer's assessment of the brand, for example, through continuously updated content or interactive applications. Content-rich information prompts a learning process about the brand, for example, about its origin and values (Pine *et al.* 1995).

- *Personalization:* In contrast to marketing a formerly broad mass brand, one-to-one marketing and the associated customer-specific information also allows an individual brand appearance to be marketed that is tailored to the individual customer. The presentation of commodities in a customized context accordingly provokes (gradually) different notions of the brand (Peppers *et al.* 2000; Strauss & Schoder 1999b). Depending on the applied context and website design, the Internet facilitates a wide range of virtual, customer-specific (one-to-one) brand experiences (Briggs & Hollis 1997; Sorrell 1997).

For most companies, the significance of known brands for product selection is still retained, despite the general low-price orientation on the Internet (Strauss & Schoder 2000). Against the backdrop of pre-established brand awareness, the decision to buy on the Internet is thereby generally reduced to the selection of a reasonably priced vendor (Strauss & Schoder 2001). The new professional and evaluation services allow for information on a broad basis with neutral, institutionalized quality tests and reviews and the experiences of other consumers, but, from the perspective of companies, still have hardly any influence on the final decision to buy with respect to the (product) brand. Accordingly, new Internet brands have so far been attributed less chance of catching up and competing with established brands sustainably and within a short period of time (Strauss & Schoder 2001).

The online purchase can be complemented by a wide range of independent quality information, for example, in the form of neutral, institutionalized test verdicts. At first, this begs the assumption that the significance of the brand will decrease. However, practical experience shows that companies tend toward the opinion that the use of neutral information services is more likely to lead to a reduced significance of (personal) purchase advice than to a reduced significance of established brands. Only intensely service-based companies (over 90% service oriented) feel threatened by external information services and expect customers to become increasingly price oriented, rather than brand oriented (Strauss & Schoder 2001). The *orientation and trust functions* of known brands apply all the more:

- the more physical products are at the focus;
- the longer companies have been represented on the web; and
- where companies had already gathered relevant experience in online branding.

Empirical analyses show that increasing pressure from international competitors affects all industry sectors, and that brands are increasingly recognized as an active instrument for competition, rather than competition revolving solely around price (Strauss & Schoder 2001).

The British bank **Prudential** followed a completely different course in 1998. With *Egg* (www.egg.com), Prudential created a new Internet brand that could be used to handle private banking services entirely on the Internet. The target groups are "young professionals" and active young people. The success proves that Prudential was right: On its first day alone, *Egg* received 1.75 million hits on its website and 100,000 calls at the call center. By 2000, the brand name *Egg* had achieved a recognition value of 75% in the target group. In the process, *Egg* combines values such as dynamism and customer orientation with reliability of services through Prudential as its parent company. To date, *Egg* has been able to win approximately 2 million customers (Beamish & Ashford 2006).

At the same time, orientation toward known brands in the decision-to-buy process directly affects the selection of the sales channel. While the newly arising market transparency does lead to the creation of an "information seeker" as well-informed (independent), differentiated and less retailer-loyal consumer (declining loyalty to sales channel), manufacturer loyalty and therefore brand loyalty are retained (Tölle *et al.* 1981; Diller 1999). For companies or areas of industry with high customer loyalty, there is consequently less danger of established brands being displaced by new Internet brands (Strauss & Schoder 2001).

With the use of personalized services and one-to-one marketing, brands receive additional meaning, for example, as a way to design a personalized brand presence. Companies that implement an individualized sales approach are more likely in business practice to prove themselves capable of securing the strength of their brands, in spite of manufacturer-independent information services (Strauss & Schoder 2001). The application of one-to-one marketing thereby furthers the significance of the brand (in other words, the brand strength) in the decision to buy, for example, using individualized information or services in the form of personalized websites or e-mails.

In addition to the known forms of Internet-based marketing, a number of innovations in the **Web 2.0** environment have newly emerged as so-called "consumer-generated content" (e.g. blogs as user-created online magazines) or have grown considerably in importance (e.g. search engine marketing, blogs or content sharing, Figure 7.30).

In the new "get involved Web", users praise and criticize products and companies without inhibition – today consumers already produce more marketing information than the companies themselves. This means that companies are increasingly losing control of their own market management. The constant increase in Internet use hides the fact that media consumption time is incrementally shifting from classic, static websites toward the "social Web". The "get involved Web" is more interesting and credible from the user's point of view, and is therefore currently growing rapidly (Li & Bernoff 2008). The new Web 2.0 portals live off user-generated content. People write their thoughts of products and companies honestly. This usually seems more credible to the reader than traditional marketing messages. From the company's point of view, intelligent use of the Internet requires and offers authentic dialog with the consumer – both individually and with the entire community (Bughin *et al.* 2007; Kreutzer & Merkle 2008b; Tapscott & Williams 2007). Applications such as www.mystarbucksidea.com or www.nikeid.com reduce the isolation between customers and cultivate groups of customers with a special interest focus. The collaborative feedback and suggestions from customers afterwards can then be incorporated into the regular

	Blogs & RSS feeds	File exchange & content sharing	Wikis	Podcasts	Mash-ups	Tagging	Social networking	Evaluation portals
Business model	• Systematization and compilation of online journals • Revenue from ad sales	• Archiving and systematization of user-generated content (e.g. videos, photos) • Revenue from banners and performance ads	• Gathering, systematization and further development of information • Revenue from donations	• Provision of audio and video content • Revenue from pay-per-use, subscriptions, and banner ads	• Aggregation and contextualiz-ation of Internet services • Revenue from placement fees and pay-for-performance ads	• Classification and systematization of Web sites • Revenue from sales of clickstreams for data mining purposes, etc.	• Compilation and provision of user-generated content on a single platform • Revenue from banner ads	• Aggregation and systematization of product and product-based information • Revenue from commission and banner ads
Services offered	• Provision of an authoring tool for writing blogs • Blog hosting • Blog categorization	• Provision of online memory space • Systematization of content, e.g. through categories and evaluations	• Tools for the user to create and edit content • Provision of a platform for finding and displaying information/ knowledge	• Topic-based audio and video content • Opportunity to subscribe	• Linking of basic data (usually maps) with additional information (addresses, images, events, etc.)	• Central archiving and ubiquitous availability of bookmarks • Bookmark indexing • Access to other users' collections of links	• User self-portrayal • Networking among users • Networking of users and content	• Aggregation of product information • User-generated product evaluations • Price comparison with links to online shops
Customer benefits	• Unfiltered and personal publication opportunities for all • Visual refinement of content	• Broadcasting for all • Provision of an audience	• Aggregation of topic-based information • Freedom in terms of content and authors • Users as collective editors	• Consumption of content independent of time and place • Automatic update	• Added value from linking relevant information • Value-added services for cross usage	• Individual editing of the Internet	• Provision of social contacts • Facilitation of social contacts through virtual interaction	• Independent product evaluations by users • Simplification and support in the decision-making and purchasing process

Figure 7.30 Examples of business models in Web 2.0 (Enderle & Wirtz 2008; reproduced by permission of *Absatzwirtschaft*).

and company official customer service Q&A area (Thomke & von Hippel 2002; Schoder *et al.* 2008).

An example of a successful corporate blog is provided by **Frosta** (www.blog-frosta.de). Employees from marketing, production, R&D, public relations, and even top-level management write a web diary. The goal of the blog is to report on Frosta openly, honestly, and first-hand – uncensored, freely and uncommentated – and to discuss current topics from the world of nutrition.

A striking example for the "get involved" Web 2.0 and the exclusion of traditional business models and sales channels is **Prosper**, a market-place for personal loans. All borrowing and lending is processed between private parties, guaranteeing better conditions as banks (www.prosper.com). One, still being regarded to be one of the most vibrant consumer communities has been formed around **Lego** products. In parallel, this example demonstrates how the boundaries between pro-ducers and consumers increasingly blur (Tapscot, Lowy, Ticoll *et al.* 2000). Lego established a model of true customer co-innovation for products and services. While Lego is certainly most famous for produc-ing little interlocking plastic bricks, the focus has been shifting over the years to high-tech toys. Using *Lego Mindstorms*, consumers can build real robots out of programmable bricks that can be turned into legged walking machines, for example. After being released, user groups sprung up and reprogrammed sensors, motors, and controller devices at the heart of *Mindstorms* robotic systems. Today – after some thinking about legal defense of intellectual property, Lego uses mindstorms. lego.com to encourage consumers tinkering with its software ("crowd-sourcing", Brabham 2007; Hempel 2006; Howe 2006). Programers find free downloadable software, software codes, programming instructions, and Lego parts that the devices require on the site.

In other cases, the collaborative features are combined with financial incentives. For example in the case of **Amazon Mechanical Turk** (www.mturk.com), a crowdsourcing platform, every task performed successfully by an individual participant is rewarded with a reward usually amounting between US $0.01 and US $10.00. Besides financial incentives, customers can also be motivated because they really like what they do ("intrinsic motivation"), and because they want to be recognized as experts or gain a certain status within a community ("social motivation"; Schoder *et al.* 2008).

Thereby, a consistent brand communication through all company areas is left exposed to a critical, public (direct) and open-form consumer opinion and has to prevail against it. What first started at Amazon with simple user content, such as book reviews, has become omniscient: users register at platforms and write their own text, evaluations, and comments. This turns brand management into a balancing act.

Frosta, for example, promotes customer dialog via a corporate web blog (www.frostablog.de/blog/). **DocMorris** founder Ralf Däninghaus runs a CEO blog with lively discussions (www.docmorris.de/blog/). Other forums with user-generated content include, for example, **Neckermann**'s model casting: women could place their photo and application online, and users were allowed to cast their ballots on the website of the mail order company (www.neckermann.de/casting; Schwarz 2007).

After the end of the new economy, a new hype has been born with **Web 2.0**: online communities are growing exponentially, surpassing coverage of established media with no end in sight. Consequently, online advertising is currently the fastest growing item in marketing budget planning. In most companies emphasis is placed on:

- *Usability:* Improving user navigation and content on the home page;
- *Search engine optimization:* Optimization of the web appearance in search engines with the objective of appearing higher up on search results lists (for example, at Google);
- E-mail marketing and efficient customer newsletters;
- *Web controlling:* Analysis of user clicks and activity on both the home page and in newsletters (Bughin *et al.* 2007).

Pelikan worked out an optimization approach after the relaunch of the *Pelikan-Hobbywelt* website (www.pelikan-hobbywelt.de) to attract even more potential customers. They used search engine optimization, keyword advertising, online PR, and their own web blog. The result: The number of visitors increased ten-fold after a short period of time. In this case, the starting point for the measures taken was search engine optimization. *Pelikan-Hobbywelt* was thereby placed higher up on the results list for the relevant search terms at Google and other providers. To reach a top position, search engines have to be able to "read" the relevant content of a website. The criteria used by search engines to make the assignment are complex and undergo constant changes. Continuous search engine optimization is therefore unavoidable. To accompany this step, Pelikan also placed (paid) advertisements for *Pelikan-Hobbywelt* in the search engines.

In the first month, the number of visitors to www.pelikan-hobbywelt.de had increased four-fold, and in the second month even ten-fold. Following this success for *Pelikan-Hobbywelt*, **Pelikan Hardcopy Deutschland GmbH** followed suit and commissioned continuous search engine optimization for their online shop. As an accompanying measure to search engine optimization, they also plan on starting AdWords campaigns with Google and specific online PR. In December 2006, a corporate blog was set up for Pelikan Hardcopy. In the Pelikan Hardcopy blog (blog.pelikan-hardcopy.de), employees report on news, products, or the company, and strive for a transparent dialog about the Pelikan brand with customers and interested parties. Because the configuration is optimized for search engines, the pages are effectively indexed. Due to the continuous blog entries, the subject relevance of the website is constantly on the rise. The generally high networking of web blogs with one another also increases link popularity, which is an additional important criterion for improving search engine ranking (Ihde 2007).

Comparatively, Web 2.0 activities are still not very widespread: only 40–50% of companies use it. However, there are substantial differences in levels of satisfaction, if the last analyses are to be believed. User-generated content is greatly preferred by both customers and companies (Bughin & Manyika 2007). In most recent times, the combination of user-generated content and other web applications has been furthered by *mash-ups*.

Mash-ups combine the content and functions of various websites to form a new type of site. The most famous mash-up is *Google Maps* (maps.google.com/maps). In spring 2005, when the search engine provider released its licensed satellite maps for use and manipulation via a user-friendly programming interface, it took only a few days for new websites to appear that exploited the supplied map material for new and unusual uses. *Housingmaps* (www.housingmaps.com), a combination of *Craigslist.org* real estate ads and city maps from *Google Maps*, is one of the earliest and most prominent examples. By using Google, real estate locations can be directly displayed online, together with additional information on the environment of each property. *Chicagocrime* does the same using the crime database of the Chicago Police Department: Immediate information on the crime rate is presented for specific city neighborhoods (www.chicagocrime.org/). Thanks to both *Google Maps* and *Google Earth*, geographic information has gained significance. From the start, the connection between an actual geographic location and its digitally geocoded image unleashed waves of enthusiasm and is now used in countless location-based mash-ups. Via *Plazes*, for example, we can track the current location of individual users or find out which persons from our own circle of acquaintances are currently nearby (plazes.com/). At *Qype*, the local search is coupled with a recommendation network to locate the best addresses and service providers for each city (www.qype.com/de). At *Flickr*, users can assign a shooting location to their photos, so that we can see precisely where each picture was taken (www.flickr.com/tour/; Figure 7.31, Westphal 2007; Tapscott & Williams 2007).

The appeal of these new platforms with user–generated content is most clearly reflected by the **YouTube** (www.youtube.com) video portal: almost 100,000 new videos are posted there each day. However, the consumer trend toward *consumer-*

Figure 7.31   Example of a mash-up with *Flickr* (Westphal 2007; reproduced by permission of Yahoo! Inc. 2008).

generated content and advertising also means that brands may be presented in a context that is not in line with the desired strategy and positioning (Schwarz 2007).

> The prototype for consumer-generated content was provided by **Mozilla**. The company behind the popular *Firefox* browser stayed true to its original open-source philosophy and advertised its first big TV campaign online – global and open to everyone to participate – to anyone who wanted to advertise. A "creative brief", which could have been sent as a job instruction to an expensive agency, was published on a separate home page. The task was to create a 30-second commercial. The core values of the brand were to be taken into account, and the focus was to be placed on the specific properties of the browser. In late 2006, four TV commercials were released in the USA with a quality that could compete with professionally produced films – not to mention the higher degree of credibility and efficiency (Karig 2007).

Companies must therefore decide: do they use and integrate customer comments profitably, or do they block expressed opinions to avoid damage to their image?

> **Time Warner** had done this already in the year 2000 and sued a number of enthusiastic *Harry Potter* fans for copyright infringement. The reason: They advertised *Harry Potter* on home-made, unauthorized websites (Karig 2007).

Taking legal steps is mostly counterproductive: this usually results in critical press coverage and calls for a boycott. Brand manufacturers, as they see themselves to be the "bringers of meaning to the lives of their customers", must allow users to grab the chance to experiment and play around with these very "meanings".

> **Apple** showed how this is done. In response to a private promotional film for the *iPod*, which caused a sensation in 2004/2005, Apple reacted perfectly. It did not react at all. In other words: why prosecute a 37-year-old teacher who is giving us free advertising for a product – even if he infringes copyrights in the process and the company achieves higher brand awareness values with *viral marketing*? (Karig 2007).

By contrast, some brand producers consider creative users to be less of an asset, and more of a threat to integrated marketing communication and brand management.

> For example, **Coca-Cola** reacted rather humorlessly to a video shot by two practical jokers. Their film showed the explosive effect of *Coke*

Light when mixed with *Mentos* and shot to the top of the *YouTube* charts, inspiring a whole host of imitators. Official statements referred only to the use of the *Coke* beverage. *Mentos*, on the other hand, was delighted about the free advertising (worth approximately USD 10 million) and followed the absurd series of tests that spread in epidemic proportions. As the reactions remained positive throughout, the company sponsored a sequel of the original version and distributed it on the Net (Karig 2007). **Dove** succeeded in reaching 4.4 million viewers on the web with its critical view of the beauty ideal of the western woman. Parody by imitators tended to increase the brand strength (Schelske 2007).

In his marketing blog, Cultureby.com (www.Cultureby.com), the anthropologist Grant McCracken writes about the learning process that a brand must undergo. He states that these kinds of open discourses are essential if a brand is to be kept vital and experienceable (Karig 2007). This inevitably leads to the democratization of brands: In Web 2.0, the Internet user is free to respond to the brand's message, with responses, which, in turn, may be so creative that the form alone carries the message. In this case, the communicative strength is based less on extensive media budgets and strategies, and much more on networks, multipliers, and communities.

Therefore, the striking difference between the more classic media/communications channels and Web 2.0 applications lies:

- in both the basic approach and usage mechanism, initiated by the company ("push") or by the user ("pull"); and
- in the question as to what extent the company's brand appearance can be followed in form and content.

In Web 2.0, the dialog partner is increasingly withdrawing from both the company-dominated communication channels ("push") and the content contained in the manufacturer's brand appearance (Figure 7.32). Users nowadays choose the most comfortable and credible communication channels and interaction points with a company or directly with a company's existing customers with greater autonomy. In other words: the focal point of communication and interaction in the illustration shifts from lower right to upper left. As a consequence, the sales approach also shifts from active "selling" by the manufacturing company to active "purchasing" by the consumer. The spectrum of rather anarchistic communication channels from brand management and communication strategy ranges from third-party blogs, search engine optimization, to so-called "RSS feeds".

RSS (Really Simple Syndication) is an electronic news format that allows the user to subscribe to a website's content, or parts of that content, as a RSS *feed* or to integrate the content in other websites. RSS is a service which, similar to a new sticker, usually only contains headings and a text teasers. It is only supposed to indicate that a change

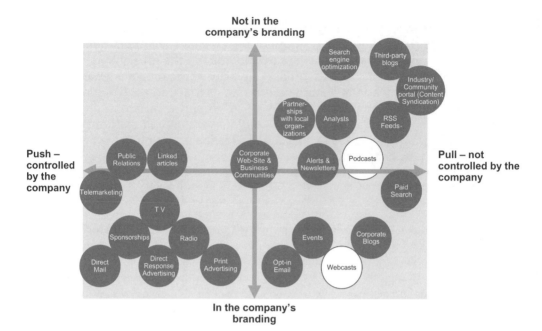

Figure 7.32   Push/pull media and integration in the company's brand management.

has been made with the intention that the recipient visits the relevant website to read the new content. The feed reader then automatically transfers newly published content in regular, user-defined intervals to the terminal devices (PCs, mobile phones, PDAs or mobile gaming platforms) of the subscribers, who thereby receive current information automatically. It is no longer necessary to visit the actual websites to check for changes. This has particularly simplified the process of keeping up to date with a large number of sources, such as blogs, in which changes are not made regularly, but users still want to know of any updates when they are made. The difference to notification by e-mail is that, with RSS, the recipient, who has subscribed to the feed, is the initiator. This means that the provider cannot select the readers but, in return, also does not have to bother with managing the reader pool (for example, with mailing list software). The reader does not have to disclose that he or she is watching the source and can subscribe to sources or cancel subscriptions much more easily by simply making the appropriate settings in his or her RSS aggregator (Wikipedia). This means that the control of the provider company over which content of the company website is reused, which context and layout is reused, and whether the brand values of the manufacturer's brand are maintained, is undermined to no small degree.

What is important here is that, with all of the media options to be used, brand owners alone are fundamentally responsible for brand management: this is the only way to ensure a consistent brand presence over time (Kreutzer & Merkle 2008b). Consequently, all current attempts to leave brand management in Web 2.0 in the hands of the user need to be rejected unambiguously. What still remains unclear, however, is which instruments can be used to influence brand management in Web 2.0 in the multilayered applications, which, by definition, cannot be controlled by the company.

Kimberly-Clark is the latest consumer company to reach out to Web 2.0 technology leaders to help to further its brand. The maker of *Kleenex* has been hooking up with **Meetup**, a company that facilitates in-person meetings of an online community of users with like interests (like parenting), in a sponsorship deal. **American Express** has a similar relationship with Meetup through its Open division, aimed at small business owners and entrepreneurs. For the deal, Kimberly-Clark is sponsoring some of Meetup's parenting groups, picking up the fees the members usually pay to Meetup. It's also sponsoring in other ways, like creating a widget that expectant mothers can use to count down to their due dates. The widget can be put on a *Facebook* or *MySpace* page or on a computer desktop (AMR Research 2008).

In this way, Web 2.0 technologies are not only used to expand brand awareness, but also cull customer feedback on consumer products. But unlike the impersonal nature of having a *Facebook* page or sponsoring online discussion forums, Meetup is fundamentally about people meeting in person, not virtually. And this is where Kimberly-Clark is hoping to find value. While physical meetings obviously don't have the reach of a purely virtual meeting, they may well prove to have a greater impact and thus greater brand value from an advertising or marketing perspective. Companies have to make a trade-off between reach and impact, and this lets them experiment with that impact even while trying to do it in a somewhat leveraged way. To effectively use social networking for marketing and sales purposes, companies and their networks have to deliver it in a way that adds value to the discussion (de Bonis *et al.* 2003; Blakely & Copeland 2007). In the case of Kimberly-Clark, the company is going to a community and starts asking for their specific requirements and the value Kimberly-Clark might add to that. The value for Kimberly-Clark is to capitalize on word of mouth; for example, if a mother at a Meetup event speaks highly of her experience with the *Huggies* sponsored events to other mothers, Kimberly-Clark's brand wins and it can build new loyal customers (de Bonis *et al.* 2003).

More recent studies show that the starting point for Web 2.0 projects in companies (similar to their subsequent use and content) is frequently not a part of formally initiated projects. Rather, smaller groups tend to launch informal pilot projects, which are only handed over to formal project organization later (Bughin & Manyika 2007).

Companies tend to stick to the claim that broad-based usage remains problematic, particularly on account of insufficient in-company knowledge and experience, and also with the lack of short-term measurability of potential success (Bughin *et al.* 2007).

The new online community, Capessa.com (www.capessa.com), where users talk about their personal experiences, such as the loss of a family member or other significant events in their life, would probably be lost in the jungle of Web 2.0 self-representations on the Internet, if it had not been created by **Procter & Gamble**. None other than the consumer goods giant commissioned the creation of this community, which targets women aged 25–49 in the "Health" area of the *Yahoo* portal. The creator, Procter & Gamble, does not even mention its brands on the site. The page was released for the US market shortly before Christmas 2006. Long gone are the days when thrilled housewives instructed viewers on the particular joys of a product.

At the same time, Procter also started a second site for a community in the USA: Pcavote.com gives the people the chance to voice their opinion on the "People's Choice Award" – an event that has been sponsored by Procter & Gamble for decades, where television stars are honored by the public. However, if you are looking for brands of the world's largest advertiser on the new pages, you're wasting your time. There is no *Pampers* blog, no *Ariel* FAQs, and no *Charmin* chat. Procter & Gamble participates in the discussions at *Capessa* only rarely, usually in the form of references to expert tips or newsletters, for example, on the subject of becoming a parent. The goal is to provide solutions for specific problems in life, without suggesting name-brand products as the solution directly, which might tend to put users off. This means that *Capessa* is not an advertising platform. Nor is it intended to replace or supplement the sophisticated Internet presence of *Pampers* and other Procter & Gamble products. The new Internet presence is rather one of the first results of the change in market research thinking by the consumer goods giant: Traditional consumer panels are supplemented by online communities, because consumers never say what they really think about products in a panel. The goal of P&G is to delve deep into the world of the female consumer. For the same reason, Procter & Gamble employees occasionally accompany perfectly normal women consumers in their everyday life, on shopping trips or cooking at home, for example. This constitutes the DILO ("Day in the Life Of") approach.

However, **Wal-Mart**, the largest retailer in the world, recently experienced first-hand that starting an online community need not necessarily be successful in an age when everyday people have so many choices for active involvement on the Internet. Last year Wal-Mart removed its community platform aimed at teenagers, *The Hub*, from the Net. Teenagers preferred to meet at other sites; traffic at *The Hub* was moderate at best (Weber 2007).

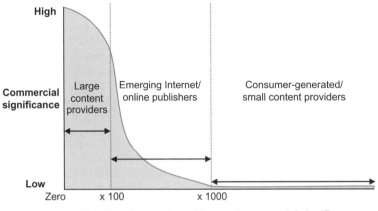

Figure 7.33   "Long tail" effect on the Internet (schematic, Anderson 2006a).

The variety and availability of products on the Internet, together with Web 2.0 functions, provides for the *long tail* effect:

> Whereas a normal, large bookseller has about 100,000 titles in stock, **Amazon.com**, as the online bookstore, earns approximately a quarter of its sales volume with books ranked far below the top 100,000 books (Ehrmann & Schmale 2008).

This phenomenon of aggregated large sales resulting from the sales of goods that are individually low in demand is called "long tail". This can be seen in a graph from the sales on the y axis and the items sold on the x axis. The curve levels out quickly, but appears to reach no end, as sales continue even in the most remote niches of a product range (Figure 7.33). A similar phenomenon appears for content offers on the Internet: whereas large content providers (e.g. media houses, publishers) used to dominate, small (private) content providers are more likely to be found in Web 2.0.

This stands opposite the *Pareto principle* – also known as the 80/20 rule – according to which 20% of products or services are responsible for 80% of sales. In practical implementation, the 80/20 rule means that companies primarily orient themselves according to "hits" and "superstars". This orientation gives way to attempts to place specific products (for example, films) with high production and advertising costs in such a way that sales and sales revenues are "hit-prone". In other words: "The winner takes it all" (Ehrmann & Schmale 2008). The core of the long-tail concept is the consideration that the long tail of the market – that is, that group of products that cannot be carried in stores because individual sales are too few – can make up a considerably greater share of the total sales volume of a company than what the Pareto principle would actually lead us to expect. As a result, a reorientation of the product range in terms of the offering would actually need to occur – away from "hits", toward the niche. Therefore, it could be lucrative for online markets to orient the product range toward less popular products intentionally. In contrast to retail stores, online markets offer almost unlimited shelf space, so that even products with low individual demand can be included in the product range. Small individual sales can only be cumulated to generate a profit with Internet sales (Ehrmann & Schmale 2008; Watts & Hasker 2006). This also has the quasi side effect of addressing customer groups that were previously small and geographically separated. Thereby, niche products can also meet a critical demand. The long-tail phenomenon is supported by a change in demand behavior: powerful search tools and recommendation systems, especially Web 2.0 applications (blogs, social networks, etc.), support this development and lower the search costs for consumers. This may make it more profitable for the customer not to buy the most well-known, popular products, but to carry out further and more detailed searches (Brynjolfsson *et al.* 2006). The emphasis is on finding a product that matches individual preferences more closely than the popular product that is principally in demand on the general market.

As the range of available movies, music, video, blogs and other media has exploded, the demand for personalized recommendations has also increased. Most media-centric e-commerce sites (like *Amazon.com*, *Netflix*, and *Rhapsody*) now offer recommendations based on users' prior behavior. The number of dedicated "discovery services" (like *Pandora, Last.fm, iLike, Flixster*, or *iRead*) has also expanded dramatically in recent years. Even while recommendation services have proven to be quite useful, users are required to provide detailed information about their preferences for each site and retailer – which can become quickly quite tedious. The user may quickly abandon the process altogether and leave the site after getting bored with filling in templates and giving away specific personal information to unknown Internet interaction partners. **Matchmine** solves this issue while neutralizing specific customer profiles. In principle, users become empowered to create an anonymous representation of their personal preferences, called a *MatchKey*, which is nothing other than a collection of numerical scores across different media types, including movies, music, blogs and video. Each colored zone on the *MatchKey* represents a media type, with crystals rising from that zone, each one representing an individual attribute score. Users create their *MatchKey* quickly and easily by rating genres in different media types and store their *MatchKey* online. Once created, a *MatchKey* evolves based on the preferences expressed – explicitly or implicitly – by its holder on any web site, widget or application in the MatchKey Partner Network. The scores in a *MatchKey* represent an abstraction of preferences derived from user actions over time, rather than scores for individual content items. Only partners retain individual item ratings from their sites (www.matchmine.com).

Important requirements for the successful use of the long-tail phenomenon in retail are, among others (Ehrmann & Schmale 2008; Anderson 2006a,b; Elberse & Oberholzer-Gee 2006):

- **Minimal storage costs:** An essential condition for exploiting long-tail opportunities is minimizing storage costs. This applies to both physical and digital products.
- **Minimal sales and marketing costs:** If individual marketing or sales efforts are necessary to generate demand for single articles, the chances of success drop considerably. An attempt to use long-tail opportunities will always imply a large number of products that do not sell at all. Success depends on how much it costs to manage these "shelf warmers".
- **Flexible sales:** The main advantage of physical dealers is that customers can satisfy their purchase needs immediately. The longer it takes for products ordered over the Internet to be delivered, the more the perceived advantage of a larger product selection fades. Furthermore, customers like to combine the advantages of online and offline channels (Ehrmann & Schmale 2008). They may choose the merchandise on the Internet, but they buy it offline in a store.
- **Virtually "unlimited" selection:** This no longer involves finding individual hits and getting consumers to buy them. Instead, a wide range of products must be made available and cost-effective tools and filters need to be installed to help consumers to find their personal favorites. These include adaptive recommendation systems, personalized home pages, user forums, and also customer reviews. However, it is crucial that maintenance overheads are kept to a minimum. Therefore, instruments that are automated or updated by the users themselves are highly recommended.

> A large part of **Amazon**'s product descriptions, search, and recommendation routines are generated automatically by analyzing the customer's behavior. Using the "wisdom of the crowd", the customers are thus guided along, starting with the "hits" and continuing along the "long tail", to find products that best meet their preferences and which they would most likely never find on their own (Ehrmann & Schmale 2008).

- **Minimal prices:** As prices drop, the willingness of customers to try out new products rises, and with that, their willingness to continue looking for specific products. In terms of the graph in Figure 7.34, this means that the customers continue to move increasingly further right. This especially holds true for entertainment products, as, in this case, it is only possible to evaluate products before purchase to a limited degree, so that there is often a high purchase risk. A penetration strategy with low prices for long-tail products can help (especially during the introductory phase of an offer like this) to reach the critical mass of customers that is required to be able to operate the indispensable collaborative filter and recommendation functions (see also Schoder 1995). On the other hand, price skimming with high prices can be successful when the quality of a product is already known and only a lack of availability has prevented higher sales numbers.

Since 2007, **Web 3.0** is a term used to describe the future of the World Wide Web. Following the introduction of the phrase Web 2.0 as a description of the recent evolution of the web, many technologists, journalists, and industry leaders have used the term "Web 3.0" to hypothesize about a future wave of Internet innovation. Views on the next evolution of the World Wide Web vary significantly. Some believe that emerging technologies such as the "Semantic Web" will transform the way the web is used, and lead to new possibilities in artificial intelligence (Copeland 2007). Other visionaries suggest that increases in Internet connection speeds, modular web applications, or advances in computer graphics will play the key role. Some predictions would be that Web 3.0 will ultimately be seen as applications that are pieced together – the transformation of the web from a network of separately siloed applications and content repositories to a more seamless and interoperable whole. Web 3.0 technologies, such as intelligent software that utilize semantic data, have been developed since the 1990s and have been implemented and used on a small scale by multiple companies for the purpose of more efficient data manipulation. In recent years – following the Internet bubble – however, there has been an increasing focus on bringing semantic web technologies to the general public. The term "Semantic Web" first gained prominence in 2001 (Berners-Lee *et al.* 2001). Here it was described as software agents roaming across the web, making travel arrangements and doctor's appointments and muting the stereo when the telephone rings. The semantic web in this vision acts more like a series of connected databases, where all information resides in a structured form. Within that structure is a layer of description that adds meaning that the computer can understand. Other definitions emphasize more on the emergence of a "Data Web" as structured data records are published to the web in reusable and remotely query-able formats, such as XML, RDF, ICDL and microformats. This is the first step on the path toward the full Semantic Web. In the Data Web phase, the focus is principally on making structured data available using RDF. The full Semantic Web stage will widen the scope of a Data Web such that both structured data and even what is traditionally thought of as unstructured or semi-structured content (such as web pages, documents, etc.) will be widely available in semantic formats.

> Large pharmaceutical companies like **Eli Lilly** have been experimenting with adding a semantic layer on top of their drug discovery databases to help scientists to discover connections between drug molecules and diseases (Farber & Dignan 2006). Similarly, **Amazon.com** is keen on using semantic technologies to help customers to search its databases. **Kodak** wants semantic tagging to help photographers to organize their snapshots online.

The shift to a semantic web is still in its very early days. In any case, the trend is clearly directed into a web that facilitates consumer interaction and collaboration in multiple communities and will further force marketing planning to systematically analyze and incorporate the "proactive, information-seeking customer" across all customer interactions and subsequent marketing planning phases (Spivack 2006).

7.4   SALES CHANNEL MANAGEMENT: DEFINING AND DESIGNING THE SALES CHANNEL

7.4.1   The sales channel: where is the added value?

Most manufacturers do not sell their goods directly to the end user. Instead, they use a variety of sales partners. With indirect sales, a distributor has different tasks (Tapscott 1995; Mougayar 1998):

- *Spatial transformation:* Making products available where they are in demand;
- *Temporal transformation:* Storing goods and ensuring a continual goods supply for physical sales, this means compensating for differences in time from manufacturing to product usage with storage;
- *Quantitative transformation:* Restructuring the diverse offers from all manufacturers into small, need-based lot sizes and goods assortments;
- *Qualitative transformation:* Combining the assortments of different manufacturers into one assortment;
- *Advertising function:* Informing potential customers of product features.

The advantages from the manufacturing point of view are a reduction of the financial resources necessary for selling the products. If a manufacturer wanted to sell products directly to the end user, the manufacturer would have to take on the sales functions listed above and, in addition, sell the products of other manufacturers (which may include competing products).

Volkswagen has several thousand dealers around the globe. Although these dealers are legally independent, they are contractually bound to the manufacturer's sales strategy. The manufacturer stipulates sales and service requirements in the contract, such as carrying only the manufacturer's brand or adopting sales measures including special sales promotion activities. **SAP** markets software business applications through several hundred partners. These "sales helpers" focus not only on distributing software licenses, but also on implementing the business applications for customers.

Other manufacturers (e.g. McDonald's) partially use their own sales channel.

McDonald's owns more than a quarter of its restaurants; the rest are involved in a franchise system.

The advantages of a company having its own – at least in part – sales channel from the manufacturer's point of view are as follows (Stern & El-Ansary 1992):

- Gaining experience in the management of all levels of a sales system;
- Better assessment of the performance of the other sales partners or franchisees involved;
- High flexibility in quickly and flexibly testing products and services;
- Establishing the manufacturer's own performance standards as the standards for all other distributors or franchisees.

Defining and designing a sales channel system should – according to the basic tasks of a sales partner – pursue at least five determining factors (Bucklin 1972):

- **Sales quantity:** While commercial recipients tend to purchase larger lot sizes, private consumers almost always purchase smaller quantities. The sales partner's ability to *adjust quantities* is more likely to increase with a decreasing issue quantity.
- **Wait time:** The wait time or delivery time is the amount of time the recipient has to wait for the delivery after placing an order. End customers prefer short delivery times, as they want to use the products immediately and future needs cannot be planned far in advance. The shorter the delivery time, the more the sales partner tends to be capable of adjusting to the respective time requirements.
- **Diversity of supply:** When the breadth and depth of a goods assortment made available to a recipient increase, the intermediary's *ability to adapt to the assortment* tends to increase.
- **Spatial presence:** This is largely determined by the number and geographic sales of potential reference points. A higher degree of decentralization means lower costs for the trip to the point of sale and the search for suitable products for the customer. Therefore, short travel times are a characteristic of an *increased ability to adapt to distance*.
- **Supporting services:** Services, such as giving credit, installation, and maintenance, broaden the services of the sales channel and sustainably strengthen customer relations.

Specificity and *complexity* of the product to be distributed are the key factors in the decision on choosing a particular distribution model. The specificity of a product is the necessary degree of adapting the product to meet specific customer needs. If a product is highly specific and complex, direct sales is often more cost-effective than sales through partners. In the same way, settling technical product specifications (in mechanical engineering, for example) would be more complicated by using intermediaries than by allowing direct interaction between manufacturer and end customer. For this reason, the industrial goods sector tends to use a direct sales approach. Even when goods are distributed through sales partners in this market segment, it usually occurs through preconfigured solutions that the sales partner can adjust to meet the needs of the customer (within certain functional limits). In this case, basic product specifications have already been predetermined directly between manufacturer and end customer. The *monetary value* of a product usually plays a decisive role in this case. If a product has a high monetary value, direct sales has relative advantages regarding transaction costs (including cost of settling product specifications, communication, and coordination with the customer as well as physical sales) when compared to product value. Conversely, products with a lower monetary value can be distributed by sales partners in a wide assortment at lower transaction costs.

Another factor in determining the sales channel is the number of customers or the number of potential customers that can be addressed. If there is a high *concentration of demand*, that is, a low number of customers, the direct sales approach has cost advantages. If there is a high number of (potential) customers, the indirect sales approach through partners usually has cost advantages. If most of the advantages of the indirect sales approach through intermediaries concern the transaction costs of the interaction between manufacturer and end customer, the direct sales approach not only offers better control of all sales activities but also has a decisive advantage for building customer relations and customer loyalty with the end customer. The closer proximity to the end customer not only allows the manufacturer to gain more accurate (unfiltered) information about "true" customer preferences, but also ensures that the provider can better influence the market presence, including established prices, other sales conditions, service conditions, or even the direct interaction with the customer, and the product's appearance on site (in terms of the brand). If goods are distributed indirectly, a substantial amount of customer information that the manufacturers receive is "pre-filtered" through the sales partner, which makes it considerably more difficult to gain customer-related information in this way than in direct sales. In the indirect sales model, the manufacturer may not even know the customer's identity.

The customer's preferences for the various components and services of a sales channel can differ greatly for various reasons. For instance, high-quality food can be bought in specialty stores, whereas the regular foods tend to be purchased in discount chain stores. The less importance a product purchase has and, therefore, the lower the (subjectively perceived) risk of a bad buy, the more this *hybrid consumer* is guided by his or her desire to save, both in selecting the product and sales channel (Schmitt 2005; Schmalen 2002; Merkle 2008). The most important maxim for shaping the sales channel system is to give the consumer the greatest possible leeway in choosing the best sales channel in his or her point of view and the channel that is best suited to his or her needs. Ultimately, it is the customer, and not the company, that determines which sales channel is used.

Decisions on sales channels significantly influence other marketing decisions. For example, decisions on the sales tasks and the advertising measures required depend on whether the selected channel approach is more of an indirect sales approach (to be supported by co-marketing measures) or whether the focus is on a direct channel. This is also a critical reason, not least because a decision in favor of a specific sales channel and the associated sales partners will entail and requires a more long-term relationship. It usually takes several years to establish an efficient (indirect) sales channel, which rules out frequent change. Ideally, the significance of an external sales channel should be set as equal to internal functions, such as human resources or production.

However, the selected sales channel is subject to limitations, on account of, for example, the product (perishable or non-standardized goods), the sales partner (such as the costs of a sales representative), competitors (existing, occupied sales channels), or a company's own characteristics (such as company size and targeted control over the sales channel). The decision on the number of partners at each sales level should take the following variations into account (Wirtz 2008):

- **Exclusive sales:** Each sales partner selected receives the exclusive right to distribute the manufacturer's products. In exchange, the manufacturer usually demands commercial exclusivity of the dealer for the manufacturer's products. Car dealerships (e.g. *VW dealer*) and luxury goods (e.g. *Boss shop*) provide good examples.
- **Selective sales:** This involves using several, albeit not all possible, sales partners to secure broad market coverage. The construction materials sector provides examples of many manufacturers who select and work with building materials traders under certain criteria.
- **Intensive sales:** Products should be readily available for the customer at all the points of sale visited. Particularly the pharmaceuticals business provides examples by using pharmacies: drugs and medication are always offered at all pharmacies at the same time.

Nike opted for selective sales with at least six different sales channels. Aside from specialized sporting goods stores (such as golf stores) that have their own shoe collections, items are also distributed through regular sporting goods stores and department stores carrying only the latest products. Reduced commodities are distributed through consumer markets and general stores. Nike stores and Niketowns, which were recently established in some major cities, offer the complete range of products and the latest trends. Finally, seconds and phase-out models are distributed through factory outlets. Conflicts constantly arise from cannibalization of the different sales channels, as is seen in the appeal made by some associations of sporting goods retailers and the European umbrella organization, **Feda**. These organizations have heavily criticized Nike's multiple channel strategy on several occasions because of the cannibalization of sales in sporting goods stores (vds 12/11/2006).

A new format has just been tested in China by Nike. Here they have launched big billboards which send out Bluetooth signals. If a customer passes by these billboards he receives the information that he has the chance to win a pair of "Zoom" sport shoes if he manages to run as fast as possible to the next Nike store. A virtual chronometer measures the the time and will – again via Bluetooth – be stopped within the store. Each day a pair of sport shoes is handed over to the fastest athlete (www.nikezoom.com.cn).

The online pharmacy, **DocMorris**, shows how a two-step sales process (wholesalers, pharmacies) can be reduced to a one-step process by using the Internet and relative cost advantages. With the exclusion of classic pharmacies (as an example of an intensive, two-level sales process), more than 100,000 customers currently receive pharmaceuticals from the Netherlands. What initially may appear to be complicated, is actually a rather straightforward procedure. The general practitioner writes a prescription for a patient and sends it by post to DocMorris. The medication is usually shipped within four to five days by courier service; DocMorris takes care of the bill directly with the health insurance company. By cutting out the middleman (pharmacies) as well as incurred prescription charges and through the relatively low cost of pharmaceuticals in the Netherlands, the price level is up to 10% lower overall than in regular pharmacies. The next step that we may expect to see as part of the present liberalization of the pharmaceutical market in other countries will provide further significant changes in both the market structure and sales channels. Furthermore, wholesalers will also establish new pharmacy chains in the future (Heiny 2007).

The advantages of an exclusive sales approach can be found in the preservation of a consistent market presence with a lower number of sales partners (often connected to the manufacturer). The intensive sales approach focuses more on broad market coverage, whereby the high number – and possibly very heterogeneous quality – of the sales partners makes it harder to control the market appearance and marketing of a company's own products. In the end, competition between sales partners can mean increased coordination and control expenditures for the manufacturer.

Besides determining the number of sales levels and the depth of the sales system, the manufacturer must also determine the breadth of the sales system to be used; concretely, the manufacturer must decide on the number of parallel sales channels to use (Wirtz 2008):

- A *single channel system* uses only one sales channel – for example, a consumer goods company that distributes its products solely through retail.
- A *multi-channel system* uses multiple sales channels simultaneously and in parallel for product sales. From the customer's point of view, this means that the customer can turn to more than one sales channel to obtain information, buy goods, and find service.

Lufthansa uses a classic multi-channel sales approach. In addition to its own sales offices in big cities, the airline also uses independent travel agencies, tour operators, online shops (www.lufthansa.com), and brokers.

Sophisticated customers with high purchasing power want a comprehensive range of products and services that they can access offline or online. Studies show that this customer layer (e.g. in retail banking) is considerably more profitable and generates two to four times the revenue than customers who rely on only one sales channel. The US retailer, **JC Penny**, was able to determine within its multi-channel activities that multi-channel customers generate a turnover of around four times as much when compared to single channel customers. Simultaneously, the multi-channel approach also serves to open new customer segments that could not be reached through previous channels. By establishing multi-channel sales, JC Penny increased the percentage of new customers by 26%. Similarly, in 2000, **Conrad Electronic** increased the number of its online customers in Germany to 900,000, which means a 60% share of new customers (Wirtz 2002).

When **Avon**, famous for that peculiar (personal) distribution channel with an extremely powerful sales force made up of half a million members, decided to start selling in small kiosks at American shopping malls, the results were amazing: 90% of the customers that purchased products in its new physical spaces had never bought Avon cosmetics on sale in their home (Gallo 2007).

The reasons that speak for setting up a multi-channel approach include broader market coverage and lower costs in reaching various types of customer segments exactly at the interaction point that each customer wants. Targeted offers can expand the individual customer portfolio of the products in demand and exploit cross-selling potentials within/between sales channels to increase the share of wallet. Simultaneously, cross-sales channel analysis of customer needs and combining the range of information and services provided based on the analysis allow multiple customer retention – i.e. customer retention that is based on a network of business relationships and interactions. More comprehensive customer support with a number of interaction points allows the customer to be connected to the company more systematically than ever before.

Multi-channel sales systems can lead to conflicts if different sales channels supply the same customer segments. A classic example of a sales channel conflict is the emergence and use of factory outlet stores as competitors to classic retail.

Hugo Boss has managed to continue significant expansion of its factory outlet in Metzingen, Germany, over the years – at the cost of critique from trade associations and specialized dealers. In the meantime, a large number of other factory outlet stores, aside from Boss, have taken root, such as **Escada** and **Cerruti**.

Major US retailers are reining in their store expansion plans in the face of a slowing economy, but one retail channel is far from short on capital fuel with upscale outlets that carry popular brands from *Gucci* to *Nike*. Among the 30 or so new shopping centers that have opened in the US in the past three years, almost one-third of them were outlet malls, the fastest-growing retail segment. Traditionally seen as a place to clear out-of-season merchandise, outlets have been transformed into a deliberate selling strategy in which companies try to design or buy in-season products specifically for that channel in hope of stoking the market. Brands from *Victoria's Secret* to designer labels like *Valentino* have also made forays into the outlet scene (Cheng 2008). These companies have put aside old fears about outlets diluting their brand image or stealing sales from regular stores. Many now believe they help companies to attract a new set of customers who don't buy at their regular-priced locations. Even as a slowing economy has helped to lure traffic to outlets, retailers say there's still little overlap between the two groups of shoppers. Rent at outlets is rated at being approximately 25% to 50% lower than that at regular stores. **Nike** reported recently that the outlets helped to widen its US unit's gross margin. In 2004, the No. 1 US luxury leather goods seller, **Coach Inc.**, installed a design team specifically to create products for the outlet channel. That outlet has helped Coach attract a different customer from its retail store shopper – a woman in her 30s without children at the regular store versus a woman in her 40s with two children and less discretionary income at the outlets (Cheng 2008).

The growing number of channels through which the customer can interact with the dealers – retail, online, call centers, kiosks, television, mobile shopping – result in an increase in consumer expectations and requirements. Customers want to be able to return or exchange an item to a store regardless of where they bought the item (online, in a store, or through a catalog). These multi-channel customers equally expect to be able to act freely within the buying process and to be able to change or cancel their order from anywhere, independent from how they initially made the order ("channel hopping"). Finally, they find it important to be able to complete an order regardless of where the order was originally started (Riedl 2007). The true challenge of a correct channel strategy is not simply saying, "the more sales channels the better", but rather orienting the right customer toward the right channel, adapting the sales resources to this strategy.

The Internet, mobile applications and other channels have paved the way for many companies to move to "multi-channelism" without meticulously planning how that change would affect their current channel structure, their sales force, the relationship between channels, as well as finally the impact on the customer. It is essential for every company to know their customer segments' composition before taking hasty action. A new channel does not necessarily constitute a threat, but it is an opportunity. The key is in the value proposal that the new channel offers the customer. If it is different, then several channels can coexist. If it is clearly superior, the challenge will be more complicated and lead to "multi-channelism".

The sector of airlines and tourism, for instance, has benefited strongly from the Internet boom, but not all companies have opted for this channel as their single option. All the studies prove that the leisure customer, primarily motivated by price and the search for bargains (even under severe restrictions on date and time for their travels), is much more prone to online purchase than the business customer. Therefore, it is only natural that "low cost" companies are focusing on the online channel, while the major airlines diversify and complement their channels, but they do not substitute them. **Ryanair** built its business model around that: a few years ago, 60% of their revenue came through travel agencies, which charged them 9% ticketing commissions. Also, managing reservations burdened them with 6% additional costs. So, 15% of the ticket price didn't belonging to Ryanair. Today, 96% of sales are through the Internet, with a cost of 1 cent per ticket. **British Airways**, like the majority of major airlines, focuses strongly on the Internet for the unquestionable advantages in terms of disintermediation, as well as cost savings and higher profits; but it doesn't play with just one card, and also utilizes other sales channels in parallel (Gallo 2007).

7.4.2   Managing the sales channel: recruiting, power, and changes

One of the first steps in deciding on a sales channel model is to recruit sales partners. Car manufacturers, for example, usually have little difficulty in finding dealers for their vehicles. The promise of exclusive or selective sales rights usually attracts many (potential) partners.

In other cases, as in the case of camera manufacturer, **Polaroid**, the search for sales partners proved to be very difficult. As sales through camera retail stores slowed, Polaroid was forced to win department stores as sales partners (Kotler & Bliemel 2001).

In most cases, a differentiated set of criteria should be established in the search for suitable sales partners. The requirement criteria for selecting a sales partner can include the installed customer base, know-how, sales strengths, financial situation and size of company, reputation or the existing assortment of the sales partner (Homburg *et al.* 2001).

Since customers view sales partners as a part of the company, it is recommended that they are trained thoroughly in the company's processes, values, and products.

Microsoft, for example, requires all retailers who sell Microsoft products or offer services for Microsoft products to attend one of their own training course series. Participants then take an examination, which, if passed, leads to the qualification of "Microsoft Certified Professional" (MCP), which in turn can be used for the retailer's own advertising purposes.

The areas of a collaboration between manufacturer and sales intermediary can exceed execution of pure sales activities to a variety of different task areas, including pursuing joint product development, offering financial solutions, carrying out sales logistics processes (such as just-in-time logistics), or conducting joint market research.

There are different types of mechanisms for structuring these relationships into legally independent sales partners and realizing interests. These can be in the form of using force, rewards, know-how, legitimation, or reputation (French & Raven 1959; Wirtz 2008).

- When *power is exercised through force*, the manufacturer, for example, threatens a sales partner to suspend delivery to the dealer in cases of non-cooperation on operational issues. Exercising power in this way is appropriate only in situations where the sales partner is highly dependent on the manufacturer. If power is exercised through force excessively, the sales channel usually responds with reactance, which is usually critical. As a consequence, several sales partners may join forces to form a community of interests.
- When *power is exercised through reward*, sales partners are offered rewards for certain services. This usually results in a situation where the partner strongly focuses their activities purely on obtaining the rewards offered.
- *Exercising power through legitimation* is based on agreements concluded between the partner and dealer to list a particular product or provide a particular service. This is the case in franchise agreements, for example.
- A situation where *power is exercised through reputation* occurs when the manufacturer has such a good reputation (brand strength) that sales partners are proud to have their name mentioned together with the manufacturer's. This situation occurs when high-quality brands (such as *Hugo Boss, Mercedes Benz,* or *McDonald's*) are involved.
- When *power is exercised through know-how*, the manufacturer's position (compared to the sales partner's) is based on specialized know-how that sales partners view as valuable. What is problematic here, is that systematic training of the sales channel and the associated transfer of the manufacturer's know-how gradually erode the manufacturer's power base, which consists of this very know-how.

Often in daily business practice, management of the sales channel is shaped by extremes. Following a search for partners in accordance with only very rudimentary partner criteria, large incentives, such as higher gross margins and market development funds, go hand-in-hand with negative sanctions and threat scenarios. Most of the time, need structures, such as the sales partner's strengths and weaknesses – unlike those of a customer – are not analyzed systematically in terms of a *channel relationship management* approach (Wirtz 2008). The subsequent, periodic assessment of the sales partner's performance is oriented toward target values, including sales quotas, the partner's customer service quality as determined by questionnaires, or training programs carried out for the partner's employees.

Experience has shown that it is rare for a specific sales channel to be ahead of the competition throughout the entire life cycle of a product and to be left as is. While buyers with a strong desire for innovation and willingness to make early product purchases are ready to pay for costly sales services (e.g. in the specialist retail sector), recipients in later phases of the product life cycle search for cheaper places to shop (e.g. department stores and special discounters).

> The product life cycle of a personal computer is a prototypical example. If a PC is distributed mainly through specialist retailers (e.g. authorized **IBM** dealers) in the introduction phase, it will move to large-volume sales channels, such as office supply stores and electronics stores during the growth phase. When growth slows down and the added value of the sales channel diminishes (due to decreasing demand for customer support and repairs), these products move increasingly to even cheaper sales channels, such as general goods stores. At the end of its life cycle, a product is distributed through the most cost-effective channels, such as mail order and specialist discounters (Kuss *et al.* 2007).
>
> Aside from the product life cycle, newly emerging sales channels also call for revision of the sales channel strategy: car manufacturers today, for example, who traditionally worked exclusively with authorized dealers, simply cannot afford to avoid activity on the Internet as well (Dirkes *et al.* 1999).

7.4.3   The sales channel: between cooperation, conflict, and competition

In practical application, a multi-channel sales system may often be preferable in order to address different target markets and customer segments. Accessing markets through as many sales channels as possible allows broader market coverage and optimal control of the sales channel costs according to customer segment and the respective customer preferences. If, for example, a classic direct channel approach is preferred for the major customer segment, a combination of sales channels with manufacturer-related telemanagement functions is required to address medium-sized businesses as well. Although there are advantages to additional sales channels, the disadvantage is that different sales channels and partners compete against one another, which can lead to conflicts and make it more difficult to control the sales channels. In practice, there will always be *sales channel conflicts* when two or more sales channels compete with one another for the same customer. In principle, there is a difference between *horizontal* and *vertical* channel conflicts (Bucklin *et al.* 1997; Wirtz 2008).

- *Horizontal channel conflicts:* There arise between sales partners at the same sales level. For example, franchisees compete with one another if they are in the same geographical areas because region or price agreements were not kept.
- *Vertical channel conflicts:* There arise between the manufacturer and its sales partners. Most conflicts arise in this case because (a) the roles and functions in the marketing and sales process were not clearly defined, (b) the manufacturer and

sales partners do not have compatible goals, (c) there are differences in how the previous and future business development is perceived, or (d) there are communication deficiencies between the sales partner and manufacturer (Bucklin *et al.* 1996). Empirical studies confirm that the three most common causes for conflict between the manufacturer and its sales partners are due to: the margin for the sales partners deemed to be insufficient; direct sales that excluded the sales partners; and the sales partner's pricing for the end customer (Homburg & Schneider 2000). Another frequent cause for channel conflicts is a lack of clarity in the assignment of customers. In most cases, customers cannot be assigned to a certain market segment or the related sales channel (direct sales vs. indirect sales) with absolute precision. Examples can be seen in the differentiation of customers between purely private customers and customers that use home offices for business purposes (small office/home office, SoHo), or in the differentiation between the mid-sized customer to be supported through partner sales and the major customer to be supported in direct sales (as with mid-sized subsidiaries of large enterprises).

Starbucks consciously takes horizontal channel conflicts into account. The Starbucks franchise system is set up to cover the largest possible geographic area. Ideally, every customer is to have a Starbucks location in their immediate environment. For this reason, Starbucks endorses the fact that new businesses are opened directly in the operating area of existing Starbucks shops, which effects cannibalization.

Vertical conflicts between manufacturer and sales partner can produce positive (functional) or negative (dysfunctional) effects. In the case of *functional* conflicts, the emerging conflict is seen as an opportunity to improve the business relationship systematically based on the emerging problems or to clear up emerging misunderstandings. In the case of a *dysfunctional* sales channel conflict, which is more likely to occur in practice, there is no cooperation in finding a solution, which consequently leads to a situation where either the desired sales targets are not met or the business relationship deteriorates systematically. Most of the time, both sides move into a classic stalemate situation, in which each side is dependent on the other, but, at the same time, hardly sees itself in a position to find a positive end to the conflict situation because each side is still focused on its own interests.

Solving the channel conflict with a simplified incentive mechanism by exercising power through rewards or force fails in most cases. Even though a business relationship conflict can be superficially solved by a power strategy (force), in reality, the conflict will continue to fester as a latent problem and to put further strain on the business relationship. More progressive sales channel management and the solution to existing channel conflicts aims at the long-term development of a trusting partnership (channel relationship management – Wirtz 2008; Kollmannsperger 2000). Clear and mutually agreed expectations – e.g. in relation to supporting sales activities, provision of market or customer information, or all other services and consulting activities – form the basis.

Acknowledging needs on both sides within the scope of a programmatic **co-marketing approach** includes joint planning of sales targets, necessary training measures, and joint specification of all advertising activities. This usually means a paradigm shift for the sales partner. Efforts should no longer be focused on gaining as many possible advantages with a manufacturer (such as in purchasing), but rather on systematically using the manufacturer for the mutual and cooperative planning and implementation of all marketing and sales activities. Organizationally, this type of cooperative marketing approach can be supported by:

- Mutual discussion groups between manufacturer and wholesalers (such as those that mostly exist in the pharmaceutical sector);
- A marketing advisory committee (such as the one SAP maintains for its mid-sized partners);
- Joint preparation of marketing plans;
- Temporary, mutual exchange of employees to work for a certain time in the role of the partner of manufacturer respectively.

Ideally, the architecture of the sales channel system is to be structured in such a way that different channels are responsible for different customer target groups. Classic direct sales is responsible for major customers, whereas telemarketing is aimed at mid-sized companies, and sales representatives serve smaller customer segments close to their respective geographic locations (Cespedes & Corey 1990).

7.4.4   Sales channel management on the internet: the end of the road for the trading partner?

Managing sales channels using modern IT and Internet-based applications is shaped by the elimination of the middleman as classic intermediaries (*disintermediation*). Faced with the possibilities of disintermediation, companies must take the necessary action to shape the actual use of different sales channels as part of sales channel integration efficiently. As a counter movement to disintermediation, new intermediaries can be created in this context through *reintermediation*.

Last year Americans spent 1.83 billion dollars on clothing, accessories, and footwear on the Internet, as opposed to the 1.72 billion dollars they invested in the purchase of hardware and software. This trend, according to most recent studies, seems unstoppable. For this year, spending on Internet clothing purchases is expected to increase to 2.21 billion dollars, which would represent 10% of the sectors' total revenue in the United States alone (Daemon Quest 2008).

Quite similarly, **Charles Schwab**, a pioneer in the use of the Internet as a successful transaction channel, has found its way to orient the right customer toward the right sales channel. The financial giant and "online broker" has learned to "educate" its customers so that they use the channels that are best suited to their interests and to those of the company – and this really binds the customer to the company. In their first contacts with the company, according to their profile, the customer is oriented by experts that guide them toward the products and services that best suit their needs, and toward the use of specific channels of contracting the company. This pattern repeats itself each time the customers financial profile changes; that is to say, according to their life cycle within the company. The focus on the customer that Charles Schwab has been utilizing for years has allowed the firm to offer service to over 7 million customers who invest in fixed and variable income, 1.1 million customers who invest in pension funds, and more than 150,000 who invest in checking accounts. In total, the company manages almost 1.5 billion dollars in assets. Charles Schwab did not begin as an exclusively online company, as it may be perceived today. The broker existed 20 years before the Internet boom. It simply knew how to take maximum advantage of a new channel's performance. It considered, as every channel strategy should, whether the new channel would replace the existing ones or simply be complementary to them, the impact that opting for it as a corporation would have, and the organizational changes that it would cause (Gallo 2007).

7.4.4.1 *Cutting out the middleman (disintermediation)*

In traditional retail structures, contact between the manufacturer and end customer only takes place over several different trading levels. The use of modern IT and the Internet in e-business allows the manufacturer to interact directly with the end customer (*disintermediation*, Figure 7.34).

Spatial transformation is not required for all products, as products can be ordered regardless of the location of demand, without the need for running a physical store at that location. This affects non-perishable goods in particular (such as books or CDs) in e-business (Bliemel *et al.* 2000). Using modern supply chain management concepts and parcel services, it is at least partially possible to compensate for the missing *temporal transformation* of direct goods receipt, which arises on account of the time between purchasing and delivering a product (Strauss & Schoder 2001). The manufacturer or a third-party logistics partner can take care of distribution.

Quantitative transformation requires adjusting distribution and storage capacities to meet the requirements of direct sales. For the manufacturer, the costs of maintaining complex logistics services often overcompensate for the advantages brought about by internalizing the margin that would otherwise be absorbed by retail. Ultimately, Internet-based direct sales can fully adopt the *qualitative transformation* and assortment creation function, either by direct access to different providers or by combining different providers or product categories within an electronic shopping mall, for example (such as in the case of Amazon).

iTunes revolutionized the way music is sold. Since its launch in April 2003, the **Apple iTunes Store** now sells approximately 3 million songs

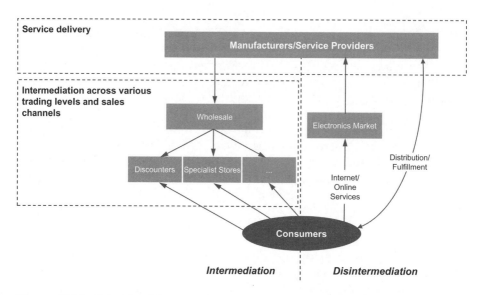

Figure 7.34 Principle of disintermediation (Kalakota & Whinston 1996; Sarkar *et al.* 1995; Schoder 2000).

a day world-wide, and the trend is rising. The iTunes Store sold its billionth song on February 24, 2006. As of April 2007, DRM-free music and videos can be purchased from Apple and EMI Music (without the restriction of the licensing model that files can be played on no more than computers at the same time) at increased bit rates of 256 kbps for DRM-free titles. The number of songs purchased exceeded the 3 million mark in July 2007, in addition to the approximately 50 million television episode and 1.3 million film purchases. Not only did *iTunes* reshape media usage and the type of media formats on the market, but its success is also a prime example of how the classic (stationary) middleman in music sales is being cut out.

The boom in trips purchased over the Internet is the clearest example of the "revolution" of a traditional channel. In the United States, approximately 300 travel agencies are closing each month, and the reservations and ticket sales per agency have been cut in half in only a few years (Gallo 2007).

From the manufacturer's point of view, the biggest incentive to eliminate traditional sales structures is usually informational in nature. As most customer information is created and stored decentrally at the retail stores in classic retail structures (such as in car sales), the manufacturer usually does not have access to a large part of this information. Decentralized retail and support structures offer better flexibility and scope for addressing, as well as advantages brought about by knowledge of local customers and markets. Possessing comprehensive qualified customer data provides possibilities for significantly superior and individualized marketing, and for the direct involvement of the customer in product development. The bookseller's sector offers prominent examples for eliminating retail using web-based direct sales (Tapscott *et al.* 2000; Mougayar 1998).

> According to the German Association of Publishers and Booksellers, book sales in 2006 generated a turnover of EUR 9.3 billion, 1.1% more than in 2005. Of all the sales channels used, the Internet enjoyed the most growth, with a sales increase from 11% to EUR 703 million or 7.6% of total book sales (Börsenverein des Deutschen Buchhandels).

7.4.4.2 Options for sales channel integration

The range of alternatives for integrating sales channels into existing sales structures can be illustrated most clearly by sales channel integration in e-business. In this area, channel management ranges …

* from *direct sales*, by-passing established sales partners, …
* through the integration of existing sales channels (*channel integration*) … to
* providing support for existing sales structures within a *channel-centered strategy*.

However, demarcation between the different approaches is not always entirely distinct and may flow into one another (Mattes 1999; De Kare-Silver 1998; Amor 1999; Hurth 2001; Strauss & Schoder 2001).

With the advantages of **direct sales**, such as being able to address customers directly, keeping otherwise incidental sales commissions, and gaining customer datasets, comes the disadvantage that the effects on the existing retail structure are hardly foreseeable. Dealers often discontinue a manufacturer's products even before an additional, complementary electronic sales channel is introduced because they expect increased competitive pressure.

> As a result of its offer of tailor-made products online (mass customization), **Levi's Jeans** was discontinued from the product range of large distributors and department store chains in the USA, such as **Sears**. As a result, Levi's put a halt to its initial direct sales, and did not reintroduce it until much later after revising the offering. Similarly, the Dutch airline, **KLM**, was forced to stop the web-based direct sales of freight space to end customers after major customers, who are also sales partners (resellers) of freight space, switched to other airlines (Mattes 1999).

This situation can also have an adverse effect: in direct sales, the manufacturer now had to handle logistics processes, previously the responsibility of sales partners, as well as the necessary sales and after-sales support services.

Option	Information	Ordering	Transaction	Delivery	Service
1. Status quo	OEM site (some dealer sites)	Dealers	Dealers	Dealers	Dealers
2. Increased frequenting of dealer sites	OEM site - primary dealer sites	Dealers	Dealers	Dealers	Dealers
3. Hosting of dealer sites	OEM site (incl. dealers)	Dealers	Dealers	Dealers	Dealers
4. "OEM inter@ctive"	OEM site (incl. dealers)	OEM site	Dealers	Dealers	Dealers
5. OEM/dealers joint trading company	OEM site/ Joint site Dealer sites	Joint site	Joint site	Dealers	Dealers
6. Direct delivery from OEM via dealer	OEM site	OEM site	OEM site	Dealers	Dealers
7. Direct from OEM	OEM site	OEM site	OEM site	Direct	Direct from dealer/third party

OEM = Original Equipment Manufacturer

Figure 7.35 Example of different models of sales channel integration taken from the automotive industry (Strauss 1999).

With *channel integration*, customer contact is established directly (Figure 7.35). However, order processing, including the required commission processing, is carried out by the respective sales partner. The advantages of directly accessing customers and collecting information are countered by the disadvantages of lower achievement of efficiency potential due to insufficient market coverage and high distribution costs with each concluded contract.

In a *channel-centered strategy*, the existing sales model is only supported, but no structural or fundamental changes are made to it. The target group of sales channel management are the established sales partners, and not the end customers. Broker portals in the insurance industry provide a good example. Insurance agents use these portals to access all required and current information and price comparisons. However, concluding insurance policies and issuing commission are carried out in the traditional way. In this instance, the offer focuses on providing comprehensive information to the existing sales partners. High acceptance from the partners is counteracted by the absence of direct customer contact and the manufacturer utilizing the potentials of directly addressing customers and prospects only to a minimal degree.

Project examples of sales channel integration in the car trade illustrate the multi-layered range of alternative models, with fluid transitions between the individual forms (De Kare-Silver 1998; Strauss & Schoder 2001).

The automotive manufacturer **Ford** provides one example for such a flexible model. Ford cooperates with dealers in the *Ford Fleet Online* program (www.fleet.ford.com), which is designed to allow business customers to configure and order cars online. The price of the products is based on the prices that have been negotiated with the dealers. The Internet front end forwards electronic orders to Ford's order management and production planning system, allowing customers to place their order directly with the manufacturer. Dealers can store individual price lists in the system for their preferred customers.

In 2000, *Ford Canada BuyerConnection* (buyerconnectioncanada.ford.com) tested a special *e-price* for their consumers, which passed a share of the lower sales expenditures to their online customers in the form of cheaper prices.

Joint ventures between dealers and the manufacturer are other solution approaches. FordDirect.com (www90.forddirect.fordvehicles.com/) is 80% owned by the manufacturer; the other 20% of ownership is at the disposal of the dealership community. After customers configure and order products, local dealers provide delivery and customer service for all cases just as they have done in the past.

A similar channel integration compromise, such as **OEM Inter@ctive**, for solving sales channel conflicts was implemented by the book wholesaler **Libri** (www.libri.de). To avoid conflicts with existing sales channels, customer orders are directly forwarded to the bookstore geographically closest to the customer. The customer can decide whether the store should ship the order or hold it for pick up. In this case, as in many others, implementing direct shipping by second brands is a consideration.

Evaluating the attractiveness of different sales channels can be oriented, among others, on *channel preference*. This can be determined from the relationship between the response in the direct channel (e.g. to a website) and the entire response to all sales channels (e.g. based on online advertising). The relative importance of the website in comparison to other customer touch points, such as call centers and store visits, can be measured using this method (NetGenesis 2000). Channel preferences can be used similarly as part of the analysis of the target group matrix.

The final decision on the best-suited sales channel strategy is usually oriented toward the company's sales strategy, the negotiating power of the company *vis-à-vis* existing channel partners, the competencies that exist within the company, and the chronological horizon of implementation.

Gateway Computer (www.gateway.de) first pursued Internet sales, and later supplemented this offering with the necessary repairs and support services by gradually opening traditional stores.

The clothing manufacturer **Gap** (www.gap.com) allows its customers to search online for all items not sold in stores, either directly in the store or at home. The customer can return products that were purchased online to any Gap store.

As is shown in these examples, the search for a (new) optimum between single channel strategy, coexistence, and complete integration of sales channels is always key (*convolution:* Amor 1999; Strauss & Schoder 2001).

7.4.4.3 *Reintermediation and the emergence of new intermediaries*

Reintermediation generally describes the current development towards disintermediation and the resulting elimination of value-adding stages in sales. *Intermediation* is understood to mean the emergence of new providers who focus on the individual stages in the value chain and their transaction phases (Sarkar *et al.* 1995). The development of a few core competencies lies at the core: usually, only a strictly limited area of adding value to the product or distribution is handled by the company (Mougayar 1998). Other tasks and sections of the value chain are outsourced to a network of partner businesses to facilitate specialization and cost benefits. In such cases, *infomediaries* generally take over the coordination of information and transaction flows between the involved parties. In reality, the infomediary concept has not been implemented extensively, at least not in its originally propagated form. Relevant service providers, such as *FireFly* or *Yoolia* were bought out or had no commercial success. In industries with established traditional retail structures, such as the car or insurance sectors, infomediaries adopt this role on electronic markets as aggregators of diverse offerings, frequently with a strong online partner to back them up (Dirkes *et al.* 1999; Kalakota & Whinston 1996).

The auto retailing business is another interesting "single traditional intermediary" example, besides the insurance sector such as **Insurancecity** (www.insurancecity.de). Traditional car dealers have felt threatened by EC-only intermediaries such as **AutoByTel** (www.autobytel.com) and Microsoft's **CarPoint** (www.carpoint.msn.com). In the case of AutoByTel, dealers soon discovered, however, that they could reintermediate by using the same kind of partnership approach that AutoByTel was providing to them. Thus, many car dealers became Internet-enabled by becoming connected to the AutoByTel website, as being their infomediary toward the customer. This enabled AutoByTel to employ technology licensing and partnering for content (Chircu & Kauffman 1999). AutoByTel's licensing approach involved requiring dealers to pay fees for being listed on the website and receiving orders, as search engines do. In addition, AutoByTel maintains large databases of available cars for dealerships that they serve, permitting dealership sharing. This sort of "virtual" product variety increases clients' ability to sell cars. This partnering for content approach on the orther side enables AutoByTel to perform product aggregation, making its service offerings all the more attractive to its clients. Other infomediaries like **schober.com** or **Dun & Bradstreet** help companies to generate and aggregate customer information; **ebay.com** offers a market platform that functions as an auction; **Partsnet.com** offers services as an information broker for electronic components (Mougayar 1998).

Beyond these business models, content marketers as a special kind of infomediary, such as **Cocomore**, provide customers a content container in an order subscription (www.cocomore.de). Similar services are carried out by publishers, such as **Gruner & Jahr**, on the basis of core competencies in content management. Another prime example of a new intermediary is **Chemplorer** (www.cc-chemplorer.com). This company combines the catalogs of various product vendors in the chemicals sector and offers them on one platform.

Furthermore, intermediaries can provide services in fulfillment or delivery, such as through bank institutes for smooth realization of business transactions. From the company's perspective, the spectrum of alternative services provided by intermediaries stretches over all transaction phases – from supporting business acquisition to online contract negotiations to processing and settlement.

The increase of intermediaries is the result of two developments. Firstly, declining customer loyalty leads companies to more intensive concentration on existing, own core competencies and, subsequently, to outsourcing services that are not part of the core competencies. Secondly, new intermediaries promote a further decline in customer loyalty through supplementary value-added services on manufacturer-independent platforms (Strauss & Schoder 2001).

7.5 ONLINE MARKETING: ATTRACTIVE OFFERINGS AND PRICING WANTED

7.5.1 The development of a range of web products and value-added services

Project examples in retail and online banking show that the definition of user offers and value-added services can orient itself on the customer experience chain (Figure 7.36). From the customer's perspective, the range of online offerings and specific value-added services is to be defined in 10 different areas. Customer services that are to be developed along the value chain include necessary communication measures for the application of the offering on the market, the structure of access requirements, active brand management using web design, added value, and potential billing procedures (Siegel 1997). Different value-adding stages, which must be maintained by the company to meet customer requirements, can be defined on a second level based on the requirements of the customer. In turn, these stages must be further specified in various work levels by concrete applications, functionalities, and process requirements.

The procedure presented here, based on the value chain from the customer's point of view, can be used as a tool for systematically defining customer-oriented services and added value. This procedure should always be supplemented by other methods,

Customer	Awareness of technology & media	Access/ availability	Brand awareness	Availability of product & services	Usability	Expected added value	Usage quality (technical)	Simplicity and security of payment process	Quality of products and services	Ease of pull-out
Value creation	Promotion	Offer of media access	Branding & positioning	Product development and management	State-of-the-art media & content design	Provision of added value	System infrastructure & processes	Billing and dunning procedures	Delivery processes	Customer care
Applications	Communication of added value	Technical product development	Brand management	Channel strategy and management	Design	Market and customer segmentation	HW/SW systems/ network mgmt.	Security mechanisms	Delivery/ distribution	Customer retention
	Training	Media selection	Market & customer segmentation	Value-added products and services	Navigation/ search options	Personalization	Technical services/ customer service	Payment options/ processes	Customer/ user tracking	Termination of service
		Pricing of access	Development of offering	Competitive analysis/ benchmarking	System support	Value-added services	Design	Credit control/fraud		
			Promotion/ database marketing	System support				Billing processes		
				Customer care						

Figure 7.36　The development of user offerings within the 10–stage customer experience chain (Strauss & Schoder 2001).

such as benchmarking or brainstorming. Ideally, external service providers, such as web design agencies, provide the final definition of the offering, specific to the company and project before implementation is commissioned and executed. Project experience shows that the boundary between the marketing approach aimed at more traditional media and the approach based on online activities can be fluid along the customer experience chain.

The methods used by **Audi** to introduce the Q7 in Great Britain with complex mailings and virtual feedback channel is a prime example of how a product can be launched using a smooth combination of offline and online media. In 2006, Audi planned a new breed of cross-media campaign for promoting the launch of the long-awaited Q7. The agency was required to develop a cross-media mailing strategy, which was to be multi-personalized and individualized. The aim was to communicate emotions (films) and individuality (360-degree views), while providing a convenient online response channel. The campaign implemented a new technology, the **n-CD** (*network connected disc*). The CD contains multi-media elements and provides the interface to the online world. The offline component for the mailings comprised a postage-optimized DIN A5 postcard that contained an n-CD. The n-CD had a personalized disc label, which included the name of the recipient, and a personalized multi-media component. As soon as the recipient inserted the disc into the PC drive, a personalized flash interface addressing the recipient by name to announce that he or she had been selected to test drive the Q7 started automatically. The recipient could then choose to either explore the Q7 interactively or reserve the exclusive test drive directly (with just one click of the mouse). The recipient was not required to fill out tedious online forms to book a personal test drive, as the n-CD technology was developed to include not only the name of the recipient, but also the recipient's telephone number and address data in the online form. With one simple click, the disc booked the test drive at the local dealer via an online connection and the response data was saved in Audi's central CRM system (Dankl 2007).

Thanks mostly to the convenience offered to the customer of pre-personalized forms, as well the physical contact established with the prospect by direct mailing and the disc, which bridged offline and online media, Audi achieved double the response rate of standard mailings. Audi was also able to carry out detailed analyses of the usage pattern (Dankl 2007; reproduced by permission of Marketing-Boerse).

7.5.2   Price management: is the price becoming even more decisive?

In comparison to traditional markets, price management in e-business is subject to drastic changes. Customer segments or even single customers can be offered individual prices (*price customization*), which can also be changed easily over the course of time (*dynamic pricing* or *real-time-pricing*; Kannan & Kopalle 2001).

Price comparison services such as **Dealtime** (www.dealtime.com) or ShopBots such as **PricingCentral.com** (www.pricingcentral.com) enable consumers to find the alternative to a product that offers the greatest value for money at little cost and in the shortest possible time. *Intelligent agents* can be used for the information search (such as www.mysimon.com) or for selecting a product (such as filter and product agents, e.g. www.linxx.de – Bocionek 1995; Maes 1994; Skiera & Spann 2001; Eymann & Vollan 2001).

When sellers and buyers use different agents, the agents can submit different offers to one another over the course of time according to the respective negotiation functions that have been saved. Modern comparison agents support the choice of product, even for highly heterogeneous products, by supplementing price criteria with a variety of predefined quality criteria and weighting the price criteria (e.g. www.frictionless. com, which is now integrated into SAP SRM). According to estimates, from the company's point of view, information transparency in the Internet will give rise to the following situations (Strauss & Schoder 2001):

- Customers will increasingly use the relevant services to compare products purely based on price;
- Particularly physical products (including a small share of services) will be the object of Internet-based price comparisons: A diversity of services and a comparability

that can only be achieved with considerable effort and expenditure allow service providers greater scope for avoiding the growing pressure of price comparisons in e-business;

- Companies in e-business will be able to implement fewer price differentiation strategies between different customer segments, and on an international scale, between different countries.

The use of the Internet allows the price-building mechanisms that are already established in the offline world, such as quantity-related price differentiation or auctions, to be implemented for dynamic price setting with real-time pricing and for automatic transfers of set prices to systems for invoice creation. Products with the following qualities are particularly suitable for flexible pricing (Shapiro & Varian 1999; Skiera & Spann 2001):

- **High fixed cost share:** As more and more products and prices are becoming digitalized, high fixed costs are still incurred for the production of the prototype, whereas there are only comparably low (variable) costs for the production of additional samples, e.g. in software manufacturing.
- **High perishability:** Products must be consumed before a specified expiration date, such as transmission bandwidth, transport capacities in airplanes, or marketing of advertising space (such as with *AdScale.de* for real-time marketing of online advertising spaces)
- **Configurable characteristics:** Different willingness to pay among consumers can be exploited with different prices for combinations of various product attributes (quality and availability of the product, whether the product is up-to-date).

The (zero) price strategy of *follow the free* has established itself online for digital products that find a special way to meet these flexible pricing criteria (Fritz 2000). Delivering cost-free products has often proved to be logical in web-based retail for a number of reasons (Skiera 2000). Firstly, free products compensate for the time it takes for new users to be incorporated in the system (e.g. registration). Additionally, high costs for future changes to other providers are established as the costs for incorporating new users recur with every additional provider change, creating the *lock-in* phenomena (Schoder 1995). At the same time, the value of many products offered on the Internet depends on the number of other users. For example, the most important factor for determining the success of discussion forums, chat rooms, or blogs is a sufficient number of participants and the associated perception of differentiated content. Similarly, the value of the offering by virtual booksellers increases with the number of visitors to the websites who comment on and evaluate the books being offered. The value for all customers increases with the number of users, which is regarded as a *positive network effect*. Similar phenomena can now be seen in Web 2.0. The number of users needed for the success of the web offering can be termed the *critical mass*. The free delivery of products facilitates reaching the critical mass through positive network effects and brings about the creation of other market entry barriers for new providers.

A "follow the free" approach is always implemented in a two-step process. The first step is to establish a rapidly growing customer basis with a high customer retention rate with a free sale (e.g. of a software product such as the McAfee antivirus software) and the network effects of the free sale. The second step is to try to generate revenue from the installed customer base by selling complementary services and the latest product versions (Skiera & Spann 2001). This is a two-edged sword from a price management point of view: although the price-setting strategy was already successfully implemented for a company's own products, the disadvantage is that a basic mindset is anchored in the customer to reject offers that require payment (also known as the "free lunch mentality").

In the early stages of e-business, it was diversely assumed that increased price transparency would move toward a perfect market with identical prices for the same products (at marginal costs). However, its use in practice paints a very different picture. Studies prove that price differences of up to 30% can occur between different providers through the implementation of service-based price comparisons, even for simple, homogeneous online products requiring little explanation, such as CDs and books (Bliemel *et al.* 2000). Therefore, in spite of the diverse possibilities for product and price comparisons, e-business is still far from the model of a perfect market. Given this context, the task of company price management is to determine the optimum price according to the chosen strategy and to implement it on the market, taking into consideration the behavior of the competition. The price, therefore, steps in the marketing mix as an active differentiating factor next to other product characteristics, and allows switching barriers to be established through price reduction when the sales quantity increases. Companies are faced with the challenge of using an active price management strategy to position and accompany product categories that are particularly suited for flexible pricing.

The mobile phone market in Germany provides one of the best examples of active (offline) price management: The **E-Plus** brand *Simyo*, which initiated price cuts on the mobile phone market, is lowering its prices again after *Bild mobil* (Vodafone network) and *Fonic* (O_2) disrupted the price structure further. E-Plus had announced that it would make further cuts in the prices of its cheap brand, *Simyo*, if the competition manages to underbid them. O_2 was able to do so with its product, *Fonic*, and the German newspaper *Bildzeitung* used its brand, *Bild mobil*, to make prices even cheaper – not necessarily very much cheaper, but nevertheless, cheaper and in large quantities. *Simyo* is now reacting and setting new prices: calls to German landlines cost only EUR 0.099 per minute, and text messages are also offered at the same price (per transmission). This applies 24 hours a day. There are no basic fees or minimum purchase requirements. By using one-minute billing increments (e.g. charging the customer for a full minute, even if only a few seconds were used), E-Plus gets back its money when short phone calls are made. In the meantime, **Deutsche Telekom** has also declared its intention to offer a 10 cent rate in the *T-Mobile* network with the discount brand *Congstar*. For the first time, every cellular network in Germany now has a prepaid rate of one minute of talk time for 10 cents.

This allows customers to remain loyal to their network and save money by switching providers. *Congstar* was launched in July 2007, with a rate of 19 cents per minute and seeks to gain roughly 1 million customers by 2010 (www.portel.de).

Similar trends can be oberserved in other countries. In the US, **AT&T** and **Verizon** offer a fixed rate of 100 US-dollars for the US market for mobile calls into all networks. **Verizon Wireless** began offering unlimited since the beginning of 2008 with a calling price at $100 a month (Kharif 2008, www.americasnetwork.com). In February the price change by Verizon Wireless was swiftly matched by AT&T *Mobility* and *T-Mobile USA*. In all, 5% to 15% of the combined customer base of these three of the four largest US cell-phone service providers will probably save by converting to the all-you-can-talk calling plans.

7.6   DEVELOPING AND EVALUATING MARKETING STRATEGIES

7.6.1   Developing the marketing strategy using key questions ... which basic questions need to be discussed?

A market strategy can be formulated by building on the analysis of the initial strategic situation, basic (business) brand strategy, preliminary considerations for using online media, and options for implementing different sales channels. In a pragmatic approach, key questions can be used to discuss the most important focal points of the marketing strategy in the following areas:

- Marketing objectives and the target groups addressed;
- Customer value and competitive positioning;
- Customer relationship management;
- Competitive behavior to be adopted, falling between cooperation and co-opetition (including the respective choice of sales channels);
- Basic marketing mix along the customer typologies and target group matrix, the use of online media, or possibilities for using standardized campaign architectures.

7.6.2   Key questions about the marketing strategy

7.6.2.1   Marketing goals and target groups

In the discussion of the *marketing objectives* and the *target groups* addressed, it is essential to define which market segments should be developed and which strategic objectives should be reached for a certain market segment and target group within a certain time period. Accordingly, the first step is to answer the question of which market segments should be handled. The customer and market segmentation that was initially conducted delivers information for identifying the market segments and, in most cases, already provides the first conclusions on respective attractiveness. A comprehensive prioritization of different market segments based on their attractiveness (in terms of market potential or growth) or on the respective competitive intensity (as a result of the competitive analysis) within the marketing strategy allows:

- Strategic prioritization of all (scarce) resources used;
- The best possible linking of the market strategy to the overall corporate strategy and other company areas;
- Precise statements on the scope of and budget for addressing certain segments with certain product categories;
- Identification of KPIs and their relative weighting in terms of market cultivation (such as revenue share or the number of qualified leads).

Empirical examples show that presenting the information in four fields according to the Ansoff matrix proves to be valuable for discussing strategic prioritization (Figure 7.37). *Market attractiveness* is determined by factors such as market size, market growth, or the average revenue of each sales transaction. *Intensity of competition* results from, among other things, factors such as existing number of competitors with relevant offerings, relative customer satisfaction in comparison to competitors, the share of wallet as a relative market share, or the costs for each qualified lead (e.g. as cost per lead). Differentiated conclusions on the necessary use of resources, such as the marketing budget or employees, can be made from evaluating these two dimensions. The four emerging fields on customer, market, or product segments can be characterized as follows:

- Segments in which there is already a high market share and in which additional growth can be generated through a straightforward allocation of resources due to the high market attractiveness are termed *growth drivers*.
- In the area of *profit drivers*, market attractiveness and the intensity of competition are rather low. Consequently, the marketing effort and expenditures used for profit drivers should be reduced.
- The area of *strategic focus topics and segments* with a high market attractiveness is different in that these represent a strategic opportunity and require a disproportionately high involvement, which may mean accepting a high intensity of competition.
- Lastly, *difficult markets* are shaped by a high intensity of competition with only low market attractiveness. Accordingly, they should be served rather selectively and, if necessary, with the objective of implementing innovative business models, within the framework of partnerships, for example.

Even if the selected approach for prioritizing along the market attractiveness/intensity of competition matrix has numerous advantages (such as offering the possibility for structured and transparent strategy discourse or highlighting the importance of a balanced portfolio structure), there are also numerous disadvantages. Several criteria must be aggregated for both dimensions to a statistical value. The aggregation of

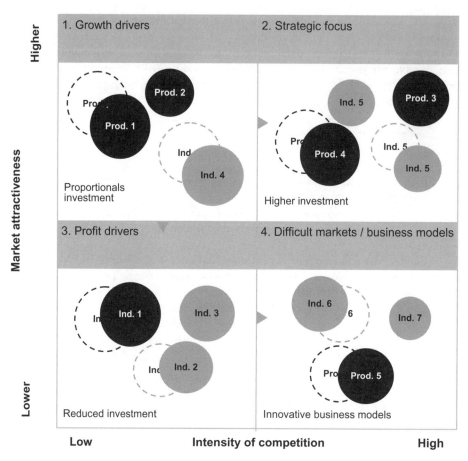

Figure 7.37 Prioritization matrix for market cultivation according to market scenarios for market segments and products (B2B example).

different data gives the user a considerable amount of leeway, which is ultimately the reason why this classification has a rather subjective nature.

Specific KPIs must be determined for each of the four fields in the next step in order to further operationalize the market cultivation strategy. The main focus here is usually on whether the available resources should be directed more toward developing the installed customer base or more toward acquiring new customers. Even though customer retention requires a significantly lower allocation of resources than gaining new customers, a certain portion of the resources should still be aimed at acquiring new customers. This type of commitment to acquiring new customers is mainly necessary in the early phases of the market/product life cycle. Similarly, it is more important to focus on acquiring new customers when it seems hardly likely that further revenue potentials can be realized in the installed customer base, due to a high share of wallet. In this case, the company can only tap new growth potential by acquiring new customers.

Marketing goals can be grouped according to each of their purposes and effects as to whether they are:

- *Informative:* For example, in the introduction phase of a new product, the goal would be to increase the awareness of the specific characteristics of the new product.
- *Perception change/attitude altering:* Fosters demand for a certain product. This may involve reducing preconceptions regarding a product or provider (lowering evaluation barriers) or directly generating qualified leads (engagement or conversion stage) along the brand funnel.
- *Retention:* Keeping a product and brand in the mind of the customer in the maturity phase of a product or customer relationship. *Confirmation advertising* produces a similar effect. This form of advertising is to counteract cognitive dissonance after the purchase (by congratulating the buyer for the product purchase, for example).

The marketing goals need to be further broken down to the level of campaigns and activities in further planning procedures (Paley 2000). For this, it is decisive to formulate KPIs from the multitude of possible KPIs that not only conform to the overall company strategy, but also support as best as possible a differentiated market address in compliance with the prioritization matrix as part of the marketing strategy. For this, the following applies: The more differently should each of the variously prioritized segments be addressed, the more differently the respective goals should be structured or weighted. How the performance objectives are formulated should be subject to diverse requirements. These should be defined according to quantity and time in order to be subsequently measurable and controllable (Diller 1998). In the majority of cases, a target system comprises several targets, such as increasing revenue, the market share, and awareness.

In order for these types of performance objectives to be operable, they should be:

- *Hierarchically structured:* All company areas involved receive the same goal, which can be further operationalized according to area;
- *Quantitatively formulated:* All performance objectives should be quantifiable, e.g. "increase the number of generated leads by 12%". If quantitative information about the KPIs within the existing processes and analyses is not available directly, it should at least be collected with sporadic analyses and market studies (on brand awareness, for example);
- *Realistic:* The requirements should be based on the opportunities analysis, within the scope of a SWOT analysis, for example, and on competitive strengths, rather than on little more than wishful thinking;
- *Balanced:* Target combinations should be weighed up against each other – this means that it is almost impossible to outline simultaneous maximization of sales and profit.

Different marketing strategies can be pursued depending on the customer or product segment. In the installed customer base market, a company is more likely to follow a customer retention strategy, whereas in the acquisition of new customers, the company would be more likely to focus on changing the brand funnel, i.e. changing perception, and gaining qualified leads, i.e. lead generation (Figure 7.38; Kotler & Bliemel 2001).

> The "men's cosmetics" market segment represents a strategic focus for **NatureLabs**. The following are the main *instrumental goals* (Figure 7.39):
>
> - Creating awareness of the new brand *alpha* ("Awareness" and "Evaluation" level in the brand funnel);
> - Initiating sample purchases ("Engagement" and "Conversion" level);
> - Achieving high customer satisfaction and repurchasing rates ("Loyalty" level).

Marketing goals	Growth drivers		Strategic focus		Profit drivers		Difficult market	
	Inst.base	New	Inst.base	New	Inst.base	New	Inst.base	New
Change in perception	10%	10%	30%	40%	0%	10%	50%	50%
Lead generation	25%	35%	15%	30%	30%	30%	0%	0%
Retention	40%	25%	40%	10%	45%	40%	0%	0%
Sales support	25%	30%	15%	20%	25%	20%	50%	50%

Figure 7.38 Marketing KPIs according to market scenario (example).

Goal	Goal weighting	Time-frame	Key activities	KPIs
Create brand awareness ("Awareness")	50%	First 6 months after launch	• Pre-launch campaign (for sales channels) • Cross-channel launch campaign • Influencer campaign	• 20% supported brand awareness in target segments 1-3
Acquire prospects, stimulate trial purchases ("Conversion")	30%	First 6 months after launch	• Promotional campaign • Recommendation campaign	• Sales figures in the first three months (300,000 products sold in the first year) • (sales revenue: EUR 5 million)
Create customer satisfaction, stimulate repeat purchases ("Loyalty")	20%	Second 6 months after launch	• Dialog campaign • Loyalty campaign	• 50% satisfied customers • Repurchasing rate: 20% • Average spend per purchase: € 15 • 5 purchases annually

Figure 7.39 Target system for launching *alpha* from NatureLabs on the market (example).

Guiding questions on *marketing objectives* and *target group selection*:

- Which market segment should be focused on? Should the focus be more on commercial customers (e.g. on small and mid-sized businesses, certain industrial segments, or companies with certain characteristics) or more on private consumers (e.g. according to micro-geographic segmentation or lifestyle typologies)?
- Which factors influence market attractiveness and the intensity of competition?
- What degree of priority do different market segments have in the dimensions of market attractiveness and intensity of competition? Which strategies should be pursued in each of the different segments?
- Is the focus more on keeping existing customers (customer retention programs) or on winning new ones (acquisition strategy)?
- Which marketing goals should be reached as part of the marketing strategy? What should be focused on more? Potential-oriented KPIs (such as achieving a certain customer satisfaction level) or market success-oriented KPIs (such as winning a certain number of new customers or reaching a certain revenue size)?
- How are targets weighted in different market segments within the prioritization matrix?
- Can marketing targets be further differentiated according to different company areas (such as business units)?
- By which point in time should marketing goals be reached?
- What relationship do all marketing efforts have to the stated KPIs? How big should the scheduled return on marketing investment foreseeably be?

7.6.2.2   Customer value and competitive positioning

Another category of key questions on devising the market strategy arises from the discussion on customer value and positioning of the competition (McDonald 2005; Paley 2000; Homburg & Krohmer 2006; Hiebing & Cooper 2000). Customer value can differ greatly within different customer segments. Usually, various value categories and needs can be determined from customer typologization or a target group matrix approach (Dibb *et al.* 1996; Kroeber-Riel 1993b). These include the following:

- *Functional value:* Basic functions of a product, associated with immediate value (such as mobility from a car);
- *Economic value:* As a result of product properties (such as efficient gas mileage);
- *Process-related value:* Amenities in acquisition and usage processes (such as service with car repairs);

- *Emotional value:* As a result of positive emotions arising from owning a product (e.g. proud to own a car or conscience of being a leader in an industry for implementing just-in-time logistics);
- *Social value:* Positive emotions arising from interaction with, and the positive behavior of, others, such as receiving admiration for owning a luxury car.

A real *competitive advantage* is created only when performance is superior to that of the competition, and so customer needs are satisfied. This performance must pertain to a product feature that the customer perceives to be and values as important, and cannot be quickly imitated or rivaled by competitors. A performance feature can only be a competitive advantage if the appropriate customer value is generated. Conversely, performance features may be able to offer noteworthy customer value, without having an actual competitive advantage.

The question on the competitive strategy within the marketing strategy originates at the core of the general competitive strategy of the company or the respective company area, e.g. within the value dimensions according to Treacy & Wiersema. When market cultivation is based on a *strategy of cost leadership*, features such as a highly aggressive low-price policy, high degree of standardization of the offering, and emphasis of attractive prices in communication (operational excellence) can be found.

Saturn, an electronics retailer in Austria and Germany, used *"Geiz ist geil"*, an idiomatic phrase meaning something along the lines of *"Cheap is hot!"* as an advertising slogan. The slogan was introduced in 2003 in a long-running advertising campaign in print media, radio, and television. Even though consumers did not view the campaign in Germany as markedly original or funny, the slogan received much attention, especially as a result of the discourse in the media. In 2004, it became the subject of public discussion, as it was said to reflect a part of the "Zeitgeist" and the current development in market competition in Germany, in which the price of a product was the only relevant factor, while other factors, such as quality, functionality, operating costs, or retail service were not taken into consideration. Critics lamented that the mentality characterized by the slogan represented the excessive thriftiness of (private) consumers. They claimed that this would lead to intensified price competition between manufacturers and retailers, which would continue the spiral of aggressive market policies, dumping prices, and cut-throat competition. The two main arguments were: (1) the economy would suffer as a whole, and, in particular, the domestic economy, which was already suffering as a result of excessive parsimony would be weakened further. Simultaneously, (2) the slogan was said to encourage the growth of the "service desert", while small and mid-sized retailers and specialized workshops would suffer further. The "cheap is hot" mentality, however, was not restricted to the end customer sector. Even manufacturers and wholesalers often feel exposed to a cut-throat price competition and do not know how to respond other than to slash prices in an attempt to win and keep customers. This type of development was seen most of all in the automotive market with competition mainly based on price arguments. According to the critics, suppliers are still put under pressure to sink prices. A common view is that Saturn's slogan reflected an unhealthy "Zeitgeist" and was representative of a period of increased, economic, social, and private self-interest. The campaign ended in 2007 (*Horizont*).

However, if a strategy with a higher degree of differentiation is adopted, the focus in the case of *product differentiation* (product leadership) is more on features, such as a continually optimizing product performance capability and comprehensive innovation activities, a variety of services accompanying the product, or on intensive (product) brand maintenance.

One example of innovative differentiation on the basis of superior products and services accompanying products is provided by **Geek Squad** in the USA. Instead of conforming to the usual clichés of IT specialists, Geek Squad is a company that has succeeded in using wit and experiences to turn a rather indistinct service, for which there are numerous providers in any city, into a successful and unique service offering. As a B2B service provider, Geek Squad supports companies that have IT problems. Services include solutions for typical network problems, printers that do not print, or files that cannot be opened. In a humorous mixture of serious service, wit, and experience, Geek Squad declared itself a type of "specialist unit" that comes to the aid of customers when they are experiencing computer problems. Geek Squad gives their customers an experience while they deliver their services: their employees are dressed in black suits with white shirts and thin black ties, white socks, and drainpipe trousers that are at least 10 centimeters too short, and carry a "special agent" ID. If you were thinking of the legendary film figures Jake and Elwood Blues from the *Blues Brothers* movie, you thought right. This is a successful attempt to make an unglamorous business more exciting from the customer's perspective. The result is strong distinction from the competition, lots of mouth-to-mouth propaganda and free advertising, a certain cult factor, and good business success. Geek Squad is a clever example of how a B2B company successfully sets itself apart from its competition by adding experiential and fun element to a purely functional offering (Internet research).

Differentiation through better customer relationships places the establishment and maintenance of long-term customer relationships in the core of the competitive strategy (customer intimacy). The features of differentiation through better customer relationships are an intensive analysis of specific customer needs, high individualization of customer address, retention of personal contacts, loyalty programs, and diverse company-internal efforts to increase customer orientation.

Empirical analyses show that companies that want to operate successfully under the conditions of increased intensity of competition must concentrate on both the cost and differentiation position simultaneously. This is the opposite of the classic, generic competitive strategies according to Porter (1980) as a differentiation or cost leadership strategy that became and remains the procedural model for numerous organizations (Kotha 1995). In his concept, Porter follows the assumption that cost leadership and differentiation strategy cannot be combined. A company must clearly decide on one type of strategy, unless it wants to run the risk of being "stuck in the middle" (Porter 1980). However, empirical studies (Gaitanides & Westphal 1991; Miller & Dess 1993; Reitsperger *et al.* 1993; Schnaars 1998) and a detailed theoretic argumentation (Corsten 1998; Fleck 1995; Piller 1998; Proff & Proff 1997) show that the competitive strategy does not mean a choice between the two extremes, cost leadership *or* differentiation. According to the *simultaneity hypothesis* (Corsten & Will 1995), companies should rather seek to realize cost leadership and differentiation in a *hybrid competitive strategy* simultaneously (Porter 1999, 2001; Piller & Schoder 1999). One example of a hybrid strategy is the previously discussed implementation of one-to-one marketing and mass customization: products that are tailored to the individual needs of each customer should be made and sold at cost-efficient prices (Piller & Schoder 1999).

The search for possibilities for changing the traditional rules of the game beyond pure cost leadership and differentiation strategies leads to strategies that are either focused on innovation in a submarket or aimed toward changing the competition of the entire market. Changing the competition with new rules and creating new markets is termed the *new game strategy* or, more recently, the *blue ocean strategy* (Kim & Mauborgne 2005; Frank *et al.* 2004).

The three most poignant examples of a *new game* or *blue ocean* strategy are provided by the **Cirque du Soleil, Southwest Airlines,** and **IKEA.**

Probably Canada's most well-known cultural export, Cirque du Soleil, started in 1984 as a group of fire eaters in Quebec and has evolved to become a global entertainment machine with a revenue of USD 600 million, and that in an industry plagued by recession and universal complaints about decreasing demand and high price sensitivity on the part of the audience. Cirque du Soleil redefined the word "circus". A combination of dance, theater, and acrobatics gave life to an entirely new business model, which addressed an adult audience willing to spend money. While other competitors in the USA outdid one another with increasingly elaborate performances and renowned attractions (such as two arenas, VIP performances, etc.), Cirque du Soleil was reinventing the circus, bringing together theater and entertainment in the style of a Broadway show. With its new approach, Cirque du Soleil was able to captivate an audience that was running away from the antiquated circus business. The secret of their success: flooding the senses with perfection in a way that can easily compete with any Hollywood film.

Moreover, the real coup of the company lies in multiplication. Every show is rehearsed by several ensembles that then each take the show on tour. Twenty casting agents are constantly traveling the world to recruit new performers. The ensembles include Olympic gold medal winners, such as the archer from Azerbaijan from the "O" show, and also the snake charmer from the Indian street circus. The direct effect of the worldwide multiplication of shows: creating a new global market (in 22nd place according to *Interbrand* and even more famous than *Disney*) while decreasing costs. Still, imagination comes before profit: 70% of the income flows back into new projects. According to Cirque president Daniel Lamarre, the brand stands for creativity and permanent innovation. The audiences let themselves be enticed into an emotional fantasy world in circus tents and sold-out long-term runs in permanent venues at a price of up to EUR 150 in Las Vegas or Tokyo (www.foerster-kreuz.com – Kim & Mauborgne 2005).

Southwest Airlines offers a similar success story. While other airlines were busy outperforming each other with additional service components such as fancy lounges, seat selection, and meal choices, Southwest was reducing all unnecessary services. Southwest passengers are not served on-board meals, cannot make seating reservations, nor does the airline provide lounges. The focus is on low prices, friendly service in a customer-oriented culture, and frequent connections – however, outside big hub airports. In the end, the former start-up from 1967 has become one of the most permanently highly rated and profitable airline businesses (Kim & Mauborgne 2005). One of the positive and interesting side effects of not offering seat reservations is that passengers show up at the departure gate earlier than those traveling with other airlines as they are motivated to get a good seat.

IKEA drastically changed furniture retail using a similar new game strategy. Using a marketing mix that clearly stood out from the traditional market norm is at the center of IKEA's strategy. While delivery and assembly by furniture dealers – covering the whole price spectrum (cheap to luxury furniture), a high degree of promotional activity, and a high degree of individual customer advice – dominate the classic furniture retail market, IKEA's basic business principle declares just the opposite: self-pick-up and self-assembly of generally cheap furniture, limitation to image advertising, and reduction of all consulting activities and compensation with self-service, catalogs, and a general informational desk (Kuss *et al.* 2007).

These types of strategies are characterized by policies such as a high focus on competition and are geared toward shaping the competitive conditions in terms of the company's top strengths. This is associated with high revenue potential, but also high risk.

An overview of the key questions for **customer value and competitive positioning** is listed below (McDonald 2005; Hiebing & Cooper 2000):

- What value should the company offer its customers? How should the company go about systematically addressing customer needs?
- How should the company position itself along these customer needs among the competition? What should positioning look like in the model according to Treacy & Wiersema?
- What competitive advantages does the company hope to achieve? What competitive strategy do other providers place at the fore?

7.6.2.3 Between competition, cooperation, and strategic alliances

The behavior *vis-à-vis* other companies should be closely discussed alongside the question of the pursued competitive strategy – respectively, to determine which companies your company would like to collaborate with and in which form within the overall scope of market cultivation. The goals of cross-company cooperation range from:

- Joint construction of market entry barriers *vis-à-vis* competitors;
- Two-way access to know-how and other resources;
- A more simple access to the market and revenue synergies, such as through cross-selling to the other company's customers;
- Expanding the company's own service offering;
- Risk distribution;
- Tapping cost reduction potentials (Barney 2003; Lensker 2008).

The spectrum of alternative forms of cross-company cooperation ranges as a continuum from purely supplier relationships to participations and acquisitions (Figure 7.40; Dull *et al.* 1995).

Companies outsourcing some marketing functions in the area of execution – such as graphic services, copy production, and event management – to external agencies, as is common practice, is an example of a tactical agreement.

One example of *product-oriented cooperation* is the collaboration between the soccer team, **FC Bayern** and the **Hypo-Vereinsbank**: the FC Bayern *SparCard* savings card gives customers interest on credit, which is, among other things, dependent on the number of goals scored by FC Bayern. The rail company, **Deutsche Bahn**, and the grocery discounter, **Lidl**, are engaged in a more *price-oriented collaboration:* in a time-limited offer, rail tickets were offered at a flat-rate price of just EUR 49.90. Due to the resonance in the media, 500,000 tickets were sold within a very short time period. **BMW Mini** and **Beck's Bier** brewery

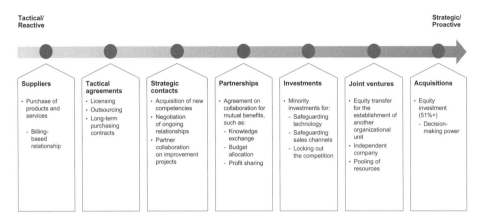

Tactical/ Reactive   Strategic/ Proactive

Suppliers	Tactical agreements	Strategic contacts	Partnerships	Investments	Joint ventures	Acquisitions
• Purchase of products and services - Billing-based relationship	• Licensing • Outsourcing • Long-term purchasing contracts	• Acquisition of new competencies • Negotiation of ongoing relationships • Partner collaboration on improvement projects	• Agreement on collaboration for mutual benefits, such as: - Knowledge exchange - Budget allocation - Profit sharing	• Minority investments for: - Safeguarding technology - Safeguarding sales channels - Locking out the competition	• Equity transfer for the establishment of another organizational unit • Independent company • Pooling of resources	• Equity investment (51%+) - Decision-making power

Figure 7.40   Continuum of possible forms of partnerships.

> formed a *communication-oriented alliance:* Beck's Bier was portrayed in a joint advertisement with BMW Mini as the only reason why Mini was not moving (Gutknecht 2008).

The term *strategic alliance* describes the voluntary, target-oriented cooperation between legally independent companies in different fields of activity, in which the affected companies at least partially limit their freedom of decision and can, if necessary, participate in the other company financially (Backhaus & Schneider 2007).

> It is, however, seldom that cross-selling effects are as close to one another as in the strategic co-marketing alliance between **Nike** and **Apple**, which started in the sales race with "hear how you run". Behind *Nike+* is software that connects the selected shoe model with the *iPod nano* to allow athletes to evaluate their performance data. To use this technology, the user needs a *Nike+* shoe that has an integrated compartment under the inner sole specially developed for the *Nike+ iPod* sensor. An *iPod nano* synchronizes the entire training data with **iTunes** and nikeplus.com. A "sport kit" facilitates communication between the *Nike+* shoe and the *iPod nano*. The sensor uses an accelerometer to measure the activity, and transfers this data wirelessly to the receiver on the customer's *iPod nano*. The sensor measures the running speed and other performance data. At the same time, the user's song selection is recorded, which in turn is made available to Apple and Nike for other analyses. This means that the songs that are heard at any time during a work-out can be determined, so that the fit and sporty Apple user can then be presented with an appropriate offering in the iTunes store (Willhardt 2007).

As regards mergers and acquisitions, it should be emphasized that they can lead to problems, especially from the marketing point of view. An acquisition may lead to the uncertainties among customers regarding the following:

* Performance and services to be expected in the future;
* Price level to be expected;
* Retention of established relationships that may be years' old with employees of the companies involved in the merger.

Actual examples show that at times of fusions and acquisitions, competitors often use aggressive and targeted methods to try to lure customers away from the merged company.

In Switzerland, the **Züricher Kantonalbank** successfully exploited the changes in the Swiss bank market a few years ago. After acquisition of the Volksbank by Credit Suisse and the merger of the Schweizer Bank-enverein (SBV) and the Bankgesellschaft (SBG) there was uncertainty in the market. While the newly merged banks announced their plans to concentrate more on profitability in the retail business and to clean up its installed customer base, staff reductions were announced and carried out at the two newly merged institutes with no small degree of public awareness and response. The Züricher Kantonalbank was able to win more than 80,000 new customers and significantly increase customer and employee satisfaction with its "welcome to the KKB" campaign in an extremely short period of time (Vogler & Lienhardt 1999; Kuss & Tomczak, Reinecke 2007).

The risk for merged companies is that too much focus on company-internal activities can lead to a significant reduction of all activities aimed at the external market (Viardot 2004).

The key questions in the area of **cooperation and strategic alliances** focus accordingly on the questions such as the following (McDonald 2005; Hiebing & Cooper 2000; Paley 2000):

* Which companies and objectives should the company select to cooperate with for market cultivation? Which criteria should be used for the discussion of joint market cultivation?
* How should the collaboration be structured? Which type of partnership should be pursued? Which complementary competencies should be brought together?

- At which company areas and market segments should the partnership be directed?
- How can the partnership be effectively implemented and then systematically and permanently accompanied?

The discussion of alternative business models and positioning options is usually associated with the decision of whether a *block strategy* (focused on actively establishing market entry barriers for competitors), a *run strategy* (focused on permanent innovation in the product environment, areas of services, and business model, e.g. Google's strategy), or a *team-up strategy* (oriented toward strategic alliances and joint ventures with competitors) should be pursued (as in the case for automotive manufacturers in Covisint; Afuah & Tucci 2000).

Covisint, as a trading platform in the automobile sector, represents the most well-known failure in the peak times of the New Economy. From 1999 onwards, Covisint haunted the business press, and a little business did actually take place on this B2B automotive platform. In 2004, the car manufacturers sold their subsidiary. The reason for its failure: the companies (Daimler Chrysler, Ford, General Motors) who wanted to do business with their suppliers and so achieve synergies of their purchasing volume, had different perspectives.

7.6.2.4 Structuring the marketing mix

Based on the prioritization of different market segments within the market attractiveness matrix and intensity of competition matrix, a company not only needs to define differentiated marketing goals, but also needs to further differentiate its market cultivation. Therefore, prioritizing different segments also entails shaping the individual components of the marketing mix into different quadrants in a differentiated way.

The key questions for the following structure of the **marketing mix** contain questions about the following (Paley 2000; Hiebing & Cooper 2000; McDonald 2005):

- To which extent should market cultivation between the individual customer segments and the segments in the quadrants of the market attractiveness matrix and intensity of competition matrix be differentiated?
- How should the company's product program be shaped with respect to the depth and breadth? What quality level should the products achieve?

- How should the company's brand(s) be structured and positioned?
- Which price positioning should the company set as a target in relation to the competition? To which extent and based on which criteria should discounts and rebates be awarded?
- Which instruments should be used as targets, particularly in communication (online, media, etc.)?
- How should the success of marketing communication be controlled in the various instruments?
- Should products be distributed directly or indirectly? How many sales channels should be used? Single or multi-channel?
- How should the different sales strategies be set apart from one another? Which criteria should be used to select the sales partner? Which sales channel conflicts are likely to arise? How can they be systematically limited?

7.6.2.5   Estimating the return-on-marketing

The company should not only formulate key questions on the marketing strategy, but it should also always write at least a rough business case. The business case should be less concerned with providing detailed analysis of all parameters, and more focused on providing a rough calculation as to what extent the initially set marketing budget is considered sufficient in terms of achieving the marketing goals, and what are the resulting implications as regards to overall profitability (Reinecke 2006). If a cooperation and acquisition strategy is also the result of the strategy planning process, the business case should be further developed to a comprehensive *business plan* including assessment procedures for potential acquisition targets. The informational value and validity of the business case, however, depends on the quality and details of the input values, e.g. business model, the definition and extent of the relevant market, the use of benchmarks, and estimation of realistic market shares (Figure 7.41). Project experience confirms that, within the development of the business case, even simple plausibility checks (e.g. as regards the average revenue/customer or the relative market share) are often not carried out. Similarly, different general conditions are often not taken into consideration in a *sensitivity analysis*, which it is highly recommended to carry out (Stevens *et al.* 2006).

For estimating the cost/benefit potential, different scenarios in terms of a *best case*, a *worst case*, and a *real case* (for the most likely event) can be evaluated, allowing the company to assess the economic risk. The business case should also re-evaluate the *price strategy*. Bearing in mind the marked low price orientation on many markets (such as automotive and electronics) and the new Internet-based business models (such as auctions), the primary question to be addressed here is: Which floor prices can/will be accepted?

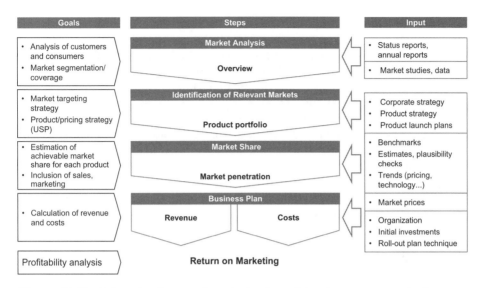

Figure 7.41 Influencing factors and results for determining the return on marketing.

The following considerations serve as some key questions for analyzing the **return on marketing** (Hiebing & Cooper 2000; Homburg & Krohmer 2006; McDonald 2005):

- To what extent are the initial marketing budgets sufficient for reaching the multifaceted objectives that are pursued with the marketing strategy?
- How can the instruments of the marketing mix or the marketing approach under discussion be evaluated in monetary terms?
- Which different KPIs (such as profitability) result when different marketing strategies are pursued?
- How valid and stable are the made assumptions in the development of the business case? Which best/real/worst case scenarios can be expected?

7.6.3   Selecting a marketing strategy

In a practical application, the analysis and subsequent discussion of strategy usually generate several alternative marketing strategies, which must then be further evaluated as a next step before a final strategy is selected. Along with the quantitative evaluation taking into account a rough business case, different aspects should be kept in mind for the qualitative evaluation of the different strategy approaches. It must first be checked whether the formulated marketing strategy coincides with the higher ranking company goals and the strategies of other business areas, such as sales without contradictions (*goal consistency*).

Additionally, it should also be checked whether the individual elements and specifications of the strategy are consistent with the results of the analysis phase, such as target group analysis, competitive positioning, and the structure of the marketing mix. In most cases, the biggest challenges lie in evaluating the content of the strategy against the background of the analyses performed, and of the key questions that emerged. Consequently, information from the strategic analysis is either weighted differently in the process of formulating the strategy, or neglected in the process of formulating the strategy and usurped by "gut-feeling" decisions. Checking and evaluating the qualitative informational basis and the *content* of the marketing strategy should be examined accordingly as to whether:

- Sufficient analyses (scope and quality) in relation to customers, the market, and competitors were made for developing the strategy. If the analysis procedure discussed above was pursued, there should be enough information available.
- The company or the company's activities have been realistically categorized and evaluated in these analyses.
- The conclusions of the marketing strategy are sufficiently precise in the context of the strategic analysis, and are structured according to the key questions appropriately for cultivating the market.

Finally, the marketing strategy is to be checked for *feasibility*. Resistance can result due to insufficient communication and management support *within* the company. Resistance can result *outside* the company from the sales partners, for example:

- Are there enough resources and competencies to implement the marketing strategy?
- Does the developed marketing strategy have enough acceptance *within* the company – among management and the affected employees?
- Does the developed marketing strategy have enough acceptance *outside* the company – among sales partners or strategic alliance partners, for example?

As target segments in the marketing strategy for **NatureLabs**, the three segments that have already been discussed ("trendsetters who like to experiment", "the undecided", and "the experienced mainstream") are the initial focus as potential customers. Simultaneously, women (as influencers) and purchasing managers (supermarkets, drug stores, cosmetics chain stores) are also a focus for sales interest. The value proposition is central to communication: The *alpha* cosmetics range offers highly effective beauty products based on natural active ingredients and modern science for an active sense of well-being (Figure 7.42). With this slogan, the product seeks a position on the existing market between luxury and consumer goods on the one hand, and between physical (image) and inner values on the other.

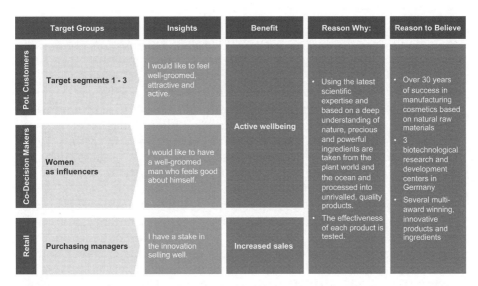

Figure 7.42 Value proposition for the *alpha* brand from NatureLabs.

More recently, the **Axe** advertisement ("The *Axe* effect") pursues a similar process and positioning. Males between the ages of 17 and 25 constitute the target group. Until now, the promise made by deodorants have tended to be more a functional promise, such as staving off sweat and odor, and giving the consumer a feeling of unbeatable confidence.

The Axe (international brand also *Lynx*) strategy is shaped to try to understand the consumer and acquire knowledge about the daily life of its target group. The focus is on knowing what moves consumers and on understanding their non-articulable desires, cares, and problems. Axe targets the consumer's "higher" goals in life. In theory, Axe promises to meet one of the most important needs of its consumers – success with the opposite sex. The message: Axe is sexy and it makes the user sexy too; men can rely on the Axe power of seduction. Implementation on the market faithfully follows the concept: with irresistible scents, and extraordinary and humorous advertising campaigns, Axe appeals to the taste of its target group time and time again, and enjoys a high level of awareness. Presented in the form of advertisements on TV and in movie theaters, the *"Bom Chicka Wah Wah"* campaign succeeded in verbalizing the Axe effect. In addition, the campaign was advertised in print, online, ambient, and mobile marketing.

A quite similar "Axe effect" took place with the international pendant of Axe within **Unilever**, with *Lynx* in Australia in 2006. While slinky imagery flogging *Lynx* deodorant on the outside of its planes has been banned in Australia, that hasn't stopped a provocative "fantasy airline" called "Lynx Jet" from triggering one of the biggest sales runs on the brand in the last 20 years. More than 1.7 million cans of *Lynx* deodorant have been purchased off supermarket shelves since the campaign started in late November in Australia and more than 500,000 people went to the "Lynx Jet" website to download a line-up of saucy TV commercials and to book tickets – while many still believe the airline is real. The public rush for "Lynx Jet" propaganda and products is due almost entirely to (testosterone-charged) adolescent males, at whom *Lynx* squarely aims its brand. To ensure the target group remains hooked, the imagery and advertising messages are laden with maidens kitted out in skimpy airline uniforms promising in-flight services unmatched by rivals. Unsurprisingly, the campaign is working. Public voting, for example, for the "flight attendant of the week" on the "Lynx Jet" website is approaching 130,000 for the leading candidate. Therefore, the campaign is working a charm with its audience and Unilever claims that most of the current "Lynx Jet" work is more efficient compared to what has been launched in the past for classical marketing campaigns. The latest "Lynx Jet" campaign has gained notoriety because the advertising was placed in mainstream media rather than niche titles. According to company figures, "Lynx Jet" has the highest sales of a limited-edition release, selling 151,000 cans in 12 weeks. *Lynx Anti-Hangover*, which was launched for three months in 2004, sold 125,000 cans. *Lynx Africa* is the biggest seller in the regular range. Overall the brand took a record 84.2 per cent of all sales in supermarkets for male deodorants in 2006 (*The Sydney Morning Herald*, February 9, 2006).

CHAPTER 8

PHASE 4: PROGRAM STRATEGY

8.1 DECISIONS ABOUT THE COMMUNICATION STRATEGY AND ADVERTISING MESSAGE

Empirical studies and interviews dealing with marketing planning show that during the definition of the marketing strategy, the focus is often placed on the product, price, and sales policy as instruments in the marketing mix, yet the formulation of a communication strategy and the associated advertising messages are neglected in comparison. The cause for this rather negligent treatment of the communication strategy includes the following reasons (see also Kotler 2005):

- Other functional areas, such as sales or manufacturing, are directly affected by the product, price, and sales policy in a similar way as marketing. In contrast, the communication strategy is primarily viewed as the domain of the marketing area or business communication (*other business areas are less directly affected*).
- In comparison, the other elements of the marketing mix are more *tangibly accessible* or require direct personal interaction (such as with the sales channel), so that they are more likely to be the subject of cross-unit discussions.
- For the same reason (better tangible accessibility), marketing communication is quickly reduced to the level of *agency presentations* with creative development suggestions, while the content details take a back seat by comparison.

For this reason, it is advisable to subsequently focus more strongly on the communication strategy and the development of advertising messages as part of marketing planning.

Project examples show that the procedure outlined here can be quickly and easily expanded to a *comprehensive marketing mix planning*. In this way, the considerations presented here regarding the communication strategy can be easily and methodically expanded to include the product concept (such as the product idea, product positioning or even assortment policy), product development, price mix (such as the price strategy, price positioning, or condition mix) or even the distribution mix (such as the channel mix or push/pull relation, Lüttgens 2000). For the launch of a new product, elements of the brand and assortment strategy or even product tests can be included in the planning procedure.

Compelling advertising messages in the communication strategy emphasize the key value of the advertised product without overloading the message with too much information or too many appeals, which would lessen the effect. According to Twedt (1969), advertising messages should be evaluated on the basis of how desirable, credible, and distinct they are from the view of the target group. Accordingly, advertising messages must:

- State something that is desirable or of interest to the target group;
- Distinguish themselves clearly or originally from the advertising messages of other products or brands in the target market segment;
- Be credible and the proposed claim must be provable.

Volkswagen offer examples of credible advertising messages. "VW. The car." The VW *Golf* gives its name to an entire generation, while the VW bus serves as the expression of an entire approach to life. In a similar way **Mercedes-Benz** is now focusing on the subject of sustainability, which the competition had adopted some time ago. And yet, Mercedes-Benz has managed to make an exciting campaign of it. This is made possible by various changes in style. For Mercedes, the color for the environment is suddenly no longer green, but blue, and the cars have no wheels. The color blue is a metaphor for clean air in a new Mercedes-Benz international advertising and brand communications campaign that focuses on sustainability. It is unusual how the campaign's focus moves toward the sky and away from the car. This gives the observer the impression that it is all about nature and not design, technology, and the joys of driving (w&v). With this, Mercedes-Benz not only clearly distinguishes itself from other suppliers, but also addresses the current debate regarding CO_2 emissions directly and in a surprising way (Figure 8.1). The sustainability campaign will then be extended in mid-2008 to include additional vehicles and developments related to Mercedes-Benz's activities, which are combined under the heading "TrueBlueSolutions".

Throughout the integrated marketing campaign, the message is simple also for the new *Jeep Liberty*. This is truly an authentic Jeep, from its classic seven-slot grille and the redesigned exterior, to its legendary off-road capability and new features designed to give owners

Figure 8.1 Communication in the CO_2 discourse at Mercedes–Benz (reproduced by permission of Mercedes–Benz).

that extra dose of fun that comes from wanting to bring more of the world into their driving experience. With off-road capability that is uniquely **Jeep** and new features, like the *Sky Slider*, which provides that open-air Jeep brand experience, the *Liberty* is said to give new meaning to "Have Fun Out There." The first spot to air, "On-Road, Off-Road," highlighted the improved on-road driving experience, while reinforcing the legendary off-road capability that can only be found in a Jeep. Online creative includes both an emotionally-driven interactive campaign and a rational product-based campaign. The emotional campaign is aligned with the "Pouring In" TV ad. It is set up to drive consumers to jeep.com/liberty/sessions where the wolf, the squirrel, and the bird each sing about their affinity for the unique features of the new *Jeep Liberty*.

The communicator must formulate and communicate product advantages, product claims, or even rationales so that the target audience is encouraged to give thought to the offering and be drawn into it further. Accordingly, it is necessary to posit a claim and also deliver a rationale which then underlines the claim for the design and content of advertising messages. For the development and weighting of communicative contents with the claim and rationale of the messages, the *value proposition*, which has been introduced above, can be applied as a central control element (Hühnerberg 1984).

As far as the formulation of the *value proposition* and the claim derived from it are concerned, "less is more". Not only is a good value proposition important, the message must also be clearly communicated to the customer. Instead of getting bogged down with many messages, the claim should concentrate on one or two fundamental points. Good marketing distinguishes itself by the consistent use of a poignant and understandable message over a longer period of time. Frequently changing advertising messages only come across as implausible, and do not stick with the buyer. **Tesco** has been using their message "Every little helps" unchanged for years, and has been able to set itself apart from the competition successfully. The impact of consistency is underestimated in many cases. In addition, it is not just restricted to the advertising message. Successful business like **Hennes & Mauritz** distinguish themselves in that their advertising promises what the store contains (Kliger & Südmeyer 2003). *Milka* ("The most delicate temptation since the invention of chocolate"), *Natreen* ("Smart self-indulgence"), *Nokia* ("Connecting People"), *SAP* ("The best-run businesses run SAP") *BMW* ("Sheer driving pleasure") and the business newspaper, *Handelsblatt* ("Substance matters").

The ultimate effect of an advertising message does not only depend on the content, but also its structure. The *design* of the advertising message can aim at either a more rational or emotional positioning with the recipient (Kroeber-Riel 1993a, b). The decision to achieve either a more rational or a more emotional address should be based on the results of the customer typology or target group matrix analysis. A more informative and rationale advertising message can be effective with target groups that are already highly involved with the product or in segments that have more "information seeker" qualities. By contrast, a more emotional message design may be appropriate in target markets in which the products are highly functionally and technically interchangeable. Studies show that even with capital goods that are technologically similar or for which a buying center is significant in defining the decision-to-buy processes in the B2B area, it is advisable to create experience profiles (Viardot 2004). Based on the value proposition, *style, word choice* (tone) and *formal elements* (such as colors, graphics, images) are to be developed for the design of the advertising message (Ogilvy & Raphaelson 1982; Hühnerberg 1984). All elements must fit together perfectly in order to convey a uniform image and an inherently consistent message.

The formulation of a specific value proposition for a certain target market can serve as the universal orientation and starting point of all communication. Based on this, a *communicative key concept* is represented in audio-visual form.

An example for a communicative key concept can be found in the **Nivea** campaign. The new key concept is based on "Beauty is ...". The key concept is broken down differently for products and media, such as in an advertisement for anti-aging care ("Beauty is knowledge"), hand care ("Beauty is a good feeling") or even an advertorial in a women's magazine ("Beauty is a moment in which we feel happiness").

A similar communicative key concept by **Dove** has been developed for *Pro-Age*, a multi-category line of products (face, body, hair care, deodorant), which is designed to expose what our anti-aging society has been hiding. *Pro-Age* celebrates women aged 50 and older by showing their honest, real beauty. This marks the first time a major consumer products brand has targeted a line across all categories of personal care to this demographic, which research quickly showed was a group of consumers that felt misunderstood. Much like the photographs in Dove's "Campaign for Real Beauty" initiative, this campaign features images of real women, literally uncovering all of their age spots, grey hair and curves, demonstrating that women are stunning – at any age. Promoting the philosophy that beauty has no age limit, the company developed a website that gained added strength from publicity direct mail, and television, radio and print ads drove visitors to the site. The campaign supports the Dove mission: to make more women feel beautiful every day by widening stereotypical views of beauty. Since launching, more than 4.5 million people have logged onto www.campaignforrealbeauty.com. Thousands have shared words of encouragement, learned about self-esteem tips and joined Dove in encouraging a wider definition of beauty (www.adverbox.com; www. brandpackaging.com; Figure 8.2).

This form has the advantage of taking the most important findings and conclusions from the (empirical) customer analyses that have been carried out and making them sustainably perceptible and understandable, even without previous strategic knowledge – not least in the briefing situation of agencies. The analyses that have been carried out (such as the target group study) and the value proposition allow communication guidelines to be derived for the use of language and images. The *communication architecture* lastly defines which message is to reach which dialog partner via which channel along the value proposition (Figure 8.3).

The closer one is to the consumer and partner of the communication dialog, the more important it is to follow value-oriented communication in the sense of the outlined value proposition. As a rule, the dialog partner should be placed in the center during discussion of the weighting of content and the design of the communication. When doing so, the following applies: The further along is the decision-to-buy process, the more concrete must be the provided communication. This can be broken down to the level of factual or objective communication. This type of staggered communication enables high market penetration with the relevant messages in all channels in each phase of the decision and with as little wastage due to stray advertising as possible. How strongly each element of the value proposition, each with which content and statement should be weighted in which channel, is derived from transferring the content and channel preferences for each dialog partner and decision phase (Figure 8.4):

Using a **content platform** (also called **editorial platform**), the contents that are to be communicated can be further differentiated by target group and communication channel (Figure 8.5).

Figure 8.2 Example of how a key concept is implemented from Dove. (Reproduced by permission of Unilever).

Synergies can be presented by networking channels and implementing the value proposition, such as for answering the questions:

- Where do different target groups expect the same message in the same communication channel?
- How strongly should the individual elements of the value proposition be weighted in relation to each other for each dialog partner and communication channel?

Similarly, **NatureLabs** can differentiate the messages for the *alpha* product launch and along the level of the brand funnel (Figure 8.6). The assortment at launch comprises 9 products (that are essential or have the highest growth rates on the target market): 1 shower gel, 1 shampoo, 1 deodorant, 4 skin care products, 2 after shave products. The packaging appears natural and scientific, in accordance with the positioning. Every product has a natural "magic ingredient", a clear statement of the effects (such as "Instantly more relaxed skin") and pinpoints a test result on an effectiveness barometer (such as "20% more ...").

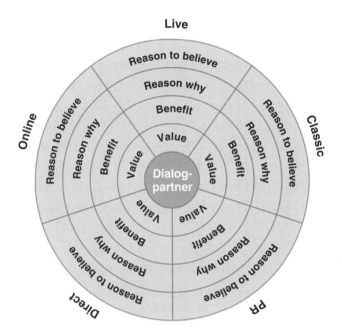

Figure 8.3 Communication architecture with the dialog partner in the center.

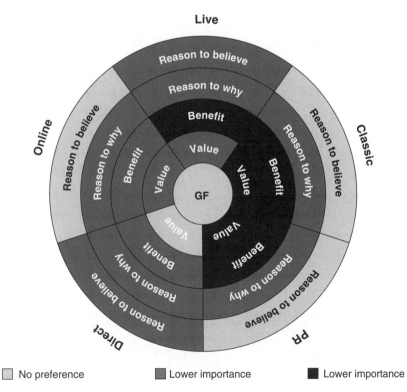

Figure 8.4 Channel preferences for each dialog partner using a managing director as an example (GF, B2B example).

	Classical advertising: print	PR	Online: Web site, campaign microsites	Live: exhibitions, roadshows, events	Direct: mailing, telephone, e-mail
Managing director	Message: "The company has market presence", "The company offers...". Effect: Sensitizes decision makers, emotional flanking throughout the decision-making process. Role-specific differentiation for different levels of the brand funnel. Summary: Permanent presence on this channel documents the necessary seriousness and manifests content.	Message: "The company has market presence", "The company offers...". Effect: Sensitizes decision makers, confirmation throughout the decision-making process. Summary: PR must support the messages of classical advertising to generate objective confirmation.	Up to now, online channel used only for superficial orientation and flanking of content for some roles.	Message: "The company focuses on the market and its needs (for example, exhibitions)", "The company has industry presence (industry exhibitions)". Effect: Evidence of being on equal terms, demonstration of tangibility. Summary: Live channel to influence the decision-making process. Live contacts as central element of future communication chains.	Message: "The company has individual and specific presence and invites dialog." Effect: Sensitization, support of willingness to enter into dialog, management of the decision-to-buy process. Channel for managing communication chains. Summary: The direct channel is the most important channel to actively shape the dialog during the decision-making process. Individual communication can be practiced only through these channels.
Further roles in the company		Message: "The company has a presence with user-friendly solutions." If appropriate, refer to channel partners and sales channels. Effect: Flanking of the messages in the classic channel, objective confirmation from user perspective. Recommended channel for phases 1 and 3. Summary: For this role too, PR must support the messages of classical advertising to provide objective confirmation of relevance.	Message: "The company has an online presence especially for the specific target group", "The company substantiates specific solutions using many testimonials," and so on. Effect: Imparts competence through additional support in answering specific questions. Summary: For some target groups, online is an important channel to gain more detailed information about content according to need.	Message: "The company focuses on the market and its needs" "The company demonstrates specific use cases." Effect: Evidence of competence, demonstration of tangibility. Recommended for some roles in the brand funnel. Summary: The live channel is the most important channel to influence the decision-making process significantly. Live contacts must be planned as a central element of future communication chains.	Message: "The company has individual and specific presence and invites dialog", "The company provides information at variable levels of detail, according to individual need." Effect: Sensitization, support of willingness to enter into dialog, management of the decision-making process. Channel for managing communication chains, in-depth support in establishing product competency. Summary: The direct channel is the most important channel to actively shape the dialog during the decision-making process. The direct channel is the most important channel to actively shape the dialog during the decision-making process. Gaining more information step-by-step and in a targeted way is only possible using this channel.

Figure 8.5 Content platform for differentiating content to be communicated by communication channel, using a B2B example.

	Classic advertising	PR	Online	Direct	POS
TG 1: Men	• Message: Discover a powerful, natural way to care for yourself – discover your nature. • Effect: Grabs attention and emotionalizes the new brand • Conclusion: An attention-grabbing campaign in this channel draws attention and creates interest.	• Message: Powerful skincare products for men's skin are created using new combinations of natural ingredients. • Effect: New knowledge gleaned from research affords proof of the company's expertise. • Conclusion: PR can provide objective information about innovative cosmetics and new ingredients.	• Message: Competition to be part of an expedition - "Discover ... - discover your nature". • Effect: Incentive to take part and discover new facets of his own personality. • Conclusion: Online advertising enables the involvement of target groups and the generation of addresses.	• Message: Competition to be part of an expedition. • Effect: Incentive to take part and discover new facets of his own personality. • Conclusion: Direct advertising enables dialog, the involvement of target groups and the generation of addresses.	• Message: Discover the new care products.
TG 2: Women			• Message: Test, competition, forum, blog: "How much grooming does a man need?" • Effect: Women concern themselves with the topic and indirectly create demand for more grooming. • Conclusion: Suggestions and findings from the target group of women as influencers.	• It is not planned to address this TG directly.	
ZG 3: Retail		• Message: A study of lifestyle trends relating to the topic of "Nature and man" • Effect: A large target group is interested in natural products. • Conclusion: Objective confirmation that sales are assured.		• Message: An invitation to become familiar with the innovative range • Effect: Incentive to take part and avail of new sales opportunities • Conclusion: Direct advertising enables dialog, the involvement of target groups and the generation of addresses.	• Effect: Stimulates a desire to try the product and triggers the initial purchase.

Figure 8.6 Content platform for differentiating the contents to be communicated by communication channel, using the *alpha* product launch from NatureLabs as an example.

8.2 THE ELEMENTS OF PROGRAM PLANNING

After the strategy for reaching the market objectives has been worked out, action programs (tactical aids for reaching the marketing objectives practically) must be developed. A *marketing program* defines the goals for a specific submarket and refines the marketing strategy and the content of communication. Each program represents a number of integrated marketing and sales activities under a single comprehensive, topic-specific, relevant concept (Nykiel 2003).

Programs operationalize which subtopics (such as individual products) are to have which focus in marketing activities within a certain customer segment or product line (Figure 8.7). If, for example, the marketing activities of a certain industry, such as wholesale, are the focus in the B2B area (the "Customer segment/target market" level), various topics (the "Topic" level) can be positioned, such as merchandise management or even human resources. In turn, one or more programs with different contents and objectives can be defined for the positioning of these topics ("Program" level).

Below programs, *marketing campaigns* specify the contact flow with the target customer segment that is required to reach the objectives of the higher-level program (Figure 8.8). A program can have one or more campaigns. While a program can comprise multiple objectives, campaigns should always focus on a single objective (such as generating leads).

Tactics ultimately describe communication measures to communicate with customers within a campaign or a campaign wave. A campaign can comprise one or more tactics (which may be connected with each other), such as holding an event, running print advertisements or even direct marketing mailings. In turn, these are connected to each other both in the definition of the content and the chronological order. At

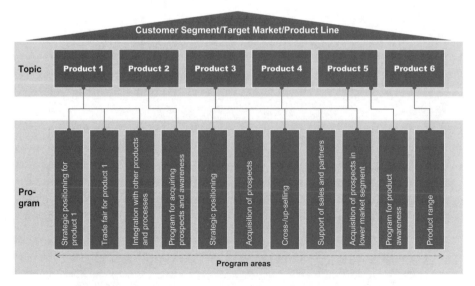

Figure 8.7 Schematic structure for categorizing programs.

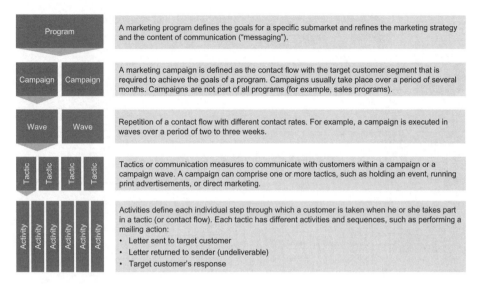

Figure 8.8 Differences between programs, campaigns, tactics and activities/measures as levels of marketing planning.

the lowest tactical level, *activities* or measures describe individual activities that are to be carried out, such as sending a letter or processing returns.

Project examples show that discussing marketing programs as part of marketing planning offers considerable advantages:

*   Clear connection as regards content between the business and marketing strategy that concerns target markets and content that is to be communicated and, subsequently, the stringent derivation of required tactical measures;
*   Avoidance of purely tactically motivated discussions about specific measures – such as the judgment of advertisements based on "gut feelings";
*   Precise agency briefings as regards content, with the consequence that the quality of the agency work increases considerably, multiple rebriefings can be avoided and cooperation in partnership with the agency is ensured.

In a first step, as part of the development of a marketing program, all information required for the target market must be summarized, such as the general market situation, the various market segments and target customers, or even the situation of the competition (Figure 8.9). In practice, it has been shown that this type of summarization is useful, as otherwise the available information and analyses are not used sufficiently in relation to the target group and the marketing activities that are to be set up, so that they are hardly considered in the discussion about the best possible marketing activities. In such a case, the information is available, but simply gathers dust in the filing cabinet of the respective planner in the form of emotive PowerPoint presentations.

It is always advisable to integrate the used *sales channels* into the description of the program level early on. The extent of inclusion in these planning levels can range

Effects on Marketing		
	Global/Regional	Country-Specific Information
Market Situation	• For example, status quo of company and products • ….	• … • …
Market Segments & Target Customers	• ….	
Market in Figures	• For example, market growth	• …
Competitors	• … • …	• …
Partners	• For example, sales partners • …	• … • …
Influencers	• Analysts • Press • Partners (multiplier effect)	• ….

Figure 8.9   Program overview (Part 1, Dibb *et al.* 1996; Hiebing & Cooper 2000).

from simple notes about the contents of the marketing programs *vis-à-vis* the phalanx of different sales partners to the direct inclusion of individual partners as part of co-marketing activities. If the sales channels and their inclusion in the marketing activities are not integrated into a program level early enough, there is a risk that they will not be considered as a significant part of marketing planning.

A conclusion about the type and meaning of the influencers (*influencer*) of the decision to buy for a certain product helps in the further design of the program. An influencer is to be understood very generally as an opinion leader who has better information about a subject area and imparts information relevant to the purchase during the purchasing process. Influencers could be tax advisers, associations, or even neutral product test information such as from Consumer Reports.

For the program design, it is crucial to know who the relevant influencers are in each case and whether they support the purchase of a certain product (*promoters*) or not (*opponents*; Witte 1976). In both cases, it must be decided how to integrate influencers into program planning as regards content or even whether additional specific influencer programs should be set up.

> Applied to the case example of **NatureLabs,** all information of the customer/market/competitive analysis can be summarized here as part of program planning (Figure 8.10).

To detail the program further, you must decide which marketing goals are to be weighted with which key activities for which sub-segments, based on the prioritization in the market attractiveness/intensity of the competition matrix (Figure 8.11). In some industry segments (such as the automotive industry), there are some unavoidable activities (such as participating in the International Motor Show in Frankfurt) that can

	Effects on Marketing
Market Situation	• NatureLabs AG's annual revenue is still only increasing by 0.5% each year. • To boost revenue, the company plans to enter the growing market segment for men's cosmetics.
Market Segments & Target Customers	• 45% of men who spend more than € 10 a month on grooming products are aged between 30 and 49. This target group equals a 37% share of the potential market (31 million). • Segment 1: Trendsetters who like to experiment: Low price elasticity, 3.46 million potential customers • Segment 2: The undecided: High price sensitivity, 3.92 million potential customers • Segment 3: The experienced mainstream: Medium price elasticity, 3.17 million potential customers
Market in Figures	• The market for men's cosmetics amounts to an annual volume of EUR 806 million. • Projected annual growth in this market is 19% up to 2008.
Competitors	• The groups experiencing the strongest growth are: L'Oréal (revenue growth of 8.9%), Procter & Gamble (not specified), Unilever (not specified), Wella (+11%), Beiersdorf (+7.2%), Henkel (+1.5%)
Partners	• Traditional sales partners: Grocery retailers, department stores, drugstore chains, perfume stores • Innovative sales partners: Internet, home improvement stores, service stations
Influencers	• Press • Wives and partners

Figure 8.10 Program overview of the *alpha* product launch from NatureLabs.

Marketing goals	Growth drivers		Strategic focus		Profit drivers		Difficult market	
	Inst.base	New	Inst.base	New	Inst.base	New	Inst.base	New
Change in perception	10%	10%	30%	40%	0%	10%	50%	50%
Lead generation	25%	35%	15%	30%	30%	30%	0%	0%
Retention	40%	25%	40%	10%	45%	40%	0%	0%
Sales support	25%	30%	15%	20%	25%	20%	50%	50%

Recommended goal allocation for marketing

Topic:	Product 1	Sub-Segment:	Private Consumption
Goal	Actual distribution	Key activities & programs in marketing	
Change perceptions	40%	Media campaign (print/TV) Address directly using sales dept. and partners	
Acquire prospects	10%	Acquisition program	
Retain customers	25%	Event for installed base Loyalty program	
Sales channel support	25%	Reference program	

Figure 8.11 Program overview (Part 2) with examples (Hiebing & Cooper 2000).

be approved and scheduled at program level before providing additional details for all activities.

Information from the following must be consolidated for the marketing and communication strategy for the target market (Figure 8.12):

• Target group analysis (such as typology or target group matrix);
• Value proposition for the most important communication contents for each target segment;
• Additionally refined KPIs from the discussion on strategic prioritization.

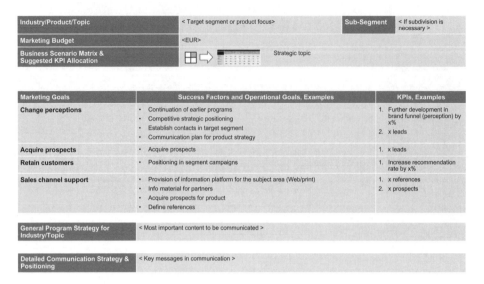

Industry/Product/Topic	< Target segment or product focus>		Sub-Segment	< If subdivision is necessary >
Marketing Budget	<EUR>			
Business Scenario Matrix & Suggested KPI Allocation		Strategic topic		

Marketing Goals	Success Factors and Operational Goals, Examples	KPIs, Examples
Change perceptions	• Continuation of earlier programs • Competitive strategic positioning • Establish contacts in target segment • Communication plan for product strategy	1. Further development in brand funnel (perception) by x% 2. x leads
Acquire prospects	• Acquire prospects	1. x leads
Retain customers	• Positioning in segment campaigns	1. Increase recommendation rate by x%
Sales channel support	• Provision of information platform for the subject area (Web/print) • Info material for partners • Acquire prospects for product • Define references	1. x references 2. x prospects

General Program Strategy for Industry/Topic	< Most important content to be communicated >

Detailed Communication Strategy & Positioning	< Key messages in communication >

Figure 8.12 General marketing and communication strategy for industry/product/topic (example, Dibb *et al.* 1996; Hiebing & Cooper 2000).

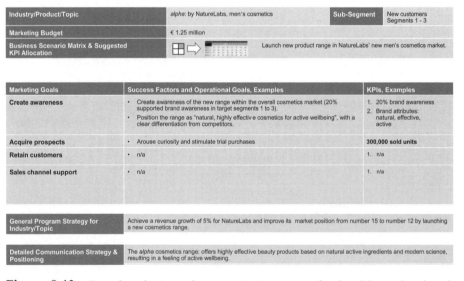

Industry/Product/Topic	*alpha*: by NatureLabs, men's cosmetics		Sub-Segment	New customers Segments 1 - 3
Marketing Budget	€ 1.25 million			
Business Scenario Matrix & Suggested KPI Allocation		Launch new product range in NatureLabs' new men's cosmetics market.		

Marketing Goals	Success Factors and Operational Goals, Examples	KPIs, Examples
Create awareness	• Create awareness of the new range within the overall cosmetics market (20% supported brand awareness in target segments 1 to 3). • Position the range as "natural, highly effective cosmetics for active wellbeing", with a clear differentiation from competitors.	1. 20% brand awareness 2. Brand attributes: natural, effective, active
Acquire prospects	• Arouse curiosity and stimulate trial purchases	300,000 sold units
Retain customers	• n/a	1. n/a
Sales channel support	• n/a	1. n/a

General Program Strategy for Industry/Topic	Achieve a revenue growth of 5% for NatureLabs and improve its market position from number 15 to number 12 by launching a new cosmetics range.

Detailed Communication Strategy & Positioning	The *alpha* cosmetics range: offers highly effective beauty products based on natural active ingredients and modern science, resulting in a feeling of active wellbeing.

Figure 8.13 General marketing and communication strategy for the *alpha* product launch from NatureLabs (example).

In the case example of **NatureLabs**, a goal of 300,000 sold products and an increase in awareness and associated attributes are central in the general marketing and communication strategy (Figure 8.13).

Lastly, it is advisable to further detail the information gained here with the company's product/service offering. Ideally, conclusions will be drawn here regarding the

Topic/Product	Program Topic, Example	Program Influence	Priority
< Sub-topic and product >	Strategic positioning	< Country or regional >	High
	Goals, example	KPIs, examples	
Program Goals & Detailed KPI Sets	• Increase willingness to buy in the brand funnel • In specific target group	• External perception (measurable using market studies) • x leads	
Budget	TBD		
Program Positioning & Key Messages	< Most important messages and precise messaging>		
Company's Product/Service Range	Additional services, supplementary products		
Offer	< Further differentiation possible according to country and sub-target segment>		
Target Group	< For example, in line with customer typology and target segments/role>		
Marketing Mix Strategy (based on proven methods)	For example, pricing policy, product features, communication measures (information platfrom: Web, event, media and so on)		
Agreed/Fixed Program Elements (such as contracts and events)	For example, product trade fairs, conferences		
Inclusion of Partners & Sales Channels	For example, sales partners		
Deliverables & Schedule	For example, concept for whole year (start on January 1)		

Figure 8.14 Program overview (example; Paley 2000; Hiebing & Cooper 2000).

Topic/Product	Program Topic, Example	Program Influence	Priority
alpha: by NatureLabs	Product launch campaign	Germany	High
Program Goals & Detailed KPI Sets	Goals	KPIs	
	• Create brand awareness • Acquire prospects • Stimulate trial purchases	• 20% supported brand awareness in target segments 1 - 3 • 300,000 sold units in the first year • Revenue of € 5 million	
Budget	€ 1.25 million		
Program Positioning & Key Messages	With the *alpha* skincare range, you experience natural, innovative and highly effective care for your skin. The products will transform your daily skincare routine into an active experience.		
Company's Product/Service Range	Free samples at POS and as tip-on advert (print)		
Offer	See above		
Target Group	**Men aged between 18 and 49** • **Segment 1: Trendsetters who like to experiment: Low price elasticity, 3.46 million potential customers** • **Segment 2: The undecided: High price sensitivity, 3.92 million potential customers** • **Segment 3: The experienced mainstream: Medium price elasticity, 3.17 million potential customers**		
Marketing Mix Strategy (based on proven methods)	Traditional (print), PR, direct mail, online, POS, free samples		
Agreed/Fixed Program Elements (such as contracts and events)	Cosmetics trade fairs: Cosmetica, Hanover (Jan.); Beauty World, Frankfurt (Jan.); Beauty International, Düsseldorf (March); Cosmetica, Wiesbaden (Sept.); Beauty Forum. Munich (Oct.)		
Inclusion of Partners & Sales Channels	Pre-launch event with trade partners		
Deliverables & Schedule	Start Jan. 2008		

Figure 8.15 Program overview for the *alpha* product launch (example).

time at which the first communication measures are expected to be carried out (first rough annual plan). If communication measures already exist (such as completed mailings or advertisements), they should also be included in the program overview (Figure 8.14; Nykiel 2003).

In most cases, it is advisable to perform an initial *program coordination* at this program level in order to:

- To check when which target groups are to be addressed with which contents, using an initial rough time plan, so that collisions in the address can be avoided early on;
- Determine which target markets and dialog partners are located in which status in the decision-to-buy process or along the brand funnel, and how the address of similar target groups can be optimally combined in the decision-to-buy process.

A *program book* can also be used for detailing the program strategy further (see Appendix, page 289; McDonald 2005). Ideally, it would also be a component of later agency briefings. The program book is used to detail the previously outlined program contents and acts as a sort of master document.

For the *alpha* product launch, some fixed program elements can already be settled, such as large cosmetic trade shows or even a necessary pre-launch event with the most important trading partners (Figure 8.15).

CHAPTER 9

PHASE 5: INTEGRATED MARKETING COMMUNICATION PLANNING (CAMPAIGN PLANNING)

9.1 FROM PROGRAMS TO CAMPAIGNS: FROM CONTENT TO IMPLEMENTATION

After program planning, the programs must be refined with concrete activities in the form of campaigns. A program, such as "Acquisition of new customers in wholesale", can have one or more campaigns with different goals, such as "Reduction of evaluation barriers in wholesale", with tactics such as advertising and direct marketing activities or even "Lead generation with reduced price offering" with mailings and an invitation to a trade show for further explanation of the offering. At this tactical level, the communication and sales promotion mix contains instruments such as:

- *Advertising:* All forms of non-personal presentation, such as advertisement placements, product packaging, brochures or the placement of emblems, symbols or logos;
- *Direct marketing instruments:* Mail, telephone (telemarketing), e-mail, online events and all other means of non-personal communication and contact;
- *Sales promotion:* Short-term incentives to purchase a product or service such as contests, discounts, financing offers, or trade-ins of used goods;
- *Personal sale:* Direct sales pitch with one or more potential buyers, such as in a sales presentation or at trade shows and events.

For the selection of the communication instrument, the effect on the recipient is influenced greatly by factors such as (Schmalen 1985; Fiske & Hartley 1980):

- The more pronounced the *uniqueness* of a communication source, the larger is the change triggered in, or effect on, the recipient.
- The communicative effect is largest when the conveyed message matches the existing opinions, beliefs, and views of the recipient (*positive confirmation*).

- The message can most effectively cause attitudes to change with topics that are not located in the **central value system** of the recipient, are not as familiar to the recipient, or are simply not as important to that person.
- The message is all the more effective when *expertise*, high status, objectivity, or even just popularity is attributed to the messenger or medium. This effect is increased when power emanates from the messenger and the recipient can identify with that person.
- The **social context** and other peer groups influence reception of a message and determine whether it is more likely to be accepted or rejected.

Accordingly, messages that come from a known and trusted messenger receive more attention and are more memorable (such as testimonial advertising). The credibility of the messenger depends greatly on the *expert competency* (such as with doctors or analysts), a *likable appearance* or even the *trustworthiness* as a measure of objectivity and integrity that is attributed to him or her. Friends and acquaintances are trusted more than strangers or sales people. Reference customers have a high degree of trust as they are already using the product and (evidently) still believe so strongly in the product and the benefits it brings that they are willing to act as reference customers for the advertising company (Helm 2000; Reingen & Kernan 1986; Misner & Davis 1998; Herriott 1992).

The current boom in *retro brands* has a strong foundation in the trustworthiness of, and experience with, old brands, such as *Agfa*, *Ahoj-Brause*, *Tri Top*, *Sinalco*, *Afri-Cola* or *Creme 21*. **Retro marketing** is "in" and many see it as a short-cut to establishing a strong brand quickly with less effort and resources. Retro marketing only makes sense when you are able to build up durable positioning – without fashion gimmicks. Ideal for this is an original position that you can revive credibly. **BMW** succeeded in doing just that with the *Mini*. This was the return of an original. Whether the *Agfa* brand can be revived is questionable. Who needs an old photo film brand in the age of digital photography? Awareness alone certainly does not justify the comeback of an old brand. Even **Kodak** has to be careful today that they do not fall by the wayside – as the majority of typewriter manufacturers have in the age of PCs. Right now, retro is "in", but everything that is "in" today will definitely be "out" tomorrow. **Jägermeister** is absolutely "in" right now for consumers in the German-speaking countries, especially among young people, thanks in part to mixed drinks such as the "Jägerbomb". But even in this case, there is considerable risk that precisely this "trendiness" will cause it to be absolutely *passé* again in a few years (Brandtner 2007).

A vivid example for the use of references to strengthen credibility can be found in Germany: the multiple award-winning advertising campaign of the **Frankfurter Allgemeine Zeitung**, which uses humorous testimonials from VIPs such as politicians and scientists for its adver-

Figure 9.1 VIP testimonial advertisement from *Frankfurter Allgemeine Zeitung* (example, reproduced by permission of *Frankfurter Allgemeine Zeitung*).

tisements: "FAZ. A clever head behind every one", using celebrities such as the German Federal Minister for Family Affairs Ursula van der Leyen (Figure 9.1). Similarly, insurance giant **Geico** is bringing back another iteration of its brand marketing: celebrity translators. The insurer announced at the end of 2007 that it will feature three new celebrities who will "translate" insurance stories from actual Geico customers. The campaign will star Grammy award-winning artist Peter Frampton, Michael Winslow, the famed "motor mouth" from the Police Academy movies, and rock star Little Richard. The campaign follows the same theme of previous efforts: real customers tell their story, and the celebrities translate that tale into something more "exciting" (www. brandweek.com).

When selecting communication paths, *personal communication*, such as in personal sales, takes on a special function, which allows for:

- *Personal interrelationships:* Direct and interactive relationship between people, where each person involved directly caters or adjusts to the desires and the behavior of the other;
- *Relationship building:* In addition to purely subject-based relationships, a personal relationship can be formed that has positive effects on customer loyalty;
- *Reaction obligation:* Perceived obligation on the side of both the buyer and seller to react to the communication and the offer of the dialog partner.

For this reason, *inter-personal communication* is of special importance if:

- The products are high priced and not often purchased, and the buyer has a high and very specific requirement for information beyond that provided in mass media. This is often the case with capital goods, for example;
- The product has a strong association with social status and peer pressure is very pronounced.

The advantages of *personal communication* can be used in marketing communication by using influential people (*testimonials*) in advertising. While in the B2B area the role of the pacesetter in the respective industry segment generally falls to *lighthouse companies* (such as Metro or Carrefour in the retail sector), in the B2C segment, you very often find *opinion leaders*. The use of and attention paid to opinion leaders arises from the insight that opinions are not influenced by mass media as instantly and as strongly as may have been originally intended. Opinion leaders belong to the core of the target group and their opinion is in demand in one or more product areas (Schmalen 1985). Behind this lies the understanding that consumers tend to interact with members of the same social stratum (in other words, people who are formally equals) and solicit their views in decision-to-buy processes (Moschis 1976). For marketing communication, you should question both at program and campaign level whether there are opinion leaders or "lighthouse companies" and how they could be integrated in the content and tactics of the communication in the best possible way.

To communicate with the communication and sales promotion instruments used consistently, cost-effectively and with the highest possible effect, they must be coordinated with others using the following:

- The **contents** to be communicated as a result of program planning: *Which contents are to be communicated with which goal?*
- The **preferences** of potential consumers regarding the communication channel: *Via which communication channel would the customer like to be addressed?*
- The (abstract) **advantages** of various communication channels for marketing communication: *Which communication channel is especially suited for the transport of which content?*
- All used **instruments** in the marketing max, for example: *Which product characteristics and price graduations are offered?*

The used communication and sales promotion instruments must also be translated into concrete campaigns and activities. As part of campaign planning, the previous *contents from program planning* and the analyses must be specified further at the level of campaigns and tactics (Figure 9.2). These may include:

- The target market;
- The contents and subjects to be positioned;
- The existing market scenario from the prioritization matrix;
- The address of existing vs. new customers;
- The KPIs desired in each case;
- The target group.

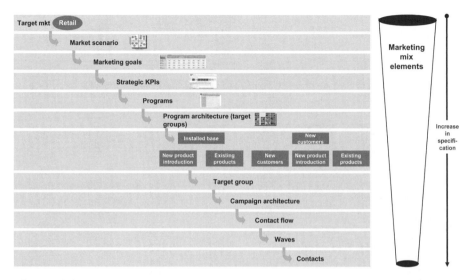

Figure 9.2   Summary overview of the structure and levels of marketing planning.

The summary in a campaign calendar is facilitated by the addition of campaign-specific information (*campaign planning*), such as the following:

- Marketing goals for each campaign;
- Budget specifications;
- Scheduled tactics (such as advertisements, mailings, events, etc.);
- The size of the respective target segment to be addressed (the "target universe");
- The time period of the campaign and various tactics;
- The repetition of the measures in "waves".

Here, *campaign architecture* refers to the selection of various communication channels, while *contact flow* describes the chronological order of various tactics within the campaign architecture (Jenner 2003).

It is advisable to consolidate all contents of a campaign, the respective goals, scheduled tactics and measures as well as the persons responsible and contact persons in detailed **campaign planning** (Figure 9.3). A risk analysis should be carried out for the execution that, for example, indicates possible delays in the campaign execution due to missing customer data.

In detailed campaign planning, some activities can be laid out for multiple target groups while other activities address a specific target group at a specific level of the brand funnel.

The *alpha* product launch accounts for both pre-launch activities with teasers and post-launch activities. Due to the high importance of influencers (women), an influencer campaign is advisable (Figure 9.4).

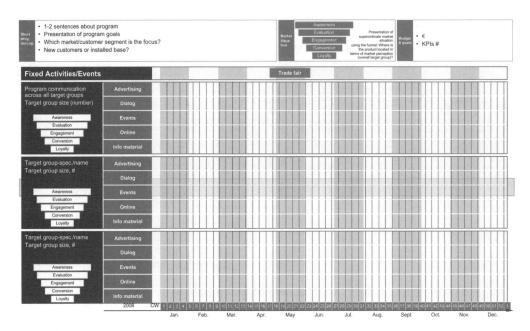

Figure 9.3 Detailed campaign planning and campaign architecture (architecture template, incl. calendar weeks).

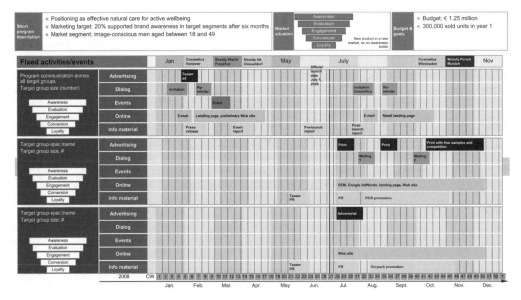

Figure 9.4 Detailed campaign planning for the *alpha* product launch on the men's cosmetics market (example).

A total of three different campaigns are planned for the **Awareness** section: (1) In Q1/2008, a *pre-launch campaign* (for sales channels) will include tactics such as a press release and a pre-launch event that is accompanied by activities such as PR announcements, event invitations and holding an event. (2) In Q3 and Q4/2008, the *cross-channel launch campaign* uses the classic channel (print), as well as dialog and online. Activities include advertisements in men's magazines and sport and automobile titles, mailings to subscribers of sport and automobile publications, as well as the design of a website with a competition and the option of requesting test packs. (3) In Q3/2008, the *influencer campaign* will be geared toward the classic and online channels with advertorials in women's titles, landing pages, requests for test packs, and the inclusion of samples with women's cosmetics.

A *promotion campaign* will begin in the **Conversion** section in the print and online areas in Q4/2008 comprising an advertorial with a competition and *participation in a personality training course*. At the same time, the *online recommendation campaign* rewards recommendations with free test products. Further *loyalty campaigns* for Q1/2009 at the *Loyalty* level can be planned as dialog campaigns at a later stage.

In any event, it is important to define specific KPIs for all tactics and activities. In this example for a direct marketing campaign, the following must be defined before the campaign execution and pursued later (Figure 9.5):

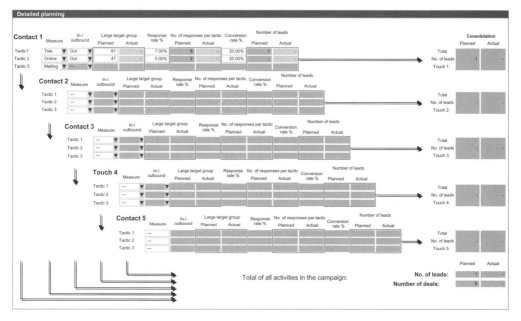

Figure 9.5   Example for detailed planning for campaign results based on leads.

- Number of contacts with the target group as part of the campaign;
- Type of tactic;
- Size of the addressed target group;
- Conversion rates;
- Generated number of leads.

Detailing KPIs is helpful both to ensure that planning is of high quality and to be able to reserve and train the required capacities (such as telemarketing resources) at an early stage.

9.2   DIFFERENTIATION AND STANDARDIZATION OF CAMPAIGN ARCHITECTURES

The further specification of dialog partners additionally requires the *differentiation of new and installed base customers* at the level of the campaign architecture. While existing customers (in the case of satisfaction and trust):

- prefer new products from companies or brands to which they already feel attached,
- generally think and speak positively about the company and its products,
- pay less attention to the brand, promotion, and price offerings of the competition,
- are less costly to be handled in marketing communication,

Addressing new customers requires significantly different campaign architectures (Bliemel & Eggert 1998). A similar phenomenon can be found along the *product life cycle*. The requirements of marketing communication change considerably along the product life cycle (Kuss *et al.* 2007; Dibb *et al.* 1996; Buzzel 1956; McDonald 2005):

- ***During the launch phase:*** In the time segment of slow growth during the launch of a product, the generation of new customers and a change in buying behavior with information of the buyers takes center stage to move them to try out the product. In terms of the brand funnel, the focus here should be placed on increasing the awareness and evaluation the product above all.
- ***During the growth phase:*** Many early adopters take to the product and with increasing market acceptance, more and more consumers begin to purchase the product. The prospect of high gains prompts the appearance of new competitors. As a consequence, not only is the product quality improved and the spectrum of product variations expanded, but new market segments are addressed, new sales channels are tapped, and the focus of advertisement shifts from building awareness of the brand to convincing the customer of the advantages of the product and to aiding transactions. The focus is on making the product known and interesting on the mass market and securing the largest possible market share in this environment. The focus of the activities is oriented toward the lower levels of the brand funnel (Engagement, Conversion, Loyalty – Wasson 1978).

- *In the maturity phase:* The slowing down of growth rates leads to overcapacities in the industry, which in turn causes increased competition. Price reductions, list price discounts, and increased advertising expenditures result. In addition to modifying the market (such as by gaining previous non-users) and modifying the product, other marketing mix elements must also be revised, such as advertising measures, distribution points in existing sales channels, or even the organizational sales set up. "Dropping" products in the maturity phase, which is quite common, fails to take into account that the success rate for new product launches is very low (less than 25%) and that many "older" products still have a considerable revenue potential (Hellbrück & Schoder 1994; Schoder 2000). Approximately three-quarters of all new product launches are "flops".

> In *grocery retailing* alone, more than 30,000 new products are launched every year – in some months, more than 600 per day. From their panels, research agencies know, for instance, that a person purchases an average of 420 different items every year. With that in mind, more products are launched in some periods than consumers can even purchase in a year.

- *In the slowdown phase:* The sales volume shrinks and profits dwindle. The marketing strategy in this phase depends on the relative attractiveness and competitive strength of the company in the respective industry. The spectrum here covers the strategy of *selective shrinkage* (in an unattractive industry with the company's own competitive position being strong) to *maintaining the present investment level* (attractive industry, company's own competitive position is strong). In this phase, in addition to eliminating low-selling products, prices are reduced and the level of advertising is lowered to the point that is necessary just to retain the most loyal customers (Doyle 1976).

Using the example of the product life cycle in the food industry, various alternative actions along the product life cycle can be represented (Figure 9.6).

As a planning instrument, the product life cycle indicates the most important tasks in each phase and simultaneously provides pointers to (possible) marketing strategies. The campaign architectures are also to be designed differently in compliance with the various marketing strategies throughout the life cycle (Figure 9.7).

In the first quadrant ("New product introduction for customer base"), the focus is on increasing the awareness of the new product and deepening customer relationships. The company's activities should be anchored as relevant in the customer's perception and should be flanked accordingly in terms of communication (support for the evaluation phase in the brand funnel). In the fourth quadrant ("New customer acquisition, existing product"), less effort is to be made raising the awareness of the product. Instead, effort is to be put into qualifying and securing leads so that they add the existing product to their personal shopping list as part of their decision-to-buy process. In this way, recommendations for campaign architectures can be differentiated

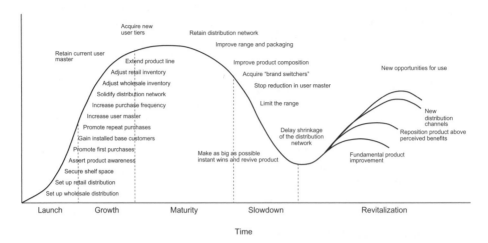

Figure 9.6 Product life cycle and the associated strategy modules using the example of the food industry (Kotler & Bliemel 2001, p. 603; reproduced by permission of Schaeffer-Poeschl Verlag, Stuttgart).

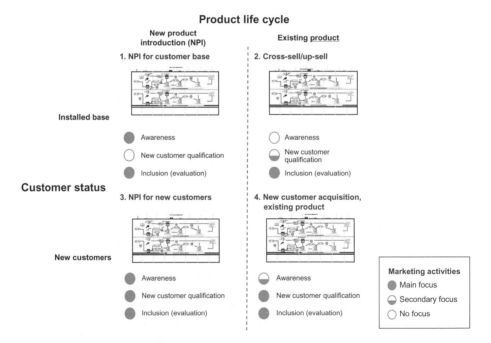

Figure 9.7 Campaign architectures for various phases of the product life cycle and customer statuses (new/existing customers; NPI = new product introduction; Beamish & Ashford 2006; Marketing Leadership Council 2006).

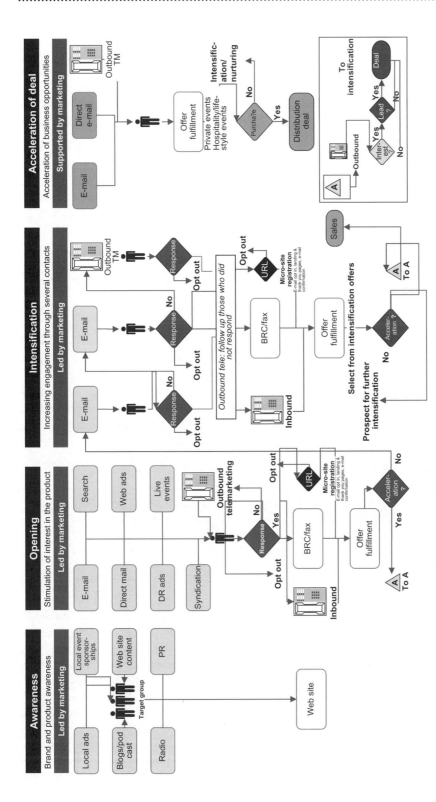

Figure 9.8 Campaign architectures for the fourth quadrant (existing product, new customer acquisition; Strauss 2007; Marketing Leadership Council 2006; example).

into different phases of the product life cycle by existing and new customers (Figure 9.8), such as:

- For raising awareness of a new product;
- Tactics for deepening existing interest in a product and anchoring the product in the decision-to-buy process via a high level of individualization in marketing communication;
- Measures and communication channels for converting leads into sales.

The development of standardized campaign architectures is based not only on the customer analyses outlined at the beginning, such as the typology and target group matrix, but also analyses of earlier campaigns and architectures used in each case. Project examples show that by standardizing campaign architectures, you can:

- Considerably reduce the costs for campaign development;
- Simultaneously avoid misdirected energies for repeated development of campaign architectures;
- Be able to place a stronger focus on the optimization of campaign contents (and less on architectures and used tactics).

Experience shows that the use of standardized campaign architectures can result in up to 30% higher results with the same budget.

The campaign architectures and the contact flow scheduled here with the target group can be further differentiated and standardized as needed for specifically addressing new markets, smaller target groups, or even for campaigns with lower budgets.

> O_2 chose the direct marketing approach of extensively industrializing O_2 communication while keeping the quality very high and avoiding "flat" communication. In processes that have been standardized to the greatest possible extent, target groups are addressed and campaigns are carried out in a predefined process sequence. Customers benefit from the right offering via the right channel at the right time (Hermes 2007).

To ensure that the target group is addressed efficiently and to prevent individual target groups from being addressed excessively in a certain period of time, a *campaign coordination* should be carried out not only at program level, but also at campaign level. Even a simple **collision matrix** provides transparency during campaign coordination, and allows you to identify additional potential for improvement (contact strategies) in the frequency that individual target groups are addressed (Figure 9.9). In the example, according to initial planning, the department head is to be approached six times in one month in January 2005.

Planning individual campaigns also points again and again to the problem that target group segments in reality are actually smaller than planned for. As an example, campaigns for the target group Human Resources Manager were designed for 2,000

KAM|PAGNEN
PLA|NUNG
Wilkommen Norbert Weber (d027485)

Datenbestand vom Montag, den 13.12.2004

Übersicht	ToDo's	Suchen	Reports	Logout	CRM-Datenimport

Ansprachen pro Mastercode im Zeitraum von [3] Monaten ab [Jan ▾] [2005 ▾] [suchen]
  Anzeigen der Top [5] Kombinationen
  Kritische Schwelle ab [4] Ansprachen
  Tabelle der "Alle"-Kriterien anzeigen ☑

Monat	Fkt. - Abt. \ MC	1	2	3	4	5	6	7	8	9	10	11	12	13	14	15	17	19	20	21	22	23	27	28	29	30	31	32	33	34
01.2005	Summe	6	5	4	6	5	7	4	8	4	6	8	3	6	4	4	4	5	5	5	6	4	4	5	4	4	4	4	3	
	Abteilungsleiter - EDV-Organisation(IT)	3	3	3	4	3	4	3	4	3	4	6	2	4	3	3	3	2	3	3	3	4	3	3	3	3	3	3	4	
	Gruppenleiter - EDV-Organisation(IT)	3	3	3	3	3	4	3	4	3	3	5	2	3	3	3	3	2	3	3	3	3	3	3	3	3	3	3	3	
	Abteilungsleiter - SAP Systembetreuung	3	3	3	3	3	3	3	3	3	3	5	2	3	3	3	3	2	3	3	3	3	3	3	3	3	3	3	3	
	Gruppenleiter - SAP Systembetreuung	3	3	3	3	3	3	3	3	3	3	5	2	3	3	3	3	2	3	3	3	3	3	3	3	3	3	3	3	
	Bereichsleiter - EDV-Organisation(IT)	2	2	2	3	2	4	2	4	2	3	4	2	3	2	2	2	2	2	2	2	3	2	2	2	2	2	2	2	
02.2005	Summe	9	8	7	9	7	8	7	9	8	8	8	5	7	7	5	4	5	5	6	6	7	5	5	8	5	5	7		
	Gruppenleiter - EDV-Organisation(IT)	6	5	5	6	5	5	5	5	6	5	5	4	5	5	5	4	3	4	4	5	4	5	4	4	5	4	4	5	
	Gruppenleiter - EDV-Organisation(IT)	6	5	5	6	5	5	5	5	6	5	5	4	5	5	5	4	3	4	4	5	4	5	4	4	5	4	4	5	
	Projektleiter - EDV-Organisation(IT)	6	5	5	5	5	5	5	5	6	5	5	4	5	5	5	4	3	4	4	5	4	5	4	4	5	4	4	5	
	Abteilungsleiter - SAP Systembetreuung	6	5	5	5	5	5	5	5	6	5	5	3	5	5	5	3	2	3	3	4	3	5	3	3	5	3	3	5	
	Projektleiter - SAP Systembetreuung	6	5	5	5	5	5	5	5	6	5	5	3	5	5	5	3	2	3	3	4	3	5	3	3	5	3	3	5	
03.2005	Summe	9	9	6	10	7	10	5	11	7	6	8	6	8	6	7	5	8	5	6	8	6	5	4	4	3	7	7	4	4
	Abteilungsleiter - EDV-Organisation(IT)	5	6	6	8	5	7	5	8	6	6	7	5	6	6	7	5	7	4	5	6	5	4	3	3	7	5	4	4	
	Abteilungsleiter - SAP Systembetreuung	5	6	6	7	5	6	5	8	6	6	6	5	6	6	6	4	5	4	5	5	5	4	3	3	7	5	4	4	
	Gruppenleiter - EDV-Organisation(IT)	5	6	5	7	5	6	5	7	5	6	6	4	5	5	5	4	5	4	4	5	5	3	3	3	5	4	4	4	
	Projektleiter - EDV-Organisation(IT)	5	6	5	7	5	6	5	7	5	6	5	4	6	4	4	4	5	4	5	4	3	3	3	6	5	4	4		
	Gruppenleiter - SAP Systembetreuung	5	6	5	7	5	6	5	7	5	6	4	5	5	5	4	4	5	4	4	5	5	3	3	3	5	3	4	4	

Figure 9.9 Example of a collision matrix for campaign planning and coordination (Strauss 2006).

contact partners yet only 100 were found in the target segment during company-internal data selection. The insufficient qualification of existing datasets causes delays in the execution of the campaign as additional data qualification measures or even the reworking of the campaign concept become necessary. Using a *target group inventory*, the currently available dataset can be analyzed in a simple search query as part of campaign planning in relation to the sought selection criteria, so that the conception of the campaign can then be reworked at an early stage, or additionally required qualification measures can be initiated.

9.3 USING MEDIA: HOW CAN I REACH THE CUSTOMER COST-EFFICIENTLY?

On the one hand, the *decisions on the use of media* within the planning at the activities level result from the analysis of the target groups and the insight gained there about media consumption habits and their preferences. At the same time, media agencies offer "target group and reach" analyses for various media (such as newspapers, magazines, TV, online, etc. – Kreshel *et al.* 1985; Sissors & Bumba 1998; Ace 2001).

When selecting the type of media, reach, frequency and the quality of impression are critical:

- **Reach:** Number of people or households that can be reached at least once by certain advertising media in a certain period of time;
- **Frequency:** Number of advertising contacts that a reached person or household is exposed to on average in a certain period of time. Analytic procedures such as the *Media Observer* from the company Mindshare are available for determining the optimum contact frequency;

- *Quality of impression:* Estimation of the level of attention to an advertising message in a certain medium. The quality of impression is determined by the editorial and attitudinal environment of the respective medium.

KPIs, such as reach, frequency, or even the quality of impression are offered by media agencies in standardized form. For the decision about both the use and weighting of all possible communication measures (such as trade fairs, events, and sponsoring), especially beyond classic media (such as print and TV), advertisers can hardly avoid the analysis procedures introduced at the beginning (typology, target group matrix). Aside from having external agencies assure and check the objectivity of the suggestion for media use, there is otherwise hardly any other necessary target-group or roll-specific information available for media use by the respective dialog partner (that is as detailed as necessary). The assessment of the advantages and disadvantages of various advertising media, and the foundation of the decision, should take criteria such as the following into account (Koschnick 2003; Böcker 1994; Kreshel *et al.* 1985):

- *Media use of the target group:* Such as the reachability of the target group by way of trade fairs or TV;
- *Product type:* Advertising media are to be chosen based on the requirements of the respective product in relation to demonstration, visualization, credibility and color effects;
- *Communication requirements and goal of the advertising message:* Rational issues and reasoning are more easily communicated through newspapers or economic magazines, while emotional messages are more easily conveyed through popular magazines and television. If the advertising message is to be effective sustainably and for longer periods, or if it above all supports the upper levels of the brand funnel (awareness or evaluation/inclusion in purchase considerations in the relevant set), specific popular magazines and television are better suited (Figure 9.10);
- *Costs:* Measured as the price for generating one thousand contacts (the *thousand contact price*);
- *Selection criteria:* Media that are more specifically directed towards the target group (such as fashion or IT magazines) or media that are more regionally directed such as local newspapers;
- *Availability:* Limited, for example, by usable airtime on TV, publication dates of magazines or existing bookings with out-of-home advertising (posters).

In the area of media planning, the *opportunity to see* (OTS) describes how often the people who were reached at least once were reached on average. It is one of the three most used values in media planning, in addition to *net reach* and *gross rating point* (GRP). With these three values, the advertising response to an advertising campaign can be at least superficially evaluated. The net reach specifies how many people of a target group were reached at least once. Multiple contacts do not count. The value is specified as a percentage. As the OTS is an average value, the contact distribution must be examined more closely. Advertising campaigns are often planned with a desired minimum number of opportunities to see in order to push the advertising

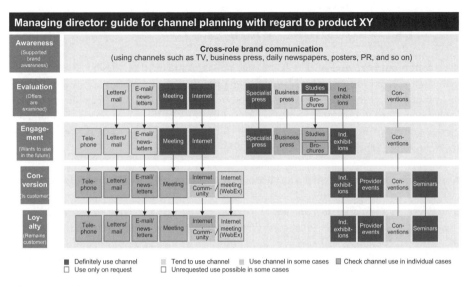

Figure 9.10 Channel mix along the brand funnel as a result of the target group matrix (example).

message on the market. The targeted reach is then called the *qualified reach*. Sometimes, contact corridors – approximately 4 to 6 contacts – are placed to generate a minimum number of contacts but also to avoid consumers having too much advertising pressure. Only people who are within this corridor are counted as qualified contacts.

The reach and number of contacts cannot be optimized simultaneously. Depending on the campaign goal, you must decide which of the two values is more valuable. Should as many consumers as possible notice the advertising message (e.g. as part of a product launch) or should the people that had contact with the message be addressed as often as possible (such as a reminder of the next purchase for often purchased products)?

Finally, the *gross rating point* (GRP) refers to the specifications for gross contacts in media planning. Every advertising contact is calculated for one person of the target group, even if he or she has been contacted on many occasions. GRPs are indexed and specified as a dimensionless number.

For example, a target group has a potential of 10 million people. Of these 10 million people, 80% (8 million) were reached at least once (= 80% net reach). These 8 million people from the target group who were reached came in contact with the advertising message an average of 3.5 times (3.5 OTS). In total: 80% × 3.5 OTS equals 280 GRP (gross rating points). In other words: As 100 GRP means that the number of gross contacts has reached the original target group size once, 2.8 (280/100) × 10 million gross contacts = 28 million contacts have been reached in total by the advertising message (Koschnick 2003).

9.4 ADVERTISING EFFECTIVENESS ANALYSIS: TEST PROCEDURE MADE EASY

The communicative ability of advertising messages and of their design as part of the campaign preparation can be analyzed using a number of procedures and metrics. Such test procedures (also called *copy tests*) can be used both before and after a certain activity has been carried out. *Direct surveys* of the consumers in the target group are generally carried out as an empirical research design. Such a survey may contain assessments of the following (Schmalen 1985; Berndt 1995):

- *Stopping power:* To what extent does the advertising material catch the attention of the addressee?
- *Effect on the desire to read on:* To what extent was the addressee stimulated to delve into the product characteristics and the concrete offering by the advertising material (reason why)?
- *Cognitive effect:* How clearly is the core statement or key benefit emphasized? Is the benefit clearly visible?
- *Action-prompting effect:* How effectively does the advertising material stimulate the addressee to accept the appeal or to change his or her attitude toward the product (roughly, the reason to believe)?

Both finalized advertising materials and concept tests can be tested before execution. Market research institutes, such as TNS Infratest offer standardized market research panels for this purpose.

While (potential) consumers from the target group or even experts evaluate various advertising materials directly in direct surveys, *portfolio tests* do not specifically indicate the advertising material that is to be tested. In these tests, the test person receives an entire portfolio with various advertising materials in which the actual test object is not immediately apparent. The test person is then asked about the signal effect, the understandability or even the memorability of all presented advertising materials. Finally, the most complex procedures, *clinical test procedures*, generally measure the efficacy of advertising in a test laboratory where the physiological reactions of the test persons (such as pupil dilation, changes in skin resistance, or heart beat) as reactions to various advertising messages are recorded (Kotler & Bliemel 2001). The advantage of clinical test procedures lies in the measurement of the activation effect of individual advertising materials, although changes to attitudes or beliefs that underlie these changes elude this test procedure.

The analysis and evaluation of the communicative effect of advertising materials and the measurement procedures used for this should meet measurement criteria such as (Rao & Miller 1975; Kroeber-Riel 1992; Schmalen 1985):

- *Activation:* The recipient of an advertising message must be "activated" not only for the absorption, processing, and memorization of information, but also for all further "activating processes" (emotion, motivation, attitude change);
- *Attention:* This is an important and necessary advertising effectiveness criterion in the early phase of processing the information of a test person. However, a high

level of attention does not guarantee a high level of effectiveness of the advertising material;

- *Poignancy:* How well an advertising message is absorbed, even under more difficult conditions, such as when an advertisement is only presented for an extremely short period of time;
- *Impression:* Concerns the feelings of the observer when the advertising material is displayed, such as "attractive", "familiar" or "competent";
- *Overall impression:* The overall impression of the advertising material as a result of the sum of all parts (content, design, concrete offer in the advertising material, etc.). The goal is to record a differentiated impression as regards credibility and informativeness. Similarly, it is possible to document the extent to which the advertising material as a whole addresses the pain points of a certain target group;
- *Recognition:* The test person must recognize advertising material that has been seen before. The effectiveness of *recall* places even higher demands – recall of both the contents and the design is tested;
- *Change of attitude:* Along the brand funnel, changes in attitude can be measured as a criterion for the assessment of the effectiveness of advertising, such as to what extent is the attitude toward a certain product changed by certain activities ("Would you now consider purchasing the product")? Such procedures are generally only useful if campaigns and activities have been used for a longer period of time.

While the measurement of the communicative effect is necessary for the advertiser to assess the fundamental elements of advertising materials, no direct conclusions regarding their actual effect on sales can be made. Even when it can be proven from the results of the test procedures that an attitude toward a product has changed, and that the product is positioned in the relevant set of the consumer, it is still not certain which indirect or direct effect on sales this has. The actual effect on sales depends on other factors: for example, the measures taken by the competition at the same time, the delay between attitude activation or change, as well as the (planned) execution of the actual act of buying (Schmalen 1985).

CHAPTER 10

PHASE 6: CAMPAIGN DEVELOPMENT AND EXECUTION

10.1 SELECTING AN AGENCY: A SYSTEMATIC APPROACH TO FINDING THE MOST SUITABLE AGENCY

The selection of one or more communication agencies is a key activity of the marketing division for developing and executing a campaign that is optimally matched to each target market. In most companies, various types of tasks are outsourced to agencies or result from the cooperation between the advertising company and the agency, such as the preparation of the value proposition, the development of communication concepts, the creation and implementation of action plans, the development of the necessary advertising materials, the implementation by a graphics agency, or even the execution (organization) of an event. The spectrum of agency services includes all possible communication measures, such as classic agencies (advertisements), as well as dialog agencies (direct marketing), trade fair stand construction, live communication (events), or even PR and online. While generally only larger *agency networks* have the infrastructure to be able to adapt and execute campaigns in various countries, experience shows again and again that highly specialized, local, generally *smaller* (owner-managed) *agencies* can deliver better results for special tasks for certain media or target groups. They strongly follow the pattern of *hidden champions* of companies in the mid-market (SMEs, Simon 2007). The advantage of international scope and the wider spectrum of experience of agency networks is often counterbalanced by a lower degree of flexibility, lower level of target group focus and the use of standard tools.

Experience also shows that *longer-term cooperation* with agencies should generally be sought. Getting to know each other and the commitment to the respective market segment, contents, ways of working and processes of the company and the establishment of personal trust requires a period of time of up to three-quarters of a year. When doing so, the following applies: the better the agency knows the commissioning company, products or target markets, the more able it is to design and implement communication instruments with precision, speed, and independence.

In an increasing number of companies, there are comprehensive efforts to make the interfaces to the commissioned agency as efficient as possible. In the course of this,

- focus is placed on fewer agencies and service providers,
- in which the tasks to be performed are combined,
- efficient workflows are established (within the company and in the interface with the agency), including a uniform workflow management for the implementation of campaigns,
- responsibilities between the agency and company are made clear with KPIs,
- measures are carried out to improve the quality of work in relation to the integral development of communication measures. The commissioned agency may even take over full responsibility and quality control. For this, fixed agency teams are generally assigned to a customer.

Although the media frequently reports on companies switching agencies, it is revealed again and again that, in reality, introducing and familiarizing a new agency with work processes and requirements runs the risk of heeding a lot of effort and being long and drawn out. To ensure that the selected service provider can actually meet the demands of the company (beyond giving impressive presentations), it is advisable to perform a *systematic agency selection procedure* (Figure 10.1).

After the analysis and consolidation of company-internal processes, tasks, and goals in the marketing strategy, detailed requirements must be stated, split by the various types of agencies. To ensure that the best service provider is found for each task area, screening of existing agencies as well as general market screening is advisable. Using a point system, the profiles of the analyzed agencies can be compared with the requirements of the company. Criteria such as the following can be used as (general) *parameters for selecting an agency* (Hartleben 2004):

- Is the agency required to carry out an individual task or a complete marketing program?
- What are the particular strengths/weaknesses (references) of the agency, such as industry expertise/knowledge of the business?
- Transparency in relation to prices and marketing behavior?

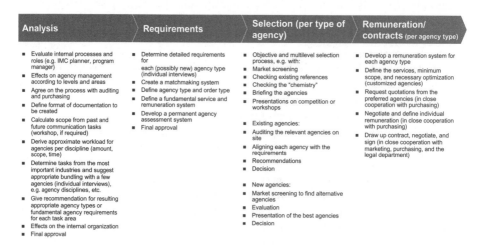

Figure 10.1 Course of action in a systematic agency selection procedure.

- More strategic or more creative expertise?
- Adherence to processes (such as, on-time delivery, quality of work)?

The development of both general and company-specific criteria and requirements facilitates clear formulation of expectations as regards cooperation, task delegation, and the necessary interfaces between the agency and the client. In extreme cases, the requirements necessitate a customer-specific organization and orientation of the agency (a *customized agency*; Harter *et al.* 2007).

Together with the requirements, a *permanent agency rating system* should be established that makes a note of all agency work and cooperation on a rotating basis. The creation of an *agency commission* can be useful, in which all involved areas analyze the quality of the work of, and the cooperation with, the commissioned agency periodically, check the conditions and, if necessary, redefine the agency pool or trigger a selection procedure.

Independent service providers can be commissioned for this kind of selection process. They can help to develop, objectively, the cross-functional criteria for the selection of the agencies. Continuous, mutual monitoring of the cooperation between the agency and service provider can be carried out using simple tools such as the *Aprais* system (www.aprais.de). To determine the agency's profit share, both economic performance criteria (such as the meeting of campaign goals for all campaigns in a planning period) and the results of the cooperation monitoring in accordance with the *Aprais* system can be used. A *pitch* only makes sense in this context if a larger account is to be assigned, and both conceptual and creative agency services are required to look after the account. The currently common practice of tendering smaller projects and accounts as part of a pitch is not generally consistent with the company-internal effort that is required.

As early as 2000, **Procter & Gamble**, the world's largest advertiser, changed the agency remuneration system on a global scale, and dedicated itself to integrated communication. Instead of the formerly common form of remuneration based on media spending, agencies now earn a share of the sales. They receive a fixed sum that is increased by a bonus as revenue increases. The amount of the bonus depends on the annual net operating sales of the brands for which they are responsible. The basic fee is based on an average value of the last three years. For the agencies, this system has the advantage that the basic fee is set at the beginning of the year. The income situation of the agencies is more plannable. Previously, they had to live with the risk that unforeseeable circumstances, such as a sudden market phase out, could put an end to the advertising project. Pegging the agency income to the revenue growth of the brands for which they are responsible is intended to stimulate the agencies to find integral communication solutions. Television, especially during the costly prime time, was preferred as a result of the traditional system. Alternative, cheaper marketing instruments such as direct marketing, public relations, and the Internet accordingly fell behind.

1 Basic fee (fixed)	**Fixed basic monthly fee (on an annual basis) for a precisely defined package of services, such as yearly strategy, weekly regular meetings, monitoring the competition, providing a fixed core team, accompanying production, and so on**	Monthly
2 Concept and idea	**Fixed project lump sum in line with price list for developing the concept and idea, including all changes**	On project basis according to price list
3 Execution	**Fixed lump sum for each measure/advertising matter or for executing measures according to the price list**	On project basis according to price list
4 Special tasks	**All tasks that do not fall within the three modules above (for example, nonstandardized measures, strategy projects, more extensive research activities) are billed by the agency according to quotation**	On project basis according to quotation

Figure 10.2 Agency remuneration model with monthly basic fee (fixed).

While remuneration systems were previously mostly based on project-oriented remuneration more than anything else, *modern* agency remuneration systems offer a combination of a monthly (fixed) basis fee with project-related remuneration for individual projects and campaigns (Figure 10.2). The advantage of such a remuneration system lies in:

- Basic and plannable provision of services and a fixed core team at the agency;
- Establishment of long-term strategic and operational cooperation with the highest possible quality;
- Reduction of agency fees with price transparency for all services rendered;
- Reduction of the agency's necessity of going on a project-by-project hunt for work;

The basic fee (level 1) covers services such as supporting the development of the yearly strategy, providing a core team, quality management for all execution processes, and critical analyses and tests of creative services (creative reviews). Below the concepts and ideas (level 2) that are to be remunerated on a project basis, is the development of main ideas (key visual, selling ideas), activity planning in a certain program area or even the layouts with headlines for all advertising materials (such as image proposals with background information and the justifying page outline). In the execution area (level 3), all services can be made transparent using a standardized service catalog including precise prices. Special tasks that cannot be standardized or planned adequately, or at all, receive separate prices for each project.

10.2 GOOD AGENCY BRIEFING: THE KEY TO SUCCESS

The function of a *briefing* is to describe tasks concretely and to give concentrated information to an external agency or service provider. Briefings are required for the creation of advertising concepts. In addition to the necessary background information about the communication strategy, a briefing should include conclusions drawn on the topical focus, relevant topics, and core messages and the optimum communication mix for the target group (Hartleben 2004; see Appendix, page 295). Quality characteristics for the requirements of a briefing include:

- *Written briefing form:* The briefing must include enough information for the commissionee to fully comprehend and manage the task;
- *Completeness:* The briefing must contain all information necessary for understanding the assigned task. This includes background information from the program strategy and customer/marketing analysis or accurate representation of measurable and comprehensible communication goals;
- *Precision and clarity:* Statements must be clear (no room for interpretation) and the schedule must be precise;
- *Concrete and understandable:* The contents must include information from program and campaign planning as well as answers to all apparent questions in sync with the developed value proposition. At the same time, the briefing must be formulated comprehensibly. Specific terminology pertaining to the respective market segment must be paraphrased for general comprehension;
- *Personal briefing:* This can be used to ensure accuracy and completeness, as well as additionally required details, which are to be further modified or added in a rebriefing as required;

Agency Briefing: launch campaign for the new *alpha* brand

Product (or service/solution and so on) (Precise description of the product, service, or solution)	The new range of cosmetics for men comprises 9 products. The range is based on high-quality, extremely effective ingredients that have proven to be effective in numerous tests...	**Tonality** (Impression made by advertising activity)	Active, questing, masculine, natural
Initial Situation (Initial situation, general market and/or sales issues, competitive environment and so on)	The entire cosmetics market is stagnating. NatureLabs' revenue is, too. The market for men's cosmetics is expected to grow by 19%...	**Product-related consumer insight** (Where will we find the target group?)	When I use cosmetics, I want to positively influence my appearance and the effect I have on others. If I am well groomed, I feel more comfortable, active, and self-assured...
Target Group (For example, demographic and socio-demographic characteristics)	TG 1: trendsetters who like to experiment TG 2: the undecided TG 3: the experienced mainstream...	**Product-related consumer benefit** (Description of the main value proposition in one sentence)	The *alpha* cosmetics range: gives me a feeling of active wellbeing.
Objective (Goal that is connected with the advertising matter to be created)	Create awareness for the new range. Position as highly effective cosmetics for a feeling of active wellbeing.	**Reason why:** (What product advantages support the value proposition?)	Valuable and highly effective ingredients from plants and the sea are processed using state-of-the-art scientific expertise. Each product is tested for effectiveness...
Timing (Campaign period, requirements for first concept presentation, deadline for final artwork, mail date)	The launch date for retail is July 1, 2008	**Restrictions** (What terms/content must not be mentioned or shown?)	n/a
Task Definition (Exact description of what must be done. Is the type or format of the advertising matter predefined?)	Development of a print campaign Development of a Web site Development of a mechanism for competitions Development of a direct mail campaign Development of POS displays	**Budget** (Are there budget restrictions?)	€ 850,000 (excl. media)
Content of Copy (Possible arguments to use in copy; is there any information on the product or target group?)	The best natural ingredients, for effective skin care and an active feeling of wellbeing. See also editorial platform...	**Measuring success** (What KPIs are used to calculate the success of advertising, such as the response rate, contacts or leads?)	Measuring brand awareness, sympathy, charisma (goal: 20% supported awareness after one year)
Call to Action (What should the addressee do?)	Buy and try out products. Check out Web site and participate in the competition.		

Figure 10.3 Briefing overview for the example of the *alpha* product launch by *NatureLabs*.

- *Preparation by the client:* Based on the contents, goals, suggested communication mix and the arguments for each core message as a result of program planning, the briefing is to be prepared by the client. The briefing forms the natural continuation of the marketing planning procedure up to the level of campaigns and tactics (Brückner & Reinert 2005; Back & Beuttler 2006). The occasionally found approach of outsourcing briefing preparation to agencies is explicitly discouraged. Only the client has the necessary knowledge and decision-making authority regarding the goals and contents of the program or the campaigns comprised in the program.

In addition to contents from program and campaign planning, a briefing should include specifications regarding the tone of the target group and the value proposition, the sought KPIs, the available budget (the funds that are available, including the agency fee, production costs, rights, expenses and so on) and the timing (completion date, time pressures such as dates for placing advertisements, delivery dates, interim coordinations and so on). It is generally advisable to give the agency a comprehensive briefing document in addition to a short overview of the discussion as part of the actual briefing (Figure 10.3, see Appendix, page 295).

CHAPTER 11

PHASE 7: ANALYSIS AND REPORTING

11.1   ANALYSIS AND REPORTING: FIGURE-BASED PLANNING AND LEARNING FROM SUCCESS (OR FAILURE)

Careful marketing planning requires diverse information on the efficiency and effectiveness of the programs and activities that have been carried out. The following are some examples of questions that need to be answered:

*   Was the market assessment carried out at the start of planning correct?
*   Which target figures are to form the basis for marketing planning and execution?
*   How do these key figures and target figures harmonize with the higher-level company goals?
*   How can these target figures from cross-area marketing planning be broken down to the level of campaigns and activities?
*   How can these key figures be measured or collected?

A systematic approach is recommended to ensure that the activities and implemented processes will run effectively. Accordingly, the main task of marketing and sales reporting or controlling consists in supplying information to marketing and sales along both the entire planning process and the final check of all measures as a "feedback loop" (Farris *et al.* 2007).

The range of tasks for the marketing analysis ranges from the definition of goals and activities to the breakdown of the budget. Consequently, in the context of strategic marketing and sales planning, the conclusions of the marketing strategy should carry over to a consistent framework of goals and budgets. In operational marketing and sales planning, the activities and underlying goals are further specified and detailed, usually for the planning period of the upcoming fiscal year.

The interaction between (a) the stated market goals, (b) the subsequently envisaged activities in campaign planning, and (c) the required budget should always be the basis.

To determine these three planning parameters, a *counter-current procedure* is recommended:

- In *top-down planning* the goals, activities and budgets are defined by a hierarchically higher level (e.g. company management or regional marketing) and gradually broken down to the downstream levels and activities;
- The ideas and desires of the downstream business levels are aggregated to higher-level master plans in a *bottom-up approach.*
- When using a *counter-current procedure* the goals specified for the upper levels are aligned with the aggregate planning of the individual sub-areas in several steps.

The use of counter-current planning ensures a high consistency of the planning contents (similar to the top-down approach), and, at the same time, planning is realistic and has high acceptance from each of the affected individual departments (similar to the bottom-up approach – McDonald 2005, Schäffer & Weber 2001). The disadvantage is that greater effort and resources are required for planning, especially when the planning and tactics designated for it here are very detailed (as in the case of highly role-specific or lifestyle typology-specific marketing planning).

For the reference object of the analysis and reporting, it must be distinguished between (Farris *et al.* 2007; Herrmann 1993; Cornelsen 2006):

- *Individual marketing activities:* for example, an increase in awareness following the placement of media advertisements, attaining a specific number of "leads" or the costs for a direct marketing campaign (examples for a *results check*);
- *The active players in the marketing and sales area:* for example, customer satisfaction in the customer care section, the number of new customers acquired, and meeting deadlines during campaign execution (examples for a *behavior check*);
- *Specific sales objects:* for example, satisfaction in a market segment, degree of loyalty (e.g. the willingness to recommend), or the profitability of a specific customer segment.

In each case, it is important to establish a *learning cycle* in which both success and failure are systematically tracked and rendered transparent, and are then available for additional activities or planning in a feedback loop (Strauss 1996).

After every promotion, the Swiss mail order company, **Damart Swiss AG**, conducts a detailed analysis of (among others) response and average order amount, profit and loss per promotion and per customer group, returns rates, as well as total back-office and marketing costs, and compares the data with other promotions from the past. All planning values are always precisely defined in the budget. After the end of a season, all campaigns are again examined and the success of the catalog is checked. How much did the catalog sell overall? Which pages sold more or less than others? Which products sell well (or poorly) to which customers? The results are then incorporated into the marketing planning for the following year. Each key figure is painstakingly evaluated in detailed planning. Usually, multiple testing procedures are used before a promotion is carried out (direct marketing report).

However, empirical studies show a completely different picture in many cases: most companies have insufficient control procedures in marketing (Geskes 1998):

- In particular, smaller companies fail to establish clearly defined goals and set up systems to assess the achievement of these goals;
- A systematic cost–benefit calculation for marketing programs and activities is not carried out;
- In the majority of companies, regular price comparisons to competitors' prices are not made and no formal assessment of the effectiveness of advertising is performed;
- Even when control reports are created, they reach the respective functional area with a delay of up to two months, and they also have great inaccuracies Subsequently, support for intermediate planning and process control can hardly be expected.

At **Kimberly-Clark**, one of the world's leading consumer goods manufacturers, the huge business area for advertising in retail sales caused problems some years ago. Each year, the manufacturer held thousands of advertising campaigns, usually offering a discount on a specific product to a specific retailer. Nevertheless, management was unable to measure the success of any of these campaigns accurately. The company did have figures pertaining to all marketing campaigns together, but these could not be broken down into individual customers, products, or deliveries. Consequently, enormous amounts were spent on marketing without knowing which campaigns resulted in more loyal customers, more shelf space, and higher sales figures, and which campaigns were completely ineffectual. The managers therefore concluded that they could significantly improve the effectiveness of their entire customer relationship cycle if they were to collect and analyze the data from their advertising campaigns using a CRM system that was somewhat limited, but tailored to their needs.

With this system, employees were able to measure the effects of a specific advertising campaign on the sales figures and profit for both Kimberly-Clark and its retail customers more accurately. By using this system and permanently tracking all campaign results, a total of USD 30 million for marketing tasks could subsequently be redistributed to the entire US private customer business to increase revenue and profit growth and continue strengthening the brand. Even though Kimberly-Clark originally only wanted to solve an urgent problem in dealing with its retailers, the company has since turned marketing into a science and success. Management now knows, for example, that the revenue from certain advertising campaigns is twice as much as that from other campaigns, which are actually supposed to achieve the same results. With this type of information, the company can determine systematically which marketing elements (e.g. gift certificates or creative ideas) lead to higher profits (Ledingham & Rigby 2005).

The discourse, which has been simmering for the last 20 years, on the connection between the creativity, content claimed and commercial success of advertising measures has received closer attention in more recent studies. With the cooperation of the Art Directors Club (ADC), more than 100 TV advertising campaigns, which had been submitted for the 2005 "GWA Effie Award" of the German Association of Communications Agencies (Gesamtverband Kommunikationsagenturen) were examined (Perrey *et al.* 2007). The submissions were evaluated in terms of advertisement recall value (psychological advertisement effectiveness) and changes in market share (commercial advertisement effectiveness). As part of the study, 13 ADC judges assessed creativity according to the following dimensions on a scale from 1 (inadequate) to 5 (excellent) (Perrey *et al.* 2007):

- *Originality:* Is the advertisement new, original, innovative? Does it break with conventional standards? Is it surprising?
- *Clarity:* Is the advertisement easy to grasp? Is its content instantly understood?
- *Power of persuasion:* Are the arguments in favor of the product plausible and convincing? Is the advertisement conclusive in itself?
- *Design and structure:* Is the advertisement structurally and technically sound? Do the elements work individually and together as a homogeneous whole?
- *"Want to see again" factor:* Is the advertisement fun? Is it entertaining? Do viewers want to see the advertisement again?

The creativity evaluations were subsequently compared with the advertisement recall values (psychological advertisement effectiveness, supported recall) and the changes in market share (commercial advertisement effectiveness) of each of the campaigns. What emerges clearly is that the more creative the advertisement, the more likely it is to (Perrey *et al.* 2007) ...

- ... have a more negative effect on advertisement recall ...
- ... but augment the likelihood of increased consumer purchases of a given product.

The "content fit" dimension then seeks to assess the quality of the structure and presentation of the content. One aspect examined here is whether there are any "boring winners", that is, campaigns, which, although not deemed particularly original or creative, are still highly effective commercially. Experts assessed "content fit" according to the following dimensions (Perrey *et al.* 2007):

- **Relevance:** Is the advertisement relevant for the respective target group and message? Does it fit in with the company strategy and the promoted product or brand?
- **Differentiation:** Does the advertising message distinguish the product from its competitors?
- **Consistency:** Does the advertisement fit in with previous campaigns? Is it in keeping with the overall product or brand communication?
- **Credibility:** Are the arguments convincing? Will the product or brand maintain the claimed value proposition?
- **Activation effect:** Will the advertisement motivate the target group to purchase?

Comparison of the content fit determined in this way with the commercial and psychological advertisement effectiveness and the changes in market share shows that a higher content fit tends to (Perrey *et al.* 2007):

- ... have a more negative effect on advertisement recall;
- ... but augment the likelihood of increased consumer purchases of a given product.

Consequently, the alignment of content, or the degree to which content "fits", has the greatest effect on the last phase of the decision-to-buy process − "content fit" evidently tends to address the rational aspect of the decision-to-buy process.

The question of whether to vest in high content fit or creativity can in turn be determined by examining psychological advertisement effectiveness (advertisement recall in the sense of supported recall) or commercial advertisement effectiveness (changes in market share) (Perrey *et al.* 2007):

- **Creativity, content fit, and psychological advertisement effectiveness:** On the one hand, this produces "exciting winners", in other words, campaigns that predominantly vest in a high degree of creativity. In these cases (as in the case of car manufacturers), content fit and relevance tend to play a subordinate role. The opposite is true for campaigns that emerged as "boring winners" from this study (usually providers of fast moving consumer goods − FMCG): a less original presentation with high content fit generates high recall value.
- **Creativity, content fit and commercial advertisement effectiveness:** Among the "exciting winners", from the car industry, for example, creative advertising guarantees that an advertisement is effective not only psychologically but also commercially (Figure 11.1). The "boring winner" campaigns of FMCG businesses predominantly achieve market success with high content fit, although they were assessed as less original and creative by the judges in the case study. The "boring losers" category comprises a high number of financial services providers, whose advertising content is usually abstract and therefore difficult to convey. Consequently, their advertising measures are deemed neither original nor fitting nor consistent. As a result, they are only marginally effective.

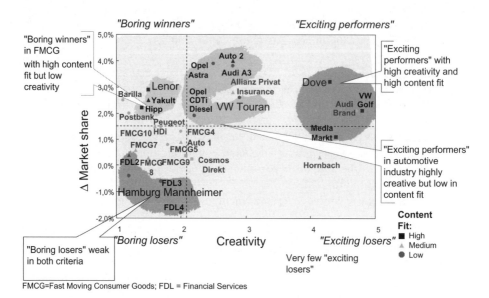

Figure 11.1   Relationship between creativity and content fit for economical success (*x*-axis: degree of creativity; *y*-axis: economical success of the campaign (change in market share; Perrey *et al.* 2007; reproduced by permission of the authors).

> In the above campaign (Figure 11.1), the **Dove** campaign is positioned in the top right, indicating that it is very creative and achieves a high degree of change in market share, while it also manifests high content fit (square in the figure).

As Figure 11.1 shows, creativity and content fit play a key role for the effectiveness and subsequent success of an advertisement. Emphasis on one or the other component should be alternated depending on a company's industry, positioning along the brand funnel and phase in the decision-to-buy process. Campaigns that satisfy both criteria achieve optimal advertising effects: a small group of "exciting winners" (in the sample study of only 100 campaigns) are successful in achieving superior advertisement effectiveness with a combination of high content fit and high creativity simultaneously. This means that creativity and fitting content need not be mutually exclusive – on the contrary, it's a combination of the two that prompts resounding success.

11.2   ANALYSIS INSTRUMENTS FOR EFFICIENT PLANNING AND IMPLEMENTATION

11.2.1   Cost accounting and profitability analysis: Is it worth the effort?

There are many methods and instruments available to perform marketing and distribution controlling and the analyses which they require: ABC and portfolio analyses,

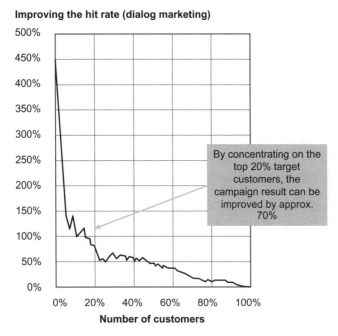

Figure 11.2 ABC analysis as part of prequalification for a dialog marketing campaign (example).

which are more for the area of planning; or cost accounting and profitability analysis, which is more for the area of control. Key figures and key figure systems can be used in both planning and the area of control, and can be tracked relatively easily up to the level of campaigns (Daum 2001; Farris *et al.* 2007):

- *ABC analysis:* The identification of important and less important products and customer segments is applied as an instrument of concentration analysis to support prioritization in marketing and sales. For example, 80% of revenue can be assigned to 20% of customers or analyzed for a dialog marketing campaign, so that by focusing on the 20% prequalified top target customers, the campaign result can be increased by approximately 70% (Figure 11.2). Despite the advantage of analyzing the economic significance of each object under consideration, it is a disadvantage that only one dimension at a time (such as revenue) is examined, and synergy effects across an entire product program, for example, are neglected.
- *Portfolio analysis:* As an instrument for analyzing individual products and customers (or customer segments), for example, in terms of customer attractiveness and vendor position (e.g. share of wallet). As with the ABC analysis, synergy effects between products and customers are also ignored here;
- *Cost accounting and performance accounting:* These allow you to assign costs to specific products or customer segments in order to determine the company's profitability in terms of individual products and customers. For this purpose, either all overhead costs are assigned to each sales object (product or customer segment) or only a part (variable costing). Cost and performance accounting procedures

have great significance for the management of a complete product portfolio (as part of *product absorption costs*), for example, or for the assessment of the financial success of individual sales channels (as part of a sales segment analysis). Finally, *activity-based costing* is appropriate for the control of in-house marketing and sales processes: in this case, overhead costs are not added to sales objects through summary overhead rates, but on the basis of the actual utilization of the applied resources instead (Recktenfelderbäumer 2006). Accordingly, a comprehensive activity analysis of all internal and external processes in product creation and marketing, and the identification of the most important cost drivers in each case, is prerequisite. The advantage of this procedure lies in the greatest possible accuracy with regard to causes in cost assignment, and the necessity of a detailed activity analysis within the company to ensure a high degree of process transparency. The latter point simultaneously represents the major disadvantage of activity-based costing: a detailed activity analysis (e.g. using the "brown paper procedure", see Figure 7.16) is associated with considerable effort and expense, as well as potential in-house resistance because individual activities and employees are measured.

11.2.2 Analysis using key figures: Less is more

Compared to the procedures for cost accounting and performance analysis or the portfolio analysis, key figure systems are usually easier to use in the day-to-day business routine. The fact that it can be easily implemented should not hide the fact that the initial determination of the key figure systems is, in turn, associated with greater effort and resources. For example, the question of which key figure should be used to measure which goal, and how these figures can be determined correctly ("Metrics that matter", Figure 11.3).

It is extremely important to select the right key figures carefully and track them consistently (Farris *et al.* 2007). Example studies in companies show that, due to the high degree of complexity and the usually limited contribution to providing an explanation, defining and tracking 20 different key figures, which is useful at least in theory, usually transitions quickly from an initial phase of enthusiasm either to being abandoned entirely or to a "natural focus" on a few selected key figures.

11.2.3 Customer lifetime value management

Whereas the focal point in classic marketing understanding is still the immediate sale of a product and the acquisition of new customers, CRM focuses on the establishment of long-term business relationships and the assessment of every single, individual customer relationship. The assessment of customer attractiveness is thereby based on the overall revenue and profit potential realized in a business relationship (Rust *et al.* 2000, Helm & Günter 2006). The reasoning behind this is that general determinants, such as market share or product life cycle, prove to be informative for determining profitable customers (Weiber & Weber 2001). A vendor's share of the overall demand of a customer is much more significant (share of wallet – Rust *et al.* 2000). Assessment

	Effectiveness	Efficiency
Potential-related KPIs	For example: ■ Customer satisfaction ■ Brand image ■ Vendor's price image ■ Product/service awareness ■ Delivery reliability	For example: ■ Number of contacts gained/promotion costs ■ Customer satisfaction with sales support/sales support costs ■ Customer satisfaction with service level/sales logistics costs
KPIs for market success	For example: ■ Number of customer inquiries ■ Total number of customers ■ Number of new customers ■ Number of lost customers ■ Number of customers won back ■ Market share of a product ■ Price level achieved on the market ■ Customer allegiance	For example: ■ Number of customer inquiries per order ■ Number of customer visits per order ■ Number of quotations per order (hit rate) ■ Number of successful new product introductions (success and flop rate) ■ Number of new customers gained/costs of activities for direct communication
Economic KPIs	For example: ■ Revenue ■ Revenue related to product or product group ■ Revenue related to customer or customer group ■ Revenue due to special offer promotions ■ Revenue due to direct communication activities	For example: ■ Profit ■ Profit margin ■ Customer profitability ■ Revenue due to discounts/costs in the form of lost revenues ■ Revenue due to participation in exhibitions/cost of participation in exhibitions

Figure 11.3   Possible key figures used in marketing analysis and reporting (Homburg & Krohmer 2006; Reinecke *et al.* 2006).

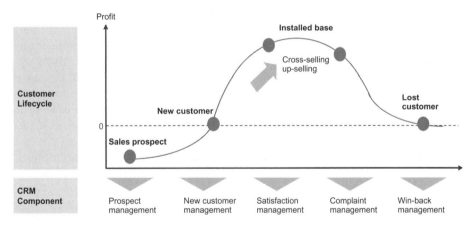

Figure 11.4   CRM – management of the stages of the customer life cycle.

of customer profitability must thereby concentrate on the *customer life cycle*, which ranges from building the relationship with a new customer, to exchanging services with installed base customers, to losing customers at the end of the life cycle (Reichheld 1997; Figure 11.4).

While the first stages of a business relationship are mostly influenced by cost factors (as a result of building the customer relationship), revenue and profit effects only start to appear later in the customer life cycle. In a CRM approach, classic *management of product life cycles* is replaced by management of customer relationships. For this reason, it is also possible, in an ideal case, to draw conclusions about the profitability of using

$$CLV_c = \sum_{t=1}^{T} \frac{\left(\sum_{U=1}^{U} R_{cut} - C_{cut} \right) - C_{ct}}{(1+r)^{t-1}}$$

where

CLV_c	CLV for customer (c)
R_{cut}	Attributable revenue from transaction u with customer c in period t
C_{cut}	Attributable costs of transaction u with customer c in period t
C_{ct}	Non-transaction based, attributable costs of the business relationship with customer c in period t
T	Length of the business relationship in periods
U	Number of transactions in a period
r	Hurdle rate

Figure 11.5 Calculation of the customer lifetime value (Weiber & Weber 2001).

one-to-one marketing or offering individualized products (Mass Customization; Rust *et al.* 2000).

The assessment of the *customer profitability* is not limited to products and services (and thereby, sales) that are in immediate demand, but also includes the buying potential that can be realized in the future and the possibility of cross-selling with a vendor's other products (Jackson 1989). These (for the most part) directly attributable revenue effects are compared against all costs that are to be attributed to a single customer relationship over time, for example, as a result of customer acquisition, customer care in customer service, and all measures taken for customer retention (Krafft 1999).

The summary evaluation of all revenue and cost effects for individual customers is carried out with a *customer lifetime value* (CLV) approach, which is derived from the difference from the net present value of all revenue minus the net present value of all investments of a customer relationship (Pepels 2001a; Jackson 1989; Weiber & Weber 2001; Dwyer 1989; Berger & Nasr 1998; Krafft 1999 – see Figure 11.5).

From the company's point of view, this generates various starting points (depending on the CLV), such as:

- Systematically *building new business relationships* with previous non-customers who, on the basis of a positive CLV, can be classified as potentially attractive;
- *Ending existing business relationships* or systematically reducing customer care expenditure and resources for existing customers with a negative CLV;
- *Increasing the profitability* (and with it, the CLV) of existing business relationships by structuring the business processes more efficiently or by increasing the revenue share of a customer through cross-selling (other products of a vendor), up-selling (higher value services), and recommendations.

Despite the advantages of the CLV approach in terms of mapping all customer interactions and the high degree of orientation toward the future within the scope of planning, there are some practical challenges (Farris *et al.* 2007; Strauss & Schoder 2001): in a relationship-oriented approach, it cannot be assumed that transactions between vendor and consumer occur in isolation. Instead, reciprocal interactions develop in a long-term relationship. Even customers who only make a few (loss-generating) transactions with a vendor may prove to be profitable, if they make *recommendations* in *virtual communities* or *blogs*, for example, and prompt other consumers to make specific transactions with a vendor.

At the same time, consumers whose opinion or actual behavior has a greater *spillover effect* can keep other customers from switching to a different vendor, persuade not-yet-customers to enter business relationships or trigger the move to another vendor by way of a negative reference. Even the *information-related behavior* of customers with a negative CLV can contribute to the initiation of improvements in the service creation and product development processes, which in turn constitutes a value over and above the actual customer relationship (Rust *et al.* 2000). The decision approach of the CLV, which is based solely on financial key figures, also finds its limitations with customers who, by virtue of an outstanding *market image*, for example, have a high degree of strategic importance for a vendor (as "lighthouse customers"), so that even if the computed CLV is negative, a continuation of the business relationship is not out of the question (Weiber & Weber 2001). For this reason, the effects of the *reference potential* (spillover effect on other customers) or the *information potential* (information provided by the customer for the purpose of improving the product quality or internal processes) of a customer should be shown separately (Rust *et al.* 2000).

Against the backdrop of these special factors or *indirect determinants*, determining the CLV and the following points can be problematic:

- Assignment of all revenue and cost factors that are relevant to the business relationship – i.e. the effort and resources required;
- Assessment of non-monetary determinants, such as the potential for recommendations;
- Necessity of taking future-oriented prognoses into account.

In each case, analysis of the costs demands a comprehensive analysis of all available customer data. Factors that are difficult to quantify (such as the likelihood of recommendation or the strategic importance of a customer for the company) can be supported or supplemented by evaluations on the basis of *micro-geographic segmentations* or *scoring models* (among others) in parallel to the CLV (Berger & Nasr 1998). One well-known scoring procedure for determining customer attractiveness is the *RFM method*, in which customers are rated by the time since their last order (recency), how often they make contact (frequency), and the purchase volume of their last order (monetary value as a percentage of revenue or transaction profit margin) (NetGenesis 2000). The forecast of future customer behavior up to the end of the customer life cycle can be obtained from *extrapolations* from the previous behavior or from *conclusions by analogy*.

Despite the conceptual limitations of the CLV approach, empirical studies have recently confirmed that a significantly higher degree of average customer profitability can be achieved by applying this method (Homburg & Krohmer 2006). The informational value of the CLV approach can be enhanced by taking real options into account (Haenlein *et al.* 2006; Schoder 2007).

11.3   DEFINING KPIs AND CONTROLLING WITH THE BALANCED SCORECARD

The traditional methods for measuring success in cost accounting, or even the use of individual key figures, often proves to be insufficient in light of more dynamic markets and more intensive competition. Besides financial key figures, the impact of marketing activities on customers (such as an improvement in the quality of service), a content-related improvement of processes, for example, in processing (e.g. a higher degree of transparency), and the effects on the motivation and learning processes of the employees, should also be shown separately. This is what the concept of the balanced scorecard seeks to address. The objective of the balanced scorecard is to provide company management a multidimensional control instrument on the basis of a manageable number of key figures (Horvath *et al.* 2001; Horvath & Partner 2000; Horvath & Kaufmann 1998): financial key figure systems are supplemented by customer–internal process, and learning/development perspectives (Schäffer & Weber 2001). By focusing on key figures in all perspectives of the balanced scorecard, it becomes a link between a still fairly abstract marketing strategy, on the one hand, and implementation on the basis of specific objectives, on the other. Anticipatory performance indicators accompany financial results figures (ex post), broaden the extremely narrow reality extract of individual key figures, and place them in the context of their relational structure.

Vision, which is to be operationalized through specific strategies and activities up to the level of key figures, is at the core of the balanced scorecard procedure (Weber *et al.* 2001; Fitz-Enz 2001; Müller & von Thienen 2001; Horvath *et al.* 2001 – see Figure 11.6):

- *Financial perspective:* Reflects the impact of all activities on profitability, as well as the company's situation with respect to assets, capital, and results. On the one

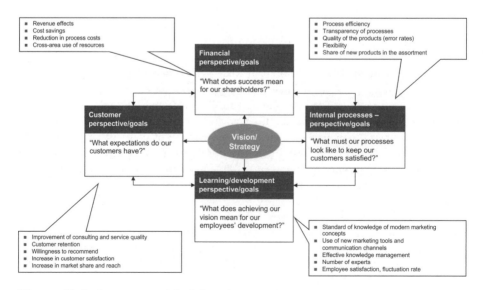

Figure 11.6   Perspectives of the balanced scorecard.

hand, financial key figures focus on performance objectives defined in the strategic planning process, and, on the other, they represent the ultimate goals of the other perspectives of the balanced scorecard. Monetary key figures that are qualified for marketing and sales control include (Jenner 2003):

— *Revenue effects* (e.g. revenue from online shop, percentage of total revenue that is marketing-induced; revenue change/channel; average order volume; "click-to-buy" conversion rate);

— *Cost savings in procurement and processing* with service providers, such as agencies (e.g. realized purchase prices vs. market prices);

— *Reduction of process costs* (e.g. resource usage for revenue, number of customers in sales or service, number of new customers generated);

— *Cross-area use of resources* (such as turnover rate of products, freight costs, profit, cash flow, total marketing costs, or "economic value added"/EVA).

• **Customer perspective:** The customer perspective emphasizes key figures, such as customer satisfaction, as a customer barometer, customer loyalty or churn rate, as well as market share in the relevant market segment. The expansion of the customer perspective to the market perspective allows the additional consideration of supplier and competition attributes. Examples of key figures for the customer perspective include (Farris *et al.* 2007):

— *Improvement in consulting and service quality* with self-service and online diagnostics (for example, measured by the extent of available information, the number of inquires arriving by e-mail, the average response time to customer inquiries);

— *Customer retention* (e.g. number of repeat buyers, sales/customer/purchase order; relationship of online/offline sales);

— Installed base customers' *willingness to recommend*, measured in the *Net Promoter Index*;

> To calculate the **Net Promoter Index**, the percentage of customers who are promoters (those who are highly likely to recommend your company or products) are subtracted with the percentage who are detractors (those who are less likely to recommend your company or products). Net Promoter Index stars are companies such as USAA 82%, Harley-Davidson 81%, Amazon 73%, Ebay 71%, Cisco 57%, or Southwest Airlines 51% (www.netpromoter.com).

— *Increase in customer satisfaction* (e.g. by measuring satisfaction);

— *Standard* of delivery service;

— *Increase in market share and reach* (distribution of customer contacts by region, growth).

• **Process perspective:** Mapping those processes required for reaching the financial and customer perspectives. Aspects that can serve as KPIs:

— *Process efficiency* (e.g. number of media switches along the processes, lead times, for example, for creating campaigns or the subsequent qualification and

tracking through sales up to contract conclusion, willingness to provide information, transparency of internal process flow or process flow with external agencies);
- *Quality* of the products (error rates);
- *Degree of integration* of marketing activities along the value chain;
- *Flexibility* (response times to inquiries/purchase orders);
- *Share* of new products in the assortment.

- **Learning and development perspective:** Describes the infrastructure required for the realization of the first three perspectives in the balanced scorecard, such as employee satisfaction, employee loyalty, or the number of incoming suggestions for improvement. This can incorporate categories such as employee qualification, information system capacity, and the goal orientation of employees. Key figures include:
  - *Standard of knowledge* with respect to modern marketing concepts (for example, following training courses);
  - *Use* of new marketing tools and communication channels (e.g. number of tools used, application methodology, use of search engine marketing);
  - Effective *knowledge management* (for example, willingness to pass on knowledge within marketing, or between marketing and sales);
  - Options for actively structuring *learning processes* (such as workshops, competence centers, training budgets, marketing circles);
  - Number of *experts* (e.g. number of employees with a marketing education, or understanding in terms of a competency profile);
  - Employee *satisfaction*, fluctuation rate.

The key figures presented here (by way of example) should not hide the fact that they should always be developed for the specific company in order to break the respective visions and strategies down to the level of quantifiable KPIs. To ensure manageability and efficient control, no more that 4–5 key figures should be derived for each of the four dimensions in the balanced scorecard (if possible).

> **E. Breuninger**, a retail company in Germany, organizes its scorecards into the areas of finance, internal processes/resources, customer/market, and goods/supplier. The entire scorecard focuses on the vision of becoming the most customer-friendly retail business in Germany.

Together with the employees affected, area-specific balanced scorecards are developed from the balanced scorecard of the overall company in a cascading process, usually in so-called *balanced scorecard workshops*. Involving the employees in the definition of goals leads to an intense communication and mobilization process within the organization and, as a result, to a significantly higher degree of identification with the defined target figures. Cause-and-effect chains between the various perspectives of the balance scorecard allow for analysis of causal relationships – for example, the impact that a reduction in lead times in production has on customer satisfaction and profit. Deviations from the objectives of the balanced scorecard can be used both to initiate immediate tactical adjustment measures and to contribute to the further development of the adopted strategy (for feedback purposes).

The use of the balanced scorecard as a strategic control instrument means supporting dynamic market and competition development with a formalized control instrument without falling into a bureaucratic trap with excessive regulation. Specification of explicit rules and key figures simultaneously ensures that coordinated and goal-oriented behavior patterns are implemented (in the sense of management by objectives) and that another extreme, the chaos trap – which is an expression of the company's loss of control – is thereby also avoided (Weber *et al.* 2001). The balanced scorecard defines the interaction of the parties using a limited, yet acceptable number of structures. Real-time information from customer interactions and processes facilitates recording time-related key figures and the implementation of online scorecards, e.g. for customer or process key figures. The (immediate) result is a higher degree of process transparency.

A *marketing audit* with checklists can be developed on the basis of the balanced scorecard (Droege & Kricsfalussy 1998). This audit comprises the levels of target achievement for the marketing strategy that was set in the strategic planning process, sales channel integration, internal processes, and the applied marketing mix. Project experience shows that, in this context, some questions must be answered, such as:

- *Strategy:* In light of the further market development and desired positioning, does the adopted strategy prove to be sustainable? To what extent were the set target parameters reached?
- *CRM:* How profitable are existing and targeted customer segments, for instance, on the basis of the customer lifetime value? What conflicts result using traditional sales channels, and how can they be resolved efficiently? How high is the customer retention and churn rate?
- *Individualization:* Which configuration patterns have been used so far, or which will be used? What impact has individualization had so far? To what extent does the use of individualization support the adopted marketing strategy?
- *Organizational structure:* To what extent does the existing organization meet the set requirements for cultivating the market? What resistance exists in the organization, and which change management measures are to be taken? How flexible is the organization in reacting to market and customer changes?
- *IT strategy:* Which IT infrastructure has been implemented? Is it an integrated, complete system, or is it more of a loose coupling of individual applications? What functions are used? Is there an IT strategy? Does the IT strategy conform to the business and marketing strategy?
- *Integration management:* Which key figures are used for permanent control and controlling? To what extent do the mainly used key figures actually map the company's strategy? How are the employees (mobilization and communication) integrated in the implementation?

The final criteria catalog should be developed for the specific company in order to be able to record and assess the particularities of each industry sector, the strategic orientation of the individual company, and the efforts that have been made so far. As with agency selection, the development of a criteria catalog should also be carried out by a neutral auditing team or accompanied by a generally accepted and neutral coordinator. Without the neutrality of the auditing team (or with the support of external experts), there is a risk that the subsequent result of the evaluation will already be prejudiced against by the affected departments during the course of the check criteria selection.

PART III

IMPLEMENTATION

CHAPTER 12

IMPLEMENTING MARKETING PLANNING

Studies show that one of the most important factors preventing successful implementation of marketing planning lies in actually executing it effectively rather than sticking to a chosen strategy. Implementing marketing planning according to the seven–phase model places requirements on:

- *Organization, management and HR:* In areas such as required skills in marketing, coordination mechanisms required to plan and execute marketing programs, and the creation of a *customer-centered* culture. When implementation involves different business areas and employees, a great deal of change is required with regard to behavior, activities and processes (Hilker 1993);
- *Customer data management:* As a prerequisite for effectively addressing target groups;
- *Deployed IT applications:* As strategic tools that enable efficient marketing processes and sales processes.

12.1 MARKETING ORGANIZATION IN A STATE OF FLUX

12.1.1 Organization and management: Getting the framework right

12.1.1.1 Requirements for marketing organization

One of the most important challenges to marketing is anchoring marketing tasks in the company. The quality of strategic marketing planning and its subsequent execution is influenced in particular by the departments that are involved in planning and execution and how they are involved, the tasks they perform during the planning process, and how well the different areas work together (Kreutzer *et al.* 2007). Converting marketing plans into tasks that can be put into action is important, because even the best strategic marketing plan is not worth much if it cannot be put into practice correctly. The interviews outlined above, as well as other detailed examinations, have revealed that the effective execution of previously defined marketing programs can be attributed in no small part to the skill of a company in four different areas (Bonoma 1985; Harter *et al.* 2007; Bucklin *et al.* 1996):

- *Identifying and diagnosing problems:* If the results of a marketing program are poorer than originally planned, the cause of the poor results needs to be diagnosed. Is the unsatisfactory outcome a result of poor strategy and planning or is it due more to poor execution within your own organization?
- *Localizing problems in the organizational structure:* The problem can lie either in a specific marketing function, in cross-department execution (such as teamwork between marketing and sales), or in marketing policies.
- *Executing the plan itself:* Managing different programs, individual functions (internal and external) and guidelines requires more than considerable skill in coordination. Good familiarity with the formal and informal relationships within the organization is often an essential prerequisite for effectively executing the programs that have been planned. Associated with that is a high degree of skill required to manage the interfaces and actively defuse conflicts between a variety of contacts in the organization.
- *Evaluating execution performance:* The results of campaigns and activities are not in themselves reliable indicators of how well marketing has been executed. It is possible that a good strategy was ruined by bad execution or that good campaign results were simply the result of fortuitous market conditions.

The structure of marketing organizations has become more important in recent years, thanks to the observation provided by practical experience that the areas of marketing and sales hold the most potential for improving productivity (Homburg & Krohmer 2006). Although optimizing horizontal *processes* normally takes center stage when implementing marketing planning, these processes must be supplemented by considerations on how to design efficient organizational *structures* and *cultures*. The pressure to make marketing efforts more efficient has ultimately led to a significant increase in attention to organizational performance. Appropriate organizational structures can be used internally and externally to ensure innovation and internal cooperation and coordination along value-adding, IT-supported processes (Strauss & Schoder 2001; Hutzschenreuter 2001).

The most important requirements and design principles for a modern marketing organization, as revealed by interviews with marketing executives, are (Hartman & Sifonis 2000; Homburg *et al.* 2000; Seybold 1998; 2001):

- *Flexibility:* Ensuring that the organization is flexible enough to adapt and react quickly to frequent changes in the market and the competition. As regards employees, this includes more flexible working times, duties, qualifications and remuneration (Drucker 1998; Gaitanides & Wicher 1986);
- *Culture:* Substituting formal organizational structures with strong "customer-oriented cultures" (Schein 1985, 1984; Ziegler 2001);

- *Innovation speed:* Being prepared to react quickly to changing market conditions and quickly introduce new products and services (Gemünden *et al.* 1992; Staudt & Schmeisser 1986);
- *Teamwork:* The ability to cooperate as applied to changing tasks, different roles and across different functional areas (Tjosvold 1990; Neck & Manz 1994);
- *Learning organization:* Establishing a learning organization as a permanent way of further developing expertise, making existing expertise available to the entire organization for the long term, and permanently aligning organizational knowledge with changing environmental and competitive structures (Daft & Huber 1987; Huber 1991; Strauss 1996; Probst & Büchel 1994; Wiegand 1995);
- *Self-organization:* A high degree of self-organization on the part of employees and the organizational structure, with a broad planning scope, particularly in executing measures and activities. This is connected with building an organization based on trust by delegating responsibilities to the lowest possible operational levels, e.g. during campaign execution (Hackman 1986; Kieser 1994; Strauss 1996; Manz & Sims 1980; Homburg & Schenkel 2005).

These requirements on marketing organizations affect more than just the conceptual phases (like working out a marketing strategy and its subsequent planning phase), they also involve the actual processes of execution and service provision (such as executing campaigns and activities, processing customer inquiries in a timely manner, and processing customer complaints).

12.1.1.2 Organizational structure on the way to customer-centered organization

There are numerous models available for embedding marketing and sales in the company organization. The most important basic variations are function-based, product-based, and customer-based organizations (Bühner 2004; Marketing Leadership Council 2005):

- *Function-oriented marketing organization:* Activities in the value chain that are similar or identical are combined in the same functional area (Figure 12.1). The advantage of a high degree of in-house specialization in relevant functional areas is usually countered by an inadequate focus on specific customer needs. As the

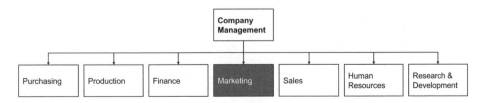

Figure 12.1 Example of function-oriented organization.

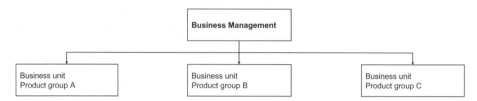

Figure 12.2   Example of product-oriented organization.

number of products increases or geographic coverage expands, the coordination effort involved soon outweighs the advantages of specialization;

- *Product-oriented marketing organization:* Business units are assigned to specific product groups (Figure 12.2). The advantages of forming business units with a high degree of product expertise are again countered by the strong tendency toward inadequate customer orientation, e.g. when customers order products from more than one area;

There is a wide range of organizational alternatives for the central advertising area of a multinational corporation like **Bayer AG**:

- A separate, central advertising department that can take over the marketing communication of individual business areas when necessary;
- A department that only buys advertising services. However, this too involves some risks. External advertising consultants do not register the complex development processes within a corporation.

That is why the chemicals corporation began to look for a synthesis of these distinct types of organizational forms several years ago. In a nutshell, the structure of Bayer's advertising area was: centralized organization, decentralized functions. The advertising department in Leverkusen (Germany) numbered around 360 employees, about 120 of whom were responsible for managing activities that related to the delivery of advertising matter. About 100 employees were responsible for coordinating advertising tasks, and 140 were directly assigned to specific business areas. For example, one team in the "Health" sector served the international "Ethical products" area (subdivided according to indication field), another served the "Ethical self-medication" area for Germany, etc.

All together, the Bayer product lineup was divided into six sectors. Naturally, business areas oriented purely around production need to invest a very small amount in advertising, while specific consumer products with media budgets received up to 10% of the revenue. These differences were reflected in the numbers of workers and degrees of specialization in the advertising teams for specific

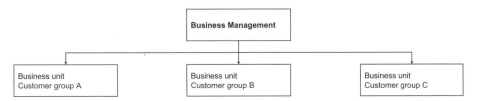

Figure 12.3   Example of a customer-oriented organization.

business areas. The job of each marketing manager was to develop a custom-tailored communication strategy for marketing a specific business area, use that for concrete planning, and initiate and monitor the required advertising measures and materials. The marketing managers were able to utilize the services of special communication departments, such as sports advertising, sales promotion, graphic design (as a contact for corporate design questions as well), film and AV, production of promotional items, advertising effectiveness (*Absatzwirtschaft* 1989).

- *Customer-oriented marketing organization:* Business units are divided up according to customer groups deemed to be relevant during market segmentation (Figure 12.3). The advantage lies in having the greatest possible focus on a customer group, yet the downside can be inadequate product expertise within individual customer segments. It is also possible that customer segments cannot be clearly divided (as in B2B). As described earlier, one need only think of the smaller subsidiaries of multinational corporations (subdivision of customer segments in large enterprises vs. small and medium-sized enterprises), or extremely small enterprises based in homes (small office/home office, SOHO) that can be assigned to either the private customer segment or the bottom SME segment. The conflicts that can be expected in a customer-oriented organization are therefore usually those that involve sales channels within the company.

One example of solid market orientation and the implementation of customer-based organization is provided by the **Sartorius Group**. Sartorius is a leading international provider of laboratory and process technology for the biotechnology and mechatronics segments. Mechatronics refers to the combination of mechanics, electronics and IT. The segment focuses on the production of scales and measuring devices for laboratories and industry. In the area of specialty scales for production in various industries and labs, Sartorius faces the growing challenge of the interchangeability of its services (Ballhaus 2008). Precise weighing and measuring, its main service, is becoming more interchangeable, removing a key distinction that existed between it and its competitors. That is why its principle for action now is to set itself apart from competitors by means of accessibility, after sales support and, of course, price. This means that price is becoming less of a critical factor when compared to developing new products in close cooperation with customers. To do that, Sartorius is divided into "core business field teams". Each team has one employee from marketing (product management) and one employee from development. Together they supervise one product. The goal is to use trends and customer needs to formulate product developments and see them through to execution.

This is how it manufactures special scales for customers such as jewelers (carat scales), pharmacies and schools. What all the products have in common is that they must all meet customer needs as closely as possible and they are offered through the most streamlined distribution network possible at an affordable price. Requirements for scales in development and quality labs in the food and life science areas are significantly higher. Besides weighing solutions, providers must also offer solutions for analytics and documentation (Ballhaus 2008). That motivates Sartorius to constantly develop its products further, taking its cue from its customers' unspoken needs. To do that, it search for solutions that will help customers with problems of which they might not even be aware. Employees take every opportunity to visit customers on location. Instead of discussing problems at meetings, they watch customers at work. This resulted in the creation of the *Acculab*-brand scales for schools, whose space-saving design allows for more convenient storage. This made Sartorius the first company on the market to offer stackable scales that store required weights in the scale itself (Ballhaus 2008).

This involved organizing "globally, functionally, and hierarchically". Stand-alone global functions for sales and marketing were assigned to each unit. A twin team consisting of a product manager and a project coordinator from the research division was responsible for revenue and returns in the segment (Ballhaus 2008). The team works the market together and converts product ideas into medium-term development plans. Sales then differentiates between a standard assortment and premium products. The standard assortment consists of technically mature products that require little consultation and are sold by specialized dealers world wide. Two-thirds of revenue comes from those standard products. Premium products, on the other hand, are solution-oriented. Regional sales representatives maintain contact with customers and receive technical support from cross-regional product specialists (Ballhaus 2008).

Optimizing products and solutions for different applications requires Sartorius to provide products for sub-segments. The more specific the requirements are in a sub-segment, the easier it is to provide a customized solution. Consequently, Sartorius established segment managers in central marketing to keep a closer eye on the market. Their challenge is to advance segment-specific product adaptation as far as possible without losing sight of the need for standardized production (Ballhaus 2008).

Sartorius uses a web-based marketing and information system to network its business areas around the world. Yet the key task of the Internet is not to disseminate information from headquarters; rather, it enables the interactive use of resources around the world. In the case of marketing, local market trends are described and discussed in a forum. Marketing activities can be evaluated and then used as a benchmark for all the regions. As a result, following an analysis, Sartorius won an award for aligning its overall corporate strategy with its marketing, sales and brand strategies. The study claims that Sartorius has demonstrated how to successfully recognize unspoken customer needs and transform them into customized solutions (Ballhaus 2008).

Other organizational forms such as the *matrix organization* attempt to mitigate the disadvantages of "pure" organizational forms in marketing by using a combination of function-oriented and product-oriented structures. Although combining function-oriented and product-oriented expertise yields high-quality decisions (at least at the theoretical level), the advantage is usually offset by immense coordination difficulties and multiple reporting lines (dotted lines) with considerable goal conflicts. Establishing independent *product management* seems to be particularly useful in companies with a complex product line. Product management would be responsible for managing the marketing of a product or product group. The range of activities covered by product management includes:

- *Analysis:* Such as positioning specific products and customer needs;
- *Planning:* Such as marketing planning and annual sales planning, as well as product innovations;
- *Implementation:* Such as executing marketing activities;
- *Checking and control:* Such as attaining goals, e.g. achieving product satisfaction, attaining a certain market share, profitability of specific brands (Kairies 2004; Matys 2005; Pepels 2000).

While product management typically relates to a specific product, *category management* relates to an entire product category. Category management is recommended especially when there are companies within a product group that offer several products with a spillover effect.

Empirical analyses and the survey taken at the CMO Summit prove that there is a growing trend among companies toward customer-oriented organization (also Homburg *et al.* 1997; Harter *et al.* 2007). Thus companies are creating appropriate organizational forms to support their endeavors to become more customer-oriented. However, shifting marketing expertise to business units increases the complexity of executing cross-area marketing planning and ensuring that business content is communicated consistently across those areas.

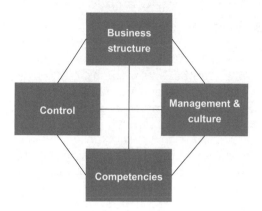

Figure 12.4 Cornerstones for implementing customer-centered organization.

12.1.1.3 Cornerstones for implementing customer-centered organization

Adjusting existing organization and management mechanisms in favor of greater customer orientation can be divided into four areas of activity: organizational structure, operational checks, available expertise, and management and culture (Figure 12.4).

Organizational structure focuses on implementing flat structures with low fixed costs and a high degree of flexibility and speed when responding to changes in the market. Partnerships and alliances allow companies to quickly develop new business fields, reduce risks, and acquire the expertise required for new task areas. Its main tasks involve improving how customer relationships are managed and improving the brand name, such as:

- by concentrating on customer contact and how to expand it;
- by determining which target groups the company should acquire and retain (for the long term);
- by employing online and offline marketing instruments.

Assuming the organization is sufficiently large and complex, the **controlling function** should be performed by special, independent organizational units (such as marketing intelligence), and the different marketing areas and cross-area support should have clearly defined decision makers (Jenner 2003). Locating them in controlling instead of marketing would certainly make them more independent from marketing and sales executives. However, this would give them an inadequate view into the processes and activities of marketing (Köhler 2006; Reinecke & Janz 2006).

The aim of organizational design measures in the area of **management and company culture** is to ensure organizational flexibility. It focuses on reducing the time needed to make decisions when operational and strategic tasks arise. Instruments for employee involvement (such as stocks or options) can help to motivate business activity at all hierarchy levels when they are designed correctly (Jost 2001; Fitz-Enz 2001). The following points summarize *framework parameters for management*:

- *Delegating* responsibility to the lowest levels possible (generally referred to as self-organization);
- All employees flexibly *adopting* personal responsibility for roles and tasks (self-coordination);
- Quickly forming *teams* that interact across all hierarchy levels and functional areas (e.g. marketing, sales, service);
- A culture that allows *mistakes* (Schein 1985; Kuss *et al.* 2007);
- *Incentive systems* for entrepreneurial thinking and activity, in the form of bonuses or stock option programs that are directly linked to the success of marketing activities or the success of the company (Jenner 2003; Witt 1998).

At least two new fields of competency emerge with regard to the competency available in the company:

- Competencies in *innovation management* safeguard the execution of the differentiation strategy that the company uses to set itself apart from competitors. At the heart of innovation management is the establishment of a standardized process for systematically developing and integrating product innovations and process innovations, such as using new media in marketing communication;
- Experience in customer retention (community management) supplements the range of required competencies. Here, the focus is on questions, such as how to systematically acquire and retain customers, e.g. by managing virtual communities, blogs, or subliminal word of mouth advertising (*viral marketing*) in Web 2.0.

A small company in Berlin with just 10 employees became wildly successful with its *K-fee* product, a coffee-based energy drink. The gruesome video clips on its website (www.k-fee.com) won awards and word of mouth drew up to 100,000 visitors per day. Visitors downloaded the clips and e-mailed them to friends an average of nine times each. The links that were integrated into the clips generated a response rate of over 10%. One clip even made it to a popular US television show, creating a huge demand. Today **K-fee** is number two on the market of ready-to-drink coffee beverages, behind the leader **Nestlé** and ahead of **Jacobs**. This proves that viral marketing can be used to beat even global players.

An entirely new form of word of mouth advertising, called **buzz marketing**, is spilling over from the US into other countries (Kreutzer *et al.* 2007). Specialized agencies plan and initiate it for a fee. These agencies have hundreds of thousands of "buzzers" in their database who selectively yet casually bring up specific products during conversations with people with whom they come into contact. They receive product samples and information about how to address customers. Buzzers do not work for pay and are under no pressure whatsoever. The ability of buzzers to stimulate the appetite of consumers for a particular product became clear in the case of a new type of sausage from the *Al Fresco* brand. The manufacturer, **Kayem Foods**, found that conventional marketing was not helping them put their product on the table of American consumers. So the company hired a group of buzz agents. They in turn organized barbecues, raved about the sausage at supermarkets and snack bars, told their friends and family about it, asked for the sausage in all kinds of stores, and complained when stores did not carry it. This generated a strong demand; sales figures jumped and revenue rose immediately after the campaign to USD 1.2 million (Schüller 2006).

12.1.1.4   Sales follows marketing – or vice versa?

Three essential options for the division of tasks and the relationship between marketing and sales emerge from real world examples (Marketing Leadership Council 2005; Homburg & Krohmer 2006; Hutzschenreuter 2001):

- *Marketing and sales have an equal division of labor and the same hierarchy:* Sales is responsible for pricing and operational sales activities, while marketing handles product management and advertising. This parallel division of labor is most common in the consumer goods industry, where there brand management is clearly established and defined;
- *Marketing as a service department in sales:* In this model, marketing performs service tasks primarily in the areas of marketing communication (esp. advertising) and market research. This model is often found in the B2B segment, such as machine engineering or technology. As personal communication plays an important role in customer interaction, sales determines the characteristics of final products in consultation with customers;
- *Sales as a fulfillment aid to marketing:* In this model, sales is primarily responsible for customer support. This is most common in companies with a very centralized approach to marketing and sales, such as in the chemicals industry.

Arcor showed how to make a virtue of necessity. As new areas were being connected successively to Arcor's network, the company fused its marketing and sales resources in those areas. It used billboards, radio, and print advertising simultaneously in each region and sent out large numbers of direct sales agents to work on-site.

The *evaluation of possible organizational models* and decisions on design options should be based on company-specific criteria. Case studies show that up to 50 different criteria need to be weighed against one another, including:

- Making the customer interface the key to understanding the needs of customers and the requirements of the market;
- Guaranteeing fast execution;

- Being able to integrate existing in-house processes and expertise;
- Offering a flexible, affordable cost structure;
- Being able to find employees who have the right expertise;
- Offering a highly adaptable, scalable organization.

12.1.2 Coordination mechanism: Self-organization and chaos?

A survey taken by the Marketing Leadership Council in 2005 revealed that 67% of marketing managers were dissatisfied with the current state of their organization. They often cited poorly defined structures and responsibilities, leading to problems with coordination, planning, and execution. Poorly defined roles and responsibilities lead to excessively burdened employees, especially when they are working with other functional areas or superiors.

Dissatisfaction with the existing organizational form is usually traced back to established, hierarchical coordination mechanisms that fail to satisfy the design principles outlined above. There is little understanding for the needs of other functional areas, just as other functional areas have little understanding for the needs of the marketing department. When used to remedy serious cases of "silo mentality", *hierarchical forms of coordination* often place excessive burdens on higher instances and official channels. This has a lasting negative impact on options for coordinating value-adding processes in marketing planning and execution, and makes them more time-consuming (Strauss 1996; Harter *et al.* 2007).

One commonly cited example of the excessive burdens on higher instances and communication channels pertains to approval procedures and clearances required for even the simplest of activities. For instance, targeted mail can only be sent once several higher instances have been consulted several times, and they all have different requirements and want different aspects changed (to suit their own purposes).

In addition to being overburdened, higher instances are far removed from the operational business, so they are often forced to make decisions whose impact they cannot accurately foresee, since they lack all the details when they make the decision. Lower levels in the hierarchy have to provide explanations, which overburdens downstream vertical communication channels even more. Furthermore, excessive area-external organization obstructs employee needs in terms of autonomy, personal responsibility and *self-realization* (Leonhard–Barton 1992; Strauss 1996).

Unlike the hierarchical coordination mechanisms often seen, **self-organization** opens up a variety of options for implementing efficient marketing organizations and cultures (Smith & Comer 1994; Manz 1992; Lant & Mezias 1992):

- It alleviates the hierarchical coordination normally required, reducing the number of formal, vertical communication processes;
- It increases employee motivation, stimulates more shared learning processes (organizational learning);
- It improves the *flexibility* of the organization as a result.

Self-organization can take on different forms (Hackman 1986; Kieser 1994; Strauss 1996 – Figure 12.5):

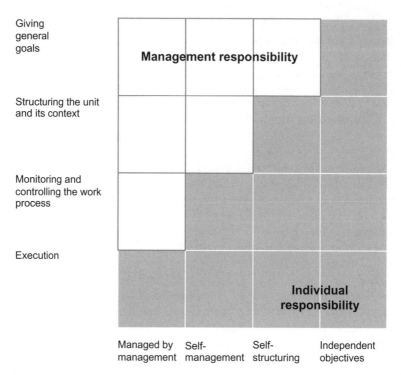

Figure 12.5　Types of self-organization as a coordination principle (Hackman 1986; Strauss 1996).

- *Self-management:* Employees are responsible for more than just correctly carrying out the tasks assigned to them (from above), they must also permanently monitor and control how those tasks are executed as part of the overall process (of campaign execution, for instance). This includes members of a working group voting on how to divide up the tasks of the group;
- *Self-structuring:* Organization members can define and design their own organizational structure and its interfaces with other groups (such as sales);
- *Units can set their own goals:* In actuality, participation in setting goals is usually kept at the management level.

Limits to self-determination and self-coordination emerge when there is competition between groups or departments – as is often the case between marketing and sales – or when specific participants in an organization act solely in their own interest (Bierhoff & Müller 1993). The basic model for self-determination does not allow for any specialized organization members; on the contrary, it is important that all employees are equally involved in coordination. In addition to taking more time, this involves considerable qualification difficulties, since strategic decisions and operational execution both require that the majority of people involved have a wide range of skills and qualifications. The wide range of decision tasks that emerge only result in at least part of the day-to-day operational tasks (such as campaign execution) being transferred to *self-coordination*, while the rest (such as the marketing strategy) is mostly left to be hierarchically controlled elsewhere.

The focus of organizational design is therefore to set framework conditions for implementing self-organization, such as planning systems and information systems, target KPIs and management structure. When self-coordination is implemented, hierarchical supervisor roles usually undergo permanent changes in their ability to shape and influence. Managing self-organizing units is transformed into the role of *facilitator* along value-adding and learning processes, and is limited to laying down formal framework conditions, in the sense of "leading others to lead themselves" (Manz & Sims 1989). Target agreements, for instance, can be used as a managerial tool (*management by objectives*).

12.1.3 Procedural model for transforming marketing organization: Market excellence

Project experience shows that executing organization principles, establishing customer-oriented organization, and introducing new processes to planning and execution usually follows a multi-stage approach (Figure 12.6). Like strategy development, after an **analysis** has been made of the existing organizational structure and (external) benchmarking has been performed, the initial options are fixed in a **macro design** and subjected to an initial evaluation. The subsequent **micro design** then gives greater depth to the design principles, including roles and responsibilities, management principles, required skills found in the competency model, and compensation models (Davenport 1993; Strauss 2006; Kreutzer 2008). A detailed **implementation plan** is developed and communicated to the entire enterprise at a kick-off. **Implementation** requires communication mechanisms and feedback mechanisms for all employees that will be

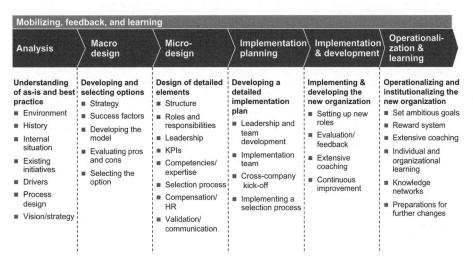

Figure 12.6 Procedure for transforming an organization.

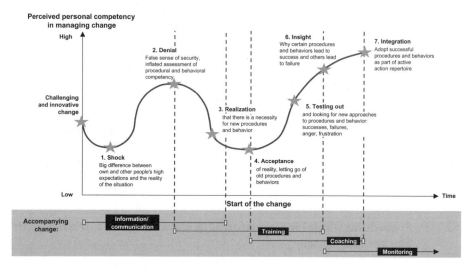

Figure 12.7   Change management cycle for implementing changes.

affected by the changes and for amassing and employing existing knowledge (***opera-tionalization and learning***, knowledge management; Davenport & Prusak 1998).

Restructuring and realignment causes *resistance*, and there are usually complex reasons for that. At the employee level there are phenomena such as:

- Old (comfortable) habits;
- Selective processing for information that does not fit in their existing frame of reference;
- A high degree of dependence on the values, attitudes and beliefs of their most important contacts;
- Insecurity and regression, such as the fear of losing their job or the danger of de-qualification;
- A socio-psychological fear of the "new" and the "unknown" (Doppler & Lauterburg 2000).

Accordingly, a change process of this type is subject to considerable fluctuations and stages in most organizations. After a stage of shock upon receiving information about changes that will take place, there is a stage of denial, which is followed by a stage of gradual realization and insight, until the planning schemas and implementation processes are ultimately accepted (Figure 12.7). The changes should be accompanied by comprehensive change management that employs different tools that fit with each stage.

Resistance at the level of the entire organization can occur as a result of (Staehle 1991; Jenner 2003):

- The changes do not conform to existing organizational norms and traditions;
- Interdependence with subsystems that are difficult to understand or delimit;
- Privileges, taboos, or resistance to external ideas ("not invented here").

Resistance is particularly strong among people who rely primarily on their own experience, who only believe in one way of doing things, and who have an extremely low tolerance for risk. Resistance is strongest in groups, on the other hand, when the group members have a strong group identity or feelings of superiority (Doppler & Lauterburg 2000).

That is why large organizations often utilize specialist *change agents* who walk the organization through restructuring; while reorganization measures are in progress, they may attend to activities such as disseminating marketing expertise and implementation, and they are not tied to any particular part of the hierarchy or any particular task. Change agents are normally not authorized to issue instructions in functional areas, but they do actively attempt to foster a customer-centered marketing organization by amassing market expertise and transferring experiences from other areas of the enterprise. Using change agents can help to overcome differences between different functional areas like sales and marketing, while also helping to establish a broad mutual understanding of the opportunities and steps in implementation. It may also be necessary to have support from *power agents*, even if they do not typically play an operational role in implementation.

In addition to agents, successful implementation utilizes a variety of measures for communicating with and mobilizing employees, as in info fairs, project journals, and workshops that get affected employees involved early on. One tried-and-tested method is called *marketing in change*, which takes place off-site with the entire marketing team and involves talks and role-playing (e.g. based on customer typologies or role profiles from the target group matrix). Training in marketing planning, project management and how to use new marketing techniques can help to further enhance existing knowledge. At the same time, human resources needs to revise existing *competency catalogs* and related *job profiles*. Both form the basis for evaluating employees during annual *functional calibration* for promotions and systematically determining areas where individuals need further development.

Project experience shows that *quick wins*, such as dramatically improved campaign results, can help to create an environment of trust on all sides (Doppler & Lauterburg 2000; Mohr & Woehe 1998). When implementation is not successful, however, it is usually due to the fact that while analytic and quantified concepts were worked out (sometimes with assistance from outside support), the organization failed when it actually tried to implement them because the people involved lacked the skills or the empathy that was required.

12.2   GATHERING AND MANAGING CUSTOMER DATA (DATABASE MARKETING)

The foundation of systematic customer relationship management is very detailed knowledge of the interests and preferences of customers, as revealed by customer data. There is a range of mechanisms available for gathering the customer data required, including:

*   Having sales associates collect data when they interact with customers;
*   Purchasing customer data from professional list brokers and address sellers;

- From information that customers enter themselves (reply forms, registration forms, and explicit filtering by selection menus on the Internet);
- Web-based, passive, implicit profiling with the help of special applications and protocols, such as analyses of server log files, cookies, and intelligent agents (Strauss & Schoder 1999b).

> The English retail chain **Tesco** focused on the interface between benefit-based customer segmentation and revenue in certain product categories. By combining (a) data from store cards about customers' current buying behavior and (b) market research on products that customers did not buy in their stores, the company was able to identify further areas of growth. Tesco found out that young mothers, for instance, tended to buy baby products at special drug stores rather than at Tesco stores. The reason was that they trusted the quality of the products at drug stores. In response, Tesco started its own *Baby Club* in which it offered information from experts as well as coupons. As a result, revenue from baby products in England increased from 16% to 24% between 2000 and 2003 (Forsyth *et al.* 2006).

One difficulty that arises when companies attempt to gather customer data systematically is that consumers are averse to providing information about themselves when there is no incentive to do so. Project experience shows that increasing the value of incentives greatly increases people's willingness to participate. There is no way to ensure that consumers are being completely truthful when they provide personal information, except when they can see obvious advantages in doing so, such as with information services like *My Yahoo!* (de.my.yahoo.com), *Facebook* (www.facebook.com), and many more Web 2.0 applications (Frazier 2001; Strauss & Schoder 2001; Tapscott & Williams 2006). People may be more willing to provide personal data if they know exactly what rules will govern how their data will be used later on (conformity with applicable laws) and if they have to give their explicit consent for their data to be used. Before registering, users should be informed about how their data will be used and they should give their permission for their user information to be used and passed on (known as *permission marketing* – Dyson 1997; Gora & Mann 2001).

> According to a study by IT associations like **Bitkom**, 61% of computer owners like to shop on the Internet and do so regularly. They normally provide their name, address, telephone number, e-mail address, and account data for the purpose of payment processing and shipping. Of course this all happens with the buyer's consent – no different from a conventional catalog order. However, many web users do not know that as they navigate through these virtual stores, they are divulging a great deal of additional information without even realizing it (Feldmann 2008).

This tracking data is normally used by those who operate the stores to get an overview of user behavior. The information is collected, made anonymous, and analyzed with regard to predefined key figures. Marketing managers for that site will then know how, when, and where the majority of visitors to the site performed certain actions.

As soon as customers' personal information is combined with key figures from site tracking for advertising purposes, the owner of the online store is on the verge of illegal activity. Personalized profiles that allow clear conclusions to be drawn about the user behavior of a specific person can only be created in accordance with strict legal regulations (Feldmann 2008). Consumers should pay close attention to who is sending them information about new products – and to how much the sender appears to know about the recipient of the promotional e-mail. In most cases, the question is how such an e-mail has been personalized and what user information forms the basis of it. As a rule, if the provider of an online store wants to e-mail an advertisement to a user based on an order that that person has made, they must have received that person's permission to do so in advance (Feldmann 2008).

One reason for the relative lack of awareness regarding which marketing measures are allowed by data protection laws and which are not, is that it is not easy to get a firm grasp of the information now circulating on the Internet. In the majority of all countries, specific legal requirements are in place, such as Germany's applicable law, the Teleservices Data Protection Act, which makes a basic distinction between *personal* and *non-personal* data (Feldmann 2008). Information that specifically refers to a person (such as name or address) clearly fits the definition of personal data. All other information that makes no reference to a specific user and is collected, saved and evaluated anonymously can be logically inferred to be non-personal.

The stipulation prohibiting data tracking has been relaxed for telephone listings, but it is still in full effect for online data. That means: shipping software and tracking software is allowed to record which e-mail addresses preferred which products on the basis of promotional e-mails that have been sent, and they are permitted to automatically divide those e-mail addresses into relevant shipping groups. However, advertisers are prohibited from extracting specific data from those pools of e-mail addresses and from shipping and tracking information, and from using saved key figures to single out individuals. Online retailers who use their software to find out items on which a specific customer clicked are violating the respective data protection acts in the particular country – unless that customer has already given explicit permission to do so (Feldmann 2008).

There are numerous cases in which the data protection act requires the customer to be informed about specific processes, such as when the customer's data is processed abroad, and sometimes customers must even give explicit permission for certain processes. An example is when personal usage profiles or interest profiles are generated and saved for CRM. If a customer finds personalized messages in his or her e-mail without having first given explicit permission, the senders of those promotional e-mails can face heavy financial penalties (Feldmann 2008). A certain degree of transparency and customer service is also required in the use of cookies. Website owners must include

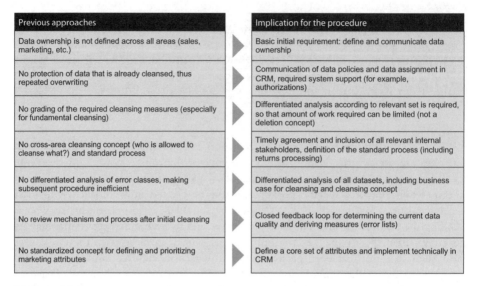

Previous approaches		Implication for the procedure
Data ownership is not defined across all areas (sales, marketing, etc.)	▷	Basic initial requirement: define and communicate data ownership
No protection of data that is already cleansed, thus repeated overwriting	▷	Communication of data policies and data assignment in CRM, required system support (for example, authorizations)
No grading of the required cleansing measures (especially for fundamental cleansing)	▷	Differentiated analysis according to relevant set is required, so that amount of work required can be limited (not a deletion concept)
No cross-area cleansing concept (who is allowed to cleanse what?) and standard process	▷	Timely agreement and inclusion of all relevant internal stakeholders, definition of the standard process (including returns processing)
No differentiated analysis of error classes, making subsequent procedure inefficient	▷	Differentiated analysis of all datasets, including business case for cleansing and cleansing concept
No review mechanism and process after initial cleansing	▷	Closed feedback loop for determining the current data quality and deriving measures (error lists)
No standardized concept for defining and prioritizing marketing attributes	▷	Define a core set of attributes and implement technically in CRM

Figure 12.8   Reasons why data quality falls short and implications for how to proceed.

notices at key places on their site indicating when, how, and why it uses cookies. This regulation, too, is only valid as long as the cookie is not being used to find clear relationships between personal data and pseudonymous usage profiles (Feldmann 2008).

While customer orientation has been a frequent topic of discussion in recent years, most companies have barely touched on the subject of how to systematically gather and utilize customer data as a foundation for all their marketing activities. They do not use the customer data they gather to identify their most important customers (like new customers and key accounts), nor do they aggregate different information sources from different functional areas in the company (like technical support hotlines, the order department, all the way to online behavior). Empirical studies show that all the theoretical and practical discussions about the necessity of systematically managing and utilizing customer data and the procedures that are built upon it, such as data mining, have been treated like mere maculation itself by the vast majority of companies. Data collected *passively* by keeping records of all sales interactions and customer data collected *actively* (using direct questions) are hardly ever used systematically or in an integrated way.

Distribution of essential customer data to different data processing systems and several functional areas has the effect of limiting the "unified view of the customer" postulated for CRM to the customer data in a single area (Forsyth *et al.* 2006). A comprehensive view of the customer that transcends the boundaries between areas in a company is rare (Figure 12.8).

Consumers around the world are familiar with tinplate in the form of beverage cans and packaging for food. Chemical companies and the automotive and construction industries are also consumers of the material, which takes its name from a gleaming white, extremely thin layer of tin that is spread on the plate by electrolysis. **Rasselstein GmbH** manufactured 1.4 million metric tons of tinplate during the 2005–2006 business year. That added up to a revenue of EUR 1.15 billion, making this subsidiary of ThyssenKrupp Steel AG the third largest tinplate producer in Europe. Rasselstein exports over 70% of the tinplate it produces to a sales market that includes approximately 80 countries around the world. Domestic and international customers trust the company for extremely high-quality products. It applies the same high standard of quality to how it manages its customer relationships. As part of a multilevel project in 2006–2007, Rasselstein changed the information technology supporting its customer relationships to a new platform. The main problem was that the applications for sales and service were separate and isolated, which prevented a unified view of customer data.

Other essential focuses of the CRM project were optimizing complaint processing and integrating IT support for sales and service. Rasselstein provides for both, using complaint management that allows all departments and employees involved to access complaint-relevant data and processes at any time. A customized workflow tailored to Rasselstein's needs ensures that information flows smoothly while also controlling and monitoring how all the stations in complaint processing work together. This includes customers, who receive a complaint confirmation that is generated as part of the workflow, giving them a secure feeling from the start that Rasselstein is dealing with their problem. In March 2007 the company moved to level 2 of its CRM optimization initiative. This level focuses on strengthening the sales force and improving sales and service integration to enhance customer service and support and further reduce process costs. Structured visit reporting will replace manual prose, and standardized quotation creation will replace the individualism of Word files (SAP 2007).

Data warehouse systems are the foundation for integrating and using customer data and for subsequent analyses. A *data warehouse* refers to a company-wide information management concept implementing a unified, consistent data basis with central logic (Wieken 1999). The focus is on bringing customer datasets that are distributed across several company areas, applications and systems into a single, unified dataset that can be accessed by the entire company. It aggregates *customer master data* (like addresses) and other sociodemographic characteristics, *promotion data* (like the company's marketing measures), *response data and transaction data* about the effects of those measures, plus any *potential data* and *success data* that is available (Löffler & Scherfke 2000; Link & Hildebrand 1993).

In-house information sources can be supplemented with external information from address publishers, list brokers and market research institutes about buying potential, patterns of behavior and product preferences (known as *microgeographic segmentation*).

These datasets can be used as a basis for prognoses about the status in the customer life cycle or aggregated customer values, for instance. Experience shows that generating addresses and additional qualification criteria over and above the data gathered during normal business processes is usually only worthwhile if the information is very particular or the customer groups are small and easy to understand (Wieken 1999).

> Germany's **Hypo-Vereinsbank (HVB)** has been using a microgeographic marketing approach since the beginning of 2007 to better adapt its marketing and its products, such as its free checking accounts, to certain target groups. It focuses on well-to-do individuals and households. The task was for 630 branches to execute a mailing adapted to the target group. The first selection criterion was distance from the branch, which reduced the target households from everyone in Germany to just under 33 million people. The second step considered demographic and economic criteria. For instance, residential streets were selected that fit the target profile, concentrating on those streets that did not have any HVB customers. This was based on data that was relevant for selecting the target group, e.g. buying power, family structure and neighborhood. Finally, a multi-criteria analysis was used to evaluate the characteristics of the units with respect to the desired profile (Brechtel 2007).

Systematic database management faces two basic challenges here. Firstly, every database *must be updated* when people move, change their names, etc. This can affect 20% or more of the dataset each year. This means that it must be ensured continually that data is current. Secondly, *duplicates* in customer data records, addresses from third parties and additional qualification criteria must all undergo continuous **alignment processes for address cleansing**:

- *Manual alignment processes* involve identifying and updating datasets by manually checking them for changes that need to be made;
- *Automated processes*, on the other hand, use IT to compare and update different datasets (Wieken 1999).

Practical experience shows that using similar entities (*key identifiers*) to compare customer data from different owners without integrated options for assignment creates serious problems for automatic alignment processes. In such a situation, automatic assignment rates can fall to less than 20% of the data record. Data cleansing applications used in *master data management* are subject to certain requirements, such as (Löffler & Scherfke 2000):

- **Flexibility:** The option of specifying tolerance limits for similarity checks that occur during comparison processes (precision level);
- **Phonetic alignment:** Alignment not just by incorrect characters, but also by addresses that sound alike, allowing for custom parameterization by each data field;

Initial		Permanent maintenance and review		
Detailed error analysis	Cleansing concept	Cleansing	Attribute maintenance	Review

• Not yet analyzed error types
• Draw up a business case
• Occurring error combinations
• Absence of most important contacts
• Segmenting acc. to customer classes
• Required technical support
	• Determine data ownership
	• Revise and communicate data policies
	• Communicate CRM authorizations
	• Define relevant set for cleansing and data maintenance (positive list), e.g.
	  • Buying centers
	  • Decision preparers
	  • Influencers
	• Concept for positive/negative lists (invoice recipients, etc.)
	• Deletion criteria and procedure
	• Customer structures (e.g. group structures)
	• Refine initial business case
	• Incentives for data maintenance
		• Draw up error lists
		• Cleanse acc. to cleansing concept:
		  • Prioritization
		  • Relevant set
		  • Data policy
		  • All contacts for each customer
		• Prepare flanking measures:
		  • Customer self-service
		  • Analyze and enter returns
		  • Online portal for simple data maintenance
		  • Improved user interface
		  • "Spring clean"
			• Maintain attributes for all customer interactions
			  • Sales contacts
			  • Customer care
			  • Marketing campaigns/data upload
			  • Active addressing (e.g. "spring clean")
			• Use customer self-service for profiling
				• Generate reports (periodically)
				  • Monitoring
				  • Quantitative syntactic/semantic
				• Checks as part of annual review
				• Automatic deletion, if no customer interaction within time interval
				• Cause/effect analysis for errors that occur

Figure 12.9 Procedural model for cleansing customer data (example).

- *Alignment across several datasets:* Several different datasets are to be aligned against each other with a different priority for each data field (e.g. dataset "A" has priority for addresses, dataset "B" has priority for names, etc.);
- *Fuzzy logic procedure:* Automatically considers different criteria during assignment, depending on degree of match. After an initial check, the system gradually and automatically adds more evaluation criteria to the comparison, allowing it to adjust itself after each run and adapt to the datasets it is currently checking.

Project experience shows that the complexity of this kind of project is initially underestimated. Instead of completing a detailed error analysis and developing a thorough cleansing concept, cleansing measures tend to be more like knee-jerk reactions that end up failing because the processes were insufficient, or cleaned data gets overwritten (Figure 12.9).

Data cleansing and the data warehouse can be used as preliminary steps for a *data mining* processes. Data mining subsumes all processes that search for information and interrelationships in large datasets. The primary purpose of data mining is the *exploratory analysis* of interrelationships about which no hypotheses can be formed in advance (Wieken 1999). For instance, multidimensional customer profiles can be used to determine which customers are most likely to buy, and then customized advertising can be used to address them. Supplementary *collaborative filtering* processes compare multidimensional profiles for different customers and identify similar interests (Runte 2000; Bocionek 1995). In this way, customers can receive recommendations for products that customers with similar interests have already purchased. The same data mining methods can used to forecast when existing customers and new customers will make purchases.

We need to think of database management as an ongoing process, not a one-time process of constructing a customer dataset − a belief often encountered during

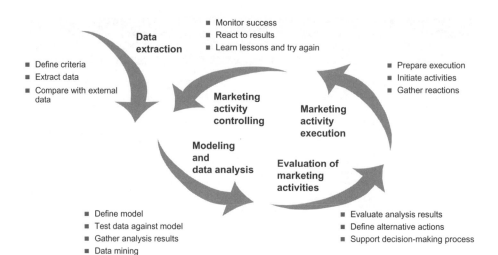

Figure 12.10 Database marketing cycle.

implementation projects. Ongoing changes to existing data and transaction data, adjusting processes that align data, and performing checks of advertising success all require an independent database marketing process. After data is extracted and analyzed, the results of marketing activities need to be permanently stored in the dataset so that customer experiences can be considered in other data analyses and the activities that build on them (Figure 12.10, Strauss & Schoder 2001).

12.3 PLANNING AND IMPLEMENTING MARKETING PLANNING: THE SECRET IS IN THE SYSTEM

12.3.1 CRM system: Requirements and basic structure

Marketing information systems and sales information systems – especially CRM systems – are intended to help decision makers to acquire, systematize, analyze, evaluate and pass on up-to-date, customer-related information. The goal is to safeguard profitable customer relationships for the long term (Uebel *et al.* 2004; Link & Hildebrand 1993). A CRM system should meet certain requirements, such as:

- *User-friendliness:* Current information should be concise, quick and easy to access, there should be different evaluation options and comprehensible displays, and information required periodically should be made available automatically;
- *Integration and coordination capabilities:* Efficient exchange of information between different IT systems, some of which may be department-specific (e.g. financial accounting and merchandising);

Twelve years ago, Munich-based **Homeshopping Europe AG** became Germany's first home shopping channel. Today it is also an Internet retailer. The channel reaches over 39 million households in Germany, Austria and Switzerland by cable and satellite. The company offers 24 one-hour sales programs each day (16 of which are live) which include items like jewelry, clothing, beauty products and consumer electronics. The company has around 1.3 million active customers. They can place orders and ask questions at no cost on the Internet, by phone, teletext, mail and fax (multi-channel system). Around 1,000 new customers are added each day. This means an average of up to 22,000 calls per day reaching a total of 14 call centers with a maximum of 800 agents. On peak days they receive over 60,000 calls.

Teleshopping means meeting the requirements of conventional mail order as well as the challenges of a media enterprise. Live retailing requires immediate processing of customer inquiries and a direct line between the live TV show and the call centers. Viewers will only be able to see how many items have been ordered and how many are still available if inventory levels (merchandising) can be retrieved in real time and updated immediately. A customized IT solution links the HSE24 customer service center with the TV program, and integrates all other internal and external functions (including logistics, accounting and vendors) on a single platform. The online store and call center, both of which are run externally, are also connected. Phone agents receive calls with browser-supported access. Customer data, product data, program data and process data is all stored centrally to improve transparency. Internal and external employees can retrieve information about stocks, order histories and specific items in real time, enabling them to assist customers quickly.

Instructions and subprocesses can be automated using workflows or by adjusting the system interface to the relevant user role. Credits, for example, can be posted so promptly to a customer's account that they will be available for the customer to use to buy another item while he or she is still on the phone. Because calls are answered automatically, customers do not even need to wait during peak times; they can speak to an agent immediately (SAP 2007).

- *Cost effectiveness:* This includes the total time and effort needed to implement and use an IT system;
- *Security:* Refers to data availability, protection from unauthorized access, different security levels for different people (authorization concept), and ensuring bindingness, e.g. with digital signatures for agreements (Eckert 2001; Grant 1998; Müller & Reichenbach 2001);
- *Acceptance among system users:* Employees may be afraid of computer-aided control (e.g. performance monitoring). Resistance comes from the fear of losing

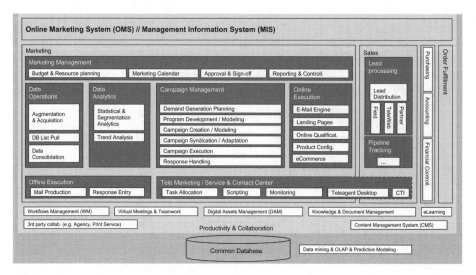

Figure 12.11 Example of a CRM system with sophisticated components for marketing and sales.

power due to the transparent, reproducible manner in which specialized knowledge is collected and saved (customer knowledge and process knowledge). This trivializes expertise that took years to acquire and makes employees more replicable, especially in their own eyes (Hummel 1996). However, like customer data maintenance, the main obstacles to systematic system maintenance are mundane, like a lack of discipline.

There are unlimited design options for how CRM systems can be used, ranging from simple customer databases to sophisticated systems that integrate a variety of functions (Figure 12.11). The functions outlined here are textbook examples and comprise the following:

- Planning components for budgets and resources, reporting (marketing management);
- Components for campaign execution, such as product development and adaptation as part of campaign management;
- The interface to sales, e.g. for transferring prequalified contacts and monitoring the sales pipeline;
- Integration of all data in a data warehouse, plus support functions for data analysis (data operations and data analytics);
- Direct support for online and offline execution, e.g. with e-mail engines or by tracking telemarketing tasks;
- Tools that support cooperation, such as workflows and content management systems (Rothfuss & Ried 2001; Koop *et al.* 2001).

Aviall, a Dallas-based provider of aftermarket parts for airplanes, began to introduce a CRM system. Their ambitious plan was to become the leading provider of supply-chain management services for the aerospace industry. The business idea: if the company could become the preferred business partner of leading manufacturers and the owners of commercial and military fleets, Aviall could secure customer demand and expand its range of coverage world wide, which would boost sales and widen profit margins (Ledingham & Rigby 2005).

Several things prevented this vision from becoming a reality. Insufficient information and inconvenient work processes slowed down company sales and services. Problems with an existing IT system increased the workload of off-site employees and kept some sales associates at their branches, helping their managers to enter order information instead of acquiring new orders by phone. In addition, the company failed to give its off-site employees adequate training in how to organize their sales regions and manage their time. The result

- Calls were forwarded inefficiently and answered almost randomly;
- Customer inquiries were forwarded to far-away call centers that did not have any current information about orders, products or prices;
- This poor customer service opened important customers up to competitors' offers;
- The company could not continue to charge the premium prices it normally charged for products that were delivered on time.

There was therefore a real need for better-trained sales personnel who would show more initiative. The company did not try to implement a comprehensive CRM program for all its departments. It took a more targeted approach. Their first step was to only introduce the applications required by sales personnel, order creation and the call center. The goal was to seamlessly move customer data from off-site sales representatives to the sales team in the office, and then to move the customer data to customer service personnel in the company's 36 regional call centers. The relatively limited scope of the new system allowed the sales personnel to quickly familiarize themselves with the programs without feeling overwhelmed. This quickly brought success, which helped to win over more managers and employees and give the project more momentum (Ledingham & Rigby 2005).

Before the CRM system was introduced, sales associates could only process customer information with an antiquated database. The system's lack of flexibility made it impossible for employees in sales and service to access even basic information about previous orders and the creditworthiness of customers. The old system did not reveal credit problems until the person creating the order tried to send it. They had to call the credit department and either wait on the line for a long time or wait for a call back. Being unable to name the price immediately and asking the customer to wait cost them the order 90% of the time. Today, the new CRM system shows the customer's creditworthiness as soon as the salesperson begins to enter the order. The system helps employees to better organize their work and motivates them to call more customers because they know they can immediately make concrete offers using customized catalogs of products and services (known as "real-time offer management"). Only four months after the CRM system was introduced, their number of daily sales calls had tripled and their customer base had grown by 33%. The productivity of the entire sales and service area had jumped dramatically. Aviall took back market share and won major contracts for new product lines. The number of orders processed each day rose from 1,000 to 25,000 while the error rate dropped – with no additional personnel (Ledingham & Rigby 2005, reproduced by permission of Harvard Business Manager).

Further case studies, e.g. at **Deutsche Bank** Private & Business Clients, demonstrate that with "real-time offer management" positive reactions can rise with up to 60% of customers in the call center interaction or 10% in an online banking scenario.

We can distinguish three different approaches for the structure of a CRM system. The *collaborative* CRM approach focuses on integrating and aligning various external contacts and interactions that the company has with customers, demanders and partners. These interactions can occur over different functional areas (marketing, sales, service and support) and communication channels (online, telemarketing, personal contact while visiting customers). In-house support for these external customer interaction processes is comprised in *operational* CRM. It can include the syndication of centrally created campaign elements and process control for complaints. Finally, *analytic* CRM refers to the detailed analyses that are performed on the basis of a data warehouse as part of ad-hoc analyses or automated analyses (Hippner & Wilde 2001).

Until now, special marketing applications were known for having or being:

- *Slow and inconvenient:* Decision making processes, review processes and release processes that took place within an operation or across several operations, for example, were drawn-out, laborious and complicated. Deep corporate hierarchies, for example, meant that many processes had to go through instance paths that wasted time (e.g. pricing processes or even mailings that had to be approved by several levels in the hierarchy);

- *Plagued with missing information and poor knowledge management:* Even basic data about the market (market volume, market share), customers (sales volume and structure, preferences, product-related and item-related revenue) and competitors is frequently not available (or no longer current). Internal information about completed activities (e.g. visits to customers, advertising, sales promotion) and related results and insights (e.g. new customer acquisitions, successful advertising, contribution margins) is spotty. Even if the required information is present in the company, the people involved in the marketing processes do not have any or only partial access to it. A lack of discipline in how data is maintained (e.g. for customer visits) goes hand in hand with high staff turnover rates, ensuring that knowledge gained from personal experience keeps getting lost;

- *No integration of marketing information systems:* IT systems that are used at many different levels are often redundant in design and poorly integrated. This leads to expensive (manual) interfaces. Some of these systems have enormous (automation) potential that is not being realized completely;

- *Poor management of multimedia assets (words, images, charts, audio and video components):* New means of communication are constantly being created, particularly when external agencies are involved (ads, brochures, websites, billboards, newsletters, etc.). Companies invest in them but rarely use them sufficiently. Employees, external service providers and agencies have them on their computers, and that is where they remain. This leads to enormous search costs and the ongoing creation of new materials instead of using the ones already available (cf. Strauss 1995a).

A new generation of software applications – *marketing resource management* MRM – attempts to address those weaknesses. MRM stands for an integrated approach in marketing for using marketing resources as effectively and efficiently as possible (this includes people, IT applications, multimedia assets, budgets and data, plus vendors and agencies) (Kleiner 2004). Planning, budgeting and controlling, for instance, use MRM applications during quantitative and qualitative planning and budgeting for marketing tasks and link them to different hierarchy levels. *Multimedia asset management* (MAM) functions and *digital asset management* (DAM) functions support the central, media-neutral storage, management and output of multimedia components (words, images, charts, audio and video components, as well as finished means of communication such as ads, brochures, mailings, etc.). Employees can use the Internet to access those functions, change content (like changing the text of a mailing themselves without having to go back to an agency copywriter again and again), and convert formats in real time. They can also exchange ideas and concrete drafts with internal and external partners. Cooperating with external agencies normally involves a great deal of coordination, numerous manual interfaces and integration gaps, but this can speed that up considerably. *Marketing portals* for individual companies support the cooperative effort and provide a place to perform all marketing tasks in an integrated manner (Kleiner 2004). Integrated process support automatically informs all employees involved when, for example, a project charter is changed or adjusted, when the project status changes, or when a creative draft arrives from an agency. This has a positive effect when used in combination with predefined sequences of subtasks, clearly assigned responsibilities, and templates that can be accessed during various marketing processes (briefing templates, guidelines, etc.). In fact, using standardized templates is usually enough to ensure that knowledge can be saved and copied. Project examples show that the use of these types of MRM applications can reduce (Kleiner 2004):

- Campaign creation by more than 70%;
- The time needed to create means of communication by more than 60%;

- Agency costs by more than 25%;
- Costs through the reuse of existing templates by more than 50%;
- Total advertising costs by 5 to 10% thanks to consolidation;
- Costs for guideline creation and distribution by more than 50% per brand.

12.3.2   The need to align IT and marketing strategies

Not having a comprehensive, coherent IT strategy becomes one of the biggest obstacles for the entire company in general and marketing in particular. A lack of IT concepts manifests itself as recurring problems when integrating different software components, security concerns, a highly complex selection of software, and inadequate knowledge of technical platforms. Strategies are often reduced to "IT plans" that focus on describing the applications, architectures and development standards being used for business activities and processes. The enterprise strategy and the IT strategy are often not developed in harmony with one another, so applications often cannot meet future business needs. Even in the rare cases when there is a strategy concept, the boundary blurs between the **IT strategy** as the basic foundation and purpose for using IT on the one hand, and operational IT **implementation planning** on the other. The concepts usually mix different levels of abstraction, infrastructure, applications, standards and products from specific providers. Consequently, there is no logical subdivision of architectures into different levels like infrastructure (network services, directory services, security services, file services), application support (workflow managers, database services, web servers) and specific applications (Koushik & Straeten 2001).

Even though people have known since the 1980s that a variety of IT concepts can have a lasting impact on competitive strategy and enterprise strategy, *technical and financial strategy concepts* have rarely been aligned or merged (Parsons 1983; Davenport & Short 1990). IT is usually seen as a tool for fulfilling strategic focuses that have already been set. Not until the strategic planning process is complete, do people begin to evaluate the ways that IT can help. The business strategy and the IT strategy are seldom integrated early on and they are almost never used to inspire one another (Meador 1999).

One reason why corporate strategies do not include enough IT is that strategic planners have insufficient *knowledge* of the broad range of technical design options (e.g. in service-oriented IT architectures). Another is that an insufficient *degree of operationalization* prevents an abstract, long-term company and marketing strategy from aligning with specific technologies and applications. Similarly, because those involved are only focusing on one aspect, they fail to directly identify *IT best practices* during competitive analysis and external benchmarking (including benchmarking with those outside the industry). The term "IT" is often understood to mean selecting *specific applications* from different manufacturers. It is more appropriate to see IT as the further strategic development of the entire IT infrastructure (Koushik & Straeten 2001). Developing an IT architecture also tends to be seen as a separate question for later, one that is answered "quasi automatically" after certain applications have been selected from a manufacturer.

The need to meet certain *service goals* (like real time read access and availability) and the *total cost of ownership* are often based more on the needs of certain users than on a profound IT strategy or an analytical evaluation of the different technical design options. A long-term migration concept to a meta-architecture – consistent with the company strategy and its marketing strategy – is often missing completely. IT executives rarely have a differentiated evaluation grid that they can use to assess the large number of new applications and technologies before they use them (Daum & Scheller 2000). Individual decisions about applications and new technologies are usually made in isolation from other decisions, so they cannot build on a long-term vision for developing the company's entire IT infrastructure. IT is used in more of a reactive fashion, reacting to developments in the company or in technology, rather than being actively designed in line with the company strategy (Strauss & Schoder 2001).

The reason for the *lack of alignment* between IT and the enterprise and marketing strategy is that IT executives often only present their arguments from a technical point of view. It is difficult for them to understand the business context in which the applications will be used, so they have little interest for it (McFarlan & McKenney 1983; Schein 1994). Various *points of conflict* arise between IT and operational departments, as evidenced by a large number of projects (Fleisch 2001; Davenport 1993; Weltz 1993; Kütz 2000; Szyperski 1980; Hummel 1996):

- The *implementation process* usually lasts longer than originally projected;
- The operational departments want a *pragmatic*, manageable solution whereas the IT executives want a *technically unique solution*;
- The main reason for delays and difficulties during implementation projects is not technical problems. It is the sluggish process of *making decisions and finding a consensus* which involves all departments and relevant decision makers;
- *Conflicts* appear unexpectedly during the planning and decision-making process, mediators and change agents are not available to balance the different interests of the departments;
- Controversies mainly emerge at the level of technical design, though the real motive lies is questions of how influence is distributed, *power*, and a lack of shared expertise and understanding (Grudin 1988; Lou & Scamell 1996).

During a project for a **financial services corporation**, the choice of a specific application was by no means based on an IT strategy, but on the desire to use certain functions in specific applications to mark out framework conditions for rival IT departments. In another example involving an **insurance company**, major differences began to arise during alignment of the user department strategy and the IT department. Without any particular strategy in mind, line-of-business executives defined a variety of requirements (wish list) for the IT area (e.g. Internet-based support for representatives, product configurators, etc.), but the IT department did not consider itself capable of estimating and judging those wishes because there was no IT strategy. The discussion of what functions were appealing was open and not moderated, with the direct result being a (political) obligation for the IT area to meet all of the haphazardly specific (and unspecific) demands. The fears of the

> IT department with regard to the unrealistic expectations of the user departments ultimately resulted in an end to alignment negotiations and a shift of orientation to implementing only what was technically feasible. As a result, the acceptance rate among users was less than 30% after the system was implemented.

12.3.3   Developing an IT strategy

Successful enterprises are characterized by the view that modern IT is an integral part of business models and business potential. They focus on using IT in a variety of ways in every value-adding process; this is only possible when the enterprise and marketing strategy are *consistent* with the IT strategy (Koushik & Straeten 2001; Fleisch 2001). IT planning needs to translate the key points of an IT strategy into concrete measures that support the company strategy (Davenport 1993). The interaction between the IT strategy and the company strategy inspires independent plans, processes and organizational structures for each company area. Ideally, this would provide consistency not only between the IT strategy and the business strategy, but also within the IT strategy and IT structure and within the business strategy and business structure (Figure 12.12 – Markus & Robey 1988; Lederer *et al.* 1997). The focus here should not be on developing a qualitatively perfect IT strategy, but rather on developing an IT strategy that is perfectly aligned with the needs of the enterprise with regard to processes, organization and competencies. A practical approach for aligning the two areas should normally be oriented around concrete questions about key issues such as required competencies and the development concept.

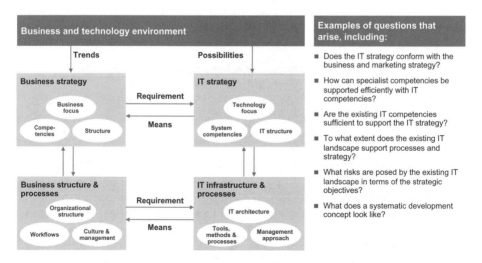

Figure 12.12   IT strategy model from Henderson & Venkatraman (1994).

Key questions that emerge from the interplay of the business and marketing strategy and the IT strategy concern (Henderson & Venkatraman 1994; Crowston & Malone 1994; Davenport 1993; Porter & Millar 1985; Rockart & Scott Morton 1984):

- **The focus of IT use:** Basic principles regarding how IT is used and how to prioritize systems and implementation projects;
- **Required competencies:** The technical side and the business side of the IT management structure, cultural guidelines, required ("TO-BE") competencies, and training required for new technologies and methods ("re-skilling");
- **The structures:** Deciding on a decision-making process for IT and who will be responsible for support (roles, responsibilities, KPIs for checks).

The answers to those questions can then be used to determine aggregated plans for developing IT in the medium to long term. Tasks and questions in the IT infrastructure need to be addressed and answered in line with the business structure, including (Mougayar 1998):

- Evaluating different organizational *structural options* (like outsourcing, simple hosting or using Software-as-a-Service concepts);
- Deciding on *development tools* and methods;
- Determining the *competencies* and personnel that will be required, including training activities;
- Defining *KPIs* for evaluating IT and for the associated check process;
- Redesigning how *IT is organized* (where applicable);
- Implementing expert *IT project management*;
- Designing the (TO-BE) *IT architecture* (data, applications, hardware).

Such an **evaluation** of IT-related tasks and functions critical to the company should consider both of the following criteria (Meador 1999):

- Current (perceived) system *performance* (e.g. availability and response time);
- Strategic significance for the future.

The tasks and functions that are most critical for the company are those that are rated as having "poor performance" and "high strategic importance". Once a combined evaluation of performance and strategic importance has been made for task areas and measures, you can address the subject of *IT effectiveness*. Areas with poor performance and high strategic importance suggest a high ROI for all the measures employed there, while areas with high performance and low strategic importance suggest a low ROI and the possibility of wasted resources (Meador 1999; Kempis & Ringbeck 1998). Differentiating this process for other company areas, such as marketing, allows for a differentiated evaluation of IT effectiveness and the creation of measures that are particular to the specific business area.

The interplay between the IT strategy and the business strategy can almost always be derived from and represented by comparing the "IT best practices" for the relevant industry segment or by using an independent IT assessment (Österle 1995). You need to keep in mind that stable, long-term IT strategy planning cannot be achieved haphazardly, since technology is developing so rapidly. Nevertheless, a *technology evaluation* needs to do more than include technologies that are currently available, it also needs to anticipate future technological developments (at least in rudimentary form).

The *IT planning* stage renders in greater detail the IT infrastructure needed to reach the goals stated at the start. A technology and data platform needs to be defined here that conforms to the business structure (understood as organizational structure, culture and processes). The architecture is subject to requirements such as (Fleisch 2001; Koushik & Straeten 2001):

- *Scalability:* A satisfactory level of performance even when user numbers grow and transaction volumes increase;
- *Flexibility:* The option of integrating new products and technologies;
- *Availability:* Keeping specific service goals ("service level agreements");
- *Enhanceability:* Flexibly expanding to support new business functions and business models.

Project examples show that while promises are often made to maintain these standards, those promises are rarely kept. In an implementation example from a printing and publishing house, things came to a climax when, shortly before the system went live, the external project coordinator decided to finally take a look at the user numbers in the business plan.

The development environment focuses on quickly implementing new applications and modifying existing applications, and qualifying IT employees. The development of IT planning is founded on the *IT assessment* of existing applications, data structures and basic technologies. The evaluation also considers IT organization and the processes to be supported (Österle 1995). This analytic foundation allows you to define the strategic IT infrastructure (TO-BE). The infrastructure contains platforms for applications and technology as well as the competencies and permanent control mechanisms required for those platforms.

When evaluating *IT effectiveness*, the focus should be on approaches that will change how IT is organized. This can include projects that improve the effectiveness of application development and system management, creating IT subplans for downstream company areas, and systematically aligning consistency in the development of the company or organization and the IT infrastructure.

PART IV

OUTLOOK

CHAPTER 13

MARKETING PLANNING 2.0

*I*t is expected that the need for marketing planning that is more content-driven, customer and market-oriented, and as a result, actually used, will most likely increase in the future. The reason:

- The increasing pressure to realize maximum results for each marketing dollar invested with a decreasing marketing budget and significantly fewer marketing employees;
- The need to differentiate the company on the market qualitatively – not only by simply increasing the number of implemented measures, but also by striving to leave qualitative "footprints" with the consumer. Various brands such as *Frosta* (purity requirements of the highest quality standards), *Bionade* (cult brand in the organic trend with the contemporary promise of fine flavor and indulgence) or *Dove* ("True Beauty" campaign speaks from the heart to consumers) show that the trend (in terms of content) is moving toward benefit- and content-oriented communication (Ziems 2008);
- Changing market conditions make it almost impossible to slavishly hold to a plan once it has been established; instead adaptation on a rolling basis is required;
- Marketing executives' desire to escape the paradox of the marketing function, and to gradually and systematically position the function higher in the company;
- A growing awareness that designing campaigns and measures without target group-specific content becomes subject to arbitrariness, regardless of how creative they may be;
- The need to interweave a much greater number of communication instruments and tactics (in the often cited "360 communication") efficiently, with regard to content, in both creation and execution.

Social communities will serve as "filters of trust" for consumers "and will be forced to make the often discussed integrated campaign mantra a reality. Studies have shown that even for stand-alone classical advertisement campaigns the respective user numbers and hits – e.g. on Google – increase significantly, even without any online campaign being in place or planned. In future all campaigns and marketing activities will be digital, whether planned by the originating companies or not. As the collaborative, actively content-producing consumer (the "prosumer", according to Tapscott & Ticoll 2003) proliferate, companies have increasingly tough choices about how to interact with them (Tapscott & Williams 2006). While previous generations spent up to 24 hours in front of the television each week, the upcoming, net-affiliated generation will grow up interacting, peering and collaborating with each other. The decline of classical media consumption is over-compensated by the use of bi-directional, collaborative interaction channels. The youth of today is constituted by active creators of media content and are hungry for interaction. While the consumption of classical media declines and has been overtaken by web-based communication and collaboration, the time spent online is already treble the time spent on classical media. In parallel, the cost per lead declines from about USD 10 in direct mailings to only USD 0.29 in search engine marketing. The paradigm shift in media consumption has to be accompanied by proper and systematical marketing plans and activities.

For this purpose, teamwork (inside and outside of marketing, e.g. with sales) and self-coordination, as the fundamental coordination mechanism for deciding and managing all pending tasks at the lowest possible hierarchical levels, will take on a significantly greater role. Although it is unlikely that hierarchies will disappear in the foreseeable future, a new form of organization is emerging that rivals the hierarchical forms by breaking up demarcated fiefdoms.

Marketing director Jim Stengel of Procter & Gamble concluded that the upcoming change in marketing will be less of a technological one, but instead much more of an "intellectual feat". According to Jim Stengel, the future belongs

> not to media models and metric marketing, but instead to the "giving mentality", commitment to the 2-way relationship with the customer. Today, more than ever, the consumer wants to know who is committed to the brand with heart, soul and integrity.

and is actually able to address the customer in a target group-specific way, and appreciate him or her as a genuine dialog partner (Stippel, 2007, reproduced by permission of *Absatzwirtschaft*). Web 2.0, with its "user-generated content", will further reinforce this trend of direct customer interaction – accompanied by new and extensive levels of freedom in favor of a more broadly and better informed customer. In the marketing of the future, brand and customer will have to share the focus equally – at eye level, so to speak. The customer requires a seamless customer experience in the Amazon. com style, connecting various communication channels and media with each other. While Mass Customization has already been discussed for some time, it is now coming into its own utilizing the long-tail effect. This implies the need for far more targeted activities and marketing campaigns per year per target group, not only yielding higher response rates but also requiring more efficient processes on managing the multitude of different campaigns, processes and workflows in parallel. Companies that know how to realize content-oriented marketing planning related to both factors have the opportunity to create intense relationships between brand and customer, and thereby considerably increase the company value. This has stringent marketing planning as its most important prerequisite.

APPENDIX: WORKSHEETS FOR MARKETING PLANNING

A.1 MARKETING PROGRAM: DETAILS (PROGRAM BOOK)

Program Book

[Name]
[Author]
[Version]
[Date]

A.1.1 Program book: objective and notes

A.1.1 Program book: objective and notes

The aim of this program book is to provide all of the necessary information, basic principles, and general conditions that are relevant for the development of a program. The program book is the basis for the development of programs/campaigns with campaign architecture and tactical planning. The planning of selected individual measures (campaign tactics) is not part of this document. The program book can also be used as briefing material for an agency involved in the development of a program or campaign.

The most important information and implications for the program/campaign are presented in the individual sections. If needed, additional sections can be added. Should further data be required, it can be added to the appendix in the form of charts or tables.

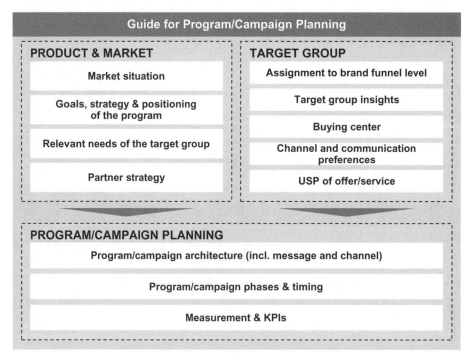

I Program overview

Note: This section is intended to provide a brief overview of the program (one-half page) and succinctly present the motivating reasons and program goals. It should summarize the current market situation and options for the company, and explain how the company can best use these options. The most important question to be answered in this section is: What is the program, and why is it important for the company seeking to advertise its products?

Program overview	
Program strategy and positioning *Define here whether "profit drivers", "growth drivers", "strategic focus topics/segments", "difficult markets" are concerned.*	▶
Program goals *For example, perception change, lead generation, customer retention, etc.*	▶
Key customer needs	▶
Countries	▶
Customer/Market segmentation	▶
Customer segment *Which segment is at the focus (installed base customers/new customers, etc.)?*	▶
Target groups involved (e.g. typologies, roles) / customer types	▶
Competitor(s)	▶
Partner(s)	▶
Influencer(s)	▶

II Market, solution portfolio and program goals

A. Starting situation on the market

Note: Description of challenges, motivating reasons, and program goals.
    Strategic classification and positioning of the program and presentation of the market and competition situations (growth drivers, strategic focus topics/segments, profit drivers, difficult markets). What is the specific market situation that we are entering with our program? Why should the program be carried out just now? What are the challenges and what are the opportunities? (market volume and potential, market trends, market development, product/topic overview ...).

B. Market segment

Note: For which market segment is this program relevant?

Which target groups and segments are the focus? And which sub-target groups and segments must be distinguished, but can be included within the scope of the program?

    Which segment does the program/campaign target?

    Where is the focus placed – on installed base customers or new customers?

    In which countries will the program be carried out? Are there any country-specific particularities?

C. Program strategy and positioning

Note: What is the program strategy to reach the goal?

D.   *Program goals*

Note: Which goals is the program to achieve? (perception change, lead generation, customer retention, distribution channel support/sales support).

E.   *Key customer needs and solution portfolio*

Note: Brief description of relevant customer needs with the corresponding company services/products targeted by the program. Any required additional information on the product, product strategy and positioning can be included here, or a reference can be made to additional documents.
As some content of this section may be generic or comprehensive, it is recommended to store it centrally.

Challenge	Implementation area	Service offering	Customer value	Target group
What is the problem ...	... that the company can solve ...	... using which features ...	... what is the result?	... and for which target groups (e.g. typologies, roles)?
▶	▶	▶	▶	▶
▶	▶	▶	▶	▶

F.   *Partner strategy*

Note: Fill in this section if the partner strategy is relevant for the program. Which sales channel facilitates optimal program results? Which types of partners are especially suited to reaching the program goals? What are some possible types of partners? Description of partners' characteristics: specialization, specialist knowledge, core competencies, offerings, references? Which joint marketing activities could be performed? Which partner levels (global, regional, local) are relevant here, and who is the contact person (if known)?

Partner marketing information overview	
Partner name	▶
Partner type	▶
Market expertise	▶
Relevant offerings	▶
References	▶
Recommended tactics	▶

III   Message and target group

A.   *Key message*

Note: Which central message should be conveyed in this program?

B.   *Brand funnel levels and marketing goals*

Note: At which brand funnel level is the target group located (with respect to the brand or product)? What do we want to achieve with our program? Which marketing goal are we pursuing? Which gaps do we want to fill (e.g. acquisition gap: The solution is known, but is not being purchased. Retention gap: customer churn/attrition is too high ...)

Brand funnel level	Marketing goal	KPIs
At which brand funnel level is the target group generally located?	Which marketing goal are we pursuing? Change perception, lead generation, customer retention, sales support	Operationalization of the goal
	►	►
	►	►
	►	►

C. Target group insights and message

Note: For considering target groups (e.g. typologies, roles), the arguments and message for the program should be entered here. Important: Always select the information that is relevant for the service portfolio. Try to provide a complete picture for all points, but state only the essentials.

Target groups (e.g. typologies, roles)	Target groups – insights	Relationship of target group to service portfolio or competition	Arguments/ USP/Value proposition/ Message
Who is the target group? To whom are we speaking?	How does the target group think, feel, and act? Brief description: self-image, core tasks, use of services, drivers, pain points, etc. →Goal: comprehensive, yet clear picture of the target group	What does the target group think and feel with regard to the company's service portfolio? Why has the target group not yet used the product/service? What does the target group think and feel with regard to the main competitors?	How can our services help to solve the pain points? How can they help the target group with their core tasks and challenges? Which argument or product feature particularly distinguishes it from the competition?

D. Buying center (in the B2B area)

Note: Describe the typical decision to buy process (buying center) and the associated consequences for the program. What type of buying center is involved?

The sought solution depicts a clearly defined and narrower customer need. How does the decision to buy process proceed (describe basic process and particularities)? Which functions do the participating roles/players have in the decision to buy process?

Based on this insight on the buying process: what should you keep in mind for communication? What must be considered in the campaign architecture in terms of key parameters?

Optional: Are there particularities? Are there external factors which influence the purchase decision/ decision to buy process?

Target groups	Functions in the buying center (B2B)	Information needs and arguments
Which roles are involved in and relevant to the buying center process?	Which function (initiator, gatekeeper, decider, etc.) do the individual roles primarily perform? Does this function change during the course of the decision process?	What needs do the target groups/roles have in terms of their function? Which contents/arguments/ measures must be offered in each case?
	▶	▶
	▶	▶
	▶	▶
	▶	▶

E. Communication and channel preferences

Note: Use this section to form the basis of the campaign architecture and to answer the following questions: WHAT (message) do I say to WHOM (target group) WHERE (in which channel) at which brand funnel level?

Target groups	Communication behavior	Importance of channels with regard to product purchase
Who is the target group? To whom are we speaking?	What information is there on the communication behavior: – Topics – Language – Content preference – Channel selection criteria – Other?	In the product search, which channels have a high significance for the target group? For which brand funnel level does this apply? If relevant: Is the use of channels possible without being asked, or only on request of the target group? (push or pull)
	▶	▶
	▶	▶
	▶	▶
	▶	▶

IV Additional program details

A. Available information material

Note: What information material is available for use within the context of the program?

B. Offers

Note: Are there specific offers for this program? List the offers here. Examples: discounts, etc.

C. References

Note: Are there references/testimonials relevant for this program? List them here.

D. Program history

Note: Which campaigns were communicated in connection with this planned program to the target group in the past? Is information material already available to the target group, and if so, what?

What message has been communicated so far?

E. Dataset and data selections

Note: How big is the target group? How many addresses exist for each segment, target group, etc.?

Check the dataset in advance and specify exact selection criteria, if possible.

F. Risks

Note: What are the risks of the program? What are the risks involved with the marketing mix guidance? What are open issues?

G. Specifications and restrictions

Note: Which specifications/restrictions have to be observed? For example: technological restrictions, guidelines, research results, legal restrictions, planned events, etc.

H. Timing

Note: Which time specifications have to be observed? Is there key data that has to be taken into account in program planning?

I. Budget

Note: What is the budget for the program?

V Appendix

Note: If necessary, additional information that is relevant for the program can be included in the appendix.

A.2 AGENCY BRIEFING DOCUMENT (DIRECT MARKETING EXAMPLE)

Agency briefing document for direct marketing

[Name]
[Author]
[Version]
[Date]

A.2.1 Objective and notes

A.2.1   Objective and notes

The aim of this briefing document is to provide all of the necessary information, basic principles, and general conditions that are relevant for the development and implementation of a tactic. The tactic to be developed is part of an overall program, which was described in detail in the program book. This program book forms the foundation for the development of the program/campaign with the corresponding architecture and the creative key concept.

The most important information and implications for the individual measure are presented in the individual sections. If needed, additional sections can be added. Should further data be required, it can be added to the appendix in the form of charts or tables.

I   Task definition

Note: Briefly describe the task to the agency in this section.

II   Contact persons

Note: List the contact persons responsible (including contact data) from planning, campaign management, and agency.

Contact persons (incl. contact data)	
Planning	▶
Campaign management/execution	▶
Agency	▶

III   Integration into overall program

Note: The following section is to provide the general context of the individual measure. Provide a brief overview of the program (one-half page) and succinctly outline the motivating reasons and program goals. The most important question that should be answered by this section is: What is the program, and why is it important for the company? This section represents a rough management summary from the corresponding program book.

Program overview	
Program strategy and positioning *Define here whether "profit drivers", "growth drivers", "strategic focus topics/segments", "difficult markets" are concerned.*	▶
Program goals *For example, perception change, lead generation, customer retention, etc.*	▶
Key customer needs	▶
Countries	▶
Products & services	▶
Customer segment *Which segment is at the focus*	▶
Target groups involved	▶
Competitor(s)	▶
Partner(s)	▶
Influencer(s)	▶

IV Campaign architecture

Note: Use the following section to briefly introduce the campaign architecture that has been decided to show how the individual measure is embedded in the overall context of a program.

V Creative key concept

Note: Briefly introduce the creative key concept of the overall program (in so far as it has been developed and decided).

VI Task details

A. Goals

Note: Which goals is the measure to achieve? (perception change, lead generation, customer retention, distribution channel support/sales support).

At which brand funnel level is the target group located?

B. Target sizes/Tactic KPIs

Note: What are the specific KPIs of the described individual measure?

VII Message and target group

A. Key message for this tactic

Note: What key message/statement should be conveyed with this tactic? Specify the key message of the overall program for the described tactic in greater detail here.

B.   Target group insights and message

Note: For considering target groups, the arguments and message for the tactic should be entered here. Important: Only select the target groups from the program book which are relevant for this specific tactic. Specify the information on the target group that was provided in the program book in greater detail with regard to the selected tactic here.

Target groups	Specific needs and pain points	Arguments/ USP/Value proposition/ Message	Call to action	Offer/ Reference
Which particular target group do we want to address with the specific tactic?	What additional, more detailed information is available on the target group that is relevant for the specific tactic? Are there further specifics? How should the address be? In what tone? →Goal: Comprehensive, yet clear picture of the target group in terms of the specific tactic.	How can our product/services help solve the needs? How can it help the target group with its core tasks and challenges/ wishes or satisfy its needs? Which argument or product feature particularly distinguishes it from the competition?	What is the target group to believe? What is it to do?	Which specific offers can we present to our target group?

VIII   Additional details

A.   Timing

Note: Which time specifications have to be observed? Are there key points in time (milestones) that must be taken into account for planning?

B.   Budget

Note: What is the budget for the tactic?

C.   Specifications and restrictions

Note: Which specifications/restrictions have to be observed? For example: technological restrictions, research results, legal restrictions, planned events, etc.

D. Risks

Note: What risks might arise during development and implementation of the tactic? What are open issues? How can these risks be dealt with? What are the alternatives?

E. Available information material/content

Note: What information material is available for use within the context of the measure to be developed?

F. Offers (description)

Note: Are there specific offers for this tactic? Describe the offers available in more detail here.
For example: discounts, test versions, etc.

G. Dataset and data selections (update)

Note: Update the information from the program book here. How big is the target group? How many addresses exist for each segment/sub-segment, etc.? Check the dataset in advance and specify exact selection criteria, if possible.

IX Specific details for online/offline dialog marketing measures

Note: If necessary, additional information that is relevant for the tactic can be included in the appendix. It is possible that not all information is known when the briefing is created and can only be added to the document successively.

A. Contact strategy

Note: Describe how the contact strategy is to be set up here. For example: in what order do online and offline tactics build on each other, what is the drive to Web mechanism, where (online or offline) does lead generation occur, and what happens after lead generation (e.g. online/offline fulfillment)?

B. Reinforcer

Note: Briefly specify whether a reinforcer is to be used (e.g. competition, prize draws, early bird, etc.). If so, give a description of the reinforcer and the incentives used. For competitions/prize draws: describe the rules and responsibilities for the drawing process and prize settlement.

C. Components – Offline

Note: List which components are to be processed or used in mailings, e.g. letter, application, fax, envelope. Also enter specifications (format, scope, colors, material) as far as is known.

D. Components – Online

Note: List which components are to be processed or used online, e.g. direct response banner, e-mailing, campaign page (simple) or microsite (complex), home page integration, contact form (with or without database connection), etc. In addition, please enter the specifications (use of Flash or GIF in banners and microsite, HTML/text e-mailing, hosting location, and back-end functions such as database availability) here, if known.

E. Versions

Note: Describe in which versions the offline/online components are to be created, and how they are different, here.

F. Data preparation

Note: Describe the preparation steps that the data still has to undergo, e.g. internal duplicate check, contact person exists yes/no, valid e-mail addresses, …

G. Ad code

Note: Describe the ad code that is to be used for response tracking here.

H. Graphical material

Note: Describe what graphical material is available or what requirements have been placed on the images/graphics to be used here.

I. Response channels

Note: Describe which response channels are at the customers' disposal, including details such as fax numbers, promotion number, URL of the campaign page, response options on the campaign page, competition/prize draw response, etc. Which interfaces are addressed? How do the processes work? Who else has to be informed?

J. Sender

Note: Enter the exact name and address of the sender here.

K. Signatures

Note: Specify the person who is to sign the document/letter here.

- ☐ Scanned: yes/no
- ☐ Data available: yes/no
- ☐ In person: yes/no
- ☐ Signer:
- ☐ Signer's title/position (if this is to be specified):

L. Text requirements★

Note: For text requirements, list additional information on the topics/contents of the tactic and on the communication focus.

Text requirements*	
Which texts are to be created in total? *(online/offline texts, forewords, etc.)*	▶
Which topics/highlights/contents should be pointed out separately?	▶
What tone should be used to address the target audience? *(Very sophisticated, elevated style, factual, sober style, promotional style, academic style, etc.)*	▶
Special focus for the cover letter	▶
Special focus for the foreword *(blurb/jacket text)*	▶
Special focus for e-mailing	▶
Final deadline for completion of text	▶
Copywriter's contact data *(telephone, cell phone, e-mail)*	▶

*Notes on text requirements:
1)   The cover letter (in print and by e-mail) and the foreword of an invitation brochure, for example, should be regarded as a single unit (contentwise). This means that, by and large, the answers to the questions above should be located in the text. However, duplication should be avoided.
2)   Formally binding criteria apply to the foreword and cover letter.

M.   Release cycles

Note: Specify how much time should be factored into timing for each release here.

N.   Check steps

Note: List the check steps in terms of goal achievement here, i.e. at which points in the process of the contact strategy can you check to see whether (and to what degree) the goal you strived for has been reached? In this context, also include possible countermeasures that can be taken if the goals have not been reached.

BIBLIOGRAPHY

Aaker, D.A. (1991) *Managing Brand Equity*. New York.

Aaker, D.A. (1996) *Building Strong Brands*. New York.

Aaker, D.A. (2001) *Developing Business Strategies*. New York.

Aaker, D.A. & Joachimsthaler, E. (2000) *Brand Leadership*. New York.

Aaker, J.L. (2000) Dimensionen der Markenpersönlichkeit, in Esch, F.-R. (ed.), *Moderne Markenführung* (2nd edition). Wiesbaden, pp. 91–102.

Abele, J.M., Caesar, W.K. & John, R.H. (2003) Re-Channeling Sales, *The McKinsey Quarterly* (No. 3), 2–13.

Ace, C. (2001) *Successful Marketing Communications. A Practical Guide to Planning and Implementation*. Oxford.

Afuah, A. & Tucci, C.L. (2000) *Internet Business Models and Strategies*. New York.

Aggert, A. (2006) Die zwei Perspektiven des Kundenwerts: Darstellung und Versuch einer Integration, in Günter, B. & Helm, S. (eds.), *Kundenwert. Grundlagen – Innovative Konzepte – Praktische Umsetzungen* (3rd revision). Wiesbaden, pp. 41–60.

Akshay, R.R. & Monroe, K.B. (1957) The Effect of Price, Brand Name, and Store Name on Buyers' Perceptions of Product Quality: An Integrative Review. *Journal of Marketing Research*, Vol. 26 (July), 205–210.

Allen, C., Kania, D. & Yaeckel, B. (1998) *Guide to One-to-One Web Marketing*. New York.

Alvarez, J.G., Raeside, R. & Jones, W.B. (2006) The Importance of Analysis and Planning in Customer Relationship Marketing: Verification of the Need for Customer Intelligence and Modelling. *Journal of Database Marketing and Customer Strategy Management*, Vol. 13 (April, No. 3), 222–230.

Amor, D. (1999) *The e-Business (R)evolution*. Upper Saddle River.

Anderson, C. (2004) *Wired*, Oct.

Anderson, C. (2006a) *The Long Tail*. Hyperion, NY.

Anderson, C. (2006b) Blog: www.longtail.com.

Argyris, C. (1952) *The Impact of Budgets on People*. New York.

Armstrong, A. & Hagel, J. (2000) Der wahre Wert von Online-Gemeinschaften, in Tapscott, D. (ed.), *Erfolg im e-Business*, Munich, pp. 196–208.

Arndt, R. (2001) Konzept- und Produkttests im Internet, in Theobald, A., Dreyer, M. & Starsetzki, T. (eds.), *Online-Marktforschung*, Wiesbaden, pp. 291–302.

Back, L. & Beuttler, S. (2006) *Handbuch Briefing* (2nd edition). Stuttgart.

Backhaus, K. & Schneider, H. (2007) *Strategisches Marketing*. Stuttgart.

Backhaus, K., Erichson, B., Plinke, W. & Weiber, R. (1994) *Multivariate Analysemethoden, eine anwendungsorientierte Einführung* (7th edition). Berlin.

Bailey, J. & Bakos, Y. (1997) An Exploratory Study of the Emerging Role of Electronic Intermediaries. *International Journal of Electronic Commerce*, Vol. 1 (No. 3), 7–20.

Bakos, Y. (1977) Reducing Buyers Search Costs: Implications for Electronic Marketplaces. *Management Science*, Vol. 43 (No. 12), 1676–1692.

Ballhaus, J. (2008) Kundenorientiertes Technologiemanagement. *Absatzwirtschaft* (No. 2), 36–38.

Barney, J. (2003) *Gaining and Sustaining Competitive Advantage* (2nd edition). Upper Saddle River.

Bayers, C. (1998) The Promise of One-to-One. *Wired* (May), 130–135, 185–187.

Beamish, K. & Ashford, R. (2006) *The Official CIM Coursebook: Marketing Planning*. London.

Benjamin, R. & Wigand, R. (1995) Electronic Markets and Virtual Value Chains on the Information Superhighway, *Sloan Management Review*, Winter, 62–72.

Berdi, C. (2006) Samsung – der zügellose Wille Erster zu werden, *Absatzwirtschaft – Zeitschrift für Marketing* (No. 5), 12–14.

Berger, P.D. & Nasr, N.I. (1998) Customer Lifetime Value: Marketing Models and Applications. *Journal of Interactive Marketing*, Vol. 12 (No. 1), 17–30.

Berke, J., Bergermann, M., Klesse, H.-J., Kiani-Kress, R., Kroker, M. & Seiwert, M. (2007) Die Welt ist flat, *Wirtschaftswoche* (No. 52), 88–94.

Berndt, R. (1995) *Marketing Management* (2nd revised edition). Berlin.

Berners-Lee, T., Hendler, J. & Lassila, O. (2001) The Semantic Web. *Scientific American* (May).

Beutin, N. (2006) Verfahren zur Messung der Kundenzufriedenheit im Überblick, in Homburg, C. (ed.), *Kundenzufriedenheit: Konzepte – Methoden – Erfahrungen* (6th edition). Wiesbaden, pp. 121–170.

Biel, A.L. (2000) Grundlagen zum Markenwertaufbau, in Esch, F.-R. (ed.), *Moderne Markenführung* (2nd edition). Wiesbaden, pp. 61–90.

Bierhoff, H.W. & Müller, G.F. (1993) Kooperation in Organisationen, *Zeitschrift für Arbeits- und Organisationspsychologie* (No. 37), 42–51.

Blakely, L. & Copeland, M.V. (2007) The Facebook Economy. *Business 2.0*, Vol. 8 (September, No. 8), 76–82.

Bliemel, F. & Fassott, G. (2000). Produktpolitik mit e-Share, in Bliemel, F., Fassott, G. & Theobald, A. (eds.), *Electronic Commerce. Herausforderungen – Anwendungen – Perspektiven* (3rd edition). Wiesbaden, pp. 191–204.

Bliemel, F.W. & Eggert, A. (1998) Kundenbindung die neue Sollstrategie? *Marketing ZFP*, Vol. 20 (No. 1), 37–46.

Bliemel, F., Eggert, A. & Adolphs, K. (2000) Preispolitik mit Electronic Commerce, in Bliemel, F., Fassott, G. & Theobald, A. (eds.), *Electronic Commerce. Herausforderungen – Anwendungen – Perspektiven* (3rd edition). Wiesbaden, pp. 205–218.

Block, C.H. (2001) *Professionell Einkaufen mit dem Internet*. Munich.

Bocionek, S.R. (1995) Agent Systems that Negotiate and Learn. *International Journal of Human-Computer Studies*, Vol. 42, 265–288.

Böcker, F. (1994) *Marketing* (5th edition). Stuttgart.

Bongartz, M., Burmann, C. & Maloney, P. (2005) Marke und Markenführung im Kontext des Electronic Commerce, in Meffert, H., Burmann, C. & Koers, M. (eds.), *Markenmanagement. Identitätsorientierte Markenführung und praktische Umsetzung* (2nd fully revised and enhanced edition). Wiesbaden, pp. 433–468.

Bonoma, T. (2006) Major Sales: Who really does the buying? *Harvard Business Review*, Vol. 36 (No. 3), 111–119.

Bonoma, T.V. (1985) *The Marketing Edge: Making Strategies Work*. New York.

Borchert, S. (2001) Einfluss von e-Commerce auf das operative Management, in Gora, W. & Mann, E. (eds.), *Handbuch Electronic Commerce*, Berlin, pp. 200–215.

Bortz, J. (1984) *Lehrbuch der empirischen Forschung*. Berlin.

Bortz, J. (1993) *Statistik für Sozialwissenschaftler* (4th fully revised edition). Berlin.

Bourne, F.S. (1966) Product, Brand and Preference-Group Influence, in Britt, S.H. (ed.), *Consumer Behaviour and the Behavioural Sciences*. New York, pp. 351–353.

Brabham, D. (2007) Crowdsourcing as a Model for Problem Solving – An Introduction and Cases. *The International Journal of Research into New Media Technologies*, Vol. 14 (February, No. 1), 75–90.

Brand, F.-J. (2008) Systematische Marktausschöpfung im Mittelstand – Wege zur Erschliessung neuer Absatzpotenziale am Beispiel der Automobilindustrie, in Kreutzer, R.T. & Merkle, W. (eds.), *Die neue Macht des Marketing*. Wiesbaden, pp. 355–368.

Brandes, D. (2005) *Einfach Managen. Klarheit und Verzicht – der Weg zum Wesentlichen*. Munich.

Brandtner, M. (2007) Retromarken-Boom. Modeerscheinung oder sinnvolle Strategie? *Diskussionsbeitrag* (June).

Brauer, W. & Saborowski, J. (1998) Internet-Branding, *Absatzwirtschaft – Zeitschrift für Marketing* (No. 11), 102–108.

Brechtel, D. (2007) Unter der Lupe. *Horizont*, (September, 20), 72.

Brehm, L. & Ferencak, R. (2001) Potenzial der SCM-Software für das Management unternehmensübergreifender Prozesse, in Dangelmaier, W., Pape, U. & Rüther, M. (eds.), *Die Supply Chain im Zeitalter von e-Business und Global Sourcing*. Paderborn, pp. 281–300.

Briggs, R. & Hollis, N. (1997) Advertising on the Web: Is there Response before Click-Through? *Journal of Advertsing Research*, (March–April), 33–45.

Brown, S.L. & Engelhardt, K.M. (1998) *Competing on the Edge*. Boston.

Brückner, M. & Reinert, R. (2005) *So Briefen Sie Richtig*. Heidelberg.

Bruhn, M. (2003) *Kundenorientierung. Bausteine für ein exzellentes Customer Relationship Management (CRM)*. Munich.

Brynjolfsson, E., Hu, Y.F. & Smith, M.D. (2006) From Niches to Riches. *MIT Sloan Management Review*, Vol. 47 (No. 4), 67–71.

Buchholz, W. (2001) Netsourcing Business Modells, in Dangelmaier, W., Pape, U. & Rüther, M. (eds.), *Die Supply Chain im Zeitalter von e-Business und Global Sourcing*. Paderborn, pp. 37–52.

Bucklin, C.B., Thomas-Graham, P.A. & Webster, E.A. (1997) Channel Conflict: When is it dangerous? *The McKinsey Quarterly* (No. 3), 37–43.

Bucklin, C.B., DeFalco, S.P., DeVincentis, J.R. & Levis, J.P. (1996) Are you tough enough to manage your channels? *The McKinsey Quarterly* (No. 1), 105–114.

Bucklin, L.P. (1972) *Competition and Evolution in the Distributive Trades*. Englewood Cliffs.

Bughin, J. & Manyika, J. (2007) How businesses are using Web 2.0. A McKinsey global survey, *The McKinsey Quarterly*, 1–16.

Bughin, J., Ebenich, C. & Shenken, A. (2007) How global companies are marketing online: A McKinsey Global survey, *The McKinsey Quarterly*, 1–10.

Bühner, R. (2004) *Betriebswirtschaftliche Organisationslehre* (10th edition). Munich.

Bullinger, H.-J. & Niemeier, J. (1993) Methodik zur Organisationsplanung im Büro, in Scharfenberg, H. (ed.), *Strukturwandel in Management und Organisation*. Baden-Baden, pp. 103–123.

Bullinger, H.-J. & Schuster, E. & Wilhelm, S. (2000) *Content Management Systeme*. Stuttgart.

Bund, M. & Granthien, M. (2001) Ganzheitliches Beziehungsmanagement im Electronic Commerce, in Walther, J. & Bund, M. (eds.), *Supply Chain Management*, Frankfurt, pp. 129–157.

Burger, P.C. & Schott, B. (1972) Can Private Brand Buyers be identified? *Journal of Marketing Research*, Vol. IX (May), 219–222.

Burmann, C. (1991) Konsumentenzufriedenheit als Determinante der Marken- und Händler-loyalität, *Marketing ZFP* (No. 4), 249–258.

Burmann, C. & Meffert, H. (2005a) Managementkonzept der identitätsorientierten Markenführung, in Meffert, H., Burmann, C. & Koers, M. (eds.), *Markenmanagement. Identitätsorientierte Markenführung und praktische Umsetzung* (2nd revised and enhanced edition). Wiesbaden, pp. 73–114.

Burmann, C. & Meffert, H. (2005b) Theoretisches Grundkonzept der identitätsorientierten Markenführung, in Meffert, H., Burmann, C. & Koers, M. (eds.), *Markenmanagement. Identitätsorientierte Markenführung und praktische Umsetzung* (2nd revised and enhanced edition). Wiesbaden, pp. 37–72.

Burmann, C. & Zeplin, S. (2005) Innengerichtetes identitätsbasiertes Markenmanagement, in Meffert, H., Burmann, C. & Koers, M. (eds.), *Markenmanagement. Identitätsorientierte Markenführung und praktische Umsetzung* (2nd fully revised and enhanced edition). Wiesbaden, pp. 115–142.

Burmann, C., Kranz, M. & Weers, J.-P. (2005a) Bewertung und Bilanzierung von Marken – Bestandsaufnahme und kritische Würdigung, in Meffert, H., Burmann, C. & Koers, M. (eds.), *Markenmanagement. Identitätsorientierte Markenführung und praktische Umsetzung* (2nd revised and enhanced edition). Wiesbaden, pp. 319–346.

Burmann, C., Meffert, H. & Koers, M. (2005b) Stellenwert und Gegenstand des Markenmanagements, in Meffert, H., Burmann, C. & Koers, M. (eds.), *Markenmanagement. Identitätsorientierte Markenführung und praktische Umsetzung* (2nd fully revised and enhanced edition). Wiesbaden, pp. 3–18.

Burr, W. (2003) Das Konzept des verteidigungsfähigen Wettbewerbsvorteils – Ansatzpunkte zur Dynamisierung und Operationalisierung, *Die Unternehmung* (No. 5), 357–373.

Buzzel, R.D. (1956) Competitive Behaviour and Product Life Cycles, in Wright, J.S. & Goldstucker, J. (eds.), *New Ideas for Successful Marketing.* Chicago, p. 56.

Cespedes, F.V. & Corey, E.R. (1990) Managing Multiple Channels – Combining Direct and Indirect Sales Channels, *Business Horizons,* (July–August), 67–77.

Chen, S. (1995) Role of Information Infrastructure and Intelligent Agents in Manufacturing Enterprises. *Journal of Organizational Computing,* Vol. 5 (No. 1), 53–67.

Cheng, A. (2008) Amid retail gloom, outlet malls a rare winner. No longer "wrecking their brands," developments shore up sagging profits, *MarketWatch* (April 4).

Chesbrough, H. (2006) *Open Business Models: How to Thrive in the New Innovation Landscape.* Boston.

Chesbrough, H.W. (2003) *Open Innovation: The New Imperative for Creating and Profiting from Technology.* Boston.

Chircu, A.M. & Kauffman, R.J. (1999) Strategies for Internet Middlemen in the Intermediation/Disintermediation/Reintermediation Cycle. *Electronic Markets,* Vol. 9 (1/2), 109–117.

Choi, S.-Y., Stahl, D.O. & Whinston, A.B. (1997) *The Economics of Electronic Commerce.* Indianapolis.

Clark, D. (1994) Intel's Name Recognition Offers a Target. *The Wall Street Journal,* Europe, (Dec. 6), 4.

CMO Council. (2007) *Define & Align the CMO.* Palo Alto.

Cohan, P.S. (1999) *Net Profit.* San Francisco.

Cohen, W.A. (2006) *The Marketing Plan* (5th edition). Hoboken.

Collins, S.R., Dahlström, P.W. & Singer, M. (2005) Managing your business as if customer segments matter, *The McKinsey Quarterly.*

Conniff, M. (1993) In Search of the Personal Newspaper, *Editor & Publisher,* (March 6), 60–64.

Consoli, J. (1993) Targeted before Tailored, *Editor & Publisher,* (June 19), S. 24.

Copeland, M. (2007) Web 3.0: No Humans Required, *Business2.com.* (October).

Cornelsen, J. (1998) Operative Analyse, in Diller, H. (ed.), *Marketingplanung* (2nd fully revised and enhanced edition). Munich, pp. 73–117.

Cornelsen, J. (2006) Kundenbewertung mit Referenzwerten, in Günter, B. & Helm, S. (eds.), *Kundenwert. Grundlagen – Innovative Konzepte – Praktische Umsetzungen* (3rd revised and enhanced edition). Wiesbaden, pp. 183–215.

Corsten, H. (1998) *Grundlagen der Wettbewerbsstrategie*. Stuttgart.

Corsten, H. & Will, T. (1995) Wettbewerbsvorteile durch strategiegerechte Produktionsorganisation, in Corsten, H. (ed.), *Produktion als Wettbewerbsfaktor*, Wiesbaden, pp. 1–13.

Court, D. (2007) The evolving role of the CMO, *The McKinsey Quarterly* (No. 3), 29–39.

Court, D.C., Gordon, J.W. & Perrey, J. (2005) Boosting returns on marketing investment, *The McKinsey Quarterly* (No. 2), 36–47.

Court, D., French, T.D., McGuire, T.I. & Partington, M. (1999) Marketing in 3-D, *The McKinsey Quarterly* (No. 4), 5–17.

Courtney, H., Kirkland, J. & Viguerie, P. (1999) Strategy under Uncertainity, in Magretta, J. (ed.), *Managing in the New Economy*, Boston, pp. 67–90.

Coyles, S. & Gokey, T.C. (2002) Customer Retention is not enough, *The McKinsey Quarterly* (No. 2), 80–89.

Crowston, K. & Malone, T.W. (1994) Information Technology and Work Organization, in Allen, T.J. & Scott Morton, M.S. (eds.), *Information Technology and the Corporation of the 1990s*. New York, pp. 249–275.

Cuningham, R.M. (1966) Consumer Loyalty to Store and Brand, in Britt, S.H. (ed.), *Consumer Behaviour and the Behavioural Sciences*, New York, pp. 342–344.

Daemon Quest (2005) Research and Insight: Marketing One-to-One Individualized Marketing Strategies (March).

Daemon Quest (2007a) Channel Strategy, 24.6.

Daemon Quest (2007b) For the first time in history, clothing outsells computer products (June).

Daemon Quest (2008) www.daemonquest.com.

Daft, R.L. & Huber, G.P. (1987) How Organizations Learn: A Communication Framework, in Ditomaso, N. & Bacharach, S. (eds.), *Research in the Sociology of Organizations*, Vol. 5, 1–36.

Dahan, E. & Hauser, J.R. (2002) The virtual customer. *Journal of Product Innovation Management*, Vol. 19 (September, No. 5), 332–353.

Dambrowski, J. (1986) Budgetierungssysteme in der deutschen Unternehmenspraxis. Darmstadt.

Dankl, C. (2007) Crossmedia-Dialogmarketing beim Audi Q7-Start, in Schwarz, T. (ed.), *Leitfaden Online-Marketing*. Hamburg, pp. 12–13.

Daum, B. & Scheller, M. (2000) *Electronic Business. Methoden, Werkzeuge, Techniken und Systeme für den Unternehmenserfolg im Internet.* Munich.

Daum, D. (2001) *Marketingproduktivität: Konzeption, Messung und empirische Analyse.* Wiesbaden.

Davenport, T.H. (1993) *Process Innovation. Reengineering Work through Information Technology.* Boston.

Davenport, T.H. & Prusak, L. (1998) *Working Knowledge.* Boston.

Davenport, T.H. & Short, J.E. (1990) The New Industrial Engineering: Information Technology and Business Process Redesign. *Sloan Management Review*, Vol. 31 (Summer, No. 4), 11–26.

Davis, J. (2000) The Net Impact, *Business 2.0*, January, 168–180.

Davis, S. & Botkin, J. (2000) Das künftige Geschäft – wissensgestützt, in Tapscott, D. (ed.), *Erfolg im e-Business.* Munich, pp. 31–41.

De Bonis, J.N., Balinski, E. & Allen, P. (2003) *Value Based Marketing for Bottom-Line Success.* New York.

De Kare-Silver, M. (1998) E-shock. *The Electronic Shopping Revolution: Strategies for Retailers and Manufacturers.* New York.

Decker, R., Klein, T. & Wartenberg, F. (1995) Marketing und Internet – Markenkommunikation im Umbruch? *Markenartikel* (No. 10), 468–472.

Dibb, S., Simkin, L. & Bradley, J. (1996) *The Marketing Planning Workbook*, London.

Diller, H. (1998) Zielplanung, in Diller, H. (ed.), *Marketingplanung* (2nd fully revised and enhanced edition). Munich, pp. 163–198.

Diller, H. (1999) Entwicklungslinien in Preistheorie und-management, *Arbeitspapier* (January, No. 76), Nuremberg.

Diller, H. (2001) Die Erfolgsaussichten des Beziehungsmarketings im Internet, in Eggert, A. & Fassott, G. (eds.), *eCRM – Electronic Customer Relationship Management.* Stuttgart, pp. 65–85.

Dirkes, M., Strauss, R.E., Brandenburg, M. & Durand, P. (1999) *Cars Online Europe 1999, Empirical Study on the Potential for Automotive Sales and Distribution in Electronic Commerce.* Bad Homburg, September.

Doppler, K. & Lauterburg, C. (2000) *Change Management.* Frankfurt.

Doringer, C. (1991) *Kundenindividuelle Fertigung.* Vienna.

Downes, L. & Mui, C. (1998) *Unleashing the Killer App. Digital Strategies for Market Dominance.* Boston.

Doyle, P. (1976) The realities of the product life cycle, *Quarterly Review of Marketing*, Summer, 1–6.

Doyle, P. (2000) Value Based Marketing. *Journal of Strategic Marketing*, Vol. 8, 299–311.

Dreihues-Uter, C. (2005) *Eine Erfolgsgeschichte der Postbank: Höchst individuell, höchst erfolgreich und höchstpersönlich.* Internet-Recherche.

Droege, W.P. J. & Kricsfalussy, A. (1998) Marketingaudit: Check up the strategic fit! in Reinecke, S., Tomczak, T. & Dittrich, S. (eds.), *Marketingcontrolling*, Thexis, St. Gallen, pp. 70–78.

Drtina, R., Hoeger, S. & Schaub, J. (1996) Continuous Budgeting at the HON Company. *Management Accounting*, Vol. 77 (No. 1), 20–24.

Drucker, P.F. (1998) The Coming of the New Organization. *Harvard Business Review*, Vol. 66 (January–February, No. 1), 45–53.

Drucker, P.F. (2000) The Emerging Theory of Manufacturing, in Gilmore, J.H. & Pine, B.J. (eds.), *Markets of One. Creating Customer-Unique Value through Mass Customization*, Boston, pp. 3–16.

Dull, S.F., Mohn, W.A. & Noren, T. (1995) Partners, *The McKinsey Quarterly* (No. 4), 63–72.

Dwyer, F.R. (1989) Customer Lifetime Valuation to Support Marketing Decision Making. *Journal of Direct Marketing*, Vol. 3 (Autumn, No. 4), 8–15.

Dyson, E. (1997) *Release 2.0. Die Internet-Gesellschaft.* Munich.

Eckert, C. (2001) *IT-Sicherheit. Konzepte – Verfahren – Protokolle.* Munich.

Eggers, B. & Hoppen, G. (2001) Strategisches e-Commerce-Management: Zentrale Aufgaben und Prozesse, in Eggers, B. & Hoppen, G. (eds.), *Strategisches e-Commerce-Management.* Wiesbaden, pp. 671–690.

Eggert, A. (2001) Konzeptionelle Grundlagen des elektronischen Kundenbeziehungsmanagements, in Eggert, A. & Fassott, G. (eds.), *eCRM – Electronic Customer Relationship Management.* Stuttgart, pp. 87–106.

Eggert, A. & Fassott, G. (2001) Elektronisches Kundenbeziehungsmanagement (eCRM), in Eggert, A. & Fassott, G. (eds.), *eCRM – Electronic Customer Relationship Management*, Stuttgart, pp. 1–14.

Eggert, A. & Helm, S. (2000) Determinanten der Weiterempfehlung: Kundenzufriedenheit oder Kundenbindung? *der markt*, Vol. 39 (No. 153), 63–72.

Ehrmann, T. & Schmale, H. (2008) Renaissance der Randsortimente, *Absatzwirtschaft* (No. 2), 44–46.

Eisenächer, H.W. (2005) Lufthansa – Excellence in Branding, in Meffert, H., Burmann, C. & Koers, M. (eds.), *Markenmanagement. Identitätsorientierte Markenführung und praktische Umsetzung*, (2nd fully revised and enhanced edition). Wiesbaden, pp. 819–836.

Elberse, A. & Oberholzer-Gee, F. (2006) Superstars and Underdogs: An Examination of the Long Tail, Phenomenon in Video Sales, *Harvard Business School Working Paper Series* (No. 07–15).

Enderle, M. & Wirtz, B. (2008) Weitreichende Änderungen, *Absatzwirtschaft* (No. 1), 36–39.

Ernst, H. (2001) *Erfolgsfaktoren neuer Produkte – Grundlagen für eine valide empirische Forschung.* Wiesbaden.

Ernst-Motz, A. (1993) Der Berg ruft immer wieder. *Top Business* (December), 58–59.

Esch, F.-R. (2007) Der Affe in uns. Worauf sich das Marketing einstellen muss, *Absatzwirtschaft – Zeitschrift für Marketing* (No. 12), 30–35.

Esch, F.-R. & Wicke, A. (2000) Herausforderungen und Aufgaben des Markenmanagements, in Esch, F.-R. (ed.), *Moderne Markenführung* (2nd edition). Wiesbaden, pp. 3–60.

Esser, H. (1974) Der Befragte, in Koolwijk, J. van & Wieken-Mayser, M. (eds.), *Techniken der empirischen Sozialforschung*, Vol. 4, *Erhebungsmethoden: Die Befragung.* Munich, pp. 107–145.

Etzel, H.-J., Faisst, D. & Richter, R. (2000) Umsetzung einer IT-Strategie in einem stark veränderlichen betrieblichen Umfeld, in Etzel, H.-J., Heilmann, H. & Richter, R. (eds.), *IT – Projektmanagement. Fallstricke und Erfolgsfaktoren.* Heidelberg, pp. 95–113.

Evans, P. & Wurster, T.S. (2000) *Web Attack. Strategien für die Internet-Revolution.* Munich.

Ewert, R. & Wagenhofer, A. (1997) *Interne Unternehmensrechnung* (3rd revised and enhanced edition). Berlin.

Eymann, T. & Vollan, B. (2001) Internetquellen zum Thema Software-Agenten. *Wirtschaftsinformatik*, Vol. 43 (No. 2), 183–188.

Farber, D. & Dignan, L. (2006) TechNet Summit: The new era of innovation. *ZDNet blog*, (November 15).

Farris, P.W., Bendle, N.T., Pfeifer, P.E. & Reibstein, D.J. (2007) *Marketing messbar machen.* Frankfurt am Main.

Federrath, H., Jerichow, A., Pfitzmann, A. & Pfitzmann, B. (1995) Mehrseitig sichere Schlüsselerzeugung, in Horster, P. (ed.), *Trust Center. Grundlagen, Rechtliche Aspekte, Standardisierung, Realisierung*, Braunschweig. pp. 117–131.

Feldmann, B. (2008) Wenn Werbung zu persönlich wird, *Absatzwirtschaft* (No. 2), 40–42.

Feldmann, K. & Grözinger, R. (2008) Geldvernichtungsmaschine Marke? – Maximierung des Return on Brand Investment am Beispiel der Finanzdienstleistungsmarken, in Kreutzer, R.T. & Merkle, W. (eds.), *Die neue Macht des Marketing.* Wiesbaden, pp. 247–266.

Fellenstein, C. & Wood, R. (2000) *Exploring e-Commerce, Global e-Business, and e-Societies.* Upper Saddle River.

Fischer, T.M. & Schmöler, P. (2006) Kundenwert als Entscheidungskalkül für die Beendigung von Kundenbeziehungen, in Günter, B. & Helm, S. (eds.), *Kundenwert. Grundlagen – Innovative Konzepte – Praktische Umsetzungen* (3rd revised and enhanced edition). Wiesbaden, pp. 483–508.

Fiske, J. & Hartley, J. (1980) *Reading Television.* London.

Fitz-Enz, J. (2001) *The e-Aligned Enterprise.* New York.

Fleck, A. (1995) *Hybride Wettbewerbsstrategien.* Wiesbaden.

Fleisch, E. (2001) *Das Netzwerkunternehmen.* Berlin.

Foltz, P.W. & Dumais, S.T. (1992) Personalized information delivery: an analysis of information filtering methods. *Communications of the ACM*, Vol. 35 (December, No. 12), 51–60.

Forsyth, J.E., Galante, N. & Guild, T. (2006) Capitalizing on Customer Insights, *The McKinsey Quarterly* (No. 3), 42–53.

Fournier, S.M. (2000) Markenbeziehungen – Konsumenten und ihre Marken, in Esch, F.-R. (ed.), *Moderne Markenführung* (2nd edition). Wiesbaden, pp. 135–164.

Frank, R.J., George, J.P. & Narasimhan, L. (2004) When your Competitor Delivers More for Less, *The McKinsey Quarterly* (No. 1), 49–59.

Frazier, C. (2001) Swap Meet. Consumers are Willing to Exchange Personal Information for Personalized Products. *American Demographics*, (July), 51–55.

French, J.R.P. & Raven, B. (1959) The Basis of Social Power, in Cartwright, D. (ed.), *Studies in Social Power*, Ann Arbor, pp. 150–167.

Freter, H. & Obermeier, O. (2000) Marktsegmentierung, in Hermann, A. & Homburg, C. (eds.), *Marktforschung: Methoden, Anwendungen, Praxisbeispiele* (2nd edition). Wiesbaden, pp. 739–764.

Fritz, W. (2000) *Internet-Marketing und Electronic Commerce*. Wiesbaden.

Gaitanides, M. & Westphal, J. (1991) Strategischer Gruppen- und Unternehmenserfolg, *Zeitschrift für Planung* (No. 3), 247–265.

Gaitanides, M. & Wicher, H. (1986) Strategien und Strukturen innovationsfähiger Organisationen. *Zeitschrift für Betriebswirtschaft*, Vol. 56 (No. 4/5), 385–403.

Gallo, M. (2007) Channel Strategy. *Daemon Quest* (24/06).

Geist & Gehirn (2006) *Das Manifest. Elf führende Neurowissenschaftler über Gegenwart und Zukunft der Hirnforschung* (25.9).

Gemünden, H.G., Kaluza, B. & Pleschak, F. (1992) Management von Prozessinnovationen, in Gemünden, H.G. & Pleschak, F. (eds.), *Innovationsmanagement und Wettbewerbsfähigkeit*. Wiesbaden, pp. 33–54.

Georg, B. (2000) Sicherheit, Recht und Steuern, in Thome, R. & Schinzer, H. (eds.), *Electronic Commerce: Anwendungsbereiche und Potentiale der digitalen Geschäftsabwicklung*. Munich, pp. 255–290.

George, M., Freeling, A. & Court, D. (1994) Reinventing the marketing organisation, *The McKinsey Quarterly* (No. 4), 43–62.

Geskes, S. (1998) Stand des Erfolgscontrollings in deutschen Industrieunternehmen: Empirische Ergebnisse, in Reinecke, S., Tomczak, T. & Dittrich, S. (eds.), *Marketingcontrolling*, Thexis. St. Gallen, pp. 334–344.

Ghosh, A.K. (1998) *e-Commerce Security, Weak Links, Best Defenses*. New York.

Gilmore, J.H. & Pine, B.J. (2000) The Four Faces of Mass Customization, in Gilmore, J.H. & Pine, B.J. (eds.), *Markets of One. Creating Customer-Unique Value through Mass Customization*. Boston, pp. 115–132.

Gleich, R. (2001) *Das System des Performance Measurement*. Munich.

Gleich, R. & Kopp, J. (2001) Ansätze zur Neugestaltung der Planung und Budgetierung – methodische Innovationen und empirische Erkenntnisse. *Controlling*, Vol. 13 (No. 8–9).

Gloor, P.A. & Cooper, S.M. (2007) The New Principles of a Swarm Business. *MIT Sloan Management Review*, Vol. 48 (Spring, No. 3), 81–84.

Goldmann, H.M. (2005) *Wie man Kunden gewinnt. Das weltweit erfolgreichste Leitbuch moderner Verkaufspraxis*. Berlin.

Goodstein, L., Nolan, T. & Pfeiffer, J.W. (1993) *Applied Strategic Planning. How to Develop a Plan that Really Works*. New York.

Gora, W. & Mann, E. (eds.) (2001) *Handbuch Electronic Commerce*. Berlin.

Görgen, W. (1995) Wettbewerbsanalyse, in Tietz, B., Köhler, R. & Zentes, J. (eds.), *Handwörterbuch des Marketing* (2nd edition). Stuttgart, pp. 2716–2729.

Gosh, A.K. (1998) *e-Commerce Security: Weak Links, Best Defenses*. New York.

Göttmann, K. (1999) Wie bette ich eCommerce in bestehende Software-Systeme ein – Software – Realisierung, in Albers, S., Clement, M., Peters, K. & Skiera, B. (eds.), *eCommerce*. Frankfurt, pp. 149–162.

Götz, P. (1998) Strategische Analyse, in Diller, H. (ed.), *Marketingplanung* (2nd fully revised and enhanced edition). Munich, pp. 33–71.

Gouillart, F.J. & Kelly, J.N. (1995) *Transforming the Organization.* New York.

Graefe, T. (1996) Marken und Internet, *Markenartikel* (No. 3), 100–103.

Gräf, H (2000) Von der Reichweitenmessung zum Marketing-Audit, *Absatzwirtschaft – Zeitschrift für Marketing* (No. 11), 48–54.

Granada Research (1999) *e-Catalog 99: Business-to-Business Electronic Catalogues.* Granada (USA).

Grant, G.L. (1998) *Understanding Digital Signatures: Establishing Trust Over the Internet.* New York.

Green, P.E. & Tull, D.S. (1982) *Methoden und Techniken der Marketingforschung.* Stuttgart.

Grossklaus, R.H.G. (2006) *Die 140 besten Checklisten zur Marketingplanung.* Landsberg am Lech.

Grudin, J. (1988) Why CSCW Applications Fail: Problems in the Design and Evaluation of Organizational Interfaces. *Proceedings of the Conference on Computer-Supported Cooperative Work,* (September), 85–93.

Gutknecht, K. (2008) Unternehmensübergreifende Marketing-Kooperationen – der Weg zum innovativen Added Value, in Kreutzer, R.T. & Merkle, W. (eds.), *Die neue Macht des Marketing.* Wiesbaden, pp. 185–200.

Hackman, J.R. (1986) The Psychology of Self-Management in Organizations, in Pallak, M.S. & Perloff, R.O. (eds.), *Psychology and Work: Productivity, Change, Employment.* Washington, pp. 89–139.

Haenlein, M., Kaplan, A.M. & Schoder, D. (2006) Valuing the real option of abandoning unprofitable customers when calculating customer lifetime value. *Journal of Marketing,* Vol. 70 (No. 3), 5–20.

Hagel, J. & Armstrong, A.G. (1997) *Net Gain.* Boston.

Hagel, J. & Rayport, J.F. (2000) Die kommende Schlacht um Kundendaten, in Tapscott, D. (ed.), *Erfolg im e-Business.* Munich, pp. 182–195.

Hamel, G.M. & Prahalad, C.K. (1994) *Competing for the Future.* Boston.

Hämmerling, A. (2001) Verkaufen ohne Grenzen, *Cybiz* (No. 05), 40–41.

Handy, C. (2000) Vertrauen: Die Grundlage der virtuellen Organisation, in Tapscott, D. (ed.), *Erfolg im e-Business.* Munich, pp. 130–143.

Hansmann, K. (1995) Prognose und Prognoseverfahren. *Betriebswirtschaftliche Forschung und Praxis,* Vol. 47 (No. 3), 269–286.

Harrington, H.J. (1991) *Business Process Improvement.* New York.

Harter, G., Landry, E. & Tipping, A. (2007) The New Complete Marketer. *Strategy & Business.*

Hartleben, R.E. (2004) *Werbekonzeption und Briefing* (2nd revised and enhanced edition). Erlangen.

Hartman, A. & Sifonis, J. (2000) *Net Ready. Strategies for Success in the e-Conomy.* New York.

Hatton, A. (2002) *Marketingplanung. Effective Marketingstrategie entwickeln und umsetzen.* Munich.

Häusel, H.-G. (2004) *Brain Script. Warum Kunden kaufen.* Freiburg.

Heiny, L (2007) Wachsende Unruhe, *FTD medbiz* (No. 16), 4–7.

Heinzel, H. (2001) Gestaltung integrierter Lieferketten auf Basis des Supply Chain Operations Reference-Modells, in Walther, J. & Bund, M. (eds.), *Supply Chain Management.* Frankfurt, pp. 32–58.

Hellbrück, R. & Schoder, D. (1994) Explaining and Forecasting Flops, *Proceedings of the "Sixth Annual Conference of the International Academy of Business Disciplines (IABD)".* Pittsburgh, PA, USA, April 7–10.

Helm, S. (2000) *Kundenempfehlungen als Marketinginstrument.* Wiesbaden.

Helm, S. & Günter, B. (2006) Kundenwert – eine Einführung in die theoretischen und praktischen Herausforderungen der Bewertung von Kundenbeziehungen, in Günter, B. &

Helm, S. (eds.), *Kundenwert. Grundlagen – Innovative Konzepte – Praktische Umsetzungen* (3rd revised and enhanced edition). Wiesbaden, pp. 3–40.

Helmke, S. & Dangelmaier, W. (2001) CRM-Audit – Grundstein für die erfolgreiche Einführung von CRM, in Helmke, S. & Dangelmaier, W. (eds.), *Effektives Customer Relationship Management*. Wiesbaden, pp. 297–290.

Helmke, S., Uebel, M.F. & Dangelmaier, W. (2003) *Effektives Customer Relationship Management*. Wiesbaden.

Hempel, J. (2006) Crowdsourcing: milk the masses for inspiration, *BusinessWeek* (September, No. 4002), 38–39.

Henderson, J. & Venkatraman, N. (1994) IT Strategy Alignment: A Model for Organizational Transformation via Information Technology, in Allen, T.J. & Scott Morton, M.S. (eds.), *Information Technology and the Corporation of the 1990s*. New York, pp. 202–220.

Hermanns, A. (1999) Electronic Commerce – Herausforderungen für das Marketing-Management, in Hermanns, A. & Sauter, M. (eds.), *Management – Handbuch Electronic Commerce*. Munich, pp. 87–100.

Hermanns, A. & Sauter, M. (1999a) Electronic Commerce – Grundlagen, Potentiale, Marktteilnehmer und Transaktionen, in Hermanns, A. & Sauter, M. (eds.), *Management – Handbuch Electronic Commerce*. Munich, pp. 13–30.

Hermanns, A. & Sauter, M. (1999b) Entwicklungsperspektiven des Electronic Commerce – Eine kritische Reflexion in die Zukunft, in Hermanns, A. & Sauter, M. (eds.), *Management – Handbuch Electronic Commerce*. Munich, pp. 427–434.

Hermes, V. (2007) Marketingplanung bei O2 – mit Zahlen allein ist es nicht getan! *Direktmarketing Report* (September), 20–21.

Herriott, S.R. (1992) Identifying and Developing Referral Channels, *Management Decision* (No. 30/1), 4–9.

Herrmann, A. (1993) Marketing-Controlling: Erläuterung der konzeptionellen Grundlagen zur Planung, Steuerung und Kontrolle der marketingpolitischen Aktivitäten am Beispiel von Unternehmen der Automobilindustrie. *Jahrbuch der Absatz- und Verbrauchsforschung*, Vol. 29 (No. 1), 4–22.

Hiebing, R.G. Jr. & Cooper, S.W. (2000) *The Successful Marketing Plan*. Lincolnwood.

Hieronimus, F. & Burmann, C. (2005) Persönlichkeitsorientiertes Markenmanagement, in Meffert, H., Burmann, C. & Koers, M. (eds.), *Markenmanagement. Identitätsorientierte Markenführung und praktische Umsetzung* (2nd fully revised and enhanced edition). Wiesbaden, pp. 365–386.

Hilker, J (1993) *Marketingimplementierung*. Wiesbaden.

Hippner, H. & Wilde, K.D. (2001) Komponenten einer CRM-Lösung, in Helmke, S. & Dangelmaier, W. (eds.), *Effektives Customer Relationship Management*. Wiesbaden, pp. 3–38.

Hoffman, D.L., Novak, T.P. & Chatterjee, P. (1996) Commercial Scenarios for the Web: Opportunities and Challenges. *Journal of Computer-Mediated Communications*, Vol. 1 (No. 3).

Hoffmann, C.P. & Klose, M. (2001) Logistik und Electronic Commerce, in Weiber, R. (ed.), *Handbuch Electronic Business*. Wiesbaden, pp. 599–622.

Holland, P. (2001) Supply Chain Optimization Systems in der Materialwirtschaft, in Walther, J. & Bund, M. (eds.), *Supply Chain Management*. Frankfurt, pp. 79–98.

Homburg, C. (ed.) (2006) *Kundenzufriedenheit: Konzepte – Methoden – Erfahrungen* (6th edition). Wiesbaden.

Homburg, C. & Krohmer, H. (2006) *Marketingmanagement. Strategie – Umsetzung – Unternehmensführung* (2nd revised and enhanced edition). Wiesbaden.

Homburg, C. & Schäfer, H. (2006) Die Erschliessung von Kundenwertpotenzialen durch Cross-Selling, in Günter, B. & Helm, S. (eds.), *Kundenwert. Grundlagen – Innovative Konzepte – Praktische Umsetzungen* (3rd revised and enhanced edition). Wiesbaden, pp. 157–182.

Homburg, C. & Schenkel, B. (2005) *Planning Excellence. Wegweiser zum professionellen Umgang mit der Marketing- und Vertriebsplanung.* Working Paper, Mannheim.

Homburg, C. & Simon, H. (1995) Wettbewerbsstrategien, in Tietz, B., Köhler, R. & Zentes, J. (eds.), *Handwörterbuch des Marketing* (2nd edition). Stuttgart, pp. 2753–2762.

Homburg, G. & Schneider, J. (2000) *Partnerschaft oder Konfrontation? Die Beziehung zwischen Industriegüterherstellern und Handel.* Arbeitspapier, Mannheim.

Homburg, C., Giering, A. & Hentschel, F. (1999) Der Zusammenhang zwischen Kundenzufriedenheit und Kundenbindung. *Die Betriebswirtschaft (DBW)*, Vol. 59 (No. 2), 174–195.

Homburg, C., Gruner, K. & Hocke, G. (1997) Entwicklungslinien der Marketingorganisation – eine empirische Untersuchung im produzierenden Gewerbe, *Zeitschrift für Betriebswirtschaft,* ZfB supplement (No. 1), 91–116.

Homburg, C., Schneider, J. & Schäfer, H. (2001) *Sales Excellence.* Wiesbaden.

Homburg, C., Workman, J. & Jensen, O. (2000) Fundamental Changes in Marketing Organization: The Movement Toward a Customer-Focused Organisational Structure. *Journal of the Academy of Marketing Science*, Vol. 28 (No. 4), 459–478.

Hope, J. & Fraser, R. (1999) Beyond Budgeting. *Management Accounting*, Vol. 79 (No. 1), 1–8.

Hope, J. & Fraser, R. (2000) *Beyond Budgeting. White paper 2. Managing in the New Economy,* Ed. v. Beyond Budgeting Round Table, CAM-I, Dorset, UK.

Hope, J. & Fraser, R. (2001) Figures of Hate, *Financial Management* (No. 2), 22–25.

Horvath & Partner (eds.) (2000) *Balanced Scorecard umsetzen.* Stuttgart.

Horvath, P. & Kaufmann, L. (1998) Balanced Scorecard. Ein Werkzeug zur Umsetzung von Strategien. *Harvard Business Manager*, Vol. 20 (No. 5), 39–48.

Horvath, P. & Meyer, R. (1989) Prozesskostenrechnung. Der Weg zu mehr Kostentransparenz und wirkungsvolleren Unternehmensstrategien. *Controlling*, 07/08, 214–219.

Horvath, P., Knust, P. & Schindera, F. (2001) Internet-Geschäfte erfordern ein wirksames e-Controlling, *Harvard Business Manager* (No. 5), 44–54.

Howe, J. (2006) The Rise of Crowdsourcing. *WIRED Magazine*, Vol. 14 (June, No. 6), 176–183.

Huber, G.P. (1991) Organizational Learning: The Contributing Processes and the Literatures. *Organization Science*, Vol. 2 (February, No. 1), 88–111.

Hühnerberg, R. (1984) *Marketing.* Munich.

Hummel, T. (1996) *Chancen und Grenzen der Computerunterstützung kooperativen Arbeitens.* Wiesbaden.

Hummel, T., Schoder, D. & Strauss, R.E. (1996) Why CSCW Applications Fail: Problems in the Support of Lateral Cooperation and the Appropriateness of CSCW Applications, in Chen, S.K. & Ebrahimpour, M. (eds.), *Northeast Decision Sciences Institute*, (April), 231–233.

Hurth, W. (2001) Multi-Channel-Marketing. *WiSt*, Heft 9 (September), 463–469.

Huston, L. & Sakkab, N. (2006) Connect and Develop. *Harvard Business Review*, Vol. 84 (March, No. 3), 58–66.

Hutzschenreuter, T. (2001) Organisation von Internet-Aktivitäten in etablierten Mehrproduktunternehmen. *Zeitschrift für Organisation*, Vol. 70 (No. 4), 206–212.

Iansiti, M. & MacCormack, A. (2000) Produktentwicklung im Internet-Takt, in Tapscott, D. (ed.), *Erfolg im e-Business.* Munich, pp. 114–129.

Ihde, T. (2007) Integriertes Online-Marketing bei Pelikan, in Schwarz, T. (ed.), *Leitfaden Online-Marketing.* Hamburg, pp. 30–31.

Im, I. & Hars, A. (2007) Does a one-size recommendation system fit all? The effectiveness of collaborative filtering based recommendation systems across different domains and search modes. *ACM Transactions on Information Systems (TOIS)*, Vol. 26 (November, No. 1),4:1–29.

Iyengar, S.S. & Lepper, M.R. When choice is demotivating: can one desire too much of a good thing? *Journal of Personality and Social Psychology*, Vol. 79 (No. 6), 995–1006.

Jackson, F.R. (1989) Customer Lifetime Valuation to Support Marketing Decision Making. *Journal of Direct Marketing*, Vol. 3 (Autumn, No. 4), 8–15.

Jacoby, J., Olson, J.C. & Haddock, R.A. (1971) Price, Brand Name, and Product Composition as Determinants of Perceived Quality. *Journal of Applied Psychology*, Vol. 55 (No. 6), 570–579.

Janetzko, D. (1999) *Statistische Anwendungen im Internet. In Netzumgebungen Daten erheben, auswerten und präsentieren.* Munich.

Jarchow, C. (2001) Werbeforschung im Internet, in Theobald, A., Dreyer, M. & Starsetzki, T. (eds.), *Online-Marktforschung.* Wiesbaden, pp. 275–290.

Jenewein, W., Kaufmann, G. & Wichert, C (2007). "Drum prüfe, wer sich bindet ..." – Eine empirische Untersuchung zur Wirkung von Markenkooperationen. *Thexis* (March), 35–39.

Jenner, T. (2003) *Marketingplanung.* Stuttgart.

Jentner, B. (1998) Praxisorientiertes Benchmarking für die gesamte Wertschöpfungskette der Vertriebsfunktion am Beispiel eines Automobilherstellers. *Zeitschrift für Betriebswirtschaft*, Vol. 68 (No. 9), 950–977.

Johnston, W. & Bonoma, T. (1981) The Buying Center, Structure and Interaction Patterns. *Journal of Marketing*, Vol. 45 (No. 3), 143–156.

Jöst, M. (1997) One-to-One-Communication – Individualisierung von Websites, in Boden, K.-P. & Barabas, M. (eds.), *Internet – von der Technologie zum Wirtschaftsfaktor, Deutscher Internet Kongress 1997.* Düsseldorf, pp. 129–134.

Jost, P.-J. (2001) *Organisation und Motivation, Eine ökonomisch-psychologische Einführung.* Wiesbaden.

Jourdan, Z., Rainer, R.R. & Marshall, T.E. (2008) Business Intelligence: An Analysis of the Literature. *Information Systems Management*, Vol. 25 (March, No. 2), 121–131.

Jung, H.-H. & Wiedmann, K.-P. (1998) Neuronale Netze im Rahmen der Automobilsegmentierung, in Hippner, H., Meyer, M. & Wilde, K.D. (eds.), *Computer Based Marketing*, Braunschweig, pp. 437–444.

Kairies, P. (2004) *Professionelles Produktmanagement für die Investitionsgüterindustrie.* Munich.

Kalakota, R. & Robinson, M. (2001) *e-Business 2.0, Roadmap for Success.* Reading.

Kalakota, R. & Whinston, A.B. (1996) *Frontiers of Electronic Commerce.* Reading.

Kaluza, B. (1996) Dynamische Produktdifferenzierungsstrategie und moderne Produktionssysteme, in Wildemann, H. (ed.), *Produktions- und Zuliefernetzwerke.* Munich, pp. 191–234.

Kannan, P.K. & Kopalle, P.K. (2001) Dynamic Pricing on the Internet: Importance and Implications for Consumer Behaviour. *International Journal of Electronic Commerce*, Vol. 5 (Spring, No. 3), 63–83.

Karig, F. (2007) Jeder kann Werbung, *Brand Eins* (No. 6), 14–15.

Karlöf, B. & Östblom, S.(1993) *Benchmarking.* Chichester.

Kaufmann, L. (1999) Purchasing and Supply Management – A Conceptual Framework, in Hahn, D. & Kaufmann, L. (eds.), *Handbuch Industrielles Beschaffungsmanagement.* Wiesbaden, pp. 3–32.

Kelly, K. (1998) *New Rules for the New Economy.* New York.

Kempis, R.-D. & Ringbeck, J. (1998) *Do IT Smart.* New York.

Kharif, O. (2008) Say hello to unlimited minutes. *BusinessWeek*, March 3.

Kieser, A. (1994) Fremdorganisation, Selbstorganisation und evolutionäres Management. *Zeitschrift für die betriebswirtschaftliche Forschung*, Vol. 46 (No. 3), 199–228.

Kim, W.C. & Mauborgne, R. (1997) Value Innovation: The Strategic Logic of Growth. *Harvard Business Review*, January–February, 103–112.

Kim, W.C. & Mauborgne, R. (1999) Fair Process: Managing in the Knowledge Economy, in Magretta, J. (ed.), *Managing in the New Economy.* Boston, pp. 115–132.

Kim, W.C. & Mauborgne, R. (2005) *Blue Ocean Strategy*. Boston.

Klein, S. & Selz, D. (1997) The impact of Electronic Commerce in the Automotive Industry. *Conference Proceedings of Association of Information Systems 1997 Americas Conference, Indianapolis, 08/97.*

Kleinaltenkamp, M. (1995) Standardisierung und Individualisierung, in Tietz, B. (ed.), *Handwörterbuch des Marketing* (2nd edition). Stuttgart, pp. 2354–2364.

Kleinaltenkamp, M. & Dahlke, B. (2006) Der Wert des Kunden als Informant – auf dem Weg zu einem "knowledge based customer value", in Günter, B. & Helm, S. (eds.), *Kundenwert. Grundlagen – Innovative Konzepte – Praktische Umsetzungen* (3rd revised and enhanced edition). Wiesbaden, pp. 217–240.

Kleiner, C. (2004) In den Marketingprozessen liegt das Gold, *Marketing & Kommunikation* (No. 5), 18–20.

Kliger, M., & Südmeyer, V. (2003) Weniger ist mehr, *Der Handel*, No. 7.

Klusch, M. (2001) Intelligente Informationsagenten für die Wissensentdeckung und Data Mining im Internet, in Meyer, M. & Wilde, K. (eds.), *Handbuch Data Mining im Marketing*. Wiesbaden, pp. 511–542.

Knapp, D.E. (2000) *The Brand Mindset*. New York.

Knapp, F. (2001) Markenführung im Internet, in Theobald, A., Dreyer, M. & Starsetzki, T. (eds.), *Online-Marktforschung*. Wiesbaden, pp. 237–248.

Koch, J. (2005) Der gefährliche Pfad des Erfolgs. *Harvard Business Manager*. pp. 97–102.

Kohl, U (1996) *Benutzerbezogene Datensicherheit in Kommunikationssystemen, VDI-Reihe* 10 (No. 446), Düsseldorf, VDI-Verlag.

Köhler, R. (2006) Marketingcontrolling: Konzepte und Methoden, in Reinecke, S. & Tomczak, T. (eds.), *Handbuch Marketing-Controlling. Effektivität und Effizienz einer marktorientierten Unternehmensführung* (2nd edition). Wiesbaden, pp. 39–62.

Köhler, T. (2000) Aufbau des digitalen Vertriebs, in Thome, R. & Schinzer, H. (eds.), *Electronic Commerce: Anwendungsbereiche und Potentiale der digitalen Geschäftsabwicklung*. Munich, pp. 107–124.

Kolbrück, O. (2007) Ein Trio mischt im Web mit – Mymuesli.com ist trotz Lieferproblemen auf Erfolgskurs, *Horizont* (June 8), 20.

Kollmannsperger, M. (2000) *Erfolgskriterien des Konfliktmanagements: eine empirische Untersuchung*. Frankfurt am Main.

Koop, H.J., Jäckel, K.K. & van Offern, A.L. (2001) *Erfolgsfaktor Content Management*. Braunschweig.

Koschnick, W.J. (2003) *Focus-Lexikon für Werbeplanung – Mediaplanung – Marktforschung – Kommunikationsforschung – Mediaforschung* (3rd edition). Munich.

Kotha, S. (1995) Mass Customization: Implementing the Emerging Paradigm for Competitive Advantage. *Strategic Management Journal*, Vol. 16, special edition "Technological Transformation and the New Competitive Landscape", pp. 21–42.

Kotler, P. (2005) *Die 10 Todsünden im Marketing*. Berlin.

Kotler, P. & Bliemel, F. (2001) *Marketing-Management: Analyse, Planung und Verwirklichung* (10th edition). Stuttgart.

Koushik, S. & Straeten, D. (2001) Eine strategische Roadmap zur Implementierung von e-Business-Lösungen, in Weiber, R. (ed.), *Handbuch Electronic Business*. Wiesbaden, pp. 91–114.

Krafft, M. (1999) Der Kunde im Fokus: Kundennähe, Kundenzufriedenheit, Kundenbindung – und Kundenwert? *Die Betriebswirtschaft*, Vol. 59 (No. 4), 511–530.

Krafft, M. & Albers, S. (2000) Ansätze zur Segmentierung von Kunden – wie geeignet sind herkömmliche Konzepte? *Zeitschrift für betriebswirtschaftliche Forschung*, Vol. 52 (No. 3), 515–536.

Kreikebaum, H. (1989) *Strategische Unternehmensplanung* (3rd edition). Stuttgart.

Kreshel, P.J., Lancaster, K.M. & Toomey, M.A. (1985) *Advertising Media Planning: How Leading Advertising Agencies Estimate Effective Reach and Frequency.* Urbana.

Kreutz, H. & Titscher, S. (1974) Die Konstruktion von Fragebögen, in Koolwijk, J. & van, Wieken-Mayser, M. (eds.), *Techniken der empirischen Sozialforschung.* Vol. 4, *Erhebungsmethoden: Die Befragung.* Munich, pp. 24–82.

Kreutzer, R.T. (2008) Passion – der differenzierende Erfolgsfaktor mit Zukunft, in Kreutzer, R.T. & Merkle, W. (eds.), *Die neue Macht des Marketing.* Wiesbaden, pp. 49–78.

Kreutzer, R.T. & Merkle, W. (2008a) Die Notwendigkeit zur Neuausrichtung des Marketing, in Kreutzer, R.T. & Merkle, W. (eds.), *Die neue Macht des Marketing.* Wiesbaden, pp. 13–20.

Kreutzer, R.T. & Merkle, W. (2008b) Web 2.0 – welche Potenziale gilt es zu heben?, in Kreutzer, R.T. & Merkle, W. (eds.), *Die neue Macht des Marketing.* Wiesbaden, pp. 149–184.

Kreutzer, R.T., Kuhfuss, H. & Hartmann, W. (2007) *Marketing Excellence. Sieben Schlüssel zur Profilierung ihrer Marketing Performance.* Wiesbaden.

Kricsfalussy, A. & Meurer, J. (2006) Marketing-Exzellenz: Basis zum Benchmarking, in Reinecke, S. & Tomczak, T. (eds.), *Handbuch Marketing-Controlling. Effektivität und Effizienz einer marktorientierten Unternehmensführung* (2nd edition). Wiesbaden, pp. 195–224.

Krishnamurthi, L. & Raj, S. (1991) An empirical analysis of the relationship between brand loyalty and consumer price elasticity. *Marketing Science*, Vol. 10 (No. 2), 172–183.

Kroeber-Riel, W. (1992) *Konsumentenverhalten* (5th edition). Munich.

Kroeber-Riel, W. (1993a) *Bildkommunikation.* Munich.

Kroeber-Riel, W. (1993b) *Strategie und Technik der Werbung* (4th edition). Stuttgart.

Krugman, H.E. (1975) What makes advertising effective? *Harvard Business Review*, Vol. 53 (March–April), 96–103.

Krumm, R. & Geissler, C. (2005) *Outbound-Praxis. Aktives Verkaufen am Telefon erfolgreich planen und umsetzen.* Wiesbaden.

Krystek, U. & Müller-Stewens, G. (2002) *Frühaufklärung für Unternehmen.* Stuttgart.

Kuhl, M. & Stöber, O. (2006) Data Warehousing und Customer Relationship Management als Grundlagen des wertorientierten Kundenmanagements, in Günter, B. & Helm, S. (eds.), *Kundenwert. Grundlagen – Innovative Konzepte – Praktische Umsetzungen* (3rd revised and enhanced edition). Wiesbaden, pp. 531–548.

Kuhlen, R. (1999) *Die Konsequenzen der Informationsassistenten. Was bedeutet informationelle Autonomie oder wie kann Vertrauen in elektronische Dienste in offenen Informationsmärkten gesichert werden?* Frankfurt.

Kuss, A., Tomczak, T. & Reinecke, S. (2007) *Marketingplanung. Einführung in die marktorientierte Unternehmens- und Geschäftsfeldplanung* (5th edition). Wiesbaden.

Küstenmacher, W., Seiwert, L.J. & Küstenmacher, T. (2004) *Simplify your life. Einfacher und glücklicher leben.* Frankfurt.

Kütz, M. (2000) Benutzerorientiertes Projektmanagement in grossen Softwareentwicklungs-und-einführungsprojekten, in Etzel, H.-J., Heilmann, H. & Richter, R. (eds.), *IT – Projektmanagement. Fallstricke und Erfolgsfaktoren.* Heidelberg, pp. 43–94.

Lammerskötter, D. & Klein, S. (2001) Neuere Entwicklungen auf elektronischen Märkten: Strategische Herausforderungen des e-Business, in Eggers, B. & Hoppen, G. (eds.), *Strategisches e-Commerce-Management.* Wiesbaden, pp. 45–71.

Lang, A. & Reich, S. (2008) "Outside-In" – die erfolgreiche Integration von Endkunden in den Innovationsprozess, in Kreutzer, R.T. & Merkle, W. (eds.), *Die neue Macht des Marketing.* Wiesbaden, pp. 131–148.

Lant, T.K. & Mezias, S.J. (1992) An Organizational Learning Model of Convergence and Reorientation. *Organization Science*, Vol. 3 (February, No. 1), 47–71.

Lederer, A.L., Mirchandani, D.A. & Sims, K. (1997) The Link between Information Strategy and Electronic Commerce. *Journal of Organizational Computing and Electronic Commerce*, Vol. 7 (No. 1), 17–34.

Ledingham, D. & Rigby, D. (2005) CRM-Systeme profitabel einsetzen, *Harvard Businessmanager* (26.04.2005, No. 5), 38.

Lensker, P.B. (2008) Marketing als Wachstumsmotor – nur die kundenzentrierte Innovation zählt, in Kreutzer, R.T. & Merkle, W. (eds.), *Die neue Macht des Marketing*. Wiesbaden, pp. 113–130.

Leonhard-Barton, D. (1992) The Factory as a Learning Laboratory. *Sloan Management Review*, Fall, 23–38.

Liautaud, B. (2001) *e-Business Intelligence*. New York.

Li, C. & Bernoff, J. (2008) *Groundswell. Winning in a World Transformed by Social Technologies*. Boston.

Link, J. & Hildebrand, V. (1993) *Database Marketing und Computer Aided Selling*. Munich.

Linthicum, D.S. (2001) B2B *Application Integration*. Upper Saddle River.

Löffler, H. & Scherfke, A. (2000) *Praxishandbuch Direktmarketing*. Berlin.

Lewis, M. (2000) Boom or Bust. *Business 2.0*, April, 193–202.

Lohmüller, T. (2008) Das Dilemma der Universalisten, der Erfolg der Spezialisten – Schritte zu einer tragfähigen Zielgruppenstrategie, in Kreutzer, R.T. & Merkle, W. (eds.), *Die neue Macht des Marketing*. Wiesbaden, pp. 291–304.

Lou, H. & Scamell, R.W. (1996) Acceptance of Groupware: The Relationships Among Use, Satisfaction, and Outcomes. *Journal of Organizational Computing and Electronic Commerce*, Vol. 6 (No. 2), 173–190.

Lüdi, A. (1997): Personalize or Perish. *EM – Electronic Markets*, Vol. 7 (No. 3), URL: http://www.electronicmarkets.org/netacademy/publications.nsf/all_pk/190.

Ludwig, M. (1999) Einführung eines WebContent Management Systems bei der Bayerischen Landesbank, in Heinen, I. (ed.), *Internet – mit e-Commerce auf dem Weg zum wirtschaftlichen Erfolg*. Heidelberg, pp. 125–130.

Lüttgens, M.R. (2000) *Marketingplanung. Von der Unternehmensstrategie zur operativen Marketingplanung. Ein Leitfaden für praxisnahes Marketing* (3rd enhanced edition). Bern.

MacMillan, I.C. & McGrath, R.G. (1997) Discovering New Points for Differentiation. *Harvard Business Review*, July–August, 133–145.

Maes, P. (1994) Agents That Reduce Work And Information Overload. *Communications of the ACM*, Vol. 37 (July, No. 7), 31–40.

Magretta, J. (1999a) Fast, Global, and Entrepreneurial: Supply Chain Management, Hong Kong Style, in Magretta, J. (ed.), *Managing in the New Economy*. Boston, pp. 213–234.

Magretta, J. (1999b) The Power of Virtual Integration, in Magretta, J. (ed.), *Managing in the New Economy*. Boston, pp. 193–212.

Malone, T.W. & Laubacher, R.J. (2000) Vernetzt, klein und flexibel – die Firma des 21. Jahrhunderts, in Tapscott, D. (ed.), *Erfolg im e-Business*. Munich, pp. 79–91.

Manz, C.C. & Sims, H.P. Jr. (1980) Self-Management as a Substitute for Leadership: A Social Learning Theory Perspective. *Academy of Management Review*, Vol. 5 (No. 3), 361–367.

Manz, C.C. (1992) Self-Leading Work Teams: Moving Beyond Self-Management Myths. *Human Relations*, Vol. 45 (No. 11), 1119–1140.

Manz, C.C. & Sims, H.P. Jr. (1989) *SuperLeadership. Leading Others to Lead Themselves*. New York.

Marketing Leadership Council (2005) *Business-to-Business Divisional Marketing Organisational Profiles. Structures, Roles and Responsibilities of the Marketing Function*. Washington.

Marketing Leadership Council (2006) *Coordinating Global B2B Marketing Campaigns*. White Paper, December.

Markus, M.L. (2000) *Paradigm Shifts – e-Business and Business/Systems Integration, Communications of the Association for Information Systems*, Vol. 4, Article 10 (November).

Markus, M.L. & Robey, D. (1988) Information Technology and Organization Change, Causal Structure in Theory and Research. *Management Science*, Vol. 34, 583–598.

Martin, W (2006) Cortal Consors: Willkommen bei der Anlagebank für Europa! *Expert sites*, 1–5.

Mattes, F. (1999) *Electronic Business-to-Business. e-Commerce mit Internet und EDI*. Stuttgart.

Matys, E. (2005) *Praxishandbuch Produktmanagement, Grundlagen und Instrumente* (3rd edition). Frankfurt.

Maxmin, J. & Zuboff, S. (2004) *The Support Economy: Why Corporations Are Failing Individuals and the Next Episode of Capitalism*. London.

Mayer, R. (1993) *Strategien erfolgreicher Produktgestaltung. Individualisierung und Standardisierung*. Wiesbaden.

McCarthy, M. (1999) *Internet and e-Commerce Services Market: A Competitive Analysis*. IDC.

McCloskey, J. (2001) The PerfectBook Machine. *Business 2.0*, July 10, 24–26.

McDonald, M. (2005) *Marketing Plans. How to Prepare Them, How to Use Them* (5th edition). Oxford.

McFarlan, F.W. & McKenney, J.L. (1983) *Corporate Information Systems Management: The Issues facing Senior Executives*. Homewood.

McKenna, R. (1997) *Real Time: Preparing for the Age of the Never Satisfied Customer*. Boston.

McKenna, R. (2000a) Marketing in an Age of Diversity, in Gilmore, J.H. & Pine, B.J. II (eds.), *Markets of One*. Boston, pp. 17–34.

McKenna, R. (2000b) Marketing in Echtzeit, in Tapscott, D. (ed.), *Erfolg im e-Business*. Munich, pp. 167–181.

Meador, C.L. (1994) *IT/Strategy Alignment. Identifying the Role of Information Technology in Competitive Strategy*. Working Paper, MIS Quarterly.

Meffert, H. & Burmann, C. (2005) Wandel in der Markenführung – vom instrumentellen zum identitätsorientierten Markenverständnis, in Meffert, H., Burmann, C. & Koers, M. (eds.), *Markenmanagement. Identitätsorientierte Markenführung und praktische Umsetzung* (2nd fully revised and enhanced edition). Wiesbaden, pp. 19–36.

Mena, J. (1999) *Data Mining Your Website*. Woburn.

Merkle, W. (2008) Der Mythos vom "Tod der Mitte" – Handlungsfelder für eine weiterhin erfolgreiche Marktbearbeitung, in Kreutzer, R.T. & Merkle, W. (eds.), *Die neue Macht des Marketing*. Wiesbaden, pp. 267–290.

Merkle, W. & Kreutzer, R.T. (2008) Emotion, Leidenschaft und Begeisterung – ein (noch immer) unterschätzter Erfolgsfaktor im Marketing, in Kreutzer, R.T. & Merkle, W. (eds.), *Die neue Macht des Marketing*. Wiesbaden, pp. 21–48.

Merz, M. (1999) *Elektronische Dienstemärkte. Modelle und Mechanismen des Electronic Commerce*. Berlin.

Miller, A. & Dess, G.G. (1993) Assessing Porter's Model in Terms of its Generalizability, Accuracy and Simplicity. *Journal of Management Studies*, Vol. 30 (No. 4), 553–585.

Misner, I. & Davis, R. (1998) *Business by Referral*. Austin.

Mohr, N. & Woehe, J.M. (1998) *Widerstand erfolgreich managen*. Frankfurt.

Moschis, G.P. (1976) Social Comparison and informal group influence. *Journal of Marketing Research*, Vol. 13, (August), 237–244.

Mougayar, W. (1998) *Opening Digital Markets: Battle Plans and Business Strategies for Internet Commerce*. New York.

Müller, A. & von Thienen, L. (2001) *e-Profit: Controlling-Instrumente für erfolgreiches e-Business*. Freiburg.

Müller, G. & Reichenbach, M. (2001) *Sicherheitskonzepte für das Internet*. Berlin.

Müller, G., Kohl, U. & Schoder, D. (1997) *Unternehmenskommunikation – Telematiksysteme für vernetzte Unternehmen*. Bonn.

Müller, G., Kohl, U. & Strauss, R.E. (1996) *Zukunftsperspektiven der digitalen Vernetzung.* Heidelberg.

Müller, G. & Strauss, R.E. (1994) *Vom Papier zur Elektronik – EDV-technische und organisatorische Weichenstellungen im Druck- und Verlagsbereich – ein Erfahrungsbericht.* Freiburg.

Müller, G. & Strauss, R.E. (1995) Medienmanagement, in Zilahi-Szabo, M.G. (ed.), *Kleines Lexikon der Informatik und Wirtschaftsinformatik.* Munich, pp. 344–348.

Müller, W. (2008) Repositionierung des Marketing – von der funktionalen Programmatik zur ganzheitlichen Managementaufgabe, in Kreutzer, R.T. & Merkle, W. (eds.), *Die neue Macht des Marketing.* Wiesbaden, pp. 231–246.

Muther, A. (2000) *Electronic Customer Care* (2nd edition). Berlin.

Myers, J.B., Pickersgill, A.D. & van Metre, E.S. (2004) Steering your customers to the right channels, *The McKinsey Quarterly* (No. 4), 37–47.

Nath, P. & Mahajan, V. (2008) Chief Marketing Officers: A Study of Their Presence in Firms' Top Management Teams, *Journal of Marketing* (No. 1).

Naudi, S. (2003) *Advanced Telesales* (2nd Edition); *The Definitive Guide to Success* (2nd edition). Warriewood.

Neck, C.P. & Manz, C.C. (1994) From Groupthink to Teamthink: Toward the Creation of Constructive Thought Patterns in Self-Managing Work Teams. *Human Relations*, Vol. 47 (No. 8), 929–952.

NetGenesis Corp. (2000) *e-Metrics. Business Metrics for the New Economy.* Cambridge.

Newell, F. (2000) *Loyalty.com. Customer Relationship Management in the New Era of Internet Marketing.* New York.

Nippa, M. (1993) Informationstechnik – Motor und Bremse des organisatorischen Wandels, in Scharfenberg, H. (ed.), *Strukturwandel in Management und Organisation.* Baden-Baden, pp. 323–345.

Nolte, H. (1976) *Die Markentreue im Konsumgüterbereich.* Bochum.

Novak, T.P. & Hoffman, D.L. (1995) *New Metrics for New Media: Toward the Development of Web Measurement Standards*, Nashville, URL: http://www2000.ogsm.vanderbilt.edu/novak/web.standards/webstand.html.

Nunes, P.F. & Cespedes, F.V. (2004) So fangen Sie Kunden, *Harvard Business Manager* (No. 5).

Nykiel, R.A. (2003) *Marketing your Business. A Guide to Developing a Strategic Marketing Plan.* New York.

o. V. (2001a) Massgeschneiderte Ersatzteile über das Internet, *Computerwoche* (No. 32), 32–33.

o. V. (2001b) Schuhkartons aus dem World Wide Web, *Logistik Heute* (No. 6), 34.

o. V. (2001c) Sealed Air reduziert Prozesskosten, *Logistik Heute* (No. 1–2), 38–39.

Oeldorf, G. & Olfert, K. (1998) *Materialwirtschaft* (8th edition). Ludwigshafen.

Ogawa, S. & Piller, F.T. (2006) Reducing the Risks of New Product Development. *MIT Sloan Management Review*, Vol. 47 (Winter, No. 2), 65–71.

Ogilvy, D. & Raphaelson, J. (1982) Research on Advertising Techniques that work – and don't work. *Harvard Business Review*, Vol. 60 (July–August), 14–18.

Oldroyd, J.B. & Gulati, R. (2005) Koordination ist alles. *Harvard Business Manager*, (June 28, No. 7), 87.

Orenstein, D. (2001) Hidden Treasure. *Business 2.0*, (July 10), 41–43.

Osel, W. (1993) Intel – vom Techniker zum Markenartikel. *Markenartikel*, (December), 574–578.

Österle, H. (1995) *Business Engineering. Prozess- und Systementwicklung*, Vol. 1. Entwurfstechniken.

Page, P. & Ehring, T. (2000) *Electronic Business und New Economy.* Berlin.

Paley, N. (2000) *A Strategic Marketing Plan. A Step-by-Step Guide.* Boca Raton.

Parsons, G. (1983) Information Technology: A New Competitive Weapon. *Sloan Management Review*, Vol. 24 (Winter), 3–14.

Pepels, W. (2000) *Produktmanagement*. Vienna.

Pepels, W. (2001a) Darstellung und Bedeutung des Kundenlebenszeitwerts im Business-to-Business Marketing, in Helmke, S. & Dangelmaier, W. (eds.), *Effektives Customer Relationship Management*. Wiesbaden, pp. 49–84.

Pepels, W.G. (2001b) Grundzüge eines Beschwerdemanagements, in Helmke, S. & Dangelmaier, W. (eds.), *Effektives Customer Relationship Management*. Wiesbaden, pp. 117–132.

Peppers, D. & Rogers, M. (1993) *The One to One Future*. New York.

Peppers, D. & Rogers, M. (1997) *Enterprise One-to-One. Tools for Competing in the Interactive Age*. New York.

Peppers, D. & Rogers, M. (1998) *The One to One Fieldbook*. New York.

Peppers, D. & Rogers, M. (1999) *The One-To-One-Manager. Real-World Lessons in Customer Relationship Management*. New York.

Peppers, D., Rogers, M. & Dorf, B. (2000) Is Your Company Ready for One-To-One-Marketing? in Gilmore, J.H. & Pine, B.J. (eds.), *Markets of One. Creating Customer-Unique Value through Mass Customization*. Boston, pp. 75–98.

Perrey, J., Wagener, N. & Wallmann, C. (2007) *Kreativität + Content Fit = Werbeerfolg*. McKinsey & Comp., Düsseldorf.

Pfannenmüller, J. (1999) Starke Schokotypen.

Pfeiffer, M. & Imhoff, J. (2008) Innovative Analysekonzepte mit neuronalen Netzen – von Daten zu Taten, in Kreutzer, R.T. & Merkle, W. (eds.), *Die neue Macht des Marketing*. Wiesbaden, pp. 325–354.

Phillips, C. & Meeker, M. (2000) *The B2B Internet Report. Collaborative Commerce*. Morgan Stanley Dean Witter, April.

Picot, A. (1993) Organisationsstrukturen im Spannungsfeld von Zentralisierung und Dezentralisierung, in Scharfenberg, H. (ed.), *Strukturwandel in Management und Organisation*. Baden-Baden, pp. 217–236.

Picot, A. & Neuburger, R. (2000) Grundzüge des Produktionsmanagements in vernetzten Organisationen, in Kaluza, B. & Blecker, Th. (eds.), *Produktions- und Logistikmanagement in virtuellen Unternehmen und Unternehmensnetzwerken*. Berlin, pp. 177–188.

Piller, F.T. (1998) *Kundenindividuelle Massenproduktion*. Munich.

Piller, F.T. (2006) *Mass Customization* (4th current edition). Wiesbaden.

Piller, F.T. & Schoder, D. (1999) Mass Customization and Electronic Commerce. *Zeitschrift für Betriebswirtschaft*, Vol. 69 (No. 10), 1111–1136.

Piller, F.T. & Walcher, D. (2006) Toolkits for idea competitions: a novel method to integrate users in new product development. *R&D Management*, Vol. 36 (June, No. 3), 307–318.

Pine, B.J., Victor, B. & Boynton, A.C. (2000) Making Customization Work, in Gilmore, J.H. & Pine, B.J. (eds.), *Markets of One. Creating Customer-Unique Value through Mass Customization*. Boston, pp. 149–166.

Pine, J. (1993) *Mass Customization – The New Frontier in Business Competition*. Boston.

Pine, J., Peppers, R. & Rogers, M. (1995) Do you Want to Keep your Customers Forever? *Harvard Business Review* (No. 3–4), 103–104.

Pletter, R. (2007) Die Biedermänner zeigen Zähne, *Brand eins* (No. 7).

Porst, A. (1999) Content Management and Workflow Computing, in Heinen, I. (ed.), *Internet – mit e-Commerce auf dem Weg zum wirtschaftlichen Erfolg*. Heidelberg, pp. 95–112.

Porter, M. (1980) *Competitive Strategy*. New York.

Porter, M.E. (1999) Clusters and the New Economics of Competition, in Magretta, J. (ed.), *Managing in the New Economy*. Boston, pp. 25–48.

Porter, M.E. (2001) Bewährte Strategien werden durch das Internet noch wirksamer, *Harvard Business Manager* (No. 5), 64–81.

Porter, M.E. & Millar, V.E. (1985) How Information Technology Gives You Competitive Advantage. *Harvard Business Review*, (July–August), 149–160.

Prahalad, C.K. & Lieberthal, K. (1999) The End of Corporate Imperialism, in Magretta, J. (ed.), *Managing in the New Economy*. Boston, pp. 49–68.

Precourt, G. (ed.) (2007) *CMO Thought Leaders: The Rise of the Strategic Marketer*. Strategy & Business.

Probst, G.J.B. & Büchel, B.S.T. (1994) *Organisationales Lernen*. Wiesbaden.

Proff, H. & Proff, H. (1997) Möglichkeiten und Grenzen hybrider Strategien – dargestellt am Beispiel der deutschen Automobilindustrie. *Die Betriebswirtschaft*, Vol. 57 (No. 6), 796–809.

Raepple, M. (2001) *Sicherheitskonzepte für das Internet*. Heidelberg.

Rahders, R. (1989) *Verfahren und Probleme der Bestimmung des optimalen Werbebudgets*. Idstein.

Raisgild, R. (1998) *Buying & Leasing Cars on the Internet*. Los Angeles.

Rao, A.G. & Miller, P.B. (1975) Advertising/Sales Response Functions. *Journal of Advertising Research*, Vol. 15 (April), 7–15.

Rappa, M. (2001) "Business Models on the Web". http://digitalenterprise.org/models/models.html.

Raub, S.P. & Probst, G.J.B. (2001) Knowledge Management and e-Business, in Weiber, R. (ed.), *Handbuch Electronic Business*. Wiesbaden, pp. 403–428.

Raulf, M. (2000) Analyse, Auswahl, Anpassung, Fehlschlag – die Historie einer Standardsoftwareeinführung, in Etzel, H.-J., Heilmann, H. & Richter, R. (eds.), *IT – Projektmanagement. Fallstricke und Erfolgsfaktoren*. Heidelberg, pp. 133–178.

Rayport, J.F. & Jaworski, B.J. (2005) *Best Face Forward. Why Companies must Improve their Service Interfaces with Customers*. Boston.

Rayport, J.F. & Sviokla, J.J. (2000) Die virtuelle Wertschöpfungskette – kein fauler Zauber, in Tapscott, D. (ed.), *Erfolg im e-Business*. Munich, pp. 59–78.

Recktenfelderbäumer, M. (2006) Prozesskostenrechnung im Marketing, in Reinecke, S. & Tomczak, T. (eds.), *Handbuch Marketing-Controlling. Effektivität und Effizienz einer marktorientierten Unternehmensführung* (2nd edition). Wiesbaden, pp. 767–794.

Reichhardt, C. (2000) *One-to-One-Marketing im Internet*. Wiesbaden.

Reichheld, F.F. (1997) *Der Loyalitäts-Effekt – die verborgene Kraft hinter Wachstum, Gewinnen und Unternehmenswert*. Frankfurt am Main.

Reichwald, R. & Piller, F.T. (2001) Mass Customization-Konzepte im Electronic Business, in Weiber, R. (ed.), *Handbuch Electronic Business*. Wiesbaden, pp. 359–382.

Reigber, D. & Spöhrer, J. (2001) Agentenbasierte Marktforschung, in Theobald, A., Dreyer, M. & Starsetzki, T. (eds.), *Online-Marktforschung*. Wiesbaden, pp. 391–406.

Reinecke, S. (2006) Return-on-Marketing? in Reinecke, S. & Tomczak, T. (eds.), *Handbuch Marketing-Controlling. Effektivität und Effizienz einer marktorientierten Unternehmensführung* (2nd edition). Wiesbaden, pp. 3–38.

Reinecke, S. & Fuchs, D. (2006) Marketingbudgetierung, in Reinecke, S. & Tomczak, T. (eds.), *Handbuch Marketing-Controlling. Effektivität und Effizienz einer marktorientierten Unternehmensführung* (2nd edition). Wiesbaden, pp. 795–820.

Reinecke, S. & Herzog, W. (2006) Stand des Marketingcontrollings in der Praxis, in Reinecke, S. & Tomczak, T. (eds.), *Handbuch Marketing-Controlling. Effektivität und Effizienz einer marktorientierten Unternehmensführung* (2nd edition). Wiesbaden, pp. 81–98.

Reinecke, S. & Janz, S. (2006) Organisation des Marketingcontrollings, in Reinecke, S. & Tomczak, T. (eds.), *Handbuch Marketing-Controlling. Effektivität und Effizienz einer marktorientierten Unternehmensführung* (2nd edition). Wiesbaden, pp. 915–932.

Reinecke, S., Tomczak, T. & Geis, G. (2006) Marketingkennzahlensysteme, in Reinecke, S. & Tomczak, T. (eds.), *Handbuch Marketing-Controlling. Effektivität und Effizienz einer marktorientierten Unternehmensführung* (2nd edition). Wiesbaden, pp. 891–914.

Reingen, P.H. & Kernan, J.B. (1986) Analysis of Referral Networks in Marketing: Methods and Illustration. *Journal of Marketing Research* (November), 370–378.

Reitsperger, W., Daniel, S.J., Tallman, S.B. & Chismar, W.G. (1993) Product Quality and Cost Leadership: Compatible Strategies. *Management International Review*, Vol. 33, (special edition 1), 7–21.

Riedl, S. (2007) Multi-Channel dominiert die Branche, *IT Business* (No. 19), 15–16.

Rieg, R. (2007) Beyond Budgeting – Ende oder Neubeginn der Budgetierung. *Balanced Scorecard*, (October 27).

Riemenschneider, M. (2006) *Der Wert von Produktvielfalt: Wirkung grosser Sortimente auf das Verhalten von Konsumenten.* Wiesbaden.

Ries, A. & Ries, L. (1998) *Die 22 unumstösslichen Gebote des Branding.* Düsseldorf.

Ries, A. & Ries, L. (2005) *Die Entstehung der Marken.* Munich.

Riesenbeck, H. & Perry, J. (2005) *Mega-Macht Marke – Erfolg messen, machen, managen* (2nd edition). Frankfurt am Main.

Ringland, G. & Young, L. (2006) *Scenarios in Marketing, From Vision to Decision.* Chichester.

Rockart, J.F. & Scott Morton, M.S. (1984) Implications of Changes in Information Technology for Corporate Strategy, *Interfaces* (No. 14), 84–95.

Rothfuss, G. & Ried, C. (2001) *Content Management mit XML.* Berlin.

Rüdiger, M. (2001) E-Customer-Innogration- Potenziale der internetbasierten Kundeneinbindung in Innovationsprozesse, in Krafft, M. (ed.), *Wissenschaftliche Schriftenreihe des Zentrums für Marktorientierte Unternehmensführung an der WHU* (July, No. 20).

Ruge, H.D. (2000) Aufbau von Markenbildern, in Esch, F.-R. (ed.), *Moderne Markenführung* (2nd edition). Wiesbaden, pp. 165–184.

Runte, M. (2000) *Personalisierung im Internet. Individualisierte Angebote mit Collaborative Filtering.* Wiesbaden.

Rust, R.T., Zeithaml, V.A. & Lemon, K.N. (2000) *Driving Customer Equity.* New York.

Sarkar, M., Butler, B. & Steinfeld, C. (1995) Intermediaries and Cybermediaries: A continuing Role for Mediating Players in the Electronic Marketplace. *Journal of Computer Mediated Communication*, Vol. 1 (No. 3).

Sauter, M. (1999) Chance, Risiken und strategische Herausforderungen des Electronic Commerce, in Hermanns, A. & Sauter, M. (eds.), *Management – Handbuch Electronic Commerce.* Munich, pp. 101–118.

Sawhney, M. (1999) The Longest Mile. *Business 2.0*, (December), 235–244.

Sawhney, M. & Kaplan, S. (1999) Let's Get Vertical. *Business 2.0*, (September), 84–92.

Schafer, J.B., Konstan, J.A. & Riedl, J. (1999) Recommender Systems in Electronic Commerce. *Proceedings of the ACM Conference on Electronic Commerce (EC-99).* Denver, pp. 158–166.

Schäffer, U. & Weber, J. (2001) Controlling von eBusiness. *Kostenrechnungspraxis.* Sonderheft 2, pp. 5–11.

Schauer, C. (2008) Mitarbeiter als Markenbotschafter – mit Leidenschaft die Marke vertreten, in Kreutzer, R.T. & Merkle, W. (eds.), *Die neue Macht des Marketing.* Wiesbaden, pp. 79–98.

Schauf, M. (2002) *Telemanagement. Telearbeit als Managementproblem.* Mering.

Schein, E. (1984) Coming to a New Awareness of Organizational Culture. *Sloan Management Review* (Winter), 3–15.

Schein, E. (1985) *Organizational Culture and Leadership.* San Francisco.

Schein, E. (1994a) Innovative Cultures and Organizations, in Allen, T.J. & Scott Morton, M.S. (eds.), *Information Technology and the Corporation of the 1990s.* New York, pp. 125–146.

Schein, E. (1994b) The Role of the CEO in the Management of Change: The Case of Information Technology, in Allen, T.J. & Scott Morton, M.S. (eds.), *Information Technology and the Corporation of the 1990s.* New York, pp. 325–345.

Schein, E.H. (1987) *Process Consultation*, Vol. 2, New York.

Schelske, A. (2007) Überallmarketing im Web 3.0, *Absatzwirtschaft – Zeitschrift für Marketing* (No. 11), 26–29.

Schmalen, H. (1985) *Kommunikationspolitik*. Werbeplanung, Stuttgart.

Schmalen, H. (2002) *Grundlagen und Probleme der Betriebswirtschaft* (12th edition). Passau.

Schinzer, H. & Steinacker, B. (2000) Virtuelle Gemeinschaften, in Thome, R. & Schinzer, H. (eds.), *Electronic Commerce: Anwendungsbereiche und Potentiale der digitalen Geschäftsabwicklung*. Munich, pp. 81–106.

Schmitt, E. (2004) *Left Brain Marketing*, Forrester Research, April 6.

Schmitt, S. (2005) *Die Existenz des hybriden Käufers. Verhaltenstheoretische Analyse und empirische Untersuchung der Preisbereitschaft von Konsumenten* (1st edition). Wiesbaden.

Schnaars, S.P. (1998) *Marketing Strategy* (2nd revised and updated version). New York.

Schnäbele, P. (1997) *Mass Customized Marketing*. Wiesbaden.

Schneider, G. & Schnetkamp, G. (2000) *e-Markets. B2B-Strategien im Electronic Commerce*. Wiesbaden.

Schoder, D. (1995) *Erfolg und Misserfolg telematischer Innovationen*. Wiesbaden.

Schoder, D. (1999) Nutzen des Electronic Commerce aus Unternehmenssicht – Eine faktorenanalytische Untersuchung. *Information Management & Consulting*, Vol. 14, 37–43, [Überarbeitete Version des Beitrages zur 4. Internationalen Tagung Wirtschaftsinformatik 1999.]

Schoder, D. (2000) Forecasting the success of telecommunication services in the presence of network effects. *Information Economics and Policy*, Vol. 12, 181–200.

Schoder, D. (2001) *Die ökonomische Bedeutung von Intermediären im Electronic Commerce*. Habil.-Schrift, Univ. Freiburg i.Br.

Schoder, D. (2007) The Flaw in Customer Lifetime Value, [Forethought], *Harvard Business Review* (December), 26.

Schoder, D. & Janetzko, D. (1998) Bots, Rubrik "Das aktuelle Stichwort". *Wirtschaftsinformatik* (April), 341–343.

Schoder, D. & Müller, G. (1999) Potentiale und Hürden des Electronic Commerce. Eine Momentaufnahme, Informatik Spektrum, Vol. 22 (August, No. 4), 252–260.

Schoder, D. & Pai-Ling, Y. (2000) Building Firm Trust Online – Barriers to E-Commerce and the Critical Role of Government. *Communications of the ACM*, Vol. 43 (December, No. 12), 73–112.

Schoder, D., Reichelt, J., Schlagwein, D. & Muhle, S. (2008) *Extending the CIO Portfolio Towards Information Management 2.0*. Working Paper, University of Cologne.

Schoder, D. & Strauss, R.E. (1997) Electronic Commerce, in Brossmann, M. & Fieger, U. (eds.), *Business Multimedia*. Frankfurt am Main, pp. 51–65.

Schoder, D. & Strauss, R.E. (1998) The Business Value of Web-Based Electronic Commerce – Empirical Evidence From Germany. *Proceedings of the Twelfth Biennal Conference of the ITS: Beyond Convergence, Communication into the Next Millennium,* Stockholm, Sweden, (June), 21–24.

Schoder, D., Strauss, R.E. & Welchering, P. (1998) *Electronic Commerce Enquête 1997/98, Empirische Studie zum betriebswirtschaftlichen Nutzen von Electronic Commerce für Unternehmen im deutschsprachigen Raum. Executive Research Report*, Stuttgart.

Schober, K.-S. (1998) Benchmarking, in Diller, H. (ed.), *Marketingplanung* (2nd fully revised and enhanced edition). Munich, pp. 199–212.

Schonfeld, E. (2005) The Flickrization of Yahoo! *Business 2.0*, Vol. 6 (December, No. 11), 156–164.

Schubert, P., Selz, D. & Haertsch, P. (2001) *Digital erfolgreich. Fallstudien zu strategischen e-Business-Konzepten*. Berlin.

Schüller, A. (2006) Empfehlungen sind planbar, *Io new management* (No. 7–8), 40–44.

Schwarz, T. (2007) *Leitfaden Online-Marketing*. Hamburg.

Sebastian, K.-H. & Simon, H. (1995) Ingredient Branding – Reift ein junger Markentypus? *Absatzwirtschaft – Zeitschrift für Marketing*, 42.

Selbmann, M. (2001) Banken – sichere Zahlungsmittel im Internet, in Gora, W. & Mann, E. (eds.), *Handbuch Electronic Commerce*. Berlin, pp. 263–277.

Seybold, P.B. (1998) *Customers.com. How to Create a Profitable Business Strategy for the Internet and Beyond*. New York.

Seybold, P.B. (2001) *The Customer Revolution*. New York.

Shapiro, C. & Varian, H.R. (1999) *Information Rules. A Strategic Guide to the Network Economy*. Boston.

Shapiro, C. & Varian, H.R. (2000) Versioning: The Smart Way to Sell Information, in Gilmore, J.H. & Pine, B.J. (eds.), *Markets of One. Creating Customer-Unique Value through Mass Customization*. Boston, pp. 133–148.

Sherrick, M. (2000) *Building and Managing the Digital Economy*. Morgan Stanley Dean Witter. April.

Siebel, T. & House, P. (2000) *Cyber Rules. Die neuen Regeln für Spitzenerfolge im e-Business*. Landsberg/Lech.

Siegel, D. (1997) *Creating Killer Web-Sites*. Indianapolis.

Silberer, G., Förster, F., Raffée, H., Fritz, W. & Hilger, H. (1984) Erfolgsrelevante Wirkungen vergleichender Warentestergebnisse auf Kaufentscheidungen der Konsumenten, in Silberer, G. & Raffée, H. (eds.), *Warentest und Konsument: Nutzung, Wirkungen und Beurteilung des vergleichenden Warentests im Konsumentenbereich*. Frankfurt, pp. 107–163.

Silverstein, B. (1999) *Business-to-Business Internet Marketing*. Gulf Breeze.

Simon, D. (1985) *Die Früherkennung von strategischen Diskontinuitäten*. Vienna.

Simon, H. (2007) *Hidden Champions des 21. Jahrhunderts. Die Erfolgsstrategien unbekannter Weltmarktführer*. Frankfurt.

Sissors, J.Z. & Bumba, L. (1988) *Advertising Media Planning* (3rd edition). Lincolnwood.

Skiera, B. (2000) *Preispolitik und Electronic Commerce – Preisdifferenzierung im Internet*. Frankfurt.

Skiera, B. & Garczorz, I. (2000) Barrieren aufbauen, Kunden binden. Wechselkosten im Electronic Commerce als strategisches Instrument. *Cybiz*, Vol. 1 (February), 52–55.

Skiera, B. & Spann, M. (2001) Flexible Preisgestaltung im e-Business, in Weiber, R. (ed.), *Handbuch Electronic Business*. Wiesbaden, pp. 539–557.

Slywotzky, A.J. & Morrison, D.J. (2000) *How Digital is Your Business?* New York.

Smith, C. & Comer, D. (1994) Self-Organization in Small Groups: A Study of Group Effectiveness within non-equilibrium conditions. *Human Relations*, Vol. 47 (No. 5), 553–581.

Sorrell, M. (1997) Riding the Rapids. *Business Strategy Review*, Vol. 8 (No. 3), 19–26.

Specht, D. & Hellmich, K. (2000) Management der Zulieferbeziehungen in dynamischen Produktionsnetzen, in Wildemann, H. (ed.), *Supply Chain Management*. Munich, pp. 89–116.

Spiliopoulou, M. (2001) Web Usage Mining: Data Mining über die Nutzung des Web, xin Meyer, M. & Wilde, K. (eds.), *Handbuch Data Mining im Marketing*. Wiesbaden, pp. 489–510.

Spivack, N. (2006) *The Third-Generation Web is Coming*, in KurzweilAI.net, December 17.

Stadelmann, M., Wolter, S., Tomczak, T. & Reinecke, S. (2003) *Customer Relationship Management*. Zürich.

Staehle, W.H. (1991) *Management – eine verhaltenswissenschaftliche Perspektive* (6th revised edition). Munich.

Staudt, E. & Schmeisser, W. (1986) Invention, Kreativität und Erfinder, in Staudt, E. (ed.), *Das Management von Innovationen*. Frankfurt, pp. 289–294.

Stauss, B. & Friege, C. (2006) Kundenwertorientiertes Rückgewinnungsmanagement, in Günter, B. & Helm, S. (eds.), *Kundenwert. Grundlagen – Innovative Konzepte – Praktische Umsetzungen* (3rd revised and enhanced edition). Wiesbaden, pp. 509–530.

Stauss, B. & Seidel, W. (1998) *Beschwerdemanagement: Fehler vermeiden – Leistung verbessern – Kunden binden* (2nd edition). Munich.

Steinle, C. (2001) Strategisches Management von e-Commerce-Geschäften, in Eggers, B. & Hoppen, G. (eds.), *Strategisches e-Commerce-Management*. Wiesbaden, pp. 329–360.

Stern, L.W. & El-Ansary, A. (1992) *Marketing Channels* (4th edition). Englewood Cliffs.

Sterne, J. (1996) *Customer Service on the Internet: Building Relationships, Increasing Loyalty and Staying Competitive*. New York.

Stevens, R., Loudon, D., Wrenn, B. & Mansfield, P. (2006) *Marketing Planning Guide* (3rd edition). New York.

Stippel, P. (2005) Alle wollen Marketing, aber warum will keiner den Job des CMO? *Absatzwirtschaft – Zeitschrift für Marketing* (No. 4), 16–20.

Stippel, P. (2007) Vom Aufschwung zum Aufbruch, *Absatzwirtschaft – Zeitschrift für Marketing* (No. 9), 14–28.

Stokburger, G. & Pufahl, M. (2002) *Kosten senken mit CRM. Strategien, Methoden und Kennzahlen.* Wiesbaden.

Strauss, R.E. (1995a) Das Medien-Management-Zentrum im Druck- und Verlagsbereich, *IM Information Management* (August, No. 3), 52–60.

Strauss, R.E. (1995b) Organizational Learning as a Cycle Between Microscopic and Macroscopic Levels, in Ebrahimpour, M. & Mangiameli, P.M. (eds.), *Northeast Decision Sciences Institute.* Proceedings, Providence, pp. 380–382.

Strauss, R.E. (1996) *Determinanten und Dynamik des Organizational Learning*. Wiesbaden.

Strauss, R.E. (1999) Von Büchern und CDs zu Automobilen – Erfolgsfaktoren und Strategien für den Electronic Commerce im Automobilhandel, *IM Information Management & Consulting* (No. 14), Sonderausgabe Electronic Commerce, (November), 51–59.

Strauss, R.E. (2006) Systematisches Marketingmanagement, in Heilmann, T. (ed.), *Praxishandbuch Internationales Marketing*. Wiesbaden, pp. 177–192.

Strauss, R.E. (2007) Transforming the Marketing Planning Process, in: Montgomery (ed.), *CRM Transformation*, Vol. 7, San Francisco, pp. 65–68.

Strauss, R.E. (2008) *Marketingplanung mit Plan. Strategien für ergebnisorientiertes Marketing.* Stuttgart.

Strauss, R.E., Padovan, B. & Schoder, D. (1995) Service Providers in Electronic Markets – Transformations in the Printing and Publishing Sector, in Dolakia, R.R. & Fortin, D. (eds.), *Living and Working in Cyberspace: New Information Technologies at Home and at Work.* Newport, pp. 144–151.

Strauss, R.E. & Schoder, D. (1999) Massenhafte Individualisierung und One-to-One-Marketing im Electronic Commerce, in Albers, S. (ed.), *Electronic Commerce*. Frankfurt, pp. 109–120.

Strauss, R.E. & Schoder, D. (1999a) Electronic Commerce – Herausforderungen für Unternehmen, in Hermanns, A. & Sauter, M. (eds.), *Handbuch Electronic Commerce*. Munich, pp. 61–74.

Strauss, R.E. & Schoder, D. (1999b) Wie werden Produkte den Kundenwünschen angepasst? in Albers, S., Clement, M., Peters, K. & Skiera, B. (eds.), *eCommerce*. Frankfurt, pp. 109–121.

Strauss, R.E. & Schoder, D. (2000) *e-Reality 2000. Electronic Commerce von der Vision zur Realität.* Frankfurt.

Strauss, R.E. & Schoder, D. (2001) *eReality. Das e-Business Bausteinkonzept. Strategien und Erfolgsfaktoren für das e-Business-Management.* Frankfurt.

Strauss, R.E. & Schoder, D. (2002) *Breitbandig zum interaktiven Endkonsumenten. Teil 1: Erfahrungen aus über 100 Feldversuchen in USA und Europa zu interaktivem Fernsehen (iTV).* Göttingen.

Strauss, R.E., Schoder, D. & Hummel, T. (1996a) The Learning Laboratory – Supporting Learning Organizations with Agent Systems, *1996 IEEE Annual International Engineering Management Conference: "Managing Virtual Enterprises: A Convergence of Communications,*

Computing and Energy Technologies", Vancouver, August 18–20, 1996, Canada, pp. 611–615.

Strauss, R.E., Schoder, D. & Müller, G. (1996b) Wired Cities – Opportunities for Small and Medium Sized Cities on the Information Highway, in Terashima, N. & Altman, E. (eds.), *Integration of Multimedia Based Applications and Information Superhighways*. Canberra (Australia), (September 2–6), 3–10.

Sydow, J. (1993) Von der Unternehmensorganisation zu Unternehmensnetzwerken, in Scharfenberg, H. (ed.), *Strukturwandel in Management und Organisation*. Baden-Baden, pp. 383–396.

Szameitat, A. (1999) Web-Content-Management-Systeme als Plattform für den Betrieb erfolgreicher Business Websites – Status, Evolution und Strategie, in Heinen, I. (ed.), *Internet – mit e-Commerce auf dem Weg zum wirtschaftlichen Erfolg*. Heidelberg, pp. 113–124.

Szuprowicz, B.O. (1995) *Multimedia Networking*. New York.

Szyperski, N. (1980) Strategisches Informationsmanagement im technologischen Wandel. Fragen zur Planung und Implementierung von Informations- und Kommunikationssystemen, *Angewandte Informatik* (No. 4), 141–148.

Tapscott, D. (1995) *The Digital Economy. Promise and Peril in the Age of Networked Intelligence*. New York.

Tapscott, D., Lowy, A. & Ticoll, D. (2000) *Digital Capital: Harnessing the Power of Business Webs*. Boston.

Tapscott, D. & Ticoll, D. (2003) *The Naked Corporation. How the Age of Transparency will Revolutionize Business*. New York.

Tapscott, D., Ticoll, D. & Lowy, A. (1999) The Rise of the Business Web. *Business 2.0*, (November), 197–208.

Tapscott, D. & Williams, A.D. (2006) *Wikinomics. How Mass Collaboration Changes Everything*. New York.

Tapscott, D. & Williams, A.D. (2007) *Wikinomics. How Mass Collaboration Changes Everything*. New York.

Thaler, K. (2001) *Supply Chain Management. Prozessoptimierung der logistischen Kette*. Cologne.

Theobald, A. (2000) Marktforschung im Internet, in Bliemel, F., Fassott, G. & Theobald, A. (eds.), *Electronic Commerce. Herausforderungen – Anwendungen – Perspektiven* (3rd edition). Wiesbaden, pp. 297–314.

Thome, R. & Schinzer, H. (2000) Marktüberblick Electronic Commerce, in Thome, R. & Schinzer, H. (eds.), *Electronic Commerce: Anwendungsbereiche und Potentiale der digitalen Geschäftsabwicklung*. Munich, pp. 1–17.

Thomke, S. & von Hippel, E. (2002) Customers as Innovators: A New Way to Create Value. *Harvard Business Review*, Vol. 80 (April, No. 4), 74–81.

Thompson, A.A. & Strickland, A.J. (1990) *Strategic Management: Concepts and Cases*. Homewood.

Thorelli, H.B., Becker, H. & Englewood, J. (1975) *The Information Seekers*. Cambridge.

Timmers, P. (1999) *Electronic Commerce. Strategies and Models for Business-to-Business Trading*. West Sussex.

Tiwana, A. (2001) *The Essential Guide to Knowledge Management*. Upper Saddle River.

Tjosvold, D. (1990) Making a Technological Innovation Work: Collaboration to Solve Problems. *Human Relations*, Vol. 43 (No. 11), 1117–1131.

Tölle, K., Hofacker, T. & Kaas, K.P. (1981) Der "Information Seeker": Konsumbegeistert oder konsumkritisch? *Marketing ZFP* (No. 1), 47–50.

Tomczak, T., Schögel, M. & Birkhofer, B. (2000) Online-Distribution als innovativer Absatzkanal, in Bliemel, F., Fassott, G. & Theobald, A. (eds.), *Electronic Commerce. Herausforderungen – Anwendungen – Perspektiven* (3rd edition). Wiesbaden, pp. 219–238.

Tomczak; T., Mühlmeier, S. & Jenewein, W. (2008) *Empirical Research on the Treacy/Wiersema Typology: A Critical Review and Proposal*, ESCP-Konferenzpapier, 7th International Conference on Marketing Trends, Paris, (January).

Treacy, M. & Wiersema, F. (1995a) How Market Leaders Keep their Edge, *Fortune*, (February 6), 88–98.

Treacy, M. & Wiersema, F. (1995b) *Marktführerschaft. Wege zur Spitze.* Frankfurt am Main.

Twedt, D.W. (1969) How to Plan New Products, Improve Old Ones, and Create Better Advertising. *Journal of Marketing*, Vol. 33 (January), 53–57.

Uebel, M.F., Helmke, S. & Dangelmaier, W. (2004) *Praxis des Customer Relationship Management.* Wiesbaden.

Ulrich, P.V., Anderson-Connell, L.J. & Wu, W. (2003) Consumer Co-design of Apparel for Mass Customization. *Journal of Fashion Marketing and Management*, Vol. 7 (February, No. 4), 398–412.

Upshaw, L.B. (1995) *Building Brand Identity.* New York.

Väthröder, D. (2005) Kein Profil – keine Chance, *Auto Service Praxis* (No. 1), 44–47.

Verband Deutscher Sportfachhandel (VDS) (2006) *Weltmarktführer Nike steuert im Internet Konfrontationskurs, vds Pressemitteilung.* (11.12.2006).

Viardot, E. (2004) *Successful Marketing Strategy for High-Tech Firms.* Boston.

Vogler, S. & Lienhardt, F. (1999) "Willkommen bei der ZKB". *Thexis*, Vol. 16 (No. 2), 34–38.

von Hippel, E. (1986) Lead Users: A Source of Novel Product Concepts. *Management Science*, Vol. 32 (July, No. 7), 791–805.

von Hippel, E. & Katz, R. (2002) Shifting Innovation to Users via Toolkits. *Management Science*, Vol. 48 (July, No. 7), 821–833.

Von Reibnitz, U. (1996) Szenario-Technik, in Schulte, C. (ed.), *Lexikon des Controlling.* Munich, pp. 747–751.

Walther, J. (2001) Konzeptionelle Grundlagen des Supply Chain Managements, in Walther, J. & Bund, M. (eds.), *Supply Chain Management.* Frankfurt, pp. 11–31.

Walther, J. & Guss, H. (2001) Supply Chain Management in Deutschland und der Schweiz – Ergebnisse der Studie 2000, in Walther, J. & Bund, M. (eds.), *Supply Chain Management.* Frankfurt, pp. 159–177.

Ware, J., Gebauer, J., Hartman, A. & Roldan, M. (1998) *The Search for Digital Excellence.* New York.

Wasson, C. (1978) *Competitive Strategy and Product Life Cycles.* Austin.

Watts, D.J. & Hasker, S. (2006) Marketing in an Unpredictable World, *Harvard Business Review*, (September), 25–30.

Weber, B. (2007) Procter & Gamble: Online Soap Opera, *Lebensmittelzeitung*, March 2.

Weber, J. (1990) *Logistik-Controlling*, Stuttgart.

Weber, J., Schäffer, U. & Freise, H.-U. (2001) Controlling von e-Commerce auf Basis der Balanced Scorecard, in Eggers, B. & Hoppen, G. (eds.), *Strategisches e-Commerce-Management.* Wiesbaden, pp. 445–464.

Webster, Wind, Y. (1972) A General Model for Understanding Organisational Buying Behaviour, *Journal of Marketing*, Vol. 36 (No. 2), 12–19.

Weiber, R. & Kollmann, T. (2000) Wertschöpfungsprozesse und Wettbewerbsvorteile im Marketspace, in Bliemel, F., Fassott, G. & Theobald, A. (eds.), *Electronic Commerce. Herausforderungen – Anwendungen – Perspektiven* (3rd edition). Wiesbaden, pp. 47–62.

Weiber, R. & Krämer, T. (2001) Paradoxien des Electronic Business, in Weiber, R. (ed.), *Handbuch Electronic Business.* Wiesbaden, pp. 149–177.

Weiber, R. & Weber, M.R. (2001) Customer Lifetime Value als Entscheidungsgrösse im CRM, in Weiber, R. (ed.), *Handbuch Electronic Business.* Wiesbaden, pp. 473–503.

Wells, T. (2006) Web 3.0 and SEO, *Search Engine News*, November 29.

Weltz, F. (1993) Konsensmanagement bei der Einführung von Informationstechnik, in Scharfenberg, H. (ed.), *Strukturwandel in Management und Organisation*. Baden-Baden, pp. 71–90.

Werbach, K. (2000) Content Syndication. The Emerging Model for Business in the Internet Area, *Harvard Business Review*, (May–June), 84–93.

Werner, A. (2000) *Site Promotion. Werbung auf dem WWW*. Heidelberg.

Westphal, F. (2007) Mashups: Remix me! *OBJEKTspektrum*, Vol. 2.

Wheelen, T.L. & Hunger, J.D. (2001) *Essentials of Strategic Management* (2nd edition). Upper Saddle River.

Whitmore, J. (1993) *Coaching for Performance: A Practical Guide to Growing Your Own Skills*. New York.

Wiedmann, K.-P., Frenzel, T. & Buxel, H. (2001) Strategisches e-Commerce-Marketing, in Eggers, B. & Hoppen, G. (eds.), *Strategisches e-Commerce-Management*. Wiesbaden, pp. 417–444.

Wiegand, M. (1995) *Prozesse organisationalen Lernens*. Wiesbaden.

Wieken, J.H. (1999) *Der Weg zum Data Warehouse. Wettbewerbsvorteile durch strukturierte Unternehmensinformationen*. Munich.

Wildemann, H. (1988) *Das Just-in-Time-Konzept. Produktion und Zulieferung auf Zuruf*. Frankfurt.

Wildemann, H. (1994) *Fertigungsstrategien* (2nd edition). Munich.

Wildemann, H. (2001) *Logistik-Prozessmanagement. Organisation und Methoden* (2nd revised edition).

Wildemann, H. (2000) Von Just-in-Time zu Supply Chain Management, in Wildemann, H. (ed.), *Supply Chain Management*. Munich, pp. 49–86.

Willhardt, R. (2007) Das seltsame Paarungsverhalten von Marken, *Absatzwirtschaft – Zeitschrift für Marketing* (No. 7), 40–43.

Wirtz, B.W. (2000) *Electronic Business*. Wiesbaden.

Wirtz, B.W. (2002) Multi Channel Management – So binden Sie Ihre Kunden auf den richtigen Kanälen, *Absatzwirtschaft – Zeitschrift für Marketing* (No. 4), 48.

Wirtz, B.W. (2008) *Multi-Channel-Marketing. Grundlagen – Instrumente – Prozesse*. Wiesbaden.

Witt, P. (1998) Was bei der Ausgestaltung von Aktienoptionen für Führungskräfte zu beachten ist. *Blick durch die Wirtschaft* (March 13), 3.

Witte, E. (1976) Kraft und Gegenkraft im Entscheidungsprozess. *Zeitschrift für Betriebswirtschaft*, Vol. 46 (No. 4/5), 319–326.

Zaltman, G. & Zaltman, L. (2008) *Marketing Metaphoria. What Deep Metaphors Reveal about the Minds of Consumers*. Boston.

Zerdick, A., Picot, A., Schrape, K., Artope, A., Goldhammer, K., Heger, D.K., Lange, U.T., Vierkant, E., Lopez-Escobar, E. & Silverstone, R. (2001) *Die Internet-Ökonomie* (3rd edition). Berlin.

Ziegler, S. (2001) Organisation der Kundenorientierung, *Absatzwirtschaft – Zeitschrift für Marketing*, 1.7.2001, 42–46.

Ziems, D. (2008) Markenmythen – die neue Bedeutung für die Markenführung, in Kreutzer, R.T. & Merkle, W. (eds.), *Die neue Macht des Marketing*. Wiesbaden, pp. 99–112.

Zmuda, N. (2008) Why Gatorade Is Losing Its Zip. Category Leader Has Been Losing Share to Upstart Rivals. *AdAge.com*, April 21.

ACKNOWLEDGMENTS

Thanks go to all colleagues who made it possible to create empirical studies, acquire the most diverse range of experience in implementing projects, and gain insight from holding workshops, additional interviews and discussions, such as Adriana Nuneva (Heidelberger Druckmaschinen, Heidelberg), Antje Feller and Stefani Spangenberg (both from SKA Agentur für Relationship Marketing, Frankfurt), Dr. Rainer Hillebrand (Otto Versand, Hamburg), Jörg Peters (IBM Deutschland, Stuttgart), Jürgen Lieberknecht (Deutsche Bank, Frankfurt), Nils Niehörster (RAAD Consult, Münster), Oliver Klein (Cherrypicker, Hamburg), Prof. Dr. Detlef Schoder (University of Cologne), Ralf Klein-Bölting (Deutsche Bahn AG, Berlin), Julia Beck (Hamburg) and Thomas Grom (Zürich Financial Services, Zürich). The feedback and multifaceted impulses from my colleagues inspired me to devote weekends and evenings to write a book that might help to take marketing to the next level and inspire a broader audience to apply its ideas, processes, and guidelines. Thanks also go to Kristin Sallai and Stephan Lindner (both from Accenture, Kronberg) for the support in the marketing planning project; to Maike Strudthoff (Accenture, Kronberg) for support in the empirical study; to my assistant, Monique Morgenstern, for her endless patience with the many revisions of the manuscript, and to my SAP colleagues, Katja Mehl, Marcus Rübsam, Frank-Uwe Joos, and Ralf Heeke, not only for numerous suggestions in the making of the book but for filtering out the most important errors and unclear points. Heartfelt thanks to my family for their understanding for all the weekends and vacations I spent working – vacations that don't really deserve that designation as they were committed to working on this book. Thanks also go to text & form for support in translation.

Thanks also go to my colleagues in SAP Germany for the many suggestions, discussions, enduring support, and constant enthusiasm during the development and implementation of some of the concepts outlined here over the last five years. The best marketing planning can only be achieved and implemented with the best team – our planning is excellent!

TABLE OF FIGURES

INDEX

DATE DUE